CW00601223

THE IRISH IN THE WE[ST OF] SCOTLAND 1797–1848

Trade Unions, Strikes and Political Movements

For my Mother and Father

THE IRISH IN THE WEST OF SCOTLAND 1797–1848

Trade Unions, Strikes and Political Movements

Martin J. Mitchell

JOHN DONALD PUBLISHERS LTD
EDINBURGH

© Martin J. Mitchell 1998

All rights reserved.
No part of this publication may be reproduced
in any form or by any means without
the prior permission of the publishers
John Donald Publishers Limited,
73 Logie Green Road, Edinburgh, EH7 5HF.

ISBN 0 85976 480 X

British Library Cataloguing in Publication Data.

A catalogue record for this book is available
from the British Library.

Typeset in Bembo by Brinnoven, Livingston.
Printed & bound in Great Britain by Bell & Bain Ltd, Glasgow.

Acknowledgements

This book is based on my 1996 University of Strathclyde doctoral thesis. Professor Tom Devine supervised my postgraduate work and I would like to express my gratitude to him for his guidance and encouragement. I would like to thank Professor Jim McMillan of the Department of History at the University of Strathclyde for appointing me to the post of Graduate Teaching Assistant in the Department for term 1995-6, and I am indebted to his colleague Professor Hamish Fraser for providing me with a number of references, transcripts and materials. Many thanks are also due to Mrs Margaret Hastie for typing both the thesis and this book. The University of Strathclyde awarded me a studentship for the period 1992-5 and the Carnegie Trust for the Universities of Scotland provided financial assistance towards the costs of travel. I wish to thank both institutions. The staff at the following archives and libraries provided much help and assistance: the Scottish Catholic Archives; the Glasgow Archdiocesan Archives; the Mitchell Library; the National Library of Scotland; and the Scottish Record Office (General Register House and West Register House). Finally, I wish to express my gratitude to my parents for their support and encouragement. This book is dedicated to them with love and thanks.

Martin J. Mitchell

Contents

Abbreviations

PP   Parliamentary Papers

SCA   Scottish Catholic Archives

SRA   Strathclyde Regional Archives

SRO   Scottish Record Office

WRH   West Register House

Introduction

In the early 1790s there were very few people of Irish birth in Scotland, of whom almost all lived in the counties of Wigtownshire, Kirkcudbright-shire, Dumfriesshire and Ayrshire. The bulk of these immigrants were employed as agricultural labourers. The rest were mostly vagrants and beggars.[1]

Fifty years later this picture of Irish immigration had changed beyond recognition. The census of 1841, the first which gave the numbers of Irish-born inhabitants of all the counties of Scotland, revealed that there were 126,321 people of Irish birth in the country, or 4.8 per cent of the total population of 2,620,184.[2] However, as the historian of the Irish in Scotland, James Handley, noted:

> The census is concerned only with the Irish-born immigrants and takes no account of the Scottish-born children of such, except to enter them as Scots. Yet by 1840 immigration into the industrial areas had persisted long enough to establish a second and even a third generation among a race of manual workers…[3]

He argued that there was little inter-marriage between the Irish and the Scots and therefore immigrants' children born in Scotland 'were of purely Irish blood'.[4] Handley suggested that because of this, 'Probably a percentage of ten to represent the proportion of Irish in Scotland in 1840 would be nearer the truth…'.[5] The census of 1851 showed that the proportion of Irish immigrants in Scotland had increased over the decade. At the time of the census there were 207,367 people of Irish birth in the country; this represented 7.17 per cent of the total population of 2,888,742. Once again, because of second and third generation Irish the figure for the Irish-born in Scotland in 1851 greatly under-represents the actual number of Irish in the country in that year.[6]

The overwhelming majority of Irish immigrants in Scotland from the second half of the 1790s to 1851 were from the nine counties of Ulster.[7] The troubles in Ireland during the late 1790s and early 1800s, and in particular the Rebellion of 1798, were chiefly responsible for the first great wave of Irish emigration to Scotland as refugees fled the province to escape the violence or the authorities. Most settled in the west of the country and were employed as weavers, labourers or as operatives in cotton factories.[8] The return of relative social and political stability to Ireland did not, however, stem the outflow from Ulster. Over the next four decades the linen industry in the province went into decline and eventually collapsed. This development coincided with the rapid expansion of manufacturing industry in Scotland. As a result, many redundant weavers and spinners left the north of Ireland and moved to Scotland to find work. Entire families emigrated as well.[9] From the mid-1840s onwards the pace of emigration to Scotland from Ulster accelerated rapidly on account of the poverty caused by the failure of the potato crop.[10]

The majority of the Irish population in Scotland during the first half of the nineteenth century lived in the west central region, namely the counties of Ayrshire, Lanarkshire and Renfrewshire. The census of 1841 showed that 88,367, or almost 70 per cent, of the 126,321 Irish immigrants in the country lived in this region;[11] ten years later the total was 135,975 out of the Irish-born population of 207,367 (65.6 per cent).[12] The figures for the three counties, hereafter termed the west of Scotland, are given in more detail in Tables 1 and 2.

Table 1: The Irish in the West of Scotland, 1841.

Counties	Total Population	Irish-born Population	Percentage of Irish-born
Ayrshire	164,356	12,035	7.3
Lanarkshire	426,972	55,915	13.1
Renfrewshire	155,072	20,417	13.2
W. Scotland	746,400	88,367	11.8

Source: James Handley, *The Irish in Scotland* (2nd edition, Cork, 1945), p.89.

Table 2: The Irish in the West of Scotland, 1851.

Counties	Total Population	Irish-born Population	Percentage of Irish-born
Ayrshire	189,858	20,967	11.0
Lanarkshire	530,169	89,330	16.8
Renfrewshire	161,091	25,678	15.9
W. Scotland	881,118	135,975	15.4

Source: James Handley, *The Irish in Modern Scotland* (Cork, 1947), p.44.

The majority of Irish immigrants settled in the west of Scotland because this was the region of the country in which the greatest expansion of industry occurred and most employment opportunities were found.

Like the Irish elsewhere in Scotland during this period, and like the Irish who lived in England and Wales, those in the west of the country were overwhelmingly working class. This is apparent from evidence given to a number of parliamentary inquiries in the 1830s and 1840s[13] , and from studies of information collected for the census of 1851.[14] In the mid-1830s most of the Irish in Lanarkshire lived in and around Glasgow.[15] Here Irish male workers were employed chiefly as handloom weavers or as labourers who made roads or railways, cut canals and served tradesmen such as masons and bricklayers. Indeed, in the city and its vicinity most of the labourers and probably the majority of the weavers were of Irish birth or descent. Furthermore, around one-half of the dyers, two-thirds of the dock labourers and most of the male workforce in the cotton mills were Irishmen. So too were the majority of workers in Dixon's large colliery at Govan. Female Irish workers in Glasgow and its neighbourhood were employed mainly in the cotton factories.[16] Most of the remainder of the Irish in Lanarkshire at this time lived in the parishes of New Monkland, Hamilton and Blantyre:[17] in New Monkland the men worked chiefly as weavers in the village of Airdrie or as colliers or labourers in the surrounding coal mines and iron works;[18] in Hamilton most Irishmen were probably weavers or labourers;[19] and in Blantyre Irish workers, both male and female, were employed mainly in cotton mills.[20] Irishmen in the towns and villages of Ayrshire were mostly weavers or labourers and Irish women in these places flowered muslin, tamboured or wove at the loom. There were also a number of Irishmen employed in some of the collieries in the county.[21] In Renfrewshire Irish male workers were chiefly labourers. In Paisley and surrounding towns and villages they cut canals, deepened rivers and served tradesmen in the building industry; in Greenock they constituted most of those employed as labourers in the sugar houses and in the building industry, and probably the majority of those who worked at the docks. In and around Paisley there were some Irishmen who were weavers of plain cotton. Furthermore, in the cotton mills of the town the bulk of the labour force was composed of Irish males and females. Indeed, it was in these establishments that most of Paisley's female Irish workers were employed.[22]

• By 1851 there had been a number of significant changes in the employment pattern of Irish male workers in the west of Scotland. During the 1840s the country's handloom weaving population declined rapidly as a result of two severe trade depressions and the increasing availability of work in the expanding heavy industry sector of the economy. In 1838 there were an estimated 84,560 weavers in the whole of Scotland; by 1850 the number had fallen to around 25,000.[23] However, from the mid-1830s onwards the coal and iron industries in Ayrshire and Lanarkshire expanded rapidly and attracted a large influx of Irish workers.[24] Moreover, the rapid development of the shipbuilding, metalworking and engineering industries in and around Glasgow during the same period led to a large increase in the number of Irishmen working in these sectors. For example, in Anderston in 1851 29.3 per cent of Irish-born male workers were employed in the metal, machine and shipbuilding sector; 13.1 per cent were in textiles; 12.7 per cent were in transport (including dock labour); and 11.5 per cent were employed in the construction industry.[25]

. Those among the Irish population in the west of Scotland during the first half of the nineteenth century who were not members of the labouring classes were mainly small shopkeepers, such as grocers, spirit dealers, pawnbrokers, fishmongers and brokers.[26] Their numbers were not great. For example, in December 1835 John Murdoch, the Catholic Bishop in Glasgow, reported that of the 43–44,000 Irish Catholics in and around the city only 200 or 300 persons were not 'of the poor or working classes'. They were mostly 'petty shopkeepers'.[27] Such a group of Irish Catholic businessmen had existed in the city since at least the 1800s.[28] Among the Irish in the towns and villages of Ayrshire and Renfrewshire in the mid-1830s there were only a few who were small shopkeepers.[29] Finally, most of the itinerant hawkers and pedlars in the region were Irish.[30]

. Irish immigration fundamentally altered the pattern of Roman Catholicism in Scotland. In the mid-1790s there were around 30,000 Catholics in the country, the vast bulk of whom resided in the western Highlands and Islands and in the north-east Lowlands. Only between 500 and 600 lived in and around Glasgow, of whom most had arrived recently from the Highlands. Elsewhere in the west of Scotland there were few Catholics. Four decades later the number of Catholics in the region had risen spectacularly to between 65,000 and 70,000.[31] Almost all were of Irish birth or descent.[32]

. However, as most Irish immigrants in Scotland during this period (c.1790–1851) came from the nine counties of Ulster a considerable number were Protestants. Historians differ in their estimates of the extent of this immigration. Gallagher suggests that 20 per cent of the total number of Irish immigrants in Scotland during the nineteenth century were Protestants;[33] Walker favours a figure of 25 per cent and claims that this is 'the generally accepted estimate';[34] Brown suggests that the proportion was at least one-third,[35] as does McFarland.[36] However, at certain times during the first half of the nineteenth century the proportion of Protestants of the total Irish population in certain areas in the west of Scotland appears to have been considerably greater. For example, in 1831 the number of Catholics in the Calton-Mile End district of Glasgow was 2,688. There were, however, 6,890 Irish residents in the area; this suggests that over 4,000 members of the Irish population were Protestants.[37] In early 1834 the manager of a cotton mill at Blantyre stated that 'almost all' of the Irish in the parish were Protestants.[38] The minister of Girvan revealed around this time that more than one-half of the Irish population of the town were non-Catholic.[39]

II

Historians have been aware for some time of the important role which Irish immigrants and Irish issues played in the various movements for political reform in England from the Jacobin organisations of the 1790s to the Chartist agitation of the late 1830s and 1840s.[40] The dominant view in Scottish historiography, however, is that there was little or no participation by the Irish in Scotland in the campaigns for political change during the same period. In his history of the Irish in Scotland, first published in 1943, James Handley argued that

> from the end of the Napoleonic War to the Chartist Risings the Irish immigrant had little active part in the political questions that agitated the bosom of the Scottish working class.[41]

According to Handley the immigrants simply did not wish to involve themselves in the reform movements of the time, as 'The fight for Catholic Emancipation and the agitation for the repeal of the Union were more important to those who still regarded themselves as exiles than the grievances of their neighbours...'.[42] He explained this attachment to Irish and Catholic issues at the expense of interest in Scottish and British affairs as being a consequence of the immigrants' belief that their stay in Scotland was only temporary. Handley argued that many crossed the Irish Sea solely to earn enough money to enable them to either depart for the New World or return home to purchase land: therefore they saw no reason to concern themselves with the political agitations of Scottish workers, except on those occasions when there could be benefits for Ireland or the Catholic Church.[43] He concluded:

> it was not until a generation of Irish, born in Scotland, had grown up to manhood that identification with the political aims of their co-workers — as, for example, during the Chartist movement of the 'forties — became a normal line of action.[44]

Leslie Wright and Norman Murray accepted Handley's argument that it was not until the final phase of Chartism, in 1847–48, that the Irish in Scotland became involved in a political campaign with native workers.[45]

Other historians have argued that the Irish — or to be exact the Catholic Irish — did not, or could not, participate in the political reform campaigns because Scottish workers were hostile towards the immigrants. For example, in his survey of the experience of the Scottish working class between 1830 and 1914, William Knox stated that 'Religious bigotry saw the Irish Catholics retreat from the embrace of the Scottish labour movement', although he acknowledged that they joined forces with the Chartists in 1847, after the death of the great Irish political leader Daniel O'Connell.[46] Elaine McFarland also accepted that Irish Catholics were involved in the final stages of the Chartist movement,[47] but argued that Scottish workers were not so friendly earlier in the century: she wrote of 'the hostile reaction of various sections of the early Scottish labour movement' to Irish immigrants which 'was based on opposition to their religion as much as economic grievances…'. According to McFarland, this 'situation was greatly exacerbated by the serious fall in real wages after 1815 and by the employment of Irish blackleg labour after 1817, particularly in the coalfields'.[48]

Despite the fact that these and other historians[49] have noted or discussed the involvement of Irish workers in Chartism in Scotland in the late 1840s, others have maintained that Irish Catholics were prevented by native hostility from participating in Scottish political reform campaigns throughout most of the nineteenth century. For example, Tom Gallagher, in his major study of the Catholic community in Glasgow during the nineteenth and twentieth centuries, argued that the Catholic Irish in nineteenth century Scotland were despised because of their religion and because they worked for lower rates of pay.[50] As a result:

> Working-class solidarity was not a strong enough impulse to bring Irish and Scottish wage labourers together even though, during the 1830s and 1840s, they were already toiling in close proximity at a time when radical movements like the Chartists enjoyed a mass following in Britain.[51]

He concluded:

> Finding religious intolerance and sectarian hate in many areas of nineteenth century Scottish life, the immigrants preferred to remain expatriate Irish rather than strive to make common cause with the Scots in their midst.[52]

Callum Brown, in *The Social History of Religion in Scotland since 1730*, argued that 'partly through the use of immigrants as strike-breakers and partly through sectarianism, Catholics were generally isolated from the trades-union and Labour movements before 1890.'[53] (The overwhelming majority of Roman Catholics in lowland Scotland throughout the nineteenth century were Irish or of Irish descent.)

˒ This view that Catholic Irish immigrants and their progeny were employed mainly as low wage labour or as strike-breakers, and were unwilling or unable to participate in strikes or trade unions during the first half of the nineteenth century, dominates historical thinking on the Irish in Scotland. In his contribution to the first volume in the *People and Society in Scotland* series Callum Brown stated that from the 1780s

> sectarian feelings strengthened amongst skilled workers in the west of Scotland. Though approximately one-third of new arrivals from Ireland were Protestant (presbyterians, episcopalians and Methodists), it was the Catholic Irish who were identified as threatening the jobs and status of native Scots.[54]

In the second volume, which examined the period 1830–1914, he asserted that 'trade unions were often overtly anti-Catholic, and Protestant working-class hostility was exacerbated when Catholics worked as strike-breakers'.[55] Tom Gallagher has argued:

> It was the Irishman's readiness to toil longer, harder, and for less remuneration which elicited the bitterest response from Scottish and English workers…the Irish undoubtedly helped to depress real wages and conditions by working longer for lower rates of pay. In Scotland, this was particularly true of the Lanarkshire coalfields…where antagonism between Scottish and Irish workers was possibly at its worst in the nineteenth century.[56]

˒ Gallagher highlighted the role of Irish workers as strike-breakers in mining disputes and stated that 'Well into the nineteenth century, plenty of Irish were to be found in those parts of the Scottish coalfields where non-union labour predominated'.[57] Furthermore, he claimed that Scottish trade unions 'were for a long time, hostile to Irish immigration', and that Irish Catholic workers played little part in trade unionism for most of the nineteenth century.[58] In his volume in the *Edinburgh History of Scotland,* William Ferguson discussed the use of Irish workers as strike-breakers in mining areas and the immigrants' role in adding greatly to the number of handloom weavers which, he argued, contributed to the decline in wages for those who worked at the loom. He stated that this 'economic rivalry gave rise to bitter resentment' which 'might well have been lost in a common struggle for improved conditions of labour but for the fierce antagonisms roused by the settlement of a large Roman Catholic population in a strongly Protestant country'.[59]

˒ Gallagher concluded that 'The widespread hostility of the host community to their presence' contributed to the formation by the Irish Catholics of a distinct community isolated from the rest of Scottish society:[60]

The community preserved its separate identity because it was a form of psychological protection. Priests and other community leaders encouraged what amounted to voluntary segregation in all the big areas of Irish settlement and in many of the smaller ones where the conditions existed for a distinct enclave community.[61]

Callum Brown has expressed similar views. He argued that 'native sectarianism helped to sustain Catholic cultural identity' during the first three decades of the nineteenth century[62] , and that from 1830–1914 the Catholic church 'was a refuge in what was frequently a hostile host society'.[63] In his survey of Glasgow working class politics between 1750 and 1914 Ian Hutchison claimed that the Irish Catholics formed a group apart:

> Throughout the nineteenth century the Irish Catholic portion of the population of Glasgow constituted a separate community within the city's social system, segregated by a whole bundle of distinguishing characteristics — race, accent, religion, occupations, residence and politics.[64]

Hutchison, however, did not state whether he believed this segregation to have been voluntary or instead a consequence of native hostility.

In several other general texts and specialised studies historians have not distinguished between Catholics and Protestants in their discussion of the effects of Irish immigration on Scottish workers, trade unionism and industrial action. For example, the Checklands, in their history of Scotland between 1832 and 1914, highlighted the role of the Irish as strike-breakers, and also stated that immigrant labour was 'so often used by employers to make effective unionism impossible'.[65] When T.C. Smout discussed the Irish in the context of industrial relations during the first half of the nineteenth century in his social histories he too focused solely on those groups of immigrants who were used as blackleg labour,[66] as did Hamish Fraser in his major study of the development of Scottish trade unionism in the period from 1700 to 1838.[67] Indeed, in another work Fraser argued that by the late 1840s, 'the Irish…were already present in such numbers as to be perceived as a major threat, and…were already identified as blacklegs and strike-breakers' by Scottish workers.[68] Clarke and Dickson in their examination of the emergence of the Scottish working class between 1760 and 1830 mentioned Irish workers twice. On the first occasion they commented on the immigrants' contribution to the labour surplus after 1815 and the problems this caused for the 'artisanal trades' in their attempts to control entry to their crafts. Clarke and Dickson then identified the 'main threat' faced by colliers unions in the 1830s — 'the influx of Irish labour used particularly as "nob" or "blackleg" labour during strikes…'.[69] Slaven and Campbell in their economic histories did not comment on Irish strike-breakers but focused instead on those Irish workers who contributed to the lowering of labour costs in the iron and textile industries.[70] Similarly, Mitchison commented on the willingness of the immigrants to accept low wages and argued that the influx of Irish workers into handloom weaving after 1816 contributed to the decline in wage-rates and working conditions in that trade.[71]

· Therefore certain views dominate historical thinking on the Irish in Scotland during the first half of the nineteenth century (and beyond): Irish immigrants, or the Catholics among them depending on which historian is being consulted, were employed mainly as low wage labour or as strike-breakers; they were despised by native workers; they played little part in political agitations alongside Scottish reformers; they were not significantly involved in trade unions or industrial action to protect or improve their wages and conditions. As has been shown, these images of Irish workers are to be found in most of the general texts on Scotland in this period and in a number of specialised works.

Yet it is surprising that such views dominate Scottish historiography. It will be recalled that Brown and Gallagher appear to have ignored the evidence of Irish participation in the final stages of the Chartist movement in Scotland. What is also strange is that they did not take into account evidence of immigrant involvement in reform agitations in Scotland prior to Chartism. The same is true of several of those who have acknowledged that the Irish were active in Scottish Chartism in the late 1840s. In a work published over eighty years ago, Henry Meikle argued that Irish immigrants were involved in the establishment and membership of the secret revolutionary United Scotsmen Society of 1797–1803,[72] and since then a number of historians including Burns, Thomis and Holt, Wells, Brims and most recently McFarland, have produced evidence of Irish involvement in this organisation.[73] Indeed, Handley, in the standard work on the Irish in Scotland, accepted Meikle's arguments and concluded that it was 'probable that many United Irishmen who had emigrated to Scotland were to be found in the ranks of the Scottish rebel society…'.[74] Furthermore, despite having argued that the Irish played little part in Scottish reform movements from 1815 to 1848, Handley stated that during the political radicalism in the west of Scotland between 1816 and 1820 'the Irish immigrant seems to have taken his share in the agitation'.[75] One of the sources he used to form this conclusion was Tom Johnston's *History of the Working Classes in Scotland*. In this book, published in 1920, the future Secretary of State for Scotland argued that during the post-Napoleonic War agitation, 'The immigrant Irish rebels were in "the troubles" — the advanced left wing of them, almost to a man…'.[76] Ellis and Mac a'Ghobhain also maintained that

Irish workers played a significant part in the radicalism of these years although they, like Johnston, did not produce any evidence to support their assertions nor provide references to the sources used to advance them.[77] William Roach provided evidence in his study of the radical movements of 1816–22 in the west of Scotland which suggests that the Irish might have been supporters of them,[78] and showed that two Irish weavers resident in Calton, a suburb of Glasgow, were heavily involved in a secret revolutionary society in 1817.[79] W.H. Fraser also noted their role,[80] but neither historian went on to examine the significance of this involvement for an understanding of the immigrant experience in Scotland at that time. In her recent study of Scottish radicalism in the late eighteenth and early nineteenth centuries Elaine McFarland argued that these two weavers, Andrew McKinlay and Hugh Dickson, were Protestants and that their society was anti-Catholic.[81] However, she also produced evidence which suggests that Irish Catholics might have participated in the agitation of 1819–20.[82]

Furthermore, there is evidence which is at odds with the view advocated by Brown and Gallagher that Scottish political reform movements were hostile to the Catholic Irish. Handley argued that the Scottish radicals 'were inclined to show themselves friendly towards the Catholic immigrants' during the 1820s and 1830s[83] and Alexander Wilson stated in his study of the Chartist movement in Scotland, published in 1970, that, 'Towards their much abused brethren, the Irish Catholics, there was a good deal of fellow feeling amongst the Chartists, but this feeling was seldom reciprocated, and it was only in the later stages of the movement that the "Irish" Catholics played any significant part.'[84] More recently, John McCaffrey has argued that the Catholic Irish 'political element' in the west of Scotland between the 1820s and 1840s established firm links with native radical movements in the region.[85]

It is also surprising that the image of the Irish as strike-breakers or workers who were content with low wages, and who were unwilling or unable to participate in trade unions or strikes, is to be found in a considerable number of major studies in Scottish history. Consider the issue of strike-breaking. It is clear from the secondary sources that immigrant workers were used as blackleg labour during the first half of the nineteenth century. The evidence of this, however, relates almost exclusively to the mining areas of Lanarkshire and Ayrshire, and mainly from the late 1830s onwards. The vast majority of Irish workers during this period were not employed in the mines and were not used as blackleg labour.[86] Treble's statement concerning the issue of the Irish and strike-breaking in the north of England is equally true of the immigrants north of the border:

the majority of Irish newcomers…had been drawn there by the 'pull' factor of higher wages and greater continuity in employment rather than recruited for the specific purpose of strike-breaking. Irish 'blacklegs' formed only an insignificant proportion of the total immigrant influx in any given year.[87]

Furthermore, it has been established that whereas some Irish workers were used as strike-breakers or as cheap labour in the north of England, others participated in strikes and trade unions, particularly in the textile industries. Indeed some immigrants, the most notable being John Doherty in Lancashire, played leading roles in workers' organisations in that region.[88] In 1963 J.A. Jackson argued that although particular economic circumstances might have made some immigrants eschew strikes and trade unions, 'given equal conditions [the Irish] were at least as active and capable as the majority of British workmen'.[89] After reviewing such evidence Dorothy Thompson stressed that, 'There is clearly…a difference between the use of fresh immigrant labour, or of labour deliberately imported to replace or dilute a difficult labour-force, and the behaviour of immigrants already a part of that force.'[90] It would appear that many writers of Scottish history have not recognised this distinction.

What is most surprising, however, is that there is evidence available in secondary sources which demonstrates or suggests that Irish workers in Scotland during the first half of the nineteenth century were involved in trade unions and strikes. D.F. McDonald in 1937, L.C. Wright in 1953, W.H. Marwick in 1967, Z.G. Brassey in 1974 and W.H. Fraser in 1976 all argued that Irish workers were heavily involved in the union of cotton spinners in Glasgow.[91] Norman Murray, the historian of the handloom weavers in Scotland, stated that Irish weavers took part in strikes and possibly trade unions as well.[92] In his study of the Lanarkshire miners Alan Campbell discussed the use of the Irish as blackleg labour but also argued that some participated in industrial action.[93] Moreover, Handley provided examples which show or suggest immigrant involvement in trade unions and strikes in a number of occupations.[94]

It is clear, therefore, that there is evidence which demonstrates that the dominant view of Irish immigrants, industrial action and political radicalism in Scotland during the first half of the nineteenth century is in great need of revision. It is strange that the examples of Irish involvement in these activities have not been incorporated into the general or specialised works of the historians discussed earlier. Nor has this evidence been brought together — until now — to suggest that the immigrant experience was perhaps somewhat different to the standard view and was in fact much like that of the Irish in England.

This book will examine in detail the issue of the Irish in Scottish political and industrial agitations. Although several historians have noted an Irish presence in these activities most mention it only in passing. The exceptions are McFarland, in her study of Scottish radicalism in the late eighteenth and early nineteenth centuries, and Campbell, in his work on the Lanarkshire miners. The study will concentrate on the west of Scotland, as this was the region in which the majority of Irish immigrants settled during the first half of the nineteenth century. It was also the part of the country which experienced most strikes, trade union organisation and political agitation. Furthermore, as has been noted, several historians have already provided examples of Irish participation in these activities in the region.

The political campaigns which were almost exclusively the preserve of the Irish community in Scotland, in particular the agitations for Catholic Emancipation and repeal of the British-Irish legislative union, will also be examined. Handley did not deal with these movements in any great detail and Montgomery and Leitch, in their theses on radicalism between 1830 and 1848 in Glasgow and Paisley respectively, did not discuss Repeal at all.[95] By examining both the 'Irish' and the 'Scottish' political movements a complete picture of immigrant political activity in this period will be given.

All the principal sources for studies of Scottish radicalism, trade unions and strikes in the first half of the nineteenth century have been consulted. These are the newspapers of the period and other contemporary publications; the parliamentary papers from the mid-1820s to the 1850s; the correspondence of government and local officials; and the legal records pertaining to arrested radicals, trade unionists, strikers and rioters. The press is also essential for the examination of the political movements dominated by the Irish in Scotland. The correspondence and papers of the Catholic clergy in the west of Scotland have been examined as well. These contain extremely valuable information on the political activities of the immigrants and on the attitudes of the priests towards them. The quality of these sources and the problems associated with them in attempting to determine the nature and extent of Irish participation in radical and industrial agitations will be considered throughout the text.

The book contains four sections. The first examines the role of Irish workers in trade unions and strikes throughout the period. The remainder of the study is concerned with the Irish and political campaigns. The first of these sections deals with insurrectionary activities, namely the United Scotsmen movement of 1797–1803 and the radical agitations of 1816–20. The chapters on these movements were originally completed before the publication of Elaine McFarland's study of Scottish radicalism in the late eighteenth and early nineteenth centuries. Although McFarland has produced a full account of the United Scotsmen society there is nothing in her work which has led me to alter my conclusions concerning this secret organisation or the extent and nature of Irish involvement in it. Furthermore, there are aspects of her discussion of the agitations of 1816–20 with which I disagree and I have included my criticisms in the text. The second section in this part of the book examines the peaceful campaigns for Catholic Emancipation and the Reform Bills. The demands for further political change in the years following the passing of the Reform Acts are also discussed. The final section is concerned with the period 1838–48 and examines the role of the Irish in the west of Scotland in the Chartist movement and in the campaign for Repeal of Union.

Notes

1. PP, 1836, (40), XXXIV, *Report on the State of the Irish Poor in Great Britain*, pp.iv, 154–5; James Handley, *The Irish in Scotland 1798–1845* (2nd edition, Cork, 1945), pp.81–5.

2. Handley, *Irish in Scotland*, p.89.

3. *Ibid*, p.90.

4. *Ibid*.

5. *Ibid*, p.91.

6. James Handley, *The Irish in Modern Scotland* (Cork, 1947), pp.44–6.

7. Brenda Collins, 'The Origins of Irish Immigration to Scotland in Nineteenth and Twentieth Centuries', in T.M. Devine (ed.), *Irish Immigrants and Scottish Society in the Nineteenth and Twentieth Centuries* (Edinburgh, 1991), pp.5–6; Handley, *Irish in Scotland*, p.108.

8. Handley, *Irish in Scotland*, pp.86–87; PP, 1836, (40), XXXIV, *Report on the State of the Irish Poor in Great Britain*, p.v. See also Chapter 2.

9. Collins, 'Origins of Irish Immigration', pp.1–10; 'Irish Emigration to Dundee and Paisley during the first half of the Nineteenth Century', in J.M. Goldstrom and L.A. Clarkson (eds.), *Irish Population, Economy and Society* (Oxford, 1981), pp.202–6; Handley, *Irish in Scotland*, p.106; PP, 1836, (40), XXXIV, *Report on the State of the Irish Poor in Great Britain*, pp.iii, vi, vii.

10. Handley, *Irish in Modern Scotland*, Chapter 2; Collins, 'Origins of Irish Immigration', pp.8–10.

11. Handley, *Irish in Scotland*, p.89.

12. Handley, *Irish in Modern Scotland*, p.44.

13. See Handley, *Irish in Scotland*, Chapter 4.

14. See Collins, 'Irish Emigration to Dundee and Paisley', pp.195–212; R.D. Lobban, 'The Irish Community in Greenock in the Nineteenth Century', *Irish Geography*, VI (1971), pp.270–81; William Sloan, 'Employment Opportunities and Migrant Group Assimilation: the Highlanders and Irish in Glasgow, 1840–1860', in A.J.G. Cummings and T.M. Devine (eds.), *Industry, Business and Society in Scotland since 1700: Essays Presented to Professor John Butt* (Edinburgh, 1994), pp.197–217; Alan B. Campbell, *The Lanarkshire Miners: A Social History of their Trade Unions, 1775–1874* (Edinburgh, 1979), Chapter 7.

15. The 1841 census revealed that of the 55,915 Irish-born inhabitants of Lanarkshire 44,345, or 79.3%, resided in Glasgow and its suburbs. In the mid-1830s the proportion of Irish in and around the city would undoubtedly have been greater, because at that time the rapid expansion of the coal and iron industries in the county, which attracted large numbers of Irish workers, had only just begun. See Handley, *Irish in Scotland*, pp.89–90, 118–21.

16. PP, 1836, (40), XXXIV, *Report on the State of the Irish Poor in Great Britain*, pp.105–17.

17. *Ibid*; PP, 1837–1838, *Reports from the Commissioners of Religious Instruction, Scotland. Second Report*, Appendix III, pp.275, 278; Handley, *Irish in Scotland*, pp.105–27.

18. SCA, Presholme Letters, PL3/120/5, Andrew Scott to James Kyle, 26 February 1827; PP, 1836, (40), XXXIV, *Report on the State of the Irish Poor in Great Britain*, pp.113–5.

19. Martin J. Mitchell, 'The Catholic Community in Hamilton, c.1800–1914', in T.M. Devine (ed.), *St Mary's Hamilton: A Social History, 1846–1996* (Edinburgh, 1995), p.31.

20. PP, 1836, (40), XXXIV, *Report on the State of the Irish Poor in Great Britain*, pp.107–8.

21. *Ibid*, pp.146–9, 158.

22. *Ibid*, pp.131–3, 139–41.

23. Norman Murray, *The Scottish Handloom Weavers, 1790–1850: A Social History* (Edinburgh, 1978), pp.21–3, 48; Anthony Slaven, *The Development of the West of Scotland: 1750–1960* (London, 1975), pp.103–5.

24. Handley, *Irish in Scotland*, pp.96–7, 118–21; Alan B. Campbell, *The Lanarkshire Miners: A Social History of their Trade Unions, 1775–1874* (Edinburgh, 1979), especially Chapter 7; Gordon M. Wilson, *Alexander McDonald, Leader of the Miners* (Aberdeen, 1982), Chapter 2.

25. Sloan, 'Employment Opportunities and Migrant Group Assimilation', pp.198–206.

26. PP, 1836, (40), XXXIV, *Report on the State of the Irish Poor in Great Britain*, pp.104–5, 139, 146; PP, 1837–1838, *Reports from the Commissioners of Religious Instruction, Scotland: Second Report*, Appendix III, p.275; *Eighth Report*,

Appendix I, pp.208, 316; PP, 1843, (115),VII, *Select Committee on Distress in Paisley*, p.120; Handley, *Irish in Scotland*, pp.274–5; Sloan, 'Employment Opportunities and Migrant Group Assimilation', p.210.

27. PP, 1837–1838, *Reports from the Commissioners of Religious Instruction, Scotland. Second Report*, Appendix III, p.275.

28. Christine Johnson, *Developments in the Roman Catholic Church in Scotland, 1789–1829* (Edinburgh, 1983), pp.176–77; SCA, Presholme Letters, PL3/28/11, William Rattray to Alexander Cameron, 19 March 1810; Blairs Letters, BL4/396/6, William Rattray to Alexander Cameron, 31 March 1812.

29. PP, 1836, (40), XXXIV, *Report on the State of the Irish Poor in Great Britain*, pp.139, 146; PP, 1837–1838, *Reports from the Commissioners of Religious Instruction, Scotland. Eighth Report*, Appendix I, pp.208, 316.

30. PP, 1836, (40), XXXIV, *Report on the State of the Irish Poor in Great Britain*, p.viii.

31. Martin J. Mitchell, 'The Establishment and Early Years of the Hamilton Mission', in Devine (ed.), *St Mary's Hamilton*, pp.1–4.

32. *Ibid*. See also PP, 1836, (40), XXXIV, *Report on the State of the Irish Poor in Great Britain*, pp.101, 139; PP, 1843 (115),VII, *Select Committee on Distress in Paisley*, p.120.

33. Tom Gallagher, 'The Catholic Irish in Scotland: in search of identity' in Devine (ed.), *Irish Immigrants*, p.20.

34. Graham Walker, 'The Protestant Irish in Scotland', in Devine (ed.), *Irish Immigrants*, p.49.

35. Callum Brown, *The People in the Pews: Religion and Society in Scotland since 1780* (The Economic and Social History Society of Scotland, 1993), p.34. See also Callum Brown, 'Religion and Social Change', in T.M. Devine and Rosalind Mitchison (eds.), *People and Society in Scotland Volume I, 1760–1830* (Edinburgh, 1988), p.154.

36. Elaine McFarland, *Protestants First: Orangeism in Nineteenth Century Scotland* (Edinburgh, 1990), p.104.

37. Handley, *Irish in Scotland*, p.108.

38. PP, 1836, (40), XXXIV, *Report on the State of the Irish Poor in Great Britain*, p.108.

39. *Ibid*, p.149.

40. John Belcham, 'England Working-Class Radicalism and the Irish, 1815–50', in Roger Swift and Sheridan Gilley (eds.), *The Irish in the Victorian City* (London, 1985), pp.130–57; Marianne Elliott, 'Irish Republicanism in England; the first phase 1797–9', in T. Bartlett and D.W. Hayton (eds.), *Penal Era and Golden Age* (Belfast, 1979), pp.204–22; Graham Davis, *The Irish in Britain, 1815–1914* (Dublin, 1991), chapter 5; A.W. Smith, 'Irish Rebels and English Radicals, 1798–1829', *Past and Present*, 7 (1955), pp.78–85; Dorothy Thompson, 'Ireland and the Irish in English Radicalism before 1850' in James Epstein and Dorothy Thomspon (eds.), *The Chartist Experience: Studies*

in Working-Class Radicalism and Culture, 1830–1860 (London, 1982), pp.120–51; E.P. Thompson, *The Making of the English Working Class* (Paperback edition, London, 1968), pp.183–88, 523–28; J.H. Treble, 'O'Connor, O'Connell and the Attitudes of Irish Immigrants towards Chartism in the North of England 1838–1848', in J. Butt and I.F. Clarke (eds.), *The Victorians and Social Protest: a Symposium* (Newton Abbott, 1973), pp.33–70; Rachel O'Higgins, 'The Irish Influence in the Chartist Movement', *Past and Present*, 20 (1961), pp.83–96; Roger Wells, *Insurrection: The British Experience, 1795–1803* (Gloucester, 1983).

41. Handley, *Irish in Scotland*, p.145. For his discussion of the immigrants and politics see pp.145–6, 313–23.

42. *Ibid*, p.313.

43. *Ibid*, pp.145–6, 313.

44. *Ibid*, p.313.

45. Leslie C. Wright, *Scottish Chartism* (Edinburgh, 1953), p.19; Murray, *Scottish Handloom Weavers*, p.233.

46. W. Knox, 'The Political and Workplace Culture of the Scottish Working Class, 1832–1914', in W. Hamish Fraser and R.J. Morris (eds.), *People and Society in Scotland Volume II, 1830–1914* (Edinburgh, 1990), p.156.

47. McFarland, *Protestants First*, p.102.

48. *Ibid*, p.52. See also E. McFarland, *Ireland and Scotland in the Age of Revolution* (Edinburgh, 1994), p.244.

49. See, for example, Alexander Wilson, *The Chartist Movement in Scotland* (Manchester, 1970), p.141, 222.

50. Tom Gallagher, *Glasgow: The Uneasy Peace: Religious Tension in Modern Scotland* (Manchester, 1987), chapter 1.

51. *Ibid*, p.13.

52. *Ibid*, p.32.

53. Callum G. Brown, *The Social History of Religion in Scotland since 1730* (London, 1987), p.164.

54. Brown, 'Religion and Social Change', p.154.

55. Callum G. Brown, 'Religion, Class and Church Growth', in Fraser and Morris (eds.), *People and Society Volume II*, p.322.

56. Gallagher, *Uneasy Peace*, pp.13–4.

57. *Ibid*, p.14.

58. *Ibid*, p.31.

59. William Ferguson, *Scotland 1689 to the Present* (Paperback edition, Edinburgh, 1978), pp.292–3.

60. Gallagher, *Uneasy Peace*, p.33

61. *Ibid*, p.18.

62. Brown, 'Religion and Social Change', p.159.

63. Brown, 'Religion, Class and Church Growth', p.322.

64. I.G.C. Hutchison, 'Glasgow Working-Class Politics', in R.A. Cage (ed.), *The Working Class in Glasgow, 1750–1914* (London, 1987), p.130.

65. Olive and Sydney Checkland, *Industry and Ethos: Scotland, 1832–1914* (2nd edition, Edinburgh, 1989), pp.17, 25, 125.

66. T.C. Smout, *A History of the Scottish People 1560–1830* (Paperback edition, London, 1972), p.407; *A Century of the Scottish People* (Paperback edition, London, 1987), p.19.

67. W. Hamish Fraser, *Conflict and Class: Scottish Workers 1700–1838* (Edinburgh, 1988), pp. 122–3, 151.

68. W. Hamish Fraser, 'The Scottish Context of Chartism', in Terry Brotherstone (ed.), *Covenant, Charter and Party: Traditions of Protest and Revolt in Modern Scottish History* (Aberdeen, 1989), p.74.

69. Tony Clarke and Tony Dickson, 'The Birth of Class', in Devine and Mitchison, *People & Society Volume I*, pp.300–1.

70. R.H. Campbell, *Scotland since 1707: The Rise of an Industrial Society* (2nd edition, Edinburgh, 1985), pp.89, 97, 141; Slaven, *Development of the West of Scotland*, pp.104, 106, 117–8.

71. Rosalind Mitchison, *A History of Scotland* (London, 1970), pp.367, 381.

72. Henry Meikle, *Scotland and the French Revolution* (Glasgow, 1912), p.186.

73. C.M. Burns, Industrial Labour and Radical Movements in Scotland in the 1790s, University of Strathclyde M.Sc. (1971), pp.205–8, 215; M.I. Thomis and P. Holt, *Threats of Revolution in Britain 1789–1848* (London, 1977), p.19; Wells, *Insurrection*, pp.72–4, 205; John Brims, 'Scottish Radicalism and the United Irishmen', in David Dickson, Dáire Keogh and Kevin Whelan (eds.), *The United Irishmen: Republicanism, Radicalism and Rebellion* (Dublin, 1993), pp.163–4; McFarland, *Ireland and Scotland*, chapters 5–8.

74. Handley, *Irish in Scotland*, p.145. See also pp.313–4.

75. *Ibid*, p.314.

76. Tom Johnston, *The History of the Working Classes in Scotland* (Glasgow, 1920), p.234.

77. Peter Berresford Ellis and Seamus Mac a'Ghobhain, *The Scottish Insurrection of 1820* (Paperback edition, London, 1989), pp.85, 114.

78. W.M. Roach, Radical Reform Movements in Scotland from 1815–1822 with Particular Reference to Events in the West of Scotland, University of Glasgow, Ph.D. (1970), pp.188, 205.

79. *Ibid*, pp.90, 100.

80. Fraser, *Conflict and Class*, pp.103–4.

81. McFarland, *Ireland and Scotland*, pp.238, 244.

82. *Ibid*, p.240.

83. Handley, *Irish in Scotland*, p.308.

84. Wilson, *Chartist Movement*, p.141.

85. John F. McCaffrey, 'Irish Issues in the Nineteenth and Twentieth Century: Radicalism in a Scottish Context?', in T.M. Devine (ed.), *Irish Immigrants and Scottish Society in the Nineteenth and Twentieth Centuries* (Edinburgh, 1991), pp.123–25. See also J. McCaffrey, 'Irish Immigrants and Radical Movements in the West of Scotland in the Early Nineteenth Century', *Innes Review*, XXXIX (1988), pp.46–60. McCaffrey's views on the Irish and radical movements in this period have been accepted by Michael Lynch in his *Scotland: A New History* (London, 1991), p.395.

86. Handley, *Irish in Scotland*, Chapter 4; *Irish in Modern Scotland*, Chapter 5.

87. J.H. Treble, 'The Attitude of the Roman Catholic Church towards Trade Unionism in the North of England, 1833–1842', *Northern History*, 5 (1970), p.96.

88. See for example, Thompson, 'Ireland and the Irish', pp.130–2; Davis, *Irish in Britain*, pp.104–5; John Archer Jackson, *The Irish in Britain* (London, 1963), pp.116–8; Duncan Bythell, *The Handloom Weavers: A Study of the English Cotton Industry During the Industrial Revolution* (Cambridge, 1969), p.184; E.H. Hunt, *British Labour History 1815–1914* (London, 1981), pp.167–8; Treble, 'Attitude of the Roman Catholic Church', *passim*; Thompson, *Making of the English Working Class*, pp.384, 472, 483–4.

89. Jackson, *Irish in Britain*, p.118.

90. Thompson, 'Ireland and the Irish', p.130.

91. D.F. MacDonald, *Scotland's Shifting Population, 1770–1850* (Glasgow, 1937), p.83; Wright, *Scottish Chartism*, p.17; W.H. Marwick, *A Short History of Labour in Scotland* (Edinburgh, 1967), p.10; Z.G. Brassey, The Cotton Spinners in Glasgow and the West of Scotland c.1790–1840: A Study in early industrial relations, University of Strathclyde, M.Litt. (1974), pp.21–5; W. Hamish Fraser, 'The Glasgow Cotton Spinners, 1837', in John Butt and J.T. Ward (eds.), *Scottish Themes: Essays in honour of S.G.E. Lythe* (Edinburgh, 1976), pp.83, 87.

92. Murray, *Scottish Handloom Weavers*, pp.201–2.

93. Campbell, *Lanarkshire Miners*, esp. chapter 7.

94. Handley, *Irish in Scotland*, pp.72–3, 77, 114, 116–7.

95. Fiona Ann Montgomery, Glasgow Radicalism 1830–1848, University of Glasgow, Ph.D. (1974); Archibald Leitch, Radicalism in Paisley, 1830–48: and its economic, political, cultural background, University of Glasgow, M.Litt. (1993).

PART ONE
IRISH WORKERS

1
Trade Unions and Strikes

This chapter will examine the role of Irish workers in trade unions and strikes in the west of Scotland during the first half of the nineteenth century. Most of the discussion will deal with cotton spinning, handloom weaving and mining, as these were occupations in which the Irish formed a large proportion of the workforce and were also those which saw most trade union activity and industrial action in this period. Furthermore, as the introduction to this study has shown, some historians have noted an Irish presence in these unions and disputes. This chapter will consider the issue in detail. Evidence concerning the Irish in several other occupations will also be presented.

I

The first cotton mills in Scotland were driven by water power and were located mostly in relatively isolated rural areas beside those rivers and streams which provided sufficient supplies of water. From the early 1790s onwards the industry was transformed by the introduction of steam-powered engines, which enabled mills to be erected in urban areas.[1] This was of great significance to cotton masters because, as Slaven states, by the early 1790s 'all the most convenient and economic water-power sites had been exploited, and only steam power, employing Watt's new rotative engine, could break the limitation on growth imposed by a shortage of power'.[2] Most of the water-powered mills had been built in Lanarkshire and Renfrewshire in order to be as close as possible to the cotton yarn merchants and weavers of Glasgow and Paisley who were so essential to the success of the industry. Glasgow, with its commercial and financial infrastructure, was particularly vital for cotton spinning. The application of the steam engine to spinning allowed new mills to be constructed in and around Paisley and Glasgow. For example, by 1833 seventy-two of the seventy-four cotton mills in Lanarkshire were in the city and its immediate vicinity.[3]

Adult workers in the urban areas in which cotton mills were constructed in the 1790s were not, however, willing to work in such establishments nor did they wish their children to be employed in them. Other work was readily available in this period and often at higher rates of remuneration, for example in handloom weaving.[4] There was also a strong aversion among the native population to working in factories. In 1834 George Miller, the manager of a cotton works at Blantyre, recalled that in those early years, 'Few Scotch families could be prevailed on to go into a cotton mill; they looked upon it as a sort of degradation'.[5]

It was fortunate for the master cotton spinners that the construction of their urban steam-powered mills in the 1790s coincided with the beginning of large scale Irish emigration to the west of Scotland. The new arrivals were not opposed to factory labour.[6] According to George Miller: 'They were glad...to take work in the cotton mills that were erecting and in course of operation, and they took their children in along with them. As the trade increased, fresh lots of the Irish came over, and were employed at once.'[7] As the cotton industry grew and the number of cotton spinning factories increased, Irish immigrants and their progeny continued to form the largest group in the labour force. For example, Miller stated in early 1834 that, 'The Irish, or descendants of Irish, are found to predominate in all spinning and weaving mills.'[8] Around this time John Orr recalled that when he opened his spinning mill in Paisley in 1810 his workforce was Irish, because the immigrants 'were the only people that asked for employment...Those who apply for work in the cotton mills are still chiefly Irish. Generally in the neighbourhood the great majority of the hands in the cotton mills are Irish'. Orr employed 279 workers in his factory in early 1834, 199 of whom were Irish.[9] A year earlier Henry Houldsworth, one of Scotland's leading cotton manufacturers, had informed a Parliamentary Select Committee that although 'a considerable number of Scotch...send their children to the mills...the greater proportion of the hands in the mills of Glasgow are either Irish themselves or of Irish parents, born in Scotland'. He added that 'a great proportion of [the spinners]...are from Irish families...'.[10] An account of the workforce in Houldsworth's spinning mills at Anderston in Glasgow in March 1834 shows that 291 of his 429 employees were of Irish birth or parentage.[11]

Given that the Irish constituted the majority of the spinning workforce in the cotton mills of Glasgow and Paisley during this period it is not surprising that there is evidence of their involvement in the Cotton Spinners' Association, which from 1816 to 1837 was the most powerful and active workers' organisation in Scotland.[12] For example, in his *Report on the State of the Irish Poor in Great Britain*, published in 1836, George Cornewall Lewis stated:

> In Glasgow and its neighbourhood, the formidable union of the cotton-spinners was first organised by the Irish, who...were at first almost exclusively employed in the cotton factories of Lanarkshire and Renfrewshire.[13]

John Orr informed Lewis that 'There were many turn-outs among the hands in the cotton mills, from 1818 down to 1828 or 1829' and added: 'The Scotch now are just as keen in combinations as the Irish'.[14] George Miller, in his evidence to the same Inquiry, stated:

> It is believed...that the union could never have acquired that degree of consistence that it now possesses had it not been for the daring character of the Irish, who scrupled at little in accomplishing their ends, even to the destruction of life and property, of which there are many miserable instances on record.[15]

By 1834, when the evidence for the Irish Poor Report was collected, the cotton spinners had indeed established a reputation for violence. During several disputes in Glasgow and Renfrewshire between 1818 and 1828 strike-breakers were threatened, intimidated and attacked. Some had vitriol thrown at them: others were shot. It is not clear, however, whether such outrages were committed by individuals or groups of spinners acting on their own, or occurred under the direction of the leadership of the union.[16] Nevertheless, there is evidence to support George Miller's claim that Irish spinners were prominent in such attacks. For example, between September 1824 and February 1825 there was a general stoppage of Glasgow spinners. After the return to work by the strikers, the new men employed during the dispute continued to be harassed. One of them, John Graham of Dunlop's Broomward Mill, was shot on 30 March 1825. John Kean, an unemployed spinner and a native of Ireland, was captured immediately and eventually found guilty of the assault. He was publicly whipped and then transported for life. Prior to the attack on Graham, Kean had attempted to shoot another strike-breaker.[17]

Four years before the attack on Graham another Irish spinner, Patrick Mellon, stood trial in Glasgow accused of the assault and burning (with vitriol) of James Cairney in late September 1820. Mellon was born in Belfast and had moved to Scotland at the age of six. He was a spinner in the mill of Robert Humphries and Co. in Hutchesontown. Cairney, who was seventeen-years-old, had been a strike-breaker at the mill for three weeks before the attack which blinded him in one eye and left his face badly disfigured. In his precognition to the authorities Cairney identified Mellon as his assailant, but at the trial the case against him was found not proven.[18] Mellon, however, was named by Thomas Stewart, a member of the Spinners' Association, as being one of a number of spinners who had been involved in assaults on strike-breakers in Glasgow and surrounding districts during the period from 1816 or 1817 to early 1821. Stewart also named the other spinners whom he believed to be prominent members of this group, including several whose surnames suggest that they were of Irish birth or descent: Owen Callaghan, Hugh Lafferty, Bernard McGeary, John McGowan and two men whose surnames only were given, Messrs. McBride and McConnell.[19] The last named was probably Henry McConnell, who, along with Callaghan, Lafferty and one Malcolm Cameron, was tried for the attempted assassination in December 1820 of John Orr, managing partner of the Underwood Mill in Paisley. The charge against Lafferty was found not proven, McConnell and Cameron were found guilty, and Callaghan was found guilty art and part. The three men were transported for life, but not before being whipped through Paisley as part of their sentence. On 5 April 1821 they each received seventy-five lashes, which were given in groups of fifteen at five different spots in the town.[20]

Malcolm Cameron was one of those spinners identified by Stewart in January 1821 as being trade unionists who participated in assaults against strike-breakers. Stewart named a number of other such activists who, like Cameron, did not have indigenous Irish names, for example Kennedy Baxter, Robert Brown, James Campbell, Paton Dunlop, John Gow, James McIntyre, Daniel Montgomery, Douglas Morrison and Robert Watson.[21] Another combined spinner, Nathaniel Donald, in a precognition given to the authorities around this time, named a number of spinners who he claimed were 'the most active in encouraging and promoting the combination about Glasgow'. He identified nineteen in total of whom three — William Burke, William Darroch and William Docharty — had recognisably Irish surnames. The surnames of the other spinners included Barclay, Blackburn, Henderson, Kee, McDonald, McKenzie, McMillan, McQuarry, Mellon, Paterson and Smith.[22] Unfortunately, nothing is known about the background of those listed by Stewart and Donald. However, given that the Irish appear to have been the predominant group in the spinning workforce in the mills during these years it is not unreasonable to assume that a number of the spinners named as being prominent union activists were Irish or of Irish descent.

After the dispute of 1824–25 it was not until 1837 that there was another general stoppage in the cotton spinning industry. In early April that year the leading cotton masters in Glasgow agreed to reduce the wage rates of their spinners and this resulted in the Spinners' Association calling out all its members. On 22 July, the one hundred and sixth day of the strike, John Smith, a strike-breaker at Houldsworth's Mill, was shot. He died three days later. The committee of the Association was soon arrested and the strike quickly collapsed. At a meeting on 3 August the spinners agreed to resume work 'unconditionally'. All but four of the committee members were eventually released. These men — Thomas Hunter, Peter Hacket, Richard McNeil and James Gibb — along with William McLean, a combined spinner who the authorities believed was the actual murderer, were charged with a number of offences. These included conspiracy to increase wages by the use of threats against workers, strike-breakers and employers; arson; assault; and the murder of John Smith. At their trial in Edinburgh in January 1838 the charges involving murder were found not proven. The five spinners were, however, found guilty of being members of a conspiracy which used 'intimidation, molestation and threats' against strike-breakers and of organising pickets to further these activities. Each was sentenced to seven years transportation to Botany Bay. However, they all remained on a prison ship on the River Thames until August 1840 when they were pardoned.[23]

As has been shown, in 1834 Irish workers were said to have formed the majority of the labour force in the cotton spinning mills in Glasgow. There is no reason to believe that this situation was any different three years later. Then there were almost a 1000 spinners in and around the city, of whom between 850 and 900 were members of the Association. Around 800 spinners stopped work in April 1837.[24] It is, therefore, probable that the majority of cotton spinners who went on strike were Irish. Furthermore, there is evidence of an Irish presence in the leadership of the Association at this time. Two of the four committee members tried in 1838 were from Ireland:[25] Thomas Hunter, the president or chairman of the union, was a native of County Antrim who had lived in Scotland for around twenty-four years[26] and Peter Hacket, the Association's thirty-six-year-old treasurer, was an immigrant from County Tyrone.[27] Hacket, who was active in the campaign for factory reform in the early 1830s,[28] was also a Roman Catholic.[29] At their trial a former combined spinner stated that Hunter had been a member of the Association for eighteen years and Hacket for twelve.[30]

The committee members of the Spinners' Association who were arrested but not charged in 1837 included James Docherty, Thomas Gallacher, Angus Campbell, Robert Johnstone, Adam Siderserff, James Munro, William Smeal, Henry Dunn and Daniel McDonald.[31] In his precognition to the authorities on 2 August 1837 Docherty stated that he was a native of County Tyrone and had left Ireland when very young. He was thirty-seven-years-old and had been a cotton spinner for about twenty years.[32] Unfortunately, the other members of the committee did not give any indication of their place of birth or ethnic background in their precognitions,[33] although from his surname it is likely that Thomas

Gallacher was Irish or of Irish descent. This can also be argued for Bernard Murphy, a former spinner aged sixty years who served as clerk to the committee.[34] With regard to Campbell, Johnstone, Siderserff, Munro, Smeal, Dunn and McDonald, and indeed to all of those who were active on behalf of the Association during 1837,[35] it is possible, perhaps probable, that some were Irish, as it is almost certain that Irish workers formed the largest ethnic group both within the spinning workforce and within the Spinners' Association. Admittedly these committee members did not have what can be regarded as indigenous Irish names. Nor had Peter Hacket and Thomas Hunter — and they were Irish immigrants. Furthermore, James Moat, a member of the committee during part of the strike and one of the chief witnesses for the Crown at the spinners' trial, declared in 1837 'That the most of the violent members are Irishmen or of Irish extraction';[36] Henry Cowan, who was a member of the Association at the time of the stoppage, informed the authorities that 'almost all the jobs done in the union...were done or originated by Catholics and Irishmen'.[37]

It must be noted that John Smith, the blackleg whose murder led to the arrest of the committee, was a native of Ireland[38] and it is likely that Thomas Donaghy, a strike-breaker assaulted by union members during the stoppage,[39] was Irish or of Irish extraction, if surnames can be a reliable guide to identifying an Irish background. Finally, James Cairney, the blackleg spinner who had vitriol thrown on his face during a strike in Glasgow in September 1820, was an Irish immigrant.[40] These examples of Irish strike-breakers being attacked by spinners from a union which had a large Irish membership demonstrate that facile generalisations cannot be made concerning the role of Irish immigrants in trade unions and industrial disputes during this period.

The Cotton Spinners Association collapsed as a result of the arrest of the leadership and the return to work in the summer of 1837. The union and its members had contracted large debts during the strike, and after the dispute ended many workers abandoned the Association. Many others were victimised by their employers; according to Fraser 276 combined spinners did not regain their positions once the strike was over. The trade depression of the following few years prevented the maintenance of an effective union organisation and any possibility of industrial action by operative spinners.[41] There was a resurgence of union activity by the spinners in 1844, including a strike at eighteen Glasgow mills in early February which ended with an agreement to increase piece rates.[42] But, as Fraser has concluded, the union 'never regained the significant, vanguard role it had achieved in the 1820s and 1830s'.[43] This was largely because its defeat in 1837 and relative weakness in the years that followed enabled the cotton masters to gain the ascendancy in the workplace and in industrial relations, with the result 'that from 1837 onwards the manufacturers exercised a very high degree of authority over wage levels and work assignment'.[44]

II

The most important figure to emerge from the ranks of the Glasgow Cotton Spinners' Association throughout its existence was an Irish Catholic named Patrick McGowan.[45] He was particularly prominent in the affairs of the union during the early 1830s. Several historians have commented on McGowan and his activities in this period: Kirby and Musson described his role in the establishment of the Grand General Union of Cotton Spinners of the United Kingdom;[46] John Ward noted the leading part which McGowan played in the Glasgow campaign for factory reform;[47] and Hamish Fraser concluded that in these years McGowan 'seems to have become a dominant and respected figure among the Glasgow Spinners...'.[48] It is evident that he was an important activist.[49] Yet there has been no attempt to present a full examination of McGowan and his role in the labour movement of the period, and evidence of his various activities has remained scattered throughout a number of articles, essays, theses and monographs. Even in these works all the surviving information concerning him is not presented. The purpose of this section, therefore, is to provide an account of McGowan's role as a labour activist from an Irish background.

Patrick McGowan was born in either 1793 or 1794. As his birth was several years before the beginning of large scale Irish emigration to Scotland it is likely that McGowan was not second generation Irish but was born in Ireland. In 1833 he told the Factory Commission that he had worked in cotton mills 'almost constantly' since the age of seven. In 1827 McGowan was employed in the Charles Todd's Mill at Springfield in Glasgow.[50] By 1830 he was active in the affairs of the Glasgow Spinners' Association.[51] In June that year he was one of the Scottish delegates to the second conference of the Grand General Union of Cotton Spinners, held in Ramsay on the Isle of Man. Here he was appointed along with Thomas Foster of Manchester to tour the various cotton spinning districts in the north-west of England to promote the Grand General Union, which had been founded the previous year largely as a result of the efforts of John Doherty, the Irish Catholic leader of Manchester's spinners. During their tour they assisted local unions during strikes and negotiations with cotton-masters, and also helped to promote Doherty's general union the National Association of United Trades for the Protection of Labour. In October 1830

McGowan was one of the participants at a meeting held in Manchester to establish a newspaper for the working classes. The outcome was the *Voice of the People*, edited by Doherty, which first appeared at the end of the year.[52]

Doherty was full of praise for McGowan's activities during the second half of 1830 — another of his publications, the *Poor Man's Advocate*, later stated that the growth of the Grand General Union in those months was largely owing to McGowan's exertions. The journal also outlined the qualities which made him such an effective representative of the Union:

> Besides the honest boldness and fearless intrepidity which is the peculiar character of Mr McGowan, there is something in his manner, his attitude, and tone, when addressing a body of workmen, which invites and carries with it the confidence of his auditors, but which is equally cutting and appalling to his opponents. The workman feels, in listening to Mr McGowan's plain, terse, but vigorous harangue, that he sees a man in whom he may safely repose the utmost confidence. There is something so resolute and bold about him, the resources of his vigorous intellect seems so abundant, that you are almost involuntarily tempted to throw the whole issue of your cause upon him, with next to a positive certainty of success.[53]

By January 1831 McGowan had returned to Scotland and the following month Foster died. These events undoubtedly led to the collapse of the Grand General Union in early 1831.[54] In June 1832 the *Poor Man's Advocate* reported that 'The union...which Mr McGowan had mainly contributed to mature, has since, from distrust or weariness, sunk into comparative insignificance'.[55]

Soon after his return to Glasgow McGowan became involved with several cotton operatives in the campaign for shorter working hours in factories. He was particularly prominent in this agitation between 1831 and 1833; for example, he spoke at or chaired meetings of the city's factory reformers.[56] He also participated in the campaign for the Reform Bill. This will be discussed in a later chapter.

McGowan, however, did not lose interest in events in England. In the summer of 1832 he launched an appeal to the cotton spinners in and around Glasgow for money for the defence fund of John Doherty, who was about to be prosecuted in London for libel as a result of an article which appeared in the *Poor Man's Advocate*.[57] In January the previous year McGowan was one of the principal speakers at a meeting of cotton workers in Glasgow held to raise funds for striking cotton spinners in Ashton, Stalybridge and Mosley.[58] In his speech that evening McGowan stated that a general union of all trades was necessary in order to prevent employers from imposing wage reductions on their workers:

without an effective union, no good could be done. We had all along been
looking on the struggles of one another as idle spectators. Why — why is it so?
Many trades from inadequate means were obliged to yield, which could have
been supported by a general union.

McGowan argued that if employers were successful in reducing wages in
one branch of industry employers in other sectors would eventually do
the same; therefore it was imperative that workers under attack should be
supported.[59] The following May the Glasgow workers' *Herald to the Trades'
Advocate* called for a general union of trades in the west of Scotland but
the proposal was not acted upon, perhaps because the city's Trades
Committee was then deeply involved in the Reform Bill campaign. The
idea revived in April 1834 as a result of the sentences imposed on the
Dorchester Labourers, but although the Glasgow Trades favoured the plan
they believed that workers in Scotland needed to be better organised before
any attempts at general unionism were made. Fraser has highlighted the
role of the Owenite Alexander Campbell in the demands in Glasgow for
general unions during this period.[60] It is evident, however, that McGowan
was prominent in calls for their establishment, and at an earlier time.

· The leading role which Patrick McGowan played in the campaign for
factory reform led to his dismissal from the Springfield Mill in September
1832 although he soon found employment in the offices of the *Liberator*,
the newspaper for the Glasgow working classes.[61] In November 1832
McGowan acted on behalf of the spinners in Houldsworth's Mill at
Anderston in negotiations held to end a strike there.[62] Curiously, after 1833,
when he gave his evidence to the Factory Commission, McGowan did
not feature in reports of working class meetings in the city.[63] By 1837,
however, he was again spinning and during the strike of that year he was
initially one of the guards, or pickets, at the Oakbank Mills, the scene of
much intimidation of strike-breakers.[64] In May, McGowan was sent to
Lancashire to raise money for the Spinners' Association. He was no doubt
chosen for this mission because of his activities in the area in 1830. In
November 1837 one union member told the authorities that McGowan
had returned to Glasgow, although he did not know where, or if, McGowan
was employed.[65] Unfortunately, no evidence has been found concerning
McGowan's activities after 1837.

McGowan was a well-informed activist. For example, in its report of a
general meeting of the Glasgow cotton spinners in August 1832, the *Scots
Times* stated:

Mr Patrick McGown, in proposing the first Resolution, entered into a clear
and minute detail of the evils of the Factory system, both in relation to its effects

on the moral and physical condition of those who were dependent upon it for their subsistence, and refuted at length the free trade opinions of McCulloch and others, from various parliamentary documents copies of which he held in his hands…

The paper added that his speech was 'replete with sound sense and true philanthropy…'.[66] In his evidence to the Factory Commission in June of the following year McGowan demonstrated his knowledge of the British cotton industry since 1803 and also provided information on the cotton industries of France and America. This impressed James Stuart, the factory commissioner who interviewed him; he informed the members of the Central Board of Factory Commissioners that they would 'find Patrick McGowan's evidence not uninteresting, and certainly of some importance, so far as respects the rates or wages paid at factories in the United States'.[67]
It is also clear that McGowan was a well-respected figure. At a crowded meeting in Glasgow in February 1833 on factory reform he 'was called to the chair amid great applause'.[68] The previous May the Glasgow working class newspaper the *Trades' Advocate* stated that McGowan

> has been many years an active, persevering, and deservedly esteemed member and conductor of the cotton-spinners' association. By his brother operatives he has been frequently engaged in missions of great importance, wherein his eloquence and perseverance have proved eminently successful.[69]

The following month John Doherty's *Poor Man's Advocate* said of the Glasgow spinners that, 'to Mr McGowan's exertions, we believe, more than those of any other man, are they indebted for the advantages which their excellent union affords them'.[70]
McGowan does not appear to have been involved in the affairs of the Catholic community in Glasgow or in campaigns concerning Catholic or Irish issues. His public activities, so far as can be judged from the sources, were concerned solely with the interests of the working classes. McGowan was one of the leading labour activists and trade unionists in Glasgow in the 1830s and, because of his work in Lancashire in 1830, he was also an important figure in the development of the British working class movement during the first half of the nineteenth century.

III

In his study of the growth and development of Scottish trade unionism up to 1838 Hamish Fraser argued that 'the spinners were an outsider group, slightly apart, because of the level of their earnings, from the rest of the working class. They were…"an aristocracy of labour"…the spinners were not a particularly well-loved group'. The evidence he used to support these arguments relates to the strike of 1837 and its aftermath:

> While the arrest and trial of the spinners undoubtedly caused much indignation, there was not that upswell of protest such as the case of the Dorchester Labourers produced in England. There was nothing comparable to the general strike in Oldham in April 1834 after police raided a cotton spinners' union. Although the spinners had given financial aid to many other groups in the past, they themselves had difficulty raising money. They had to look to fellow spinners in Lancashire rather than to unions of other craftsmen. It was five weeks after the arrest of the spinners that the Glasgow Trades Delegates issued an appeal on their behalf. There was only one mass meeting to rally support during the strike and that was addressed by Dr. Taylor, not by any working men...[71]

Now that it has been demonstrated that there was a large Irish presence both in the leadership and in the membership of the Cotton Spinners' Association, some may argue that the lack of sympathy and financial support from other groups of workers could perhaps have been a consequence of the ethnic composition of the spinners' union; after all, as the introduction to this book has shown, some historians have argued that the Irish in Scotland were a despised and isolated community. The purpose of this section is to examine the relationship between the cotton spinners and the other trades in the city to determine the validity of Fraser's assessment of the position of the cotton spinners in Glasgow.

The response of Glasgow workers to the spinners' strike of 1837 will be examined first. There were several reasons why the Spinners' Association failed to gain overwhelming support for its struggle and these had little to do with whether or not the spinners were 'a particularly well-loved group'. The spinners went on strike at a time when the west of Scotland was experiencing a slump in trade.[72] Archibald Alison, the Sheriff of Lanarkshire who led the police when they arrested the Spinners' Committee, recalled that 'April 1837 was a period of unexampled suffering and distress...'.[73] Even before the Association called out its members there were, according to the *Glasgow Courier*, nearly 3000 unemployed handloom weavers in Glasgow and its vicinity. The paper also reported that the city's power-loom factories had reduced output with the result that some workers were made redundant while others had their hours of work reduced.[74] This downturn in the economy continued throughout the summer. For example, the secretary of the committee established in Glasgow in May to administer relief to distressed workers, by providing either work or food, estimated that around one half of the 8000 or so weavers in and around Glasgow were assisted by his organisation.[75] In June the *Courier* reported that the number of workers receiving relief in Paisley was continuing to increase and presently numbered around 2,100. But, as the paper explained, this figure greatly under-represented the number of those out of work, as only one person from each family was allowed assistance from the Relief Fund, 'and several other restrictions are imposed for keeping the numbers down'.[76] Given the grim economic situation which affected workers, especially cotton workers, in the west of Scotland, it is not surprising that the Spinners' Association found it difficult to raise funds during its strike.[77]

Other work groups in and around the city, such as the masons, bricklayers and quarrymen, had been involved in strikes not long before the spinners began their struggle in April 1837. Moreover, during the spinners' stoppage industrial disputes raged throughout the coal and iron districts of the west of Scotland, the Glasgow sawyers were out, and there was a major iron-moulders strike at a works in the city.[78] It is unlikely that workers who had recently been on strike or who were engaged in industrial action would have spare funds to donate to the spinners during their conflict with their employers.

It would also appear that sections of the working class in Glasgow were hostile to the spinners' strike because it added to the distress which already existed in the city. As Fraser noted, the strike had serious repercussions for textile workers such as weavers and those in the finishing trades, and the result was that the numbers of unemployed and underemployed increased.[79] Furthermore, the stoppage meant that the other occupational groups in the cotton spinning mills, such as piecers, carders and reelers, were unable to work. Sheriff Alison informed a parliamentary committee that:

> Every cotton-spinner threw out of employment from six to ten other persons, for whom there was not a shadow of relief of any kind, and those persons were kept for four months in a state of perfect idleness wandering about the streets…and their indigence was indescribable.

He also claimed 'The feeling of horror excited in the community by this dreadful addition to public suffering was indescribable…'.[80]

The number of violent incidents during the spinners' strike, such as the intimidation of and attacks on strike breakers, the threats to employers and the acts of arson,[81] also seem to have alienated many of the city's workers. James Burn, who was active in working class radicalism in Glasgow during the 1830s and who will be discussed in a subsequent chapter (he was of Irish birth), recalled that the stoppage

> was conducted upon a very reprehensible principle. Intimidation was practised, and several persons were said to have been injured, and the consequence was

that the people who were out on strike lost much of the public sympathy which
their condition would otherwise have commanded.[82]

Indeed the violence associated with the strike was probably the principal
reason why the Glasgow Trades Delegates did not immediately make an
appeal on behalf of the arrested spinners. Andrew Gemmill, the
Association's solicitor, told the 1838 Select Committee on Combinations
that once he was satisfied that the committee members were innocent, and
was made aware that they and their union had no funds, he suggested to
the Glasgow Trades Committee that it launch an appeal on behalf of the
arrested men. Gemmill also informed the Trades Committee that he
believed the Government was contemplating measures against trade unions
and therefore the case of the cotton spinners was, 'in some measure, the
case of all working men'.[83] On 29 August, thirty one days after the Spinners'
Committee was arrested, the Glasgow Trades Committee, which had
perhaps at first been convinced of the spinners' guilt given the violence
associated with the strike, resolved to investigate the conduct of the cotton
spinners both before and during the dispute.[84] One week later the
Committee reviewed the evidence it had collected and passed a motion
which stated that it was

> perfectly satisfied of the open and honourable conduct of the cotton-spinners,
> and that they deserve the sympathy and support of all the working classes while
> suffering under their present unmerited persecutions; that an address to that
> effect be immediately circulated, to disabuse the public mind from the prejudice
> which has existed against them by the misrepresentation of a hireling press...

Four delegates were appointed to prepare the address, which was circulated
around Glasgow several days later. This appeal for contributions to the
spinners' legal fund also stated that the authorities had acted against the
spinners 'for the purpose of destroying all trades' unions'.[85] The belief that
the forthcoming spinners' trial was to be a prelude to a general attack on
trade unionism, along with the findings of the Glasgow Trades Committee
that the arrested men were innocent, resulted in various protest meetings
in Glasgow, Paisley and elsewhere in the country. Funds were raised and
twenty thousand signatures were collected in Glasgow for a petition to
Parliament supporting the spinners. After the trial the agitation continued
and was eventually taken up by the Chartist movement.[86]

- It would appear, therefore, that the Glasgow spinners were unable to
win much support for their strike, and for the arrested committee members
during their first few weeks of imprisonment, not because they were an
'outsider group', who were not 'particularly well-loved'. Workers suffering
as a result of the trade recession did not have spare funds to give to the

spinners nor had those who were or had recently been on strike. The spinners' stoppage was unpopular among some because it added to the economic misery of the city. The incidents of violence during the dispute appalled many. Yet despite all this the Spinners' Association did receive some financial assistance from several trades in the west of Scotland.[87]

Furthermore, when the activities of the spinners prior to the 1837 strike are examined it becomes impossible to accept the argument that they were an 'outsider group'. The Spinners' Association was represented on the Glasgow Trades Committees of the 1820s and 1830s.[88] Moreover, as subsequent chapters will demonstrate, groups of spinners were involved in the political radicalism of 1816–20, and the union participated with the other trades in the city in the campaign for the Reform Bills and in subsequent political agitations, including Chartism. The spinners were at the forefront of the Glasgow campaign for factory reform, which sought to improve the conditions and reduce the hours of work not solely for cotton spinners but for all workers in all factories.[89] The Spinners' Association gave financial assistance to other trades[90] and received aid during its own struggles, as occurred, for example, during the Glasgow lock-out of 1824–25.[91] The union appears to have been the principal backer of the *Liberator*, the newspaper for the Glasgow working classes founded in November 1832.[92] From then until the strike of 1837 the Association contributed £978 to the paper.[93] The union had also helped to establish and finance the *Liberator's* predecessor, the *Trades' Advocate*.[94] It is evident, therefore, that the spinners cannot be regarded as an outsider group. Individual spinners and the Spinners' Association, which throughout the first four decades of the nineteenth century had a large Irish presence both in its membership and in its leadership, were an important part of the labour movement in the west of Scotland from the mid-1810s to the late 1830s.

IV

As was shown in the introduction to this study, several historians have highlighted the role of Irish immigrants as strike-breakers. Almost all the examples they provided relate to the mining industries. This is not surprising, since from the mid-1820s immigrant labour was frequently used by employers during disputes with their workers. For example, during a stoppage by the colliers at his pits at Faskine near Airdrie in October 1825 William Dixon brought in new workers, some of whom were Irish.[95] The following April, workers at Colin Dunlop's Clyde Iron Works went on strike to oppose wage reductions. Dunlop dismissed them and employed new men, many of whom were Irish.[96] By the 1840s Irish workers constituted a large proportion of the labour force in the Lanarkshire mines. Most had entered the pits during recent industrial disputes. In 1844 Robert Lumsden, oversman at the Dundyvan Works, informed the Mining Commissioner that:

> Every year there is an accumulation of new hands as colliers, caused by strikes; these hands, in the course of six weeks, will become colliers, i.e. able to put out the 'darg'; they are mostly Irish labourers. I believe that since 1837, the first large strike, at least 4,000 men have come in and stuck to the trade...[97]

The Commissioner reported that some had estimated that these new workers formed between a fifth and a quarter of the total number of colliers and miners in Lanarkshire.[98] In the Coatbridge district, one of the two major coal and iron mining areas in the county (the other was around Airdrie), Irish workers formed almost one-half of the total collier and miner workforce in 1851: a decade earlier they had constituted just over thirteen per cent of the total.[99]

The introduction of Irish workers into the pits during strikes often resulted in acts of violence against them by local colliers. In September 1827 the houses of almost every one of the Irish workers residing in the village of Faskine were attacked by a large mob. All the windows were broken as the workers, their families and lodgers remained locked inside in a state of terror.[100] The houses of two native colliers were also attacked as these men were 'friendly to the Irishmen'.[101] According to Daniel Johnston, overseer and manager of the coalworks, the Irish colliers had 'been occasionally molested' since 1825 when, as strike-breakers, they first entered the pits, the reason being that the Scottish colliers wished 'to compel the Irishmen to leave the works altogether, conceiving that thereby they would be enabled to raise their wages'.[102] It would appear, however, from the declarations made by three of those whose houses were attacked, that the abuse they were subjected to was more frequent than occasional. One of them, George Laird, stated 'That the Irish colliers working there...have experienced a good deal of molestation and threatenings of personal violence from the Scotch Colliers...'.[103] For example, William Hannigan, one of the victims of the mob in September 1827, had previously been assaulted 'for no reason that could be conceived except that he, being an Irishman, dared to remain in Mr Dixon's employ'...'.[104]

The ringleaders of the Faskine mob absconded and the Irish workers remained.[105] Just over a year later, however, the native population succeeded in driving the Irish colliers out of the village and the pit at Faskine. On Monday 11 November a large mob attacked the house of Thomas Murphy and that of the unfortunate William Hannigan. The windows, doors, household goods and parts of the roofs were broken during the riot and the men's lives threatened.[106] As before, the aim of the attack was to expel the Irish workers.[107] Hannigan stated that as the mob approached his house he heard someone shout 'let us take out the Buggar Hannigan and tear the puddings out of him that he may be an example to every Irish Buggar living'.[108] Hannigan and Murphy fled from their houses but did not immediately leave the area. According to Hannigan, he and 'the other Irishmen remained about the works for a few days, but during night they slept in concealed places and afterwards were obliged to flee the place having received repeated warnings that their lives were in danger...'.[109] Both Hannigan and Murphy soon found employment in Dixon's works at Govan.[110]

Three years later at Cuilhill Colliery near Coatbridge a dozen Irish drawers at the pit were used to replace the Scottish colliers who had gone on strike.[111] After they finished a shift on 24 October 1831 the strike-breakers went to a house for a drink. On leaving it they were attacked by a number of the combined colliers. The following night the men on strike stoned the houses of some of the Irish workers, calling out that they would 'put the Irish B——rs from ever working another shift after that night'. Joseph McKelvy, one of the lodgers in the house of James Courtney, stated that stones continued to be thrown 'until they demolished every article of furniture in the house'. Courtney was badly injured in the attack, and he and the other Irish strike-breakers did not resume work until after several days had passed. The ringleaders of the mob absconded.[112]

Violence also occurred as a consequence of the various strikes in the Lanarkshire coalfield during the late 1830s and the 1840s. In April 1837 two hundred miners at Baird's works at Gartsherrie stopped work. Irish labourers who were working in the pits as roadsmen filled their places. The company was 'obliged to protect them day and night' as the dismissed men 'were very savage...'.[113] In 1844 Robert Brown, factor to the Duke of Hamilton, stated of the new men introduced during the strikes of the previous few years that: 'There is sometimes a struggle before they are allowed by the other men to pursue their work quietly; but, in the end, law gains the day, and the new hands become permanently engrafted on the trade'.[114]

It would be wrong to conclude that Irish workers employed to break strikes were always the victims of violence: there is evidence that some fought back. For example, in Coatbridge in 1840 there was a running battle between the new Irish colliers and the old colliers.[115] In the same town two years later the police were withdrawn at the end of the miners' strike, as the funds which had been voted for their maintenance had run out. The following evening, Saturday 8 October,

> a great number of drunken and infuriate colliers and miners assembled in this quarter, and having quarrelled among themselves, and split into two factions, distinguished as Scotch and Irish, they first fought with each other for possession of the bridge, and in the general confusion which ensued, assaulting every respectable-looking person who came in their way. The riot continued for several hours, during which the town was completely in the hands of the mob.

The *Glasgow Chronicle* reported that on the following Monday evening twenty Glasgow policemen were sent to the town and peace was restored.[116]

After examining both the incidents of strike-breaking by Irish workers in the Lanarkshire mining districts and the violent disputes between the Catholic and Protestant Irish immigrant miners in the county, Alan Campbell, the historian of the Lanarkshire miners, concluded that 'the coming of the Irish created a number of impediments to the solidarity of the mining communities which made trade union organisation more difficult'.[117] He demonstrated that, once part of the labour force, Irish miners were seemingly reluctant to join their district unions; for example, there was an underpresentation of Irish miners among trade union activists in the Coatbridge area. Campbell offered several possible explanations for this lack of unionisation among the immigrant colliers and miners: the Irish probably did not have any prior experience of trade unionism and therefore had not the same cultural traditions as the Scottish miner — the 'independent collier' — who regarded himself as a skilled worker and who wished to control the work process and regulate entry to the trade, preferably to members of his own family; the Catholic Church might have been hostile to trade unions and discouraged its adherents from joining them, as occurred in the north of England; and the segregation of Irish workers in the mining districts, itself a legacy of their introduction to these areas as strike-breakers, 'may well have prevented their integration into the union'.[118] It might also have been that Irish workers were unwilling to join unions whose members had attacked or intimidated them when they first became employed as miners or colliers. Furthermore, the Irish workers 'appear to have been more mobile than the Scots'. In 1842 the Roman Catholic priest at Airdrie told the Children's Employment Commission that:

> Young single men come from Ireland to work here and consider themselves quite disconnected with the general population of the place, intending often to return to Ireland with a little money to pay their rent.

Seven years later the Mining Commissioner for Lanarkshire reported that 'the Irish are a comparatively fluctuating body'.[119] Michael Condon, the priest in charge of St Mary's in Hamilton from 1850 to 1859, had a large number of Irish miners among his congregation who were employed not only in Hamilton but also in several other civil parishes in the middle ward of the county. In 1857 Condon noted that his 'mining population, like the herring-shoals, is ever on the move, after better pay'.[120] Campbell concluded:

> The evidence of high rates of mobility among the Irish permits some speculation as to the motivations of the transients while they were in the district. Men who were working in the mines only to raise money to pay rent in Ireland or emigrate to America could scarcely have been attracted to the union by a policy of output restriction.[121]

Miners were paid according to the amount of coal they produced. Their unions believed that a successful policy of output restriction would create a shortage of coal which would result, eventually, in an increase in coal prices and also in miners' wages. They were also convinced that output restriction should be used to prevent coal prices and thus wage levels from falling. For the policy to work all miners had to agree to produce a certain amount of coal and for most this would mean a reduction in their output. In the short term this would also result in a reduction in their wages.[122] This was something which Irish workers, who appear to have intended their stay in the mines to be as brief as possible, did not want. They sought to produce as much as they could in order to maximise their earnings.

Campbell, however, revealed that one of the leading trade union activists among the miners in the 1840s was an Irishman named William Cloughlan, who was the secretary of the Holytown Miners' Union. He edited *The Colliers' and Miners' Journal*, which had a wide circulation in the county during its brief existence in 1841. He was also the principal promoter in Scotland of the Miners' Association of Great Britain and it was largely owing to his efforts that miners in the districts of Airdrie, Coatbridge and Holytown became involved in the organisation. By mid-1845, however, the Scottish miners had abandoned the Association as had Cloughlan, who then became prominent in the National Association of United Trades for the Protection of Labour. He also lectured, published pamphlets on union policies and strategies, and aided miners in districts throughout Scotland, for example during strikes. Cloughlan emigrated to America in 1848.[123] Campbell described him as 'one of the most articulate of the Lanarkshire miners' leaders of the 1840s'.[124] Gordon Wilson went further. He concluded that Cloughlan was, 'the most consistent, influential and well-known union leader among the miners' of Scotland during that decade. Indeed, Wilson ranked Cloughlan as one of the 'three most distinguished' miners' leaders in nineteenth century Scotland: the other two he named were Alexander McDonald and Keir Hardie.[125]

Although there is little evidence of Irish involvement in miners' unions in Lanarkshire in this period there are, as Campbell acknowledged, statements from contemporary observers which insist that Irish workers were involved in industrial action. In 1834 Alexander Christie, manager of Dixon's Iron Works at Calder, told the Inquiry into the Irish Poor in Great Britain that his

> Irish labourers require more looking after…If anything like a combination gets a footing they seem more forward and active in taking a lead than the Scotch.

Nine years later an engineer at the same works stated that during strikes 'the uneducated Irish collier is generally the worst'. In 1853 'A traveller underground' wrote: 'The reason that the Union is so strong in some parts of Scotland, as in Lanarkshire, is because in the latter place the pitmen are one third Irish, and others are the worst of the Scotch'.[126] In his account of his period in charge of St Mary's in Hamilton Michael Condon recalled that during the Scottish miners' strike of 1856

> the colliers and miners of my mission had refused to work, unless their employers increased their wage. Sooner than give in, they preferred, many of them, to live on a meal or two of porrige daily. You might meet their famished faces, here, there and everywhere, collecting subscriptions or asking for a morsel of bread.[127]

Such evidence led Campbell to conclude that a 'clear distinction' needed to be 'maintained between the participation of the "turbulent Irish" in a strike or riot, and their involvement in organising stable and enduring unions'.[128]

There is, however, no direct evidence of Irish involvement in the strikes which occurred in the Lanarkshire mining areas between 1837 and 1848. Newspaper reports of the stoppages give no indication of the ethnic composition of those on strike. It is probable, however, that some of the Irish who were already part of the mining workforce at the time of industrial disputes became involved in them. For example, in 1834, 79 of the 269 colliers at Dixon's Govan colliery were Irish. Three years later there was an eight week strike at the works against wage reductions.[129] During the widespread miners' strikes of 1837 Irish workers were used as blackleg labour, for instance at the Clyde Iron Works and at Baird's Works at Gartsherrie. Five years later both establishments were affected by the miners' strike.[130] In 1843, 1844 and 1847, major stoppages again occurred in the mining areas of Lanarkshire. In all of these disputes the Coatbridge district, which it will be recalled had a large Irish mining population, 'figured prominently'.[131] Of course, there are no means of establishing whether some or all of the Irish workers introduced into the mines as strike-breakers during a major dispute were still present in the same works or districts at the time of the next stoppage. Even if they were it is impossible to determine whether they participated in the strike. However, given the evidence of contemporary observers as well as that of the major disputes, it is likely that whereas most Irish miners in Lanarkshire during the 1830s and 1840s were unwilling or unable to join their local unions, some participated in strikes at their individual places of work when wage-rates or conditions came under threat.[132]

The discussion thus far has centred on Lanarkshire. Irish colliers were also present in Ayrshire at this time, although very little is known about them or the Scottish colliers working there. There is also a paucity of secondary work on trade unionism and industrial action in the county. A study of the Ayrshire colliers similar to Campbell's work on Lanarkshire is badly needed.

Irish workers were used as blacklegs during colliers' disputes in Ayrshire. In December 1824 members of the Ayrshire Colliers Association went on strike at the Ayr collieries of George Taylor. He brought in new workers, mainly Irish labourers, to fill their places and by mid-February 1825 most of the strikers were back at work having renounced the union.[133] In early 1841 an Ayr doctor stated: 'During a strike a few years ago, the coal-master sent a number of Irish labourers down into the pits, and since that time a considerable portion of the colliers have been Irishmen'.[134] If this was indeed the case then it is probable that many of the miners in Ayrshire who participated in the major strike of 1842 were from Ireland.[135]

There is in fact evidence which shows the involvement of Irish colliers in that dispute. The colliers and labourers at the works of John Taylor Gordon in the parish of St Quivox struck work in the autumn.[136] Most were from Connaught.[137] Strike-breakers were introduced and almost immediately the houses in which they were placed 'were visited by a mob of about two hundred persons, armed with firearms, pickshafts, iron pins, bludgeons and other lethal weapons, and several of them with their faces blackened, and disguised dresses'. Members of the mob broke into the house where the new men resided, 'and assaulted them with pickshafts, iron pins, bludgeons and stones in a most violent and brutal manner...'. One of the strike-breakers fled from the house but was seized and shot, and also beaten while lying on the ground. He died of his injuries two days later.[138] At the end of December 1842 four of the workers who had gone on strike were tried at the High Court in Edinburgh charged with mobbing, rioting, intimidation and murder. The case against one was abandoned and the charge against the rest of murder was found not proven, although they were convicted of mobbing, rioting and assault. The three were each sentenced to ten years' transportation.[139] The following June, Michael McMorrow or Murray and Daniel McAulay, two of the Irish strikers at Gordon's pit,[140] were tried at the High Court in connection with the events of November 1842. The charge against them of murder was dropped and they pleaded guilty to the charges of mobbing and assault. They too were sentenced to transportation for ten years.[141]

Of the ten strike-breakers attacked that November evening in Ayrshire two, Hugh Boyle and the murder victim John Dawson, were Irish.[142] Four of the remaining blacklegs — Barnard Boyle, Charles Donnelly, James Divine and Michael Brady — had names which suggest they were of Irish birth or descent.[143] It was noted in a previous section that there is evidence that Irish workers were used as blacklegs during strikes involving the Glasgow Cotton Spinners Association, which had a large Irish membership. Clearly a distinction has to be made between the behaviour of Irish workers who were already part of a labour force and that of those who were brought over from Ireland by employers to break strikes or who were already in the west of Scotland but wanted employment, for whatever reason, in an establishment at which industrial action was taking place.[144] That most of the striking miners at Gordon's works in St Quivox were Irishmen from Connaught suggests that they might have initially been brought over to work in the Ayrshire mine as low-wage labour or as strike-breakers. But, and this argument has already been advanced for some of the Irish colliers and miners in Lanarkshire, once established in the workforce they were just as willing as Scottish workers to act to protect their wages or conditions.

V

Many of the Irish immigrants in the west of Scotland in the 1790s found employment as handloom weavers and throughout the following four decades many more took to the loom.[145] A large number of these new arrivals had been linen weavers in the north-eastern counties of Ireland.[146] Others learned the trade once they settled in Scotland. In 1834 the Glasgow cotton manufacturer Hugh Cogan stated:

> The Irish send over for their relations, or acquaintances, or town's people, and take them in as lodgers, and train them to weaving, which is now so easily

acquired, that a person of ordinary acuteness can do common work in a very short time...

According to Cogan this was one of the reasons why 'the absolute number of Irish hand-loom weavers, and still more their proportion to the Scotch, is constantly on the increase'; another was that by this time many Scottish weavers were not bringing their children up to work at the loom as they realised that the occupation would never regain the high level of wages once earned, because of the number of workers employed in the trade and as a result of the powerloom becoming more widely used.[147]

By the 1830s Irish and second (and possibly third) generation Irish workers formed a significant part of the weaving labour force. Norman Murray has suggested that 'by 1838 some thirty per cent of Scottish hand loom weavers were born in Ireland. If second generation Irish are included, the percentage would undoubtedly be higher'.[148] As most immigrants during this period settled in the west of Scotland, it is not surprising that in several weaving centres in the region estimates of the proportion of Irish websters were higher. For example, Glasgow was the major centre of low-grade plain cotton work and 'this was the sector of the trade to which the immigrant Irish were above all attracted'.[149] During the trade recession of 1837 2,884 distressed weavers were supplied with work in the summer by the city's Relief Committee: 1,103, or 38.2 per cent, were of Irish birth.[150] Many of the other weavers given relief might have been second or third generation Irish. Three years earlier Hugh Cogan had stated that he employed between 600–800 weavers in Glasgow, of whom about one-half were Irish.[151] Irish weavers were also prominent in several towns in Ayrshire at this time. It was reported that in Kilmarnock and Ayr most of the Irish were employed in cotton weaving and an estimate for Girvan put the proportion of Irish weavers as four-fifths of the total.[152] Throughout this period, however, Irish workers formed only a small percentage of the weavers in Paisley, as this town was the centre of the fancy weaving trade in which native workers retained the dominant position.[153]

There is evidence from the 1830s of the involvement of Irish weavers in trade unions and strikes. In 1833 George Allen, a Glasgow book-muslin weaver, told the Select Committee on Manufactures, Commerce and Shipping that he had been selected by his fellow weavers to 'represent their condition' to the Committee and that both Irish and Scottish weavers were present at the meeting which chose him.[154] This delegate was probably the same George *Allan* who was active in the weavers' unions of the time.[155] Even if it was established that he was not the same person and that it was not a union meeting which selected him, Allen was still a representative chosen by a group of weavers in Glasgow to put their case before a

Parliamentary Inquiry and Irish weavers were part of that group. A year later Hugh Cogan told the Irish Poor Inquiry:

> With regard to combination among the weavers, the Irish are rather urged on by the more acute and thinking among the Scotch; but when the emergency comes the Irish are the more daring spirits; and as they are in themselves less reflective, and worse educated, they are more prone to use violence, without regard to consequences.[156]

Evidence given to the same Inquiry from Kilmarnock, Ayr and Girvan stated that the Irish there had 'taken a more prominent part in trade unions...than the natives'.[157] As has been shown, most Irishmen in these towns were employed as handloom weavers. Of those 1,103 Irish-born weavers given relief work in Glasgow in 1837 595, or over half, were members of trade unions. The number of weavers born in Scotland who were aided by the Relief Committee was 1,739, of whom 938 were unionised, an almost identical proportion to that of those born in Ireland. Irish-born workers formed just under 40 per cent of the total number of combined weavers given relief. The actual proportion of Irish weavers who were trade unionists and who were given relief work at this time was probably higher as some of the Scottish-born weavers who were in trade unions were almost certainly second or third generation Irish.[158]

Unfortunately, no evidence has been found which shows the involvement of Irish weavers in strikes or combinations prior to the 1830s, although it is highly unlikely that it was not until the fourth decade of the century that they decided to become organised and take action. Reports of the meetings of delegates of the Scottish Weavers' Association during 1824 and 1825, the years during the 1820s when unionisation was strongest among the weavers, give no indication whether Irish workers were involved. Nor do they give information on the numbers of weavers from Ireland in the districts represented or on what proportion of the membership were Irish.[159] Similarly, the sources relating to the weavers union of 1808–13 and the great strike of 1812–13 do not reveal Irish participation.[160]

Indeed, it is impossible to establish with any degree of certainty the number of Irish weavers in the west of Scotland during 1808–13 and therefore the proportion they formed of the total weaving workforce: the sources do not enable this to be done. What is certain, however, is that there were Irish weavers in the region at that time and it would appear they formed a significant part of the immigrant male workforce in certain areas. For example, the Catholic priest at Paisley informed a colleague in 1810 that there were perhaps thousands of Catholic Irish weavers in and around

Glasgow.[161] The baptismal register for the Glasgow chapel for the period from 30 June 1808 to 28 December 1815 lists the occupations of most of the fathers whose children were christened. During 1812, 334 Catholic men, practically all of whom were Irish, had their children baptised. The occupations of 300 of them were recorded. The majority, 157, were employed as labourers. The second largest group was the handloom weavers with 71, or just under one-quarter, of those men whose occupations were noted.[162] Of course, this does not necessarily mean that the same proportion of all male Irish Catholic workers in and around Glasgow were handloom weavers. What the figure merely suggests is that handloom weaving was a trade which employed a large number of Irish Catholic workers during 1812, the year of the great weavers' strike. By contrast, there were few Irish Catholic weavers in Paisley at this time as the town specialised in the fancy weaving branch of the industry, which immigrant weavers were not trained in and could not gain entry to without serving an apprenticeship. Such Irish workers therefore went to Glasgow, where plain weaving dominated.[163] With regard to the Protestant Irish immigrants, it is likely that a large proportion of male workers among them at this time were handloom weavers.[164]

It is probable that a number of Irish weavers were involved in the activities of 1808–13. In July 1812 the Lord Advocate wrote to Lord Sidmouth, the Home Secretary, concerning the associations of operative weavers in the country:

> The operatives in Scotland consist of natives and of a numerous body of Irishmen. The last although they shewed some disposition to riot and tumult have been kept quiet and peaceable by the former, and at present I am disposed to hope from information I have received from different quarters that no acts of violence are to be apprehended.[165]

This hints at some Irish involvement in the Weavers' Association. Furthermore, practically all the weavers in Scotland participated in the great strike which began in November 1812. After a few days forty thousand looms were reported to be silent and the stoppage was general.[166] Andrew Scott, the Roman Catholic priest at Glasgow, wrote on 19 November that the streets of the city were 'completely filled with idle people' and that there was 'Not a *weaver working within ten miles* of Glasgow...'.[167] Three days later the Marquess of Douglas and Clydesdale informed Sidmouth that

> the weavers have struck work, not only over all Lanarkshire, but over all that very extensive district of country that is employed by the Glasgow and Paisley manufacturer. I am sorry to say this whole population is now wandering about

quite idle, refusing work at a lower rate than the minimum unfortunately fixed by the Justices…[168]

The strike lasted until the end of February 1813 and according to Alexander Richmond, one of the weavers' leaders, 'half of which time, the whole looms, engaged in the cotton manufacture in Scotland, (with a few trifling exceptions,) were at a stand'.[169] Therefore if the strike was so widespread and general, particularly at the beginning, it is not unreasonable to suggest that Irish weavers in Scotland at that time also stopped work. Admittedly there were a few non-strikers and strike-breakers,[170] but there is nothing in the available sources to indicate or suggest that Irish weavers were prominent among them.

There were certainly no barriers to Irish workers joining the Weavers' Association of 1808–13, or indeed any of the weavers' organisations which existed throughout the first half of the nineteenth century. The aim of these unions was to include all weavers who would abide by their rules and regulations. Only by so doing could they even hope to be effective.[171] As Murray has shown, 'the process of undercutting could not be effectively curbed so long as a sizeable portion of the labour force remained unorganised'.[172] It would have been a foolish union which sought to exclude, for example, those Irish workers who formed an estimated one-third of Glasgow's weaving force in 1819[173] or who formed around 40 per cent (or even more) by 1837. In the latter year the organ of the three weavers' unions in the west of Scotland, the *Weavers' Journal*, emphasised this in an *Address to the Operative Weavers of Maybole*:

> Fellow operatives, it is time we were laying all our petty differences aside. We have a common enemy to oppose. Let us unite in common to oppose them. "Let their rule of tactics" be the example which we will follow. Do they pay any deference to the nationality of a man, or the predominance of a political party? Do they refuse giving a man the twist sent to his web, because he is an Irishman? Or do they charge a man one-third more carriage than what they give the carrier because he is a Radical? No. Then why let such interfere with the social intercourse of the operatives of this place? Why let the poisonous influence of the bigots of party interfere with the energies of your minds, that when called upon by the most pressing emergency to bring them into active operation, they are sapped and powerless?[174]

Unfortunately, it is not known what was occurring in Maybole at this time to elicit such an address. Moreover, the same edition of the *Journal* published an article entitled 'There is no religion in trade'. It stated:

> might we not reasonably expect that those who have to labour for their daily bread, would not make religion an opposing barrier to the protection of that

labour. Shall we indeed convert that heavenly messenger, which carries the tidings of peace and goodwill to mankind, into a firebrand? May we not, whether churchmen or voluntaries, Calvinists or Arminians, members of the Catholic faith or of the Episcopal Church of England, support our principles in proper time and place, without injuring our mutual friendship, 'that sweetener of life and solder of society'. Can we not, as citizens of the world, and contemporaries in existence, maintain our political rights as patriots, and our industrial rights as labourers, although our religious opinions are not all in unison. The enjoyment of liberty and of our daily bread, are our unalienable birthrights; and if the former is wrested from us by feudalised aristocrats, and the latter reduced to a miserable pittance by greedy taskmasters, will we allow the difference in our religious opinions to prevent us from regaining both? If we do, mere opinions constitute all the religion we have, for we are strangers to its humanising influence, and have formed a religion and a deity for ourselves.[175]

This article likewise appears to have been published in response to religious divisions among some weavers. What is clear, however, is that the three weavers' unions in the west of Scotland at this time wanted all weavers to become members, regardless of race, nationality or religion. By the end of 1837, however, the weavers' unions had collapsed and were never again to reach the degree of organisation or level of membership of the mid-1830s. As has been shown, the trade recession of 1837 particularly affected the weavers and plunged many into even greater poverty and distress than that to which they had been accustomed. It was impossible for them to sustain effective union organisations in such dire economic circumstances, which lasted for several years. In the more prosperous years of the 1840s there is little evidence of trade union activity among handloom weavers: many had abandoned the trade and those who remained had neither the funds nor it would appear the inclination to re-establish unions which, it must be said, had for a number of reasons been of little benefit to them in the 1830s.[176]

VI

There is evidence that Irish workers in a number of other occupations were involved in trade unions and industrial action. Irish railway navvies provide several examples of the latter. In February 1834 some of the workmen labouring at Holytown on the Wishaw and Coltness Railway stopped work over wage levels. They visited other workers on the line and used threats to force them to strike. Two of the ringleaders, William Gallacher and William Dorran, were arrested and soon convicted and imprisoned for their actions.[177] In July 1838 around sixty of the labourers on the Glasgow and Ayrshire Railway went on strike for a wage increase and the rest of the workers, who were fearful of the combined men, stayed away from work as well. The contractors responded by dismissing those on strike. The *Glasgow Chronicle* thought it 'worthy of remark that the strike was almost exclusively confined to the Irish labourers, and that all the Scotchmen are again re-employed'.[178] Nearly three years later 'no fewer than 100 Irishmen' working between Cowlairs and Springburn on the Edinburgh and Glasgow line marched their sub-contractor to the Glasgow police station for not having paid them and demanded the matter be dealt with by the captain of the police. The sub-contractor had not received money from the principal contractor and so could not pay his own men. The *Glasgow Chronicle* stated that 'Captain Miller, to allay the storm which might have risen, induced the keeper of the store, where they are usually supplied, to grant a sufficient supply of provisions to last the men and their families till Monday, with which arrangement they were perfectly contented'.[179] In February 1842 a number of Irish labourers employed in Mearns parish went on strike after not receiving their wages. Five of these workers assaulted their contractor the following day. Three of the assailants were soon apprehended. It is not known at what type of work these labourers were employed.[180]

In his evidence to the Irish Poor Inquiry in 1834 Charles Scott, a Greenock shipyard owner, stated the following:

> Last August the sawyers in my yard struck, fourteen couple of whom were Irish. The Irish were not the ringleaders…We refused their terms, and employed common labourers, chiefly Irish, to fill the pits; by degrees they learnt the trade…The hands who struck are now begging to be employed on their former wages, and have entirely dissolved the union then formed.[181]

In the same report Joseph Browne, a Glasgow dyer who employed twenty workers, one-half of whom were Irish, also gave evidence of Irish involvement in strikes:

> I had a turn-out some years ago, in which the Irish were fully more to blame than the Scotch; they staid about a week, and came back on the same terms, when they saw the determined spirits of the masters; on this occasion, two men, who worked for me in the place of those who had turned out, were ill used and beaten; the suspicion fell upon Irish: at that time all the dyers in Glasgow turned out — there are 200 or 300 dyers in Glasgow, and probably near the half are Irish.

According to Browne these 200–300 men were employed in general dyeing as opposed to the dyeing of Turkey red, which also occurred in and around the city.[182] There is also evidence of Irish women workers striking. In early 1829 the women in a powerloom weaving factory in Glasgow stopped work for three weeks before returning on their employer's terms; a large number of those who went on strike were Catholics and almost certainly from Ireland.[183]

. It would appear that there were instances in which Irish workers simply took action at the workplace against management decisions. It is unlikely that they were members of structured combinations similar to those which existed for the cotton-spinners, colliers and weavers in the 1830s. There is evidence, however, of Irish workers in trade unions other than those already discussed. James Burn, born in Ireland of Irish parents, was a well-known working class radical in Glasgow during the 1830s and a leading member of the city's hatters' organisation.[184] The Irish Catholic Chartist Con Murray was the secretary of the Glasgow Operative Nailmakers Society in early 1841 and had been involved in the union since its establishment the previous September.[185] The roles which Burn and Murray played in radical politics will be discussed in later chapters.

VII

It is now evident that Irish workers participated in trade unions and strikes in the west of Scotland during the first half of the nineteenth century. But might it have been that most were Protestants? After all, historians such as Brown and Gallagher have argued that it was the Catholic Irish who were identified as being strike-breakers and cheap labour, and consequently were despised by the native workforce. Indeed, Gallagher argued that the Protestant Irish immigrants

> felt far more at home in Scotland than the more numerous Catholic Irish, since they were familiar with Scottish customs and institutions, shared the Protestant faith and were, in many cases, returning to the land of their forefathers. These ties of kinship enabled local workers and Protestant immigrants to display solidarity with one another. They made common cause against the Catholic immigrant Irish, who threatened working-class living standards by swamping the labour market and selling their labour at low rates.[186]

He also stated that the Protestant Irish 'fitted in so successfully that they were often able to bequeath their anti-Catholic Orange symbols to native Scots in order to make common cause against the despised Catholic Irish'.[187] T.C. Smout expressed a similar view in his social history of the Scottish people between 1830 and 1950.[188]

Indeed there is some evidence which, at first glance, could be used to support the view that the Catholic Irish played little part in the trade unions of the period. One of the questions asked in early 1834 by the Inquiry into the Irish Poor in Great Britain was: 'Have the Irish...taken a more prominent part in trades' unions, combinations, and other secret societies than the natives?' Answering with regard to Glasgow, Andrew Scott, by that time Vicar-Apostolic of the Western District of the Catholic Church in Scotland, stated:

> there are scarcely any of the Irish immigrants who learn any trade in this country, and scarcely any among them belong to the trades' unions. Trades' unions and combinations in this country are carried on by the natives; scarcely is there one Irishman out of a hundred among them. When any strike for wages takes place in a cotton manufactory, the Irish are then obliged to join their Scotch brethren, who are always the most numerous party.[189]

Asked the same question the priest in charge of the Catholics in and around Paisley gave a similar reply: 'They have not; indeed few of them have it in their power to do so, with the exception of some cotton-spinners, and they are forced to go along with their brethren in trade'.[190]

Scott's statement concerning disturbances in cotton works is clearly incorrect. As has been demonstrated, Irish workers were prominent in the Cotton Spinners Association in the city in this period. It may, of course, be argued that Scott was referring solely to the Catholic Irish with whom he was well acquainted; it was to this group that the priest at Paisley limited his evidence. Even if this was the case Scott was still wrong, as Irish Catholics were active in the union and some, most notably Peter Hacket and Patrick McGowan, were leading figures in it.

It is apparent from Scott's evidence that he did not consider weaving to be a trade and therefore his remarks do not concern the weavers' unions which were then re-emerging. Furthermore, there is nothing in the sources to suggest that those Irish weavers who were involved in trade unions or industrial action in this decade were overwhelmingly Protestant. It has been argued that there were no barriers to Catholics becoming members of the Weavers' associations and therefore it is most unlikely that only the Protestants among the Irish weavers acted to protect or improve their wages and conditions.

Similarly, there is no evidence to suggest that of the Irish workers who were miners or colliers, the strike-breakers among them were all Catholic and those who engaged in industrial action all Protestant. The sources for these disputes and indeed for most of the other occupations in which there is evidence of Irish participation — or non-participation — in strikes or trade unions, usually mention only the nationality of the Irish workers and not the religious denomination to which they belonged. However, as the Catholic miners and colliers in the middle ward of Lanarkshire in 1856 demonstrated, Catholic Irish workers in the mining industry were involved in strikes once they were part of the labour force.[191] Also, the evidence relating to the Glasgow Cotton Spinners Association, and to the textile industries in the north of England,[192] demonstrates that Irish Catholics were just as forward as native workers in engaging in collective action.

It is probable, therefore, that most of the examples which show that 'Irish' men or women participated in strikes or trade unions do not refer solely to Catholic or to Protestant workers. Likewise with the evidence of Irish workers being used as strike-breakers or as cheap labour. After all, Protestant immigrants did not come to Scotland to join trade unions or strikes. They, like Catholic workers, came over to escape poverty and find employment. It would be remarkable if none of the Protestant Irish immigrants were employed as strike-breakers or as cheap labour during this period.

VIII

There is, of course, evidence that Irish workers did not participate in industrial action or trade unionism in the west of Scotland during the first half of the nineteenth century. It has already been shown that many Irishmen entered the coal and iron mines as strike-breakers or as cheap labour and afterwards played little part in the colliers' and miners' combinations, although some appear to have been involved in strikes. Of the destitute Irish-born weavers given relief in Glasgow in 1837 nearly one-half were not members of the weavers' associations. Some Irish cotton spinners were strike-breakers. Furthermore, a large proportion of the Irish male workforce in the region were employed as labourers and there is little evidence of trade unionism or strike activity among them. The same is true of Irish females who worked in cotton factories.

Indeed, several employers from Glasgow, Renfrewshire and Ayrshire gave evidence in 1834 to the Inquiry into the Irish Poor in Great Britain which revealed that their Irish employees were rather docile at the workplace. One Kilmarnock builder stated that his Irish labourers were 'more obedient and serviceable' than his Scottish workers.[193] Others shared this view.[194] For example, James Coats, the leading sewing thread manufacturer, employed 150 workers in his Paisley mill, around a quarter of whom were Irish. He told the Inquiry that he had 'found the Irish hands more easy to manage, and more fond to please, than the natives, and equally industrious and well-behaved in the mill'.[195] However, such evidence cannot be used to argue that the Irish *en masse* were not involved in strikes or trade unions in the west of Scotland during these years. It merely reveals that by that particular moment in time some Irish workers had not yet engaged in industrial action.

The evidence presented in this chapter suggests on the other hand that whereas some Irish workers were employed initially as strike-breakers, others — and even some of the blacklegs — joined unions or participated in strikes once they were established in the workforce. Individual circumstances determined whether an Irish worker, or indeed a Scottish worker, became a union member, a striker or a blackleg. Throughout most of the period under examination Irish workers formed a large proportion of the membership and leadership of the Cotton Spinners' Association; by the 1830s Irish weavers were prominent in the rank and file of the weavers' associations and it is probable that some were involved in earlier combinations and strikes; in the 1840s groups of Irish colliers and miners were involved in industrial disputes. Irish workers in other occupations took action when the need arose. The Irish in the west of Scotland were not isolated from economic forces and, like Scottish workers, many of them acted to protect wages, conditions and living standards as best they could by collective action.

Notes

1. W. Hamish Fraser, *Conflict and Class: Scottish Workers, 1700–1838* (Edinburgh, 1988), p.97; Anthony Slaven, *The Development of the West of Scotland: 1750–1960* (London, 1975), pp.93–6; R.H. Campbell, *Scotland since 1707: The Rise of an Industrial Society* (2nd edition, Edinburgh, 1985), pp.81–91.

2. Slaven, *Development of the West of Scotland*, p.95.

3. W.H. Fraser, 'The Glasgow Cotton Spinners', in G. Menzies (ed.), *History is my Witness* (BBC, 1976), p.70; Slaven, *Development of the West of Scotland*, pp.93–6.

4. PP, 1836, (40), XXXIV, *Report on the State of the Irish Poor in Great Britain*, pp.v, 108, 132.

5. *Ibid*, p.108. See also pp.v, 108.

6. *Ibid*, pp.v, 108.

7. *Ibid*, p.108.

8. *Ibid*. See also Z.G. Brassey, The Cotton Spinners in Glasgow and the West of Scotland c.1790–1840: a Study in Early Industrial Relations, M.Litt., University of Strathclyde (1974), pp.21–4.

9. PP, 1836, (40), XXXIV, *Report on the State of the Irish Poor in Great Britain*, p.132. A cotton thread spinner in Paisley offered the following reason why the natives of the town in the 1830s continued to object to factory labour: 'The Irish in Paisley almost uniformly belong to the poorer classes...They

are employed in the most disagreeable and lower descriptions of labour; the employment in the cotton mills in considered of this class. Most natives of Paisley would, I believe, sooner earn 12s. a-week at weaving with their own looms, having the command of their own time, and their ingenuity exercised in their own profession, than work in a cotton factory for 20s. or 25s. per week: our weavers, however destitute, seldom think of applying for employment in cotton factories. A cotton spinner does not hold the same rank in society as a fancy weaver…'. *Ibid.*, p.133. For a similar view see PP, 1833, (450), XX, *First Report of the Central Board of His Majesty's Commissioners for Inquiring into the Employment of Children in Factories,* Appendix 2, p.82.

10. PP, 1833, (690), VI, *Select Committee on Manufactures, Commerce and Shipping,* pp.311–13. See also Fraser, 'Glasgow Cotton Spinners', p.72; W.H. Fraser, 'The Cotton Spinners, 1837', in John Butt and J.T. Ward (eds.), *Scottish Themes: Essays in Honour of S.G.E. Lythe* (Edinburgh, 1976), pp.83, 87; Brassey, *Cotton Spinners in Glasgow,* p.24.

11. PP, 1836, (40), XXXIV, *Report on the State of the Irish Poor in Great Britain,* p.107.

12. There is evidence of a combination of cotton spinners in the early 1800s and again between 1810 and 1811. The union re-emerged in 1816 and took on a permanent form. For the Spinners' Association see Brassey, *Cotton Spinners in Glasgow, passim*; Fraser, 'Glasgow Cotton Spinners, 1837', pp.80–97; John Butt, 'Labour and Industrial Relations in the Scottish Cotton Industry during the Industrial Revolution', in John Butt and Kenneth Ponting (eds.), *Scottish Textile History* (Aberdeen, 1987), pp.149–60.

13. PP, 1836, (40), XXXIV, *Report on the State of the Irish Poor in Great Britain,* p.xxiii.

14. *Ibid,* p.132.

15. *Ibid,* p.108.

16. Butt, 'Labour and Industrial Relations', pp.151–56; Fraser, 'Glasgow Cotton Spinners, 1837', pp.85, 96–7; Fraser, *Conflict and Class,* p.118.

17. WRH, Lord Advocate's Papers, AD14/25/192, Declaration of John Kean, 31 March 1825; Butt, 'Labour and Industrial Relations', pp.155–6; Fraser, *Conflict and Class,* p.118.

18. WRH, Lord Advocate's Papers, AD14/38/502, Declaration of Patrick Mellon, 2 October 1820; Declaration of James Cairney, 29 February 1821; Brassey, *Cotton Spinners in Glasgow,* p.47.

19. WRH, Lord Advocate's Papers, AD14/38/502, Declaration of Thomas Stewart, 19 January 1821.

20. Brassey, *Cotton Spinners in Glasgow,* pp.50–1; Robert Brown, *The History of Paisley From the Roman Period down to 1884, Vol.II* (Paisley, 1886), pp.151–3.

21. WRH, Lord Advocate's Papers, AD14/38/502, Declaration of Thomas Stewart, 19 January 1821.

22. *Ibid*, AD14/38/502, Declaration of Nathaniel Donald, 19 January 1821. Donald lists four spinners who were named by Stewart as being among the most violent of the unionists, viz., Kennedy Baxter, James McIntyre, Lachlan McQuarry and Robert Watson.

23. For the strike and trial of the cotton spinners see Fraser, 'Glasgow Cotton Spinners, 1837'; 'Glasgow Cotton Spinners'; *Conflict and Class*, chapter 9. There are three published reports of the trial: A. Swinton, *Report of the Trial of Thomas Hunter, Peter Hacket, Richard McNeil, James Gibb and William McLean, Operative Cotton Spinners in Glasgow…* (Edinburgh, 1838); *Trades Edition of the Cotton Spinners Trial* (Glasgow, 1838); *The Trial of Thomas Hunter, Peter Hacket, Richard McNeil, James Gibb and William McLean, the Glasgow Cotton Spinners…Reported by James Marshall…* (Edinburgh, 1838).

24. PP, 1837–1838, (488), VIII, *First Report from the Select Committee on Combinations of Workmen*, pp.44, 209; Fraser, Conflict and Class, p.154; Fraser, 'Glasgow Cotton Spinners, 1837', p.81.

25. PP, 1837–1838, (488), VIII, *First Report from the Select Committee on Combinations of Workmen*, p.208.

26. Swinton, *Report of the Trial*, p.174; Marshall, *Trial of Thomas Hunter*, p.51.

27. Swinton, *Report of the Trial*, p.108.

28. John T. Ward, 'The Factory Movement in Scotland', *Scottish Historical Review*, XLI (1962); Fraser, *Conflict and Class*, p.146.

29. PP, 1837–38, (488), VIII, *First Report from the Select Committee on Combinations of Workmen*, p.208.

30. Marshall, *Trial of Thomas Hunter*, p.44.

31. Swinton, *Report of the Trial*, p.xix.

32. WRH, Lord Advocate's Papers, AD14/38/503, Declaration of James Docherty, 2 August 1837.

33. These are located in WRH, Lord Advocate's Papers, AD14/38/503. No precognitions are available for four of the Committee members: Robert Greenhill, Daniel Walker, John McCaffer and John Bunyan.

34. WRH, Lord Advocate's Papers, AD14/38/503, Declaration of Bernard Murphy, 31 July 1837.

35. For those who were active during May and June 1837 in meetings, raising funds and support etc see Swinton, *Report of the Trial*, pp.xiii–xix.

36. WRH, Lord Advocate's Papers, AD14/37/453, Declaration of James Moat 28 July 1837. Earlier in this precognition Moat stated 'That Peter Hackett…is one of the most violent of the Association as well as Angus Campbell, John McAffer, John Bunyan, Richard McNeil, James Docherty, Daniel Walker, Henry Dunn, Thomas Hunter and James Gibb'.

37. *Ibid*, AD14/37/453, Declaration of Henry Cowan, 15 November 1837.

38. *Ibid*, AD14/39/460, Declaration of John Smith, 23 July 1837.

39. *Ibid*, AD14/37/453, Declaration of Thomas Donaghy, 1 July 1837; *Glasgow Courier* 12 and 19 December 1837; Fraser, 'Glasgow Cotton Spinners', pp.79, 88.

40. WRH, Lord Advocate's Papers, AD14/38/502, Declaration of James Cairney, 29 February 1821.

41. Fraser, *Conflict and Class*, pp.162, 167; Butt, 'Labour and Industrial Relations', pp.159–60.

42. *Glasgow Saturday Post*, 3 and 10 February 1844. For the cotton spinners and their union after 1837 see Per Bolin-Hort, 'Managerial Strategies and Worker Responses: A New Perspective on the Decline of the Scottish Cotton Industry', *Journal of the Scottish Labour History Society*, 29, (1994), pp.67–9; Eleanor Gordon, *Women and the Scottish Labour Movement in Scotland 1850–1914* (Oxford, 1991), pp.44–54; W.W. Knox, *Hanging by a Thread: The Scottish Cotton Industry, c. 1850–1914* (Preston, 1995), pp.148–150.

43. W. Hamish Fraser, 'The Scottish Context of Chartism', in Terry Brotherstone (ed.), *Covenant, Charter and Party: Traditions of Revolt and Protest in Modern Scottish History* (Aberdeen, 1989), p.67.

44. Bolin-Hort, 'Managerial Strategies', p.67.

45. Although he has been known to historians for some time it was only recently that it was revealed by John McCaffrey that McGowan was an Irish Catholic. The source which McCaffrey cited for information concerning McGowan's religion and nationality is the statement which he, McGowan, gave to a factory inspector in 1833. In this, McGowan stated that he was a Roman Catholic but did not mention his nationality or ethnic background. McCaffrey probably assumed that McGowan was Irish because of his name, occupation and religion. Evidence which almost certainly confirms that McGowan was indeed Irish or of Irish descent comes from the Glasgow working-class newspaper the *Trades' Advocate*, which in the summer of 1832 offered the following, somewhat bizarre, description of McGowan as part of a short article on him: 'In Patrick, the warmth, generosity, and rashness of the Hibernian is finely blended with the cool caution of the canny Scot; and though in his countenance you may trace the Milesian descent, yet it is shaded down into the agreeable, and his frontispiece is altogether favourably disposed.' John F. McCaffrey, 'Irish Immigrants and Radical Movements in the West of Scotland in the Early Nineteenth Century', *Innes Review*, XXXIX (1988), p.49; John F. McCaffrey, 'Irish Issues in the Nineteenth and Twentieth Centuries: Radicalism in a Scottish Context?', in T.M. Devine (ed.), *Irish Immigrants and Scottish Society in the Nineteenth and Twentieth Centuries* (Edinburgh, 1991), p.123; PP, 1833, (450), XX, *First Report of the Central Board of His Majesty's Commissioners for Inquiring into the Employment of Children in Factories*, Appendix 1, p.103; *Trades' Advocate*, quoted in *Poor Man's Advocate*, 23 June 1832.

46. R.G. Kirby and A.E. Musson, *The Voice of the People: John Doherty, 1798–1854, Trade Unionist Radical and Factory Reformer* (Manchester, 1975), pp. 100, 103, 195, 108, 113–4.

47. J.T. Ward, *The Factory Movement 1830–55* (London, 1962), pp. 53, 113; 'Factory Reform Movement', p.103.

48. Fraser, *Conflict and Class*, p.151.

49. Apart from in the works referred to in notes 45–48, references to McGowan are found in Sydney J. Chapman, *The Lancashire Cotton Industry: A Study in Economic Development* (Manchester, 1904. This reprint Clifton 1973), pp.202–3; Fiona A. Montgomery, 'The Unstamped Press: the Contribution of Glasgow 1831–36, *Scottish Historical Review*, LIX (1980), p.166; 'Glasgow and the Struggle for Parliamentary Reform', 1830–32', *Scottish Historical Review*, LXI (1982), p.139; Brassey, Cotton spinners in Glasgow, pp. 152, 158–9, 178, 187.

50. PP, 1833, (450), XX, *First Report of the Central Board of His Majesty's Commissioners for Inquiring into the Employment of Children in Factories*, Appendix 1, p.103.

51. No evidence has been found of McGowan playing any role in the Association during the industrial unrest in the Glasgow spinning districts between 1816 and 1827. This suggests that he had either not yet become active in trade unionism or was not yet working in the city's cotton mills.

52. For the Grand General Union, the N.A.P.L. and McGowan's activities in England at this time, see Kirby and Musson, *Voice of the People*, chapters 4–7.

53. *Poor Man's Advocate*, 23 June 1832.

54. Kirby and Musson, *Voice of the People*, p.141.

55. *Poor Man's Advocate*, 23 June 1832.

56. Ward, 'Factory Reform Movement', pp.103, 107 and *Factory Movement*, pp.53, 75–6, 113; Fraser, *Conflict and Class*, pp.146–7; PP, 1833, (450), XX, *First Report of the Central Board of His Majesty's Commissioners for Inquiring into the Employment of Children in Factories*, Appendix 1, p.103; *Poor Man's Advocate*, 2 February 1832; *Glasgow Free Press*, 27 February 1833; *Scots Times*, 4 August 1832.

57. *Poor Man's Advocate*, 30 June 1832.

58. *Scots Times*, 29 January 1831; *Glasgow Courier*, 27 January 1831; *Herald to the Trades' Advocate*, 29 January 1831.

59. *Herald to the Trades' Advocate*, 29 January 1831.

60. Fraser, *Conflict and Class*, pp.147–8. W. Hamish Fraser, *Alexander Campbell and the Search for Socialism* (Manchester, 1996), pp.43, 44, 48–9, 51.

61. PP, 1833, (450), XX, *First Report of the Central Board of His Majesty's Commissioners for Inquiring into the Employment of Children in Factories*,

Appendix 1, pp.101, 103; WRH, Lord Advocate's Papers, AD14/37/453, Declaration of Charles Hassan, 14 November 1837; *Glasgow Courier*, 24 August 1833.

62. Fraser, *Conflict and Class*, p.151.

63. It must be noted, however, that there was not as much activity among the spinners or the rest of the Glasgow trades during 1834–36 compared with 1831–33. Also, no copies of the newspaper for the Glasgow working classes in this period, the *Liberator*, appear to have survived.

64. *Trades Edition of the Cotton Spinners' Trial*, p.98; Marshall, *The Trial of Thomas Hunter*, p.64; Butt, 'Labour and Industrial Relations', p.158; Fraser, 'Glasgow Cotton Spinners, 1837', pp.87, 92.

65. WRH, Lord Advocate's Papers, AD14/37/453, Declaration of Charles Hassan, 14 November 1837; Swinton, *Report of the Trial of Thomas Hunter*, pp.xxiii–xxiv, reprints a letter from McGowan in Manchester to Peter Hacket, dated 10 July 1837, which gives an account of his fund-raising activities.

66. *Scots Times*, 4 August 1832. See also *Glasgow Free Press*, 1 August 1832 and *Glasgow Chronicle*, 3 August 1832.

67. PP, 1833, (450), XX, *First Report of the Central Board of His Majesty's Commissioners for Inquiring into the Employment of Children in Factories*, Appendix 1, p.99.

68. *Glasgow Free Press*, 27 February 1833. See also *Scottish Guardian*, 26 February 1833.

69. Quoted in *Poor Man's Advocate*, 23 June 1832.

70. *Poor Man's Advocate*, 23 June 1832.

71. Fraser, *Conflict and Class*, p.161. See also Fraser, 'Glasgow Cotton Spinners, 1837', pp.93–4; 'Scottish Context of Chartism', p.67.

72. Norman Murray, *The Scottish Handloom Weavers, 1790–1850: A Social History* (Edinburgh, 1978), pp.56–7; C.R. Baird, 'Observations upon the Poorest Class of Operatives in Glasgow in 1837', *Journal of the Statistical Society in London*, I, (July, 1838), p.167. James Dawson Burn, *A Glimpse into the Social Condition of the Working Classes during the Early part of the Present Century* (London, 1868), p.44.

73. PP, 1837–38, (488), VIII, *First Report from the Select Committee on Combinations of Workmen*, p.114.

74. *Glasgow Courier*, 1 April 1837.

75. Baird, 'Observations', pp.170–1. See also *Glasgow Courier*, 24 June 1837.

76. *Glasgow Courier*, 20 June 1837.

77. In the minute book of the Spinners' Association three entries for June 1837 show that some groups of workers were unable, because of their own difficult

economic position, to donate money to the spinners. These were the carters, potters, mechanics and engineers. Swinton, *Trial of Thomas Hunter*, pp.xvi–xviii.

78. Fraser, *Conflict and Class*, pp.155–56; Alan B. Campbell, *The Lanarkshire Miners: A Social History of their Trade Unions, 1775–1874* (Edinburgh, 1979), pp.81–3; PP, 1837–38, (488), VIII, *First Report from the Select Committee on Combinations of Workmen*, pp.114, 209, 226–8.

79. Fraser, *Conflict and Class*, p.161.

80. PP, 1837–38, (488), VIII, *First Report from the Select Committee on Combinations of Workmen*, p.114. See also Burn, *Glimpse into the Social Condition*, pp.44–5.

81. Fraser, *Conflict and Class*, p.154.

82. Burn, *Glimpse into the Social Condition*, pp.44–45. Burn also stated that had it not been for the charges made against the five spinners by the authorities 'which turned the anger of the public into a feeling of warm sympathy, it would have taken years to have enabled that body of men to stand well with the people of the west of Scotland'. *Ibid*, p.81.

83. PP, 1837–38, (488), VIII, *First Report from the Select Committee on Combinations of Workmen*, pp.209–10.

84. *Ibid*, pp.210–1.

85. *Ibid*, pp.210–1. The text of the address is reprinted on pp.211–2. See also *Glasgow Courier*, 12 September 1837.

86. *Glasgow Courier*, 26 October, 14 and 16 December 1837; *Glasgow Evening Post*, 28 October 1837; *Scots Times*, 28 October 1837; *Glasgow Chronicle*, 5 February 1838, 25 March 1839, Alexander Wilson, *The Chartist Movement in Scotland* (Manchester, 1970), pp.36–7, 39; Fraser, *Conflict and Class*, pp.161–2.

87. For example, the union received money from the masons, joiners and potters of Greenock, the joiners and sawyers of Glasgow, the Anderston potters and from some coal and iron-stone miners. Swinton, *Trial of Thomas Hunter*, pp.xiv–xviii.

88. Fraser, *Conflict and Class*, pp.90, 128, 148, 152.

89. Ward, 'Factory Reform Movement', *passim*; Edinburgh University Archives, S.R.C.1.3, Addresses to the Earl of Durham, f.17, Address of the Operative Cotton Spinners of Glasgow and Neighbourhood, October 1834.

90. Swinton, *Trial of Thomas Hunter*, p.xxii; Fraser, *Conflict and Class*, p.161.

91. Fraser, *Conflict and Class*, p.119.

92. The paper was renamed the *New Liberator* in November 1836. (James Dawson Burn), *The Autobiography of a Beggar Boy* (edited with an introduction by David Vincent, London, 1978), p.140; Leslie C. Wright, *Scottish Chartism* (Edinburgh, 1953), pp.28–30; Wilson, *Chartist Movement in Scotland*, pp.31,

34, 37; Fraser, *Conflict and Class*, pp.140, 155; James D.Young, *The Rousing of the Scottish Working Class* (London, 1979), pp.83, 85.

93. Swinton, *Trial of Thomas Hunter*, p.xxii.

94. Fiona A. Montgomery, 'The Unstamped Press: the Contribution of Glasgow', *Scottish Historical Review*, LIX (October, 1980), pp.162–8.

95. Fraser, *Conflict and Class*, p.123; Alan Campbell, 'The Scots Colliers' Strikes of 1824–26: the Years of Freedom and Independence', in John Rule (ed.), *British Trade Unionism 1750–1850: the Formative years* (London, 1988), p.156; WRH, Lord Advocate's Papers, AD14/28/139, Declaration of Daniel Johnston.

96. Fraser, *Conflict and Class*, p.123; Campbell, 'Scots Colliers' Strikes', p.156; PP, 1845, XXVII, *Report of the Mining Commissioner*, p.11.

97. PP, 1844, XVI, *Report of the Mining Commissioner*, p.37. See also the evidence of Robert Brown on the same page.

98. *Ibid*, p.37.

99. Campbell, *Lanarkshire Miners*, p.178.

100. The various precognitions concerning the incident are in WRH, Lord Advocate's Papers, AD14/28/139.

101. *Ibid*, Declaration of John MacShira. See also the Declarations of Michael Burk and James Moffat.

102. *Ibid*, Declaration of Daniel Johnston.

103. *Ibid*, Declaration of George Laird. See also the Declarations of John MacShira and Michael Burk.

104. *Ibid*, Dugald McCallum, Procurator Fiscal at Hamilton to Sheriff Robinson, 4 October 1827.

105. WRH, Lord Advocate's Papers, AD14/29/281, Declarations of James Hogg and William Hannigan.

106. The various precognitions and material concerning the incident are contained in WRH, Lord Advocate's Papers, AD14/29/281.

107. *Ibid*, Declarations of James Hogg, Thomas Murphy and William Hannigan.

108. *Ibid*, Declaration of William Hannigan.

109. *Ibid*.

110. *Ibid*. See also the Declaration of Thomas Murphy.

111. Campbell, *Lanarkshire Miners*, p.181.

112. WRH, Lord Advocate's Papers, AD14/31/302, Declarations of James Courtney and Joseph McKelvy.

113. PP, 1844, XVI, *Report of the Mining Commissioner*, p.37; Fraser, *Conflict and Class*, p.156; Campbell, *Lanarkshire Miners*, p.81. Roadsmen cleared up and stowed away anything which fell and impeded the work of the miners and colliers.

114. PP, 1844, XVI, *Report of the Mining Commissioner*, p.37.

115. Campbell, *Lanarkshire Miners*, p.181.

116. *Glasgow Chronicle*, 12 October 1842; Campbell, *Lanarkshire Miners*, p.181.

117. Campbell, *Lanarkshire Miners*, p.194.

118. *Ibid*, pp.195–7.

119. Quoted in *ibid*, p.200. See also the Table on p.199.

120. Glasgow Archdiocesan Archives, Michael Condon Diaries, Hamilton 1850–59, p.442.

121. Campbell, *Lanarkshire Miners*, p.200.

122. For the policy of output restriction see *ibid.*, pp.70–3, 265–67; Gordon M. Wilson, *Alexander McDonald, Leader of the Miners* (Aberdeen, 1982), pp.59–60.

123. Wilson, *Alexander McDonald*, chapters 3–5 *passim*; Campbell, *Lanarkshire Miners*, pp.137, 195, 200, 211, 220, 251–3, 165, 168, 270.

124. Campbell, *Lanarkshire Miners*, p.195.

125. Wilson, *Alexander McDonald*, pp.60, 85.

126. Quoted in Campbell, *Lanarkshire Miners*, pp.194–5.

127. Glasgow Archdiocesan Archives, Michael Condon Diaries, Hamilton 1850–59, p.392; See also Campbell, *Lanarkshire Miners*, p.194. For the 1856 strike see Wilson, *Alexander McDonald*, pp.74–8.

128. Campbell, *Lanarkshire Miners*, p.195.

129. PP, 1836, (40), XXXIV, *Report on the State of the Irish Poor in Great Britain*, p.113; Fraser, *Conflict and Class*, p.156.

130. PP, 1845, XXVII, *Report of the Mining Commissioner*, p.11; PP, 1844, XVI, *Report of the Mining Commissioner*, p.37.

131. Campbell, *Lanarkshire Miners*, p.137. See also pp. 210, 214, 249, 253; Gordon M. Wilson, 'The Strike Policy of the Miners in the West of Scotland', in Ian MacDougall (ed.), *Essays in Scottish Labour History* (Edinburgh, 1978), pp.30, 32, 48.

132. The evidence examined so far has been mainly from the late 1830s and 1840s. From the legal records in West Register House it may be suggested that even as early as the 1820s some Irish colliers were involved in industrial action. On 13 June 1826 two miners were assaulted at Airdrie by four men for having been strike–breakers the previous November. The assailants were Terence Braidy, Donald or Daniel McKillop, Daniel or Donald O'Hara and Michael O'Neill. The first three 'were combined miners' and the last named was a drawer and also a union member. The sources do not reveal whether these men were Irish, although the surnames of three of them suggest strongly that this was indeed the case. With regard to trade unionism, the evidence does not make it clear whether these men were members of the

district or regional union or were simply combined in the pit in which they were employed. WRH, Lord Advocate's Papers, AD14/26/247.

133. Fraser, *Conflict and Class*, p.122; Campbell, 'Scots Colliers' Strikes, pp.151–52; PP, 1825, (417/437), IV, *Report from the Select Committee on Combination Laws*, pp.67–8, 74.

134. *Reports on the Sanitary Condition of the Labouring Population of Scotland...* (London, 1842), p.23.

135. Wilson, 'Strike Policy of the Miners', pp.32, 48.

136. *Glasgow Chronicle*, 2 January 1843.

137. WRH, Lord Advocate's Papers, AD14/43/375, Declaration of Hugh Crawford, 5 April 1843; Declaration of Elizabeth Caldwell.

138. *Glasgow Chronicle*, 2 January 1843.

139. *Ibid*.

140. WRH, Lord Advocate's Papers, AD14/43/375, Declarations of Hugh Crawford, 5 April 1843; of Hugh Boyle, 11 May 1843; of Elizabeth Caldwell; and of Thomas Naggle.

141. *Glasgow Chronicle*, 7 June 1843.

142. WRH, Lord Advocate's Papers, AD14/43/375, Declaration of Hugh Boyle, 11 May 1843; Declaration of Daniel McAulay, 25 November 1842; *Glasgow Chronicle*, 23 November 1842.

143. *Glasgow Chronicle*, 18 November 1842.

144. From the Declarations of strike-breakers at Taylor's mine in Ayrshire it would appear that several left their jobs in the west of Scotland and arrived at the pit to find employment after seeing an advert for new workers in newspapers. It might have been that they were not aware that a strike was taking place until they had left their previous employment and arrived in Ayrshire. See, for example, WRH, Lord Advocate's Papers, AD14/43/375, Declaration of Peter Burns, 30 April 1843; Declaration of Charles Donnelly, 22 November 1842.

145. Murray, *Handloom Weavers*, pp.32–33.

146. PP, 1836, (40), XXXIV, *Report on the State of the Irish Poor in Great Britain*, pp.vii, xxxv.

147. *Ibid*, p.109. See also the evidence given by James Thompson on p.110.

148. Murray, *Handloom Weavers*, p.33.

149. *Ibid*.

150. Baird, 'Observations upon the Poorest Class of Operatives', p.168.

151. PP, 1836, (40), XXXIV, *Report on the State of the Irish Poor in Great Britain*, p.109.

152. *Ibid*, pp.143, 146–7, 149.

153. Murray, *Handloom Weavers*, p.32.

154. PP, 1833, (203),VI, *Report from the Select Committee on Manufactures, Commerce and Shipping*, p.697.

155. Strathclyde Regional Archives, Papers of Sir John Maxwell, 9th Bt. of Pollock,T–PM 117/3/209, *Address to the Operative Weavers of Glasgow, and the Surrounding Country Districts, in connection with the trade, dated Glasgow, 9 February 1833*; Edinburgh University Archives, S.R.C. 1.3, Addresses to the Earl of Durham, October 1834, f.17. Address of the Handloom Weavers of Scotland; *Glasgow Chronicle*, 30 March, 24 April 1829.

156. PP, 1836, (40), XXXIV, *Report on the State of the Irish Poor in Great Britain*, p.109.

157. *Ibid*, pp.145, 147, 149.

158. Baird, 'Observations upon the Poorest Class of Operatives', pp.168–69. Baird was the secretary of the Glasgow Relief Committee. Each applicant for assistance was required to answer a number of questions. That which asked whether the applicant was a trade unionist 'was inserted at the request of some of the members of the committee, in order to learn, as far as possible, the extent of Trades' Unions among the operatives, and to enquire how far such Unions tended to increase or diminish distress among these classes'. *Ibid*, p.168.

159. See the numerous reports in the Glasgow press during these years.

160. The materials relating to the weavers' union and strike are in WRH, Lord Advocate's Papers, AD14/13/8. These include precognitions, letters, accounts, minute books etc. Minutes of the Weavers' Association of this period are also located in WRH, Justiciary Court Records, JC45/39 and JC45/12.

161. SCA, Presholme Letters, PL3/28/11, William Rattray to Alexander Cameron, 19 March 1810. See also PL3/29/11, Andrew Scott to Alexander Cameron, 17 April 1810.

162. Glasgow Archdiocesan Archives, Baptismal Register, 30 June 1808–28 December 1815.

163. SCA, Presholme Letters, PL3/28/11, William Rattray to Alexander Cameron, 19 March 1810; Blairs Letters, BL4/396/2, William Rattray to Alexander Cameron, 5 February 1812.

164. Graham Walker, 'The Protestant Irish in Scotland', in T.M. Devine (ed.), *Irish Immigrants and Scottish Society in the Nineteenth and Twentieth Centuries* (Edinburgh, 1991), pp.45–49.

165. SRO, Home Office Correspondence, Scotland, RH2/4/98, A. Colquhoun to Viscount Sidmouth, 4 July 1812.

166. Alexander B. Richmond, *Narrative of the Condition of the Manufacturing Population and the Proceedings of the Government which led to the State Trials in*

Scotland 1820 (London, 1824), p.29; Fraser, *Conflict and Class*, Chapter 5; W.H. Fraser, 'A Note on the Scottish Weavers Association, 1808–1813', *Journal of the Scottish Labour History Society*, 20 (1985), pp.33–42; Murray, *Handloom Weavers*, pp.186–89; A. Aspinall (ed.), *The Early English Trade Unions* (London, 1949), pp.137–38, 143.

167. SCA, Blairs Letters, BL4/398/13, Andrew Scott to Alexander Cameron, 19 November 1812. See also BL4/398/14, Scott to Cameron, 4 December 1812.

168. Quoted in Aspinall (ed.), *Early English Trade Unions*, p.138.

169. Richmond, *Narrative*, pp.33–34.

170. There is evidence of strike-breakers and non-strikers in the numerous precognitions contained in WRH, Lord Advocate's Papers, AD14/13/8. See also Fraser, *Conflict and Class*, pp.92, 94.

171. Murray, *Handloom Weavers*, pp.196, 200–01. For the Articles and regulations of the Weavers' Unions over this period see the material in WRH, Lord Advocate's Papers, AD14/13/8; *Glasgow Chronicle*, 9 September 1824; Strathclyde Regional Archives, papers of Sir John Maxwell, 9th. Bt. of Pollock, T-PM 117/3/287, *Articles of the General Union of Weavers in Scotland Instituted 1832* (Paisley, 1834).

172. Murray, *Handloom Weavers*, p.196.

173. *Ibid*, p.32.

174. *Weavers' Journal*, 1 February 1837.

175. *Ibid*.

176. Murray, *Handloom Weavers*, pp.195–203 for a discussion of the reasons for the failure of the weavers' unions.

177. *Glasgow Courier*, 2 February 1834.

178. *Glasgow Chronicle*, 27 July 1838.

179. *Ibid*, 17 May 1841.

180. *Ibid*, 28 February 1842.

181. PP, 1836, (40), XXXIV, *Report on the State of the Irish Poor in Great Britain*, p.141.

182. *Ibid*, p.112.

183. SCA, Blairs Letters, BL5/248/11, Andrew Scott to James Kyle, 17 February 1829.

184. Burn, *Autobiography of a Beggar Boy*, pp.139, 144.

185. *Scots Times*, 3 March 1841.

186. Tom Gallagher, *Glasgow: The Uneasy Peace: Religious Tension in Modern Scotland* (Manchester, 1987), p.2. See also p.27.

187. Tom Gallagher, 'The Catholic Irish in Scotland: in Search of Identity' in Devine (ed.), *Irish Immigrants*, p.20.

188. T.C. Smout, *A Century of the Scottish People* (Paperback edition, London, 1987), pp.22–3.

189. PP, 1836, (40), XXXIV, *Report on the State of the Irish Poor in Great Britain*, p.105.

190. *Ibid*, p.131.

191. As has already been noted, the Irish colliers in the parish of St Quivox in Ayrshire who went on strike in the autumn of 1842 were mainly from the province of Connaught; moreover, they 'generally conversed in Irish'. This suggests that most were Roman Catholics. WRH, Lord Advocate's Papers, AD14/43/375, Declaration of Elizabeth Caldwell.

192. J.H. Treble, 'The Attitude of the Roman Catholic Church towards Trade Unionism in the North of England, 1833–1842', *Northern History*, 5 (1970), pp.93–113. There was no similar campaign by the Catholic clergy in the west of Scotland against Catholic trade unionists in this period.

193. PP, 1836, (40), XXXIV, *Report on the State of the Irish Poor in Great Britain*, p.143.

194. *Ibid*, pp.116, 140–1, 143.

195. *Ibid*, p.133.

PART TWO
INSURRECTIONARY ACTIVITIES

2
The United Scotsmen, 1797–1803

As has been shown, Irish emigration to Scotland on a significant scale began in the second half of the 1790s. This development, which occurred at a time of social and political upheaval in Ireland, coincided with the formation in Scotland of the revolutionary Society of United Scotsmen. As the introduction to this study noted, several historians have argued that some of the immigrants were involved in this new organisation although most did not deal with the matter in any great detail. This chapter discusses the reactions of the Scottish authorities to the Irish influx of the late 1790s and early 1800s and examines the issue of the Irish and the United Scotsmen. It then looks at several aspects of the organisation, such as its membership, aims, strategies and links with similar insurrectionary societies in Ireland and England.

I

Irish emigration to Scotland in the late 1790s and early 1800s greatly alarmed the Scottish authorities, who were convinced that most, if not all, of the new arrivals were or had been engaged in seditious or treasonable activities. In the spring of 1797 the Lord Advocate Robert Dundas was made aware of the existence in the west of Scotland of a secret society which was in correspondence with the United Irishmen, the revolutionary organisation which wanted to establish an Irish Republic[1]. Dundas was told that the letters from the Irish radicals were brought over by some of those who arrived at Portpatrick from Donaghadee, the principal sea route from Ulster to Scotland at this time.[2] He passed this information on to his superiors at the Home Office in London in early May, and was informed immediately that the Home Secretary the Duke of Portland thought

> it so material, that every possible exertion should be made, for the purpose of preventing the mischievous intentions, which these people have in view, that he cannot but think it advisable, that some persons, in whom you can confide, should be stationed at Portpatrick, and give an account of every individual, who may pass over from Ireland, as it may be the means of getting at some important intelligence.[3]

Dundas had in fact employed men to do exactly this the previous December and January but had been forced to withdraw them as they were needed elsewhere and also because their cost was 'considerable'.[4] He was now informed, however, that Portland had decided that, 'The expence, when weighed with the utility of the measure, should not be any consideration' and that the secret service fund would finance the operation.[5] The following month Dundas reported that he had stationed 'proper persons' at Portpatrick to watch the new arrivals and gave the assurance that 'no person of a suspicious character in any respect will be permitted in future to pass from Ireland into this country, without the purport of his journey being detected…'.[6]

In July Dundas transmitted to the Home Office a copy of a report he had recently received from William McConnell, the Sheriff of Wigtown, concerning the Irish who had landed at Portpatrick.[7] McConnell stated that during April, May and June a total of 912 passengers 'of low condition and mean appearance' arrived in the holds of the packets. Furthermore, during the same period almost the same number came over in 83 boats which transported cattle, as the fare on these vessels was cheaper.

McConnell had been asked by Dundas' men at Portpatrick to assist them in their examination of the passengers and on 28 June they all arrived in the town to begin their work. Over the following few days they interviewed all the new arrivals, except those 'people of genteel appearance or who were known upon the ferry'. On 3 July McConnell submitted his report. In it he stated that those examined were, in general, 'miserable looking wretches', although most were permitted to enter the country as they had the relevant documents and were able to give a good account of themselves. Those who were returned to Ireland 'had no fixed object in view' in coming to Scotland and some were in such poverty that their return fare was paid by the Revenue Officers employed by Dundas. Most of those who were allowed entry stated that they were going to Glasgow, Paisley, Ayr, Kilmarnock and Irvine, 'in search of employment as weavers, etc'. McConnell, however, remained suspicious, and warned the magistrates of these towns of the impending arrival of the 'low Irish'. He also wrote to several Justices of the Peace in Counties Down, Antrim, Armagh and Tyrone asking if they would put their seals on the certificates they were issuing to emigrants, as he had noted several forgeries during his investigations at Portpatrick.

By the time McConnell and his colleagues arrived at Portpatrick the number of Irish entering Scotland had increased dramatically.[8] This development greatly heightened the authorities' fears about the nature of Irish immigration. They were convinced that many among the influx were rebels fleeing Ulster as a result of the Government's campaign to crush the United Irishmen in the province during the spring and summer of 1797. Measures used included the imposition of martial law, mass arrests and the disarming of the population.[9] McConnell reported that he had been informed by 'the persons of good appearance' who disembarked at Portpatrick that 'there was much reason to apprend that many of the inferior Irish who came here, were either flying from the consequences of their conduct in the other side, or were in absolute poverty.' He believed that the decision to examine the new arrivals and the fact that some had been returned had resulted in a decline in the numbers travelling to Portpatrick from Donaghadee.[10]

These measures did not, however, result in a decrease in the numbers of Irish entering Scotland. McConnell learned that 'some persons of suspicious appearances' had not taken the normal ferry route to Portpatrick but had instead 'landed from Ireland in small vessels and boats upon different parts of the coast and immediately proceeded into the country...'.[11] It would appear that many more decided to do the same rather than be interrogated at Portpatrick. In the letter to the Home Office which was sent with McConnell's report Dundas stated that the authorities were concentrating their efforts on the various seaports on the west of Scotland. He revealed that the magistrates in these places were encountering tremendous difficulties as they did not have the power to detain those who could not be legally classified as vagrants.[12] Such legal niceties were soon dispensed with, as Dundas was convinced that the situation merited drastic action. On 14 July he informed John King, an under secretary at the Home Office, that: 'We still have swarms from Ireland but have sent back as many, indeed more persons, than in strict law we are authorised to do. But we must not stop at trifles.'[13] A similar message was sent by Dundas to King the following month.[14]

Even greater numbers arrived in the west of Scotland in June 1798 during the Irish Rebellion. On this occasion the authorities were far more alarmed, as they believed that most of the influx were not refugees fleeing the troubles but were in fact United Irishmen escaping after their defeats. One government official stationed at Portpatrick reported on 13 June that 'The numbers that are hourly arriving at this and different ports of this coast exceeds all conception', although no figures are available for those who came at this time.[15] He informed Robert Dundas that, in his opinion, some of the Irish 'may be good, but in general they are suspicious characters',[16] and 'Many...no doubt have been in the Rebel army'.[17] Troops were stationed at the various ports and creeks along the west coast to prevent the Irish entering Scotland.[18] On 15 June Dundas wrote to

Portland informing him that he had instructed the sheriffs and magistrates of the western counties 'to seize and detain all persons lately appearing in their Districts who are not possessed of passports from Ireland...'. He admitted to the Home Secretary that he was 'not sure if this is perfectly legal: But in such an emergency there is no help for it'.[19] Shortly afterwards, Dundas ordered the authorities in Ayrshire and Galloway 'to take up all Irish without Distinction...'.[20] A considerable number of those who left Ireland for Scotland in June 1798 were seized by the authorities.[21] Some were imprisoned or were interned on a prison ship; others were returned to Ireland to serve in the British army.[22]

Despite the failure of the Irish Rebellion and the disintegration of the United Irish movement, the authorities remained very concerned about those who crossed the Irish Sea to settle in Scotland in the years immediately following 1798. In April 1799 the Earl of Eglinton, who was Lord Lieutenant of Ayrshire, informed the Secretary for War Henry Dundas that people from Ireland continued to arrive in the county, sometimes in large groups. He added that they often landed at small bays on the coast in order to avoid the larger towns, presumably to escape the attention of the authorities. Eglinton ordered these places of entry watched and those 'who could not give a proper account of themselves' were to be detained.[23] In late July 1803 there was a sharp increase in the numbers arriving from Ulster. This occurred at a time of increased tensions in the province, caused in part by Robert Emmet's failed rising in Dublin that month.[24] Acting on information received from the authorities in Dublin, Charles Hope, Dundas' successor as Lord Advocate, ordered port officials on the west coast of Scotland to adopt 'every precautionary measure in regard to Irishmen arriving on that coast, which were followed during the former Rebellion'.[25] This resulted in a number being detained. Hope, however, wrote to the then Home Secretary, Lord Pelham, requesting

> instructions as to others, who, coming without passports, and landing from open Boats, are plainly fugitives, but who all pretend they come over for work, and bringing no papers with them we can have no evidence against them, altho' they may be notorious Rebels, and well known in Ireland.

He wished to know whether Pelham wanted such people returned to Ireland in custody or given to the Navy instead. It is not known what the outcome of this correspondence was or indeed whether many of those who arrived from Ireland were detained.[26]

It is evident, therefore, that the Scottish authorities were extremely concerned about the Irish who entered Scotland during the first few years of large scale sustained immigration. They were convinced that most of the new arrivals were rebels escaping from their native land. But this was not all that worried those in charge of Scottish affairs. They also believed that many of the Irishmen who settled in Scotland were, or were likely to become, engaged in seditious or treasonable activities. In June 1797 the Earl of Galloway, who was Lord Lieutenant of Wigtownshire, informed Robert Dundas that there were 'large numbers of disaffected Irish' in the county.[27] Four months later the Earl remarked that these 'ill disposed' people had been 'peaceable' only because they were aware that the authorities were watching them.[28] Six years later, in a letter to Lord Pelham, Charles Hope stated that he had been informed by the Lord Provost of Glasgow that there were

> not less than 10,000 Irish in Glasgow and its immediate vicinity almost all of them of the most suspicious character, and very many of them known to be old Rebels, not in the least reformed.

The Lord Provost also reported that he had received information from a private in the city's Volunteer Regiment that

> several concealed Irish papists had entered into the Regt. merely for the purpose of mischief and to get arms in their hands and that they had been attempting to seduce him and some more of their country men. The informer is himself an Irishman, but a Protestant. He says these men were all in former Rebellion, and are now keeping up a daily correspondence with Traitors there.

The Lord Provost was, according to Hope, extremely perturbed about the Irish in and around Glasgow, as he and others believed that if France, currently at war with Britain, landed a force on the east coast of Scotland these immigrants 'would rise to a man, all over the west' of the country, where government forces were meagre. These reports, which came at a time when the Scottish authorities were attempting to deal with a large influx of Irish immigrants arriving in the wake of Emmet's failed rising, greatly alarmed Hope. He told Pelham that he too was convinced that a French invasion in the east would place the west in great danger, as would a renewal of disturbances in Ireland. The Lord Advocate requested that the magistrates in the west of Scotland be given more powers to deal with those suspected of seditious or treasonable activities and suggested that the numbers in the Volunteer Regiments in Glasgow, Renfrewshire and Ayrshire be increased. Hope also reported that the letters to the Irish volunteers in Glasgow were to be intercepted and opened as he believed they could contain 'very material information relating to Ireland...'.[29] The issue of Irish immigrants in the Volunteers was clearly one of much concern around this time; Hope revealed to Pelham that he had received several letters on 'the evident danger in training and putting arms into the hands of the numerous body Irish in the west...'.[30] France, however, did not attempt an invasion and as a result the Scottish authorities' fears concerning Irish immigrants were reduced, although they never disappeared.

Many of those who came to Scotland from Ireland between 1797 and 1803 had emigrated simply to find employment or to escape the troubles in their native land. Some were Loyalists. Indeed it was in this period that the first Orange Lodges in Scotland were founded, by Irish Protestants. Yet given the scale and timing of the large Irish influx some of the new arrivals were undoubtedly members of the United Irishmen. Moreover, some of these rebels became members of the secret society which Robert Dundas was made aware of in spring 1797. This organisation was the Society of United Scotsmen.

II

The United Scotsmen Society was a secret insurrectionary organisation dedicated to the attainment of radical political reform, notably universal male suffrage, annual parliaments and a republican system of government. Although it first came to the attention of the Scottish authorities in spring 1797, it is possible that it was founded during the second half of 1796. By the end of 1797 United Scotsmen societies had been established in Glasgow and in the counties of Ayr, Renfrew, Lanark, Dumbarton, Fife and Perth. Despite Government repression, which included arrests and trials of members of the society, particularly during 1797–98, the organisation was still active as late as autumn 1803. Thereafter the United Scotsmen disappeared from the scene and demands for major political reform were not made in Scotland to any significant extent for more than a decade.[31]

The organisation was unlike any which had previously existed in Scotland, although it was not the first to agitate for annual parliaments and universal male suffrage. The Scottish Association of the Friends of the People, which was active from 1792 to 1794, campaigned for these changes. This society, however, was not a secret revolutionary conspiracy nor was it republican. The Friends of the People believed that through peaceful agitation, including public reform meetings and petitions, the Government would be persuaded by their arguments and therefore introduce the desired reforms.[32] The British authorities, however, were convinced that the society and similar reform organisations in England at the time were revolutionary movements intent on overthrowing the existing political and social order.

The Government knew that these groups were inspired by the aims and ideals of the French Revolution; it was equally aware of the progress of events in France after 1789 which culminated in the overthrow of the monarchy and the establishment of a radical republic. Furthermore, by February 1793 Britain and France were at war and a French–style reform movement was regarded as a potentially serious threat to internal security. Consequently, during 1793 and 1794 the authorities in Scotland and England waged a campaign of repression which included arrests, trials and transportations of reformers. This onslaught resulted in the break–up of the societies and the collapse of the British reform movement.[33]

In Ireland in the early 1790s the Society of United Irishmen publicly and peacefully campaigned for political change. The Government of Ireland did not introduce the reforms the United Irishmen wanted and attempted to crush the organisation. Unlike in Great Britain, repression by the authorities in Ireland did not lead to the disintegration of the movement for reform. In 1795 the Society of United Irishmen reconstituted itself as a secret organisation dedicated to the establishment of an Irish Republic by revolutionary means.[34]

The United Irishmen were convinced that they would not be able to stage a successful revolt by themselves. They concluded that assistance from Britain's enemy France, particularly military support and possibly an invasion, was essential. Emissaries were sent to Paris during 1795 and 1796 to convince the French Government that it was in France's interests to support a rebellion in Ireland.[35] The society also believed that its cause would be furthered by political instability in Great Britain, as a similar revolutionary movement there would inevitably result in the Government in London retaining a large military presence on the British mainland which would otherwise be used to assist in the preservation of order in Ireland or fight in the war with France. Such a development, it was believed, would force the authorities to come to an agreement with the United Irishmen. It was probably also felt that a successful revolution in Britain would lead to the establishment of an Irish Republic, particularly if the British insurgents achieved their aims with United Irish assistance.[36]

In 1796 the United Irishmen decided to rouse the British reformers, quiescent since 1794, into action. Agents were sent to England and Scotland to urge known radicals to adopt the secret oath–bound revolutionary system of the United Irishmen.[37] For example, in the summer of 1796 emissaries from Belfast brought the United Irish Constitution to Scotland for her reformers' 'inspection and approbation...'. Their mission was not immediately successful. One Belfast United Irishman reported to his colleagues at home that 'the Scotch were not possessed of sufficient energy;

but their [*sic*] was decent fellowes among them, and they were coming on surprisingly'.[38] Within a year, however, the Society of United Scotsmen was established and United societies were also founded in England. These secret organisations were modelled on the Irish system.[39] Indeed, Robert Dundas noted 'how exactly they [the United Scotsmen] had copied the proceedings of the United Irishmen'.[40] The structure and oath of the Scottish society were almost identical to those of its Irish counterpart and both organisations sought to forcibly overthrow the existing political order. So too did the Society of United Englishmen. The United Irishmen wanted Ireland to become an independent republic. It would appear, however, that the United Scotsmen did not desire an independent Scotland, but instead wished to remain united with the English in a British Republic.[41]

Few details are extant on the United Scotsmen and the full extent and nature of their activities will probably never be known. As one historian of the society acknowledged, 'any analysis…is gravely hampered by the very nature of the evidence'.[42] The Society of United Scotsmen was through necessity a secret organisation which ensured that no materials were retained which could lead to its members or activities being made known.[43] The principal sources for any examination of the organisation are the reports of Government spies and informers, the judicial declarations, or precognitions, of arrested United Scotsmen and the evidence given by witnesses in their declarations or at the trials of members of the society. All groups almost certainly contained some who were not entirely accurate in their accounts. Spies might have exaggerated or fabricated the information they transmitted to the authorities in order to be deemed indispensable and thus remain in employment; United Scotsmen most probably did not reveal the full or true extent of their operations; trial witnesses might not have told the entire truth, depending on their attitude to the organisation or to those on trial. The precognitions and the reports of spies and informers form the bases of two other important sources of evidence for the United Scotsmen, namely the correspondence of the authorities and the indictments made against arrested members of the society.

Most of the available evidence concerns the activities of the movement in the east of Scotland. Furthermore, the major trials of United Scotsmen, which were few in number compared with those involved in the radical agitations of 1816–20, were of members from Perth and Fife such as George Mealmaker and Angus Cameron. Indeed, because of this some historians have suggested or implied that the society and its activities were located mainly, or exclusively, in the east of the country.[44] However, the authorities were fully aware that United Scotsmen societies existed in the west and that the organisation was in fact established first in Ayrshire and

Glasgow and then spread eastwards.[45] Indeed, throughout the United Scotsmen's existence their headquarters were located in Glasgow and it was from this city that orders, instructions and information were issued to societies elsewhere in the country.[46] Why most of the available evidence concerning the activities of the organisation should come from the east is not clear. It might simply have been that the Government's spy system operated better in that region. For example, although the Scottish authorities were aware that the United Scotsmen's Executive Committee met in Glasgow, they were never able to infiltrate it or gain any information about its operations.[47]

Despite the paucity of the sources, and their limitations, there is evidence which demonstrates that some of the Irishmen who came to Scotland during the 1790s were involved in the United Scotsmen. A Dunfermline weaver arrested for his involvement in the society between August 1797 and June 1798 told the authorities that 'persons from Ireland…were the original founders of the Society of United Scotsmen'. It would also appear that he was initiated into the organisation by an Irishman who was travelling the country trying to establish United societies.[48] Evidence from a spy in Perth who ingratiated himself with the radicals there suggests that reformers from Ireland played a leading role in promoting the new system. He reported that at a meeting he attended an Irishman named James Craigdallie, who had 'for a considerable time been settled at Perth', attemped to enlist recruits for the cause. Craigdallie boasted to those present that 'in the west country [west of Scotland] they were pursuing the true Robertspierrian system, for if any man deserted the cause there or betrayed it, *he was never more heard of*'. Also present at this gathering was an Irish radical named Winlach. He, however, was not at that time an initiated member of the United Scotsmen. The spy reported that Winlach stated that

> no body needed to doubt his attachment to the cause, but that really he cou'd see no good that was to be arising from *uniting* — but much mischief especially to one so *noted* as himself not only as a friend to liberty but as a Irishman…No oath he added could bind him more to the cause than he was already bound — But the taking an unlawful oath (as Government reckon it) might subject him to trouble — or even to death.

Winlach also spoke of one Edward Dogherty, an Irishman and 'a true Democrate', who had been in the area advocating reform.[49]

This spy's report was from the summer of 1797 when United Scotsmen societies were first established in the east of Scotland.[50] Winlach was soon accused of being 'a Traitor and Turn-coat' because he did not join the organisation.[51] Later evidence suggests, however, that he eventually became a member of the society. A spy's report from 1802 concerning the activities of the United Scotsmen in Fife stated that 'an Irishman of the name of Winlock a Hatter was a very active hand' in the organisation in Perth.[52] Over a year later the Lord Advocate requested that the letters of John Wenlock, a Perth hatter, be intercepted as his spies had informed him that Wenlock was 'deeply concerned with the United Scotsmen here, and in close correspondence at present with Ireland'.[53] Despite the differences in the spelling of the surname, it would not be unreasonable to conclude that the Perth hatter Winlock or Wenlock who was active in the United Scotsmen in 1802 and 1803 was the same individual as the Irishman Winlach discussed in the spy's report of July 1797 on reformers' activities in Perth.

There is also evidence of Irish involvement in the United Scotsmen in the west despite the fact that the sources are poorer for this area. A member of the Thornliebank Society who was arrested in April 1798 declared in his precognition that at a delegate meeting he attended at Pollockshaws 'it was reported that some of the best people of the country were united', but that he 'never saw any but of the lowest order, and mostly Irishmen'. At least one member of his own society was an Irishman.[54] In Maybole in Ayrshire two Irish weavers, Archibald Deary and James Andrew, initiated workers into the United Scotsmen.[55] Indeed, the society in this village was reported to be 'exclusively Irish'.[56]

Given the nature and extent of Irish immigration to Scotland in the late 1790s, and the aims and strategies of the United Irishmen, it is not surprising that there is some evidence that Irishmen were involved in establishing, promoting and manning societies of United Scotsmen. Irish exiles also founded and formed part of the membership of societies of United Englishmen and United Britons.[57] These revolutionaries undoubtedly engaged in these activities in the belief that they were furthering the cause of Irish Republicanism. This does not mean, however, that the Society of United Scotsmen was an organisation dominated by immigrants and run solely for the benefit of the United Irishmen. As Brims argues, 'the growth of the United Scotsmen in areas such as Fife, Angus and Perthshire where Irish immigration was very limited suggests strongly that the movement remained essentially indigenous in character'.[58] Irishmen such as James Craigdallie and John Wenlock were certainly prominent in the society in the east but so too were Scotsmen such as Angus Cameron[59] and George Mealmaker. The latter appears to have been a major figure in the organisation in the region. In January 1798 he was convicted of sedition and sentenced to fourteen years transportation.[60] Furthermore, there is nothing in the reports of spies, the correspondence of the authorities, the reports of trials of United Scotsmen, the declarations of suspects or in the evidence of witnesses which demonstrates or suggests that there was a significant Irish presence in the societies in Perthshire, Fife and Angus. In the west of Scotland the proportion of Irishmen in the membership was probably greater given that this was the region in which most of the Irish influx settled. However, there is not enough information available to make any meaningful estimate of the extent of Irish participation in the west. What is evident, however, is that in this region and in the eastern counties Scottish workers were involved in the society.

III

Most United Scotsmen societies were located in those parts of lowland Scotland in which handloom weaving was the principal form of employment.[61] Members of these weaving communities had been active in the Friends of the People society and in fact played the predominant role in that organisation after middle class reformers abandoned it because of its increasingly radical demands, and because the progress of the French Revolution convinced them that reform would lead to violent political and social upheaval.[62] When the United Irishmen resolved to spread their system to the British mainland they naturally had to approach known radicals. In Scotland these men resided almost exclusively in weaving areas. Some of those Scots who became convinced of the need for the United system — whether they were informed of it by emissaries from the United Irishmen, or by Irish immigrants or learned of it by other means — then undertook to establish or help form societies of United Scotsmen. Such individuals would recruit from among trusted friends and associates.[63] As handloom weaving was the main occupation in practically all of these communities it is not surprising that the vast bulk of the membership of the United Scotsmen appear to have been weavers.[64] Some of these workers might have been former Friends of the People who had come to the conclusion that the only way by which they could obtain their demands was revolution; others might have regarded drastic political change as the best way to improve their social and economic position, which had been declining for some time.[65] Members of the United Scotsmen in these communities who were not weavers probably had similar reasons for becoming involved.

However, not every reformer in these communities was attracted to the United system. It will be recalled that in Perth in the summer of 1797 the Irishman Winlach did not wish to be initiated into the society because he feared that he would be executed if it were discovered that he had taken an unlawful oath. The authorities were informed that this view was held by many in the region at the time:

> That there are a considerable number of disaffected at Perth and still more in Dundee is a melancholy truth, at the same time they in general are not disposed to go into the Irish system of *Uniting* which among the…disaffected is termed *planting Irish Potatoes*.

These people shared the fears of Winlach concerning the possible consequences of taking illegal oaths.[66] Both cities, however, soon became important centres of United Scotsmen activity which suggests that many of the 'disaffected' were able to overcome their initial reluctance to the new system. Also in the summer of 1797 a newly initiated member of the United Scotsmen in Fife was informed by the man who administered the society's oath to him that: 'it was a difficult matter to deal with people of contrary dispositions and that he was therefore obliged to give them their own way as some of them had refused to take his test [oath].'[67] In Maybole around this time activists experienced problems in persuading people to join.[68] The idea of engaging in revolutionary activity might simply have been too terrifying for some.

No reliable figures are available for the membership of the society. Meikle suggested that the total never amounted to more than a few hundred.[69] At a meeting of the national committee of the United Scotsmen in May 1797, however, it was reported that there were 2,871 members.[70] Another source states that the following year there were around 30,000 United Scotsmen.[71] In 1802 a spy estimated that the total membership for Fife and Perth combined was around 2,000.[72] It is impossible to establish the accuracy of such figures. It is probable, however, that the Society of United Scotsmen did not have a large number of activists. The United Irishmen were able to build up a mass membership largely by allying with the Defenders, the secret Catholic agrarian society which was opposed to the existing social, economic and political order.[73] No similar rural, or urban, movement existed in Scotland for the United Scotsmen to join with. Furthermore, it would appear that the United Scotsmen did not to any significant extent attempt to spread their organisation to areas outwith the weaving communities, for example to mining or to agricultural districts. This was probably because they wanted to lessen the chance of their

activities being discovered by the authorities. It has been suggested that
Scots who were involved in establishing local United Scotsmen societies
recruited from among those whom they knew and trusted in their weaving
communities. If these activists had ventured outside their localities and
attempted to promote the society in areas where they were not known,
they would have run the risk of endangering the organisation.

.IV

One approach which several historians have adopted in trying to assess the
impact of the United Scotsmen is to establish how influential the
organisation was during the rioting against the raising of a Scottish militia
in 1797[74] and against food shortages and high prices in 1800.[75] Both Lynch
and Fraser concluded that the society was unable to capitalise on these
disturbances,[76] as did Smout. He claimed that the United Scotsmen's
'complete failure to start anything of significance even in the year of the
Militia Riots underlined again both the success of the government's
repression and the uninflammable character of the Scottish populace as a
whole'.[77]

Kenneth Logue has argued that the United Scotsmen might in fact have
been involved to some extent in agitation in parishes in Fife and Perthshire
against the attempts to implement the terms of the Scottish Militia Act.[78]
There is also evidence, not cited in his study of popular disturbances, which
suggests that the meal riots in Glasgow, Renfrewshire and Ayrshire in late
1800 were instigated, or the rioters inflamed, by seditious handbills. It is
possible that some of these were produced by members of the United
Scotsmen or by the society itself.[79] In England at this time radicals were
certainly involved in stirring up discontent against the shortages of
food.[80]

Although the United Scotsmen appear to have been involved to some
extent in the opposition towards the Militia Act, and possibly in the riots
over food shortages and prices as well, it is almost certain that it was not
their intention to ignite these protests into revolutionary action. The society
regarded itself as being part of a British-Irish-French conspiracy in which
co-ordinated activity was essential. It will be recalled that in the spring of
1797 the Lord Advocate was made aware of a correspondence between
the disaffected in Ireland and Scotland. That summer communication was
maintained with the United Irishmen and established with United societies
in England.[81] By the end of the year the United Scotsmen had made
contact with the French Government.[82] Representatives from the society

also visited Ireland and England and in return the organisation received emissaries from the United societies in those countries.[83] An alliance was being established.

. The English and Scottish radicals did not, however, rise with the Irish in 1798. Their societies do not seem to have been sufficiently prepared or developed, and had in fact been weakened by the arrests of members of their leadership during 1797 and 1798. Moreover, by the summer of 1798 no single body had been established to co-ordinate the activities of the British and Irish radicals and the French, though discussions had been underway to effect this since the previous year.[84]

Plans for joint action were again made in 1802 and 1803. A spy's report from April 1802 states that the United Scotsmen were arming and preparing for a rising. The spy, who had infiltrated one of the societies in Fife, reported that a regiment of dragoons which had been lately quartered in the area contained 'a number of very bad and disloyal subjects…'. These soldiers, who were Irish and probably members of the United Irishmen, attended meetings of the local United Scotsmen society. The spy revealed that at these meetings he had seen letters 'of a very improper kind' to the soldiers from their friends in Ireland, the tendency of which 'was to urge a rising in England and Scotland, assuring them that the Irish Boys in the Morning were impatient for it…'. The informer also revealed that radicals in England had a plan for an insurrection and were acting in concert with the United Scotsmen. He was convinced that the rising would occur within a month. The Lord Advocate Charles Hope informed the Home Secretary that he was certain this spy could be trusted because his information corresponded with reports he, Hope, had received from other areas. Hope, however, did not believe that a rebellion was imminent as he was confident the societies were not sufficiently prepared for such an undertaking. Nevertheless, he introduced a number of security measures in response to the information received from this spy in Fife and from others in the employ of the authorities.[85]

Throughout the summer and autumn of 1802 plans for risings in Britain and Ireland continued to be made. Furthermore, the United societies were determined not to act until the French invaded. The Home Office was aware of the plot and in November several of the revolutionaries were arrested in London.[86] This, however, did not end the conspiracy and it would appear that the United Scotsmen continued to be involved. For example, the following summer Charles Hope informed the Home Secretary that the United Scotsmen societies were 'all alive again' and in correspondence with the disaffected in Ireland.[87] The planned British-Irish rising did not, however, take place. In July 1803 Robert Emmet commenced the Irish insurrection prematurely in Dublin soon after learning that the authorities had become aware of his activities. The rising was crushed before France and the United societies in Britain could react.[88] Emmet's rebellion was 'the last fling of the remnants of the United Irishmen'[89] and its failure accelerated the disintegration of the movement.[90] This in turn resulted in a rapid decline in the activities of the revolutionaries in England and Scotland; indeed, after August 1803 there were no more reports on the United Scotsmen in Government correspondence.[91]

Any discussion of the Society of United Scotsmen must, therefore, take into account the fact that it was part of a wider conspiracy, the other members of which were France and the United societies in Ireland and England. In order to understand the 'failure' of the reform movement in Scotland during this period it must be realised that the United Scotsmen never intended to stage an insurrection by themselves. Why then do they appear to have been involved in disturbances against the Militia Act, and possibly in the Meal Riots as well? It was argued earlier that the Society of United Scotsmen did not attempt to become a mass organisation. It therefore probably regarded the opposition to the Militia Act and the discontent caused by the food shortages as opportunities to politicise the disaffected, so that when the joint rising was eventually launched such people would be sufficiently hostile to the Government and the authorities to support a call to arms.[92] During the post-Napoleonic Wars agitation in the west of Scotland radicals used similar tactics to foment popular hostility towards the existing political system.[93]

The United Scotsmen never had the opportunity to bring their plans into the open and it is therefore fruitless to speculate about how popular their Irish-style revolutionary republicanism could have been. It must be stated, however, that it does not necessarily follow that those who had grievances against the authorities were all potential revolutionaries. Indeed, popular loyalism at a time of war with France might have had a stronger appeal for many. For example, in Glasgow in January 1797 fears about a French invasion 'had no effect…but to increase the spirit of loyalty and to add considerably to the number of Volunteers…'.[94] A member of the United Scotsmen at Thornliebank declared in his precognition to the authorities in April 1798, 'That before the Volunteer Corps was raised at Thornly bank one would have thought the whole people there were United Scotsmen together, but the volunteering made a great change in their sentiments there, and was one of the causes of the plans of the United there being broke.'[95] Clarke and Dickson noted that Paisley provided many recruits for the army in the late 1790s and also held large loyalist demonstrations during these years.[96] Unfortunately, little more is known about popular loyalism in this period.

It is evident that Irish immigrants were involved in the Society of United Scotsmen between 1797 and 1803. The structure of the organisation was modelled on that of the United Irishmen. The available evidence, however, does not reveal the exact scale of Irish participation. The secret nature of the Society means that the United Scotsmen and the full extent and nature of their activities remain largely shrouded in mystery.

Notes

1. SRO, Home Office Correspondence, RH2/4/84, R. Dundas to J. King, 6 May 1797. See also SRO, Melville Castle Muniments, GD51/5/29, Earl of Eglinton to Henry Dundas, 10 May 1797.

2. SRO, Home Office Correspondence, RH2/4/80, R. Dundas to John King, 9 May 1797.

3. *Ibid*, RH2/4/80, Charles Grenville to The Lord Advocate, 9 May 1797.

4. *Ibid*, RH2/4/80, R. Dundas to John King, 9 May 1797.

5. *Ibid*, RH2/4/80, Charles Grenville to The Lord Advocate, 9 May 1797.

6. *Ibid*, RH2/4/80, R. Dundas to Charles Grenville, 24 June 1797.

7. *Ibid*, RH2/4/80, Report of William McConnell, Wigton, 3 July 1797. The information in the following discussion comes from this report.

8. *Ibid*. See also RH2/4/80, R. Dundas to Charles Grenville, 7 July 1797.

9. Gearoid O'Tuathaigh, *Ireland before the Famine 1798–1848* (Dublin, 1990), pp.17–8; Nancy J. Curtin, 'The United Irish Organisation in Ulster 1795–98', in David Dickson, Dáire Keogh and Kevin Whelan (eds.), *The United Irishmen: Republicanism, Radicalism and Rebellion* (Dublin, 1993), pp.209, 217, 219; E.W. McFarland, *Ireland and Scotland in the Age of Revolution: Planting the Green Bough* (Edinburgh, 1994), p.144.

10. SRO, Home Office Correspondence, RH2/4/80, Report of William McConnell, Wigton, 3 July 1797.

11. *Ibid*.

12. SRO, Home Office Correspondence, RH2/4/80, R. Dundas to Charles Grenville, 7 July 1797.

13. *Ibid*, RH2/4/80, R. Dundas to John King, 14 July 1797.

14. *Ibid*, RH2/4/80, R. Dundas to John King, 2 August 1797.

15. *Ibid*, RH2/4/84, Robert Carmichael to R. Dundas, 13 June 1798.

16. *Ibid*, RH2/4/84, Robert Carmichael to R. Dundas, 12 June 1798.

17. *Ibid*.

18. SRO, Home Office Correspondence, RH2/4/84, R. Abercromby to R. Dundas, 13 June 1798; RH2/4/84 Robert Carmichael to R. Dundas, 12 June 1798.

19. *Ibid*, RH2/4/84, R. Dundas to The Duke of Portland, 15 June 1798.

20. *Ibid*, RH2/4/84, R. Dundas to The Duke of Portland, 17 June 1798.

21. *Ibid*, RH2/4/84, R. Dundas to The Duke of Portland, 24 June 1798.

22. *Ibid*. See also RH2/4/84, Robert Carmichael to R. Dundas, 12 June 1798.

23. SRO, Melville Castle Muniments, Earl of Eglinton to Henry Dundas, 5 April 1799.

24. McFarland, *Ireland and Scotland*, pp.224–5.

25. SRO, Home Office Correspondence, RH2/4/88, C. Hope to Lord Pelham, 29 July 1803.

26. *Ibid*, RH2/4/88, C. Hope to Lord Pelham, 6 August 1803.

27. *Ibid*, RH2/4/80, Earl of Galloway to 'My Lord', 26 June 1797.

28. *Ibid*, RH2/4/212, Earl of Galloway to 'My Lord', 19 October 1797.

29. *Ibid*, RH2/4/88, C. Hope to Lord Pelham, 4 August 1803.

30. *Ibid*, RH2/4/88, C. Hope to Lord Pelham, 6 August 1803. See also SRO, Melville Castle Muniments, GD51/5/44, Earl of Eglinton to Henry Dundas, 5 April 1799: 'Numbers of Recruits have been landed lately for some Regiments now raising for his Majesty's service. I am informed many of these are of the very worst description of men — in fact United Irishmen.'

31. For the United Scotsmen see M.I. Thomis and P. Holt, *Threats of Revolution in Britain, 1789–1848* (London, 1977), pp.19–22; John Brims, 'Scottish Radicalism and the United Irishmen', in Dickson, Keogh and Whelan (eds.), *United Irishmen*, pp.163–6; Henry W. Meikle, *Scotland and the French Revolution* (Glasgow, 1912), pp.186–193; Roger Wells, *Insurrection: The British Experience, 1795–1803* (Gloucester, 1983), pp.72–4, 124–5, 167–9, 235; C.M. Burns, Industrial Labour and Radical Movements in Scotland in the 1790s, M.Sc. Thesis, University of Strathclyde (1971), pp.205–19; Peter Berresford Ellis and Seumas Mac a' Ghobhainn, *The Scottish Insurrection of 1820* (paperback edition, London, 1989), chapter 4; McFarland, *Ireland and Scotland*, chapters 5–8.

32. Meikle, *Scotland and the French Revolution*; John Brims, 'The Scottish "Jacobins", Scottish Nationalism and the British Union', in Roger A. Mason (ed.), *Scotland and England 1286–1815* (Edinburgh, 1987), pp.247–60; 'From Reformers to "Jacobins": The Scottish Association of the Friends of the People', in T.M. Devine (ed.), *Conflict and Stability in Scottish Society 1700–1850* (Edinburgh, 1990), pp.31–50.

33. For the British reform movement of the early 1790s and Government responses towards it see H.T. Dickinson, *British Radicalism and the French Revolution, 1789–1815* (Oxford, 1985), chapters 1–2; Thomis and Holt, *Threats of Revolution*, pp.5–16.

34. O' Tuathaigh, *Ireland Before the Famine*, pp.10–16; Dickinson, *British Radicalism*, pp.44–9; Marianne Elliott, 'The Origins and Transformation of Early Irish Republicanism', *International Review of Social History*, 23 (1978), pp.405–28; Nancy J. Curtin, 'The Transformation of the Society of United Irishmen into a mass-based revolutionary organisation, 1794–6', *Irish Historical Studies*, xxiv (1985), pp.463–92; McFarland, *Ireland and Scotland*, pp.133–6.

35. Dickson, *British Radicalism*, pp.46–7.

36. *Ibid*, p.49.

37. *Ibid*, pp.49–51.

38. Quoted in Brims, 'Scottish Radicalism and the United Irishmen', p.163. See also McFarland, *Ireland and Scotland*, p.237.

39. Dickinson, *British Radicalism*, pp.49–51; Marianne Elliott, 'Irish Republicanism in England: The First Phase, 1797–9', in Thomas Bartlett and D.W. Hayton (eds.), *Penal Era and Golden Age: Essays in Irish History 1690–1800* (Belfast, 1979), pp.204–9.

40. SRO, Home Office Correspondence, RH2/4/83, R. Dundas to 'My Lord Duke', 13 January 1798.

41. For the aims, structure, oath and constitution of the United Scotsmen *see Report of the Committee of Secrecy of the House of Commons, 1799*, pp.11–2, 20–1; Burns, Industrial Labour and Radical Movements, pp.205–19; Brims, 'Scottish "Jacobins" ', pp.261–2; McFarland, *Ireland and Scotland*, pp.153–7. For the United Societies in England see Dickinson, *British Radicalism*, pp.49–51; Elliott, 'Irish Republicanism', pp.208–10.

42. Burns, Industrial Labour and Radical Movements, p.206.

43. See, for example, SRO, Home Office Correspondence, RH2/4/87, Report of a spy, enclosed with C. Hope to Lord Pelham, 2 April 1802; T.B. Howell and Thomas Jones Howell, *A Complete Collection of State Trials…Vol. XXVI* (London, 1819), pp.1146, 1148.

44. Michael Lynch, *Scotland: A New History* (London, 1991), p.389; W.H. Fraser, 'Patterns of Protest', in T.M. Devine and Rosalind Mitchison (eds.), *People and Society in Scotland, Volume 1, 1760–1830* (Edinburgh, 1988), p.285; Thomis and Holt, *Threats of Revolution*, p.20.

45. *Report of the Committee of Secrecy*, p.11.

46. SRO, Home Office Correspondence, RH2/4/83, Declarations of James Jarvie, 13 April 1798 and of Daniel Couston, 14 April 1798; RH2/4/87, 'Copy of an Examination lately taken by the Sheriff of Fife, enclosed with

C. Hope to Lord Pelham, 2 April 1802; RH2/4/88, C. Hope to Lord Pelham, 4 August 1803; SRO, Justiciary Court Records, JC26/297, Declaration of David Black, 20 September 1798. *Report of the Committee of Secrecy*, pp.11–2.

47. SRO, Home Office Correspondence, RH2/4/88, C. Hope to Lord Pelham, 4 August 1803.

48. SRO, Judiciary Court Records, JC26/297, Declaration of David Black, 20 September 1798.

49. SRO, Melville Castle Muniments, GD51/5/30/2, 'Excerpt from a report of a spy' enclosed with GD51/5/30/2, William Scott to Henry Dundas, 19 July 1797.

50. *Report of the Committee of Secrecy*, p.11.

51. Quoted in Wells, *Insurrection*, p.74.

52. SRO, Home Office Correspondence, RH2/4/87, 'Copy of an Examination lately taken by the Sheriff of Fife', enclosed with C. Hope to Lord Pelham, 2 April 1802.

53. *Ibid*, RH2/4/88, C. Hope to Lord Pelham, 4 August 1803.

54. *Ibid*, RH2/4/83, Declaration of James Jarvie 13 April 1798. See also the Declaration of David Couston.

55. SRO, Justiciary Court Records, JC26/298, Declarations of John Kennedy, 5 and 11 April 1799.

56. Burns, Industrial Labour and Radical Movements, p.215.

57. Dickinson, *British Radicalism*, pp.49–52.

58. Brims, 'Scottish Radicalism, and the United Irishmen', p.164. See also McFarland, *Ireland and Scotland*, pp.158–61.

59. Ellis and Mac a'Ghobhainn, *Scottish Insurrection*, pp.77–8; Kenneth J. Logue, *Popular Disturbances in Scotland 1780–1815* (Edinburgh, 1979), pp.110–12.

60. Howell and Howell, *State Trials*, pp.1135–64.

61. Burns, Industrial Labour and Radical Movements, pp.206–7, 215; Norman Murray, *The Scottish Handloom Weavers, 1790–1850: A Social History* (Edinburgh,1979), p.212; McFarland, *Ireland and Scotland*, p.161.

62. Murray, *Scottish Handloom Weavers*, pp.208–10.

63. See, for example, SRO, Home Office Correspondence, RH2/4/83, Declarations of Daniel Couston, 14 April 1798 and James Jarvie, 13 April 1798; Justiciary Court Records, JC26/297, Declaration of David Black, 20 September 1798; JC26/298, Declaration of John Kennedy, 3 April 1799.

64. Murray, *Scottish Handloom Weavers*, p.212; Burns, Industrial Labour and Radical Movements, pp.206, 214–5. Most of those United Scotsmen arrested or tried appear to have been weavers.

65. Murray, *Scottish Handloom Weavers*, pp.231–4.

66. SRO, Melville Castle Muniments, GD51/5/30/1, William Scott to Henry Dundas, 22 July 1797.

67. SRO Justiciary Court Records, JC26/297, Declaration of David Black, 20 September 1798.

68. *Ibid*, JC26/298, Declaration of John Kennedy, 5 April 1799.

69. Meikle, *Scotland and the French Revolution*, p.192.

70. McFarland, *Ireland and Scotland*, p.168.

71. Elliott, 'Irish Republicanism', p.221.

72. SRO, Home Office Correspondence, RH2/4/87, 'Copy of an examination lately taken by the Sheriff of Fife', enclosed with C. Hope to Lord Pelham, 2 April 1802.

73. Elliott, 'Origins and Transformation', *passim*; Curtin, 'Transformation of the Society', *passim*. McFarland, *Ireland and Scotland*, p.135; Thomis and Holt, *Threats of Revolution*, p.21.

74. Meikle, *Scotland and the French Revolution*, pp.178–85; Burns, Industrial labour and Radical Movements, chapter 4; Logue, *Popular Disturbances*, chapter 3; McFarland, *Ireland and Scotland*, pp.136–7.

75. Logue, *Popular Disturbances*, pp.30–3; McFarland, *Ireland and Scotland*, pp.216–9.

76. Lynch, *Scotland*, p.390; Fraser, 'Patterns of Protest', p.285. See also, Thomis and Holt, *Threats of Revolution*, p.20.

77. T.C. Smout, *A History of the Scottish People 1560–1830* (paperback edition, London, 1972), p.417.

78. Logue, *Popular Disturbances*, pp.110–3.

79. SRO, Home Office Correspondence, RH2/4/86, Earl of Eglinton to Robert Dundas, 13 November 1800 and William McDowell to Robert Dundas, 5 November 1800 enclosed with Robert Dundas to the Duke of Portland, 15 November 1800; William McDowell to Robert Dundas, 16 November 1800 enclosed with Robert Dundas to the Duke of Portland, 18 November 1800; McFarland, *Ireland and Scotland*, pp.216–28.

80. John Stevenson, *Popular Disturbances in England 1700–1832* (Second edition, London, 1992), pp.188–9, 221–2.

81. Elliott, 'Irish Republicanism', pp.208–11; Mary Thale (ed.), *Selections from the Papers of the London Corresponding Society, 1792–99* (Cambridge, 1983), p.298; Brims, 'Scottish Radicalism', p.163; McFarland, *Ireland and Scotland*, pp.155, 160.

82. Brims, 'Scottish Radicalism', p.165; McFarland, *Ireland and Scotland*, pp.169–75, 180–3.

83. Brims, 'Scottish Radicalism', pp.163, 165.

84. Elliott, 'Irish Republicanism', pp.211–15; Dickinson, *British Radicalism*, pp.52–5; McFarland, *Ireland and Scotland*, pp.183–8.

85. SRO, Home Office Correspondence, RH2/4/87, Charles Hope to Lord Pelham, 2 April 1802 and enclosed 'Copy of a declaration lately taken by the Sheriff of Fife'. See also McFarland, *Ireland and Scotland*, pp.219–23.

86. Marianne Elliott, 'The "Despard Conspiracy" Reconsidered', *Past and Present*, 75 (1977), pp.46–61; Dickinson, *British Radicalism*, pp.53–4; McFarland, *Ireland and* Scotland, pp.221–2.

87. SRO, Home Office Correspondence, RH2/4/88, Charles Hope to Lord Pelham, 4 August 1803; McFarland, *Ireland and Scotland*, pp.223–4.

88. Elliott, 'Despard Conspiracy', pp.60–1.

89. O'Tuathaigh, *Ireland before the Famine*, p.35.

90. Boyce, *Nineteenth Century Ireland*, pp.26–7; Dickinson, *British Radicalism*, pp.48–9; McFarland, *Ireland and Scotland*, p.228.

91. Elliott, 'Despard Conspiracy', p.60; McFarland, *Ireland and Scotland*, p.228.

92. Brims and McFarland also take this view. Brims, 'Scottish Radicalism', pp.164–5; McFarland, *Ireland and Scotland*, pp.166–7, 216–8.

93. See, for example, SRO, Home Office Correspondence, RH2/4/126, Andrew Scott to Lord Sidmouth, 22 September 1819; Alexander Richmond, *Narrative of the Condition of the Manufacturing Population* (1971 reprint, New York, First published London, 1824), p.62.

94. SRO, Home Office Correspondence, RH2/4/80, Henry Campbell to Henry Dundas, 14 January 1797.

95. *Ibid*, RH2/4/83, Declaration of James Jarvie, 13 April 1798.

96. Tony Clarke and Tony Dickson, 'Class and Class Consciousness in Early Industrial Capitalism: Paisley 1770–1850', in Tony Dickson (ed.), *Capital and Class in Scotland* (Edinburgh, 1982), p.36.

3
The Radical Years, 1816–1820

I

The last report in Government correspondence relating to the Society of United Scotsmen is from August 1803. Eight years later the Lord Advocate Archibald Colquhoun told the Home Office that he had been 'informed of the existence of an association for seditious or treasonable purposes similar to those entered into by the individuals called United Scotsmen...'.[1] Unfortunately, there are only three letters concerning this new society in the Government papers. It was not until September 1811 that the Lord Advocate decided to inform London about the organisation, despite having been aware of it for some months. Colquhoun stated that since the society came to his attention he had occasionally received information about its nature and proceedings. He considered these reports to be reliable. Regrettably, they were not sent to the Home Secretary and the first letter from the Lord Advocate was merely a summary of the reports he had been given. This is a major problem with the Home Office Correspondence, not only for this organisation but also for the United Scotsmen societies and for the agitations of 1816–20. Most of the letters sent to London were reports and summaries of information received by the authorities in Scotland. Only occasionally were copies of the actual information given by spies and informers sent with the reports. The same problem exists for much of the information received by the Lord Advocates, as most spies and informers were employed not by them but by third parties, such as the Lord Provost of Glasgow or the Sheriff of Renfrewshire. These individuals would receive the information concerning radical activities and would then usually send only condensed accounts to the Lord Advocates. Most of the original reports of spies and informers appear to have been either lost or destroyed and much valuable information on secret radical societies is therefore not available. Nevertheless, the historian must make full use of the evidence which has survived.

The society which Colquhoun was made aware of in 1811 was called the Defenders. A secret Catholic agrarian organisation with this name had, of course, existed in Ireland since the 1790s, and its members were active on the side of the United Irishmen during the Rebellion of 1798, although it seems that the society declined to a considerable extent during the 1800s.[2] Colquhoun believed that it was from Ireland the Defenders Society in Scotland originated and that 'many Irishmen' were members. There are, however, no details available on the size of its membership, where it was located or on which groups of workers were involved. It was an underground association which acted with 'considerable caution' and used secret signs and oaths of secrecy. Such actions were essential — the society's declared aim was 'with determined resolution to procure our lost rights either by petition or the point of the Baynot not sparing any traitors that may come in the way'.[3] According to the Lord Advocate the Defenders Society was also active in England and in Ireland, and it would appear that the organisation in the latter country had strong links with the Defenders in Scotland.[4]

Five months passed before Colquhoun again wrote to the Home Office about the Defenders. He stated that he had made further inquiries about the society since his previous report and he

> was satisfied that although a dangerous institution was in contemplation and had been to a certain extent carried into effect yet that no immediate danger was to be apprehended with respect to the disturbance of the public peace or any act of violence. I therefore deemed it sufficient to adopt such measures as were calculated to give me such information as would enable me to know if the association should attempt to reduce itself into a more regular form or to proceed to any acts inconsistent with the preservation of the public peace or the safety of the Government of the country.[5]

The association was mentioned by the Lord Advocate in a letter to the Home Secretary in July 1812.[6] Although the organisation still existed at this time the fact that after February 1812 Colquhoun did not send any more reports of its activities to the Home Office suggests that the Society of Defenders in Scotland did not, or probably was not able to, 'reduce itself into a more regular form' or stir up any discontent or disorder. There were no more references to the Defenders in Scotland in Government correspondence after July 1812. Unfortunately, the lack of information concerning the society and its activities means that the reasons for its apparent disappearance cannot be determined.

From around 1812 economic difficulties began to build up in many parts of Great Britain. These intensified after 1815. The west of Scotland was an area which suffered at this time as its industries were particularly vulnerable to the workings of the trade cycle. In particular, the region was greatly affected by the severe recessions of 1816–17 and 1819–20. Widespread unemployment was a feature of these years and the problems faced by those in the industrial areas of the western counties were exacerbated by the increasing supply of labour, caused by the post-war demobilisation, continuing Irish immigration and rural-urban migration from the Highlands and Lowlands, and by the increasing trend of natural population growth. Furthermore, there was a steep rise in food prices and the abolition of the income tax resulted in taxes on working-class essentials such as salt, tea, tobacco, sugar, candles and soap. The years from 1816 to 1820 saw great hardship and suffering among many workers in the industrial areas of the western counties.[7]

The period was also one of much political activity among the unenfranchised in the towns and villages of the west of Scotland. In the summer of 1815 the veteran English radical John Cartwright toured the lowland counties promoting the cause of parliamentary reform and urging those in favour of political change to form Hampden Clubs to put pressure on the Government. These organisations, which already existed in England, were soon established in many of the areas visited by Cartwright that summer. Their principal activity was organising petitions to Parliament requesting political reforms.

Those who were active in the campaign for parliamentary reform in 1815 were mainly from the middle classes. By the autumn of 1816, however, support for the movement had increased dramatically. Large numbers of workers suffering as a result of the deepening economic crisis had become convinced by the arguments of writers such as William Cobbett who condemned the Government and its policies, and who argued that only radical changes such as the introduction of universal suffrage and annual parliaments would lead to an improvement in the condition of the distressed working classes. Large reform meetings were held in Paisley and at the Thrushgrove estate outside Glasgow. The latter demonstration, which took place in October 1816, was attended by around forty thousand people. These meetings, and numerous others which occurred in Scotland at this time, organised petitions to parliament calling for major reforms. They were not successful.

One consequence of the failure of the petitioning movement was that some working class radicals in and around Glasgow abandoned peaceful agitation and formed secret societies which sought to achieve their objectives by revolution. The authorities became aware of this development and used spies to keep track of the activities of the organisations. In February 1817 the leading members of the conspiracy were apprehended. These arrests, the sedition trials which followed and continuing Government repression ensured that the reform movement in Scotland went into rapid decline, and it remained dormant for the next two years. A slight improvement in the state of the economy also contributed to the lack of radical activity.

The campaign in the west of Scotland for political reform revived in 1819, largely as a result of a severe downturn in the state of the economy. On this occasion there was little middle class participation. The increasingly radical demands of workers during 1816–17 and the revolutionary conspiracy of that period convinced most members of the middle classes that agitation for parliamentary reform was a Pandora's Box. Workers in the western counties in 1819 became involved in the Union Societies introduced to the region by Joseph Brayshaw, a reformer from England. These organisations placed great emphasis on political education and argued that if workers boycotted exciseable goods such as tea, spirits, beer and tobacco, the Government would be forced to deal with the political demands of the reformers. In June the Societies helped to organise large public meetings in Paisley and Glasgow which called for parliamentary reform. The campaign intensified after the 'Peterloo' massacre in Manchester in August. Mass demonstrations in Glasgow and outside Paisley condemned the Government and the behaviour of the authorities in Manchester, and riots followed both these events. Protest meetings occurred elsewhere in the region. From August to December 1819 numerous demonstrations demanding political reform took place in the west of Scotland.

As in 1816, the Government at this time had no intention of extending the franchise or of introducing other political reforms. It was, however, greatly alarmed at the revival of radicalism throughout Great Britain. In December Parliament passed Sidmouth's Six Acts, which gave local authorities the powers to effectively crush the reform movements. The Scottish authorities, who were equally concerned about the resurgence of political agitation, and who were alarmed at reports that some workers had once again decided to adopt the secret insurrectionary strategy, implemented these 'Gagging Acts', and in that month public meetings of over fifty people were banned in Scotland.

Reformers in Scotland were now faced with a stark choice. They could either abandon their campaign or, as in late 1816, become involved in an insurrectionary conspiracy. A number decided to follow the latter course of action. By the end of December 1819 secret revolutionary societies existed in towns and villages throughout the west of Scotland and a central committee planned and co-ordinated their activities. The authorities had some knowledge of these developments and soon received information that the radicals were arming and drilling, and were also attempting to establish links with similar organisations in England in the hope of staging a joint rising. In February 1820 Glasgow magistrates, backed up by police and soldiers, raided a meeting of the central committee which was taking place in the Gallowgate and made around thirty arrests.

Unlike in 1817, the capture of the general committee of the secret societies in February 1820 did not lead to the collapse of the insurrectionary conspiracy. Radicals in Glasgow and its vicinity continued to meet and decided to proceed with their rising. Between the night of Saturday 1 April 1820 and the following morning they posted up the *Address to the Inhabitants of Great Britain and Ireland* on buildings in most of the industrial towns and villages in the west of Scotland. The *Address* announced that the radicals had taken up arms and were about to rebel to gain their desired political changes. It also called on the people to strike in order that they would be ready and able to assist and support the imminent revolution. The Scottish radicals appear to have acted in the belief that a rising of radicals in the north of England was currently taking place. Confirmation of this was to be the non-arrival of the mail coaches from Manchester on the morning of Tuesday 4 April; when it was evident that the coaches had been prevented from reaching Glasgow the radicals in the west of Scotland would launch their revolt. It has been estimated that around sixty thousand men and women in the region stopped work in support of the plan of the radicals. In some areas, most notably in and around Glasgow and Paisley, there appears to have been almost unanimous support for the general strike. Radicals began drilling openly and the authorities received reports of pikes being made and of attempts to seize or procure arms. In Paisley troops were attacked by a mob. On the morning of 4 April the mail coaches arrived and it soon became known that no general rising had occurred in the north of England. The Scottish insurrection was therefore aborted and leading radicals fled from their towns and villages. By this time the authorities had moved into action and were already searching for arms and arresting suspected revolutionaries.

Two groups of workers did, however, take up arms in revolt. On the night of 4 April around twenty-five Glasgow radicals left the city to raise support from workers in Stirlingshire and then attempt a raid on the Carron Iron Works near Falkirk, in order to seize arms, ammunition and artillery. They did not know that the insurrection had been abandoned and were persuaded to proceed by information, given perhaps by *agent provocateurs*, that risings had in fact taken place in England and in other parts of Scotland. On their journey they were joined by about fifteen men from Condorrat but few from elsewhere. Eventually this group stopped at Bonnymuir to rest and consider their next move. They were discovered by some yeomanry and hussars and a skirmish ensued between the two parties. Eighteen radicals were captured. On 6 April about two dozen Strathaven radicals, who were unaware that the planned rising had been called off, marched to the Cathkin Braes in the expectation that they were going to join part of the radical army. When they finally arrived they found no-one there. They soon obtained from locals reports of events at Bonnymuir and of the situation in Glasgow and elsewhere. The Strathaven radicals quickly decided to disperse and return to their village. Twelve of them were apprehended on their journey back and another was captured in his house.

The failure of the radicals to launch a general rising and the news of the 'Battle of Bonnymuir' convinced those who had gone on strike as a result of the *Address* that there was not going to be a revolution. By the end of the week almost all had returned to work. There was, on Saturday 8 April, one more major incident, at Greenock, where a mob broke into the town's jail and released some Paisley radicals who had just been imprisoned there. By the beginning of the following week, however, the 'Radical War', as the events of the first week of April 1820 were to become known, was over and peace and order were restored. The authorities continued to search for arms and radicals and many arrests were made. Trials for treason resulted and twenty-two rebels were found guilty. Three were executed and the remainder transported to Australia.

II

Unlike for the United Scotsmen Society and its activities, there is a wealth of sources available concerning the reform agitations of 1816–20. Newspapers published reports of the public reform meetings and riots of this period, and the events of April 1820 received much coverage. The spy system operated by the authorities during this post-Napoleonic War agitation performed far better than in 1797–1803; for example, in February 1817 and February 1820 the leading members of the secret radical organisations were arrested. Many activists were apprehended both during and after the 'Radical War' of April 1820 and there were far more trials of radicals in this period compared with the United Scotsmen years. Several workers produced accounts of the agitations and the roles which they played in them and therefore it is not only the writings of those in authority and their spies that historians are able to examine. There are, however, problems associated with the available sources and these are particularly evident when trying to establish the extent and nature of Irish participation in the radical activities and organisations of this period. These difficulties will be discussed in the text when the need arises.

There is evidence of Irish involvement in the reform agitations of 1816–20. In late 1816 Alexander Richmond, who had been one of the weavers' leaders during the strike of 1812–13, was employed by the Town Clerk of Glasgow and the city's Member of Parliament to spy on the secret radical society which had recently been brought to their attention. Richmond soon ingratiated himself with two of the leading figures in this organisation in order to obtain information from them about it. In his account of the events of 1816–17 Richmond claimed that among those who were active in the revolutionary conspiracy in and around Glasgow

> were some men, who had been members of the unions in Ireland and Scotland, at the periods formerly alluded to [late 1790s/early 1800s], and something upon a similar principle to the affiliated societies of that time naturally suggested itself; but, although the plan they adopted was nearly the same, it attained nothing like the extent or perfection of organisation of those associations.[8]

The structure of the secret societies of 1816–17 was indeed almost identical to that of the earlier United societies as was the oath which their members had to take.[9] Of the thirty or so leading members of the conspiracy arrested in February 1817 the precognitions of twenty-four have survived. It has not been possible to establish the place of birth or ethnic background of eleven of them. Of the remaining thirteen radical leaders eight were natives of Scotland and five were Irishmen.[10] It is impossible to determine whether any had, as Richmond claimed, been involved in either the United Irishmen or the United Scotsmen. One of the five Irishmen was James McTear, who was around thirty-five years old and a teacher of English and Arithmetic in the Calton district. He was born in County Down and had left Ireland in 1797.[11] George Biggar, another spy employed by the authorities, reported that he had been informed that McTear had been active in the United Irishmen.[12] The remaining four Irish radicals were weavers. Roger Gordon lived in Anderston and had arrived in Scotland two years previously from County Antrim.[13] Hugh Cochrane was around thirty-eight years old and was a native of County Down.[14] Hugh Dickson came to Scotland in the early 1800s and stayed in Glasgow for two years. He then enlisted in the Dumfries Militia and remained in it until he was discharged in January 1810. He then moved to Calton to resume his trade.[15] Dickson later published a reply to Alexander Richmond's narrative of the events of 1816–17.[16] Andrew McKinlay, a native of County Armagh, also lived in Calton. He left Ireland in 1799. In his precognition to the authorities McKinlay stated that he was a private both in the Volunteers and in the local militia and had been for the past fourteen years.[17] Biggar informed the authorities that John Campbell, a leading member of the secret organisation, had told him that McKinlay had held a captaincy in the United Irish army.[18]

McKinlay was one of the most important figures in the conspiracy. Like Campbell and the four radicals already discussed, he was a member of the 17–18 man general committee of delegates which sought to co-ordinate and lead the secret societies in and around Glasgow and elsewhere in the west of Scotland. McKinlay was the treasurer of the group.[19] Both Richmond and Biggar were aware of the prominent position McKinlay held in the organisation.[20] Furthermore, James Hood, one of the radicals arrested with McKinlay in February 1817, told the authorities, 'That from any thing he saw he considered…McKinlay as the most active and knowing of the association and of promoting the object and business of the meetings…'[21]

In July 1817 McKinlay stood trial accused of administering treasonable oaths. The Crown's star witness was John Campbell, McKinlay's erstwhile colleague on the general committee. In March he had given a full account of the conspiracy in return for guarantees for his safety and assistance for his wife to move to Ayrshire. At the trial, however, Campbell declared that he had been promised not only protection but also a position in the excise by one of the Advocates' Depute in return for giving evidence.[22] Roach has suggested:

> Campbell was very cleverly sabotaging the crown's case. If his statement were true his evidence was inadmissible and doubts were cast on the methods employed by the crown to prepare a case; while if it were not true he was guilty of perjury and nothing else he might say could be accepted.[23]

Campbell did not give his testimony. This greatly weakened the prosecution's case as it was relying heavily on Campbell because of the leading role he played in the revolutionary organisation and the quality of the information he had given in his confession in March. Although others gave evidence at the trial, the case against McKinlay was found not proven. This failure to convict and the circumstances of the trial resulted in the release of the other prisoners.[24]

There is, therefore, evidence that Irish immigrants were involved in the leadership of the revolutionary conspiracy of 1816–17. It is impossible, however, to determine whether they founded it or dominated its proceedings. It is likely that other Irishmen were members of the local branches of the organisation, but unfortunately the available evidence does not reveal the extent of such participation.

In his account of the reform agitation of 1819–20 Richmond stated of the secret societies of the period that their

> organisation was formed strictly on the model of the Irish in 1798…The minor details were, indeed, chiefly concocted and carried into execution by emigrants, who had been engaged in that rebellion in Ireland.[25]

Richmond, however, was not a Government informer in these years. In the summer of 1817 it became public knowledge that he had been employed by the authorities; indeed, he was labelled not simply a spy but an *agent provocateur*.[26] As Richmond had not the same access to the secret societies of 1819–20 as he had to those of the earlier period, how could he have stated with such certainty that Irish immigrants were so heavily involved in the insurrectionary activities of 1819–20? In his book Richmond stated that he 'was not an inattentive observer' of events, and that he had also obtained information 'from various sources since the ferment subsided'. Furthermore, he claimed that he had 'been at considerable pains to obtain information from several of the prominent actors' in both England and Scotland. Richmond believed that the intelligence he received was reliable.[27] He did not, however, give any further information on involvement by Irish workers.

It is impossible to establish the accuracy of Richmond's statement about the role of Irish workers in the secret societies of 1819–20. There are several reasons for this. Many of the leaders of the conspiracy were not captured. Three months after the 'Radical War' of April 1820 the Lord Advocate William Rae, writing from Glasgow, complained to Lord Sidmouth about

> the state of the police of this part of the country. From this cause the cases which we had to bring to trial at this place were comparatively in number few, weak in their circumstances, and in almost all, the principal leaders had been allowed to make their escape.[28]

In Ayrshire and Renfrewshire many of the leading radicals also managed to flee from the authorities.[29] If such individuals had been apprehended the precognitions they would have given might have revealed information about their nationality or ethnic background. In February 1820 the members of the Central Committee of the radical organisation were arrested in Glasgow.[30] These men were never tried. Furthermore, the precognitions taken after their capture appear to have been either destroyed or lost. The same is true of the dozens of activists arrested during April 1820. Invaluable information about the radicals and their activities is therefore not available. The published reports of the trials of those involved in the 'Radical War' do not mention the nationalities of the accused.[31] The spy system of the authorities did not operate as efficiently as in 1817. Although the Central Committee of the radicals was captured in February 1820 the events of April took the authorities by complete surprise.[32] Furthermore, the reports they received during 1819–20 rarely named individual activists, let alone their nationalities. It must be stated, however, that if the leadership of the conspiracy consisted mainly of Irishmen, this surely would have been mentioned in the spies' reports, in the correspondence of the authorities, or in the accounts of the events of 1819–20 written by those who participated in them.[33] That it was not, would appear to contradict the claims made by Richmond. Yet, as has been shown, many of the leading radicals avoided capture and the available information concerning those who were apprehended is not sufficient to make any firm conclusions about the role of Irish workers in the leadership of the secret societies of 1819–20.

Although there is not enough evidence to support Richmond's claims concerning the leading role of Irish immigrants in these societies and in the 'Radical War', there is evidence that Irishmen were involved to some extent in the agitation of the time. It is, however, impossible to establish how representative such examples are. In his memoirs James Paterson, a newspaper proprietor in Kilmarnock, described the activities of one of the town's political associations in 1819, when he was employed as an apprentice printer.[34] Its members, with one exception, were handloom weavers:

> All were keen Reformers; some carried their notions so far, as to come under the denominations of *Blacknebs*, which latter were understood to stop short at nothing less than an absolute and *bona fide* division of property. Old Paisley, and his next door neighbour *Glasgow*, were among the latter; and these two were warmly supported by Peter Kelly, an Irishman, who had been a soldier. He had a great dislike to the Duke of Wellington, because, as Sandy Slyman intimated, he had been whipped and dismissed the service for some rather uncommon misdemeanour...

According to Paterson these men advocated not only the standard radical programme of annual parliaments, vote by ballot and universal suffrage but also desired 'that there should be no king, no lords, no gentry, no taxes!'.[35] He did not state, however, whether this group was active during the 'Radical War'. Two Irishmen who did take up arms in April 1820 were Thomas McCulloch, a stocking maker in Glasgow, and William Smith, a weaver in Condorrat. Both were born in County Down: McCulloch in 1787, Smith in 1781. They were the only men of Irish birth among the sixteen radicals tried and transported for their skirmish with Government forces in the 'Battle of Bonnymuir'.[36] It would appear that Irish immigrants were involved in events in Ayrshire during the 'Radical War'. The Commander of the county's yeomanry, Colonel Alexander Boswell, noted how widespread the 'poison' of radicalism had spread in Ayrshire,[37] to 'as many as were debauched in *every* village...'.[38] He reported that he had to deal not only with the county's 'own natural population' but also with 'a very great influx of Irishmen, who are bad subjects and not easily controlled'.[39]

There is also evidence which suggests that there was an Irish presence in the mob which broke into Greenock Jail on 8 April 1820 and liberated the Paisley radicals who had only just been incarcerated there.[40] According to several witnesses the crowd contained a great number who were not residents of the town but who were strangers.[41] Many of them might have been in the town 'for the purpose of emigration…'.[42] James Oughterson, a merchant, declared 'That a number of the people composing the mob were dressed in corduroy jackets which is a very uncommon dress in the town of Greenock and a number of them were Irishmen'.[43] Another of the town's merchants informed the authorities that he observed that an Irishman was one of the leaders of the mob which broke down the door of the prison.[44]

Seven men were arrested in connection with the riot. They were not, however, strangers to Greenock but lived and worked in the town. At least two, Edward McGowan and Darby Canning, were Irishmen. McGowan was a labourer who worked about the quays and vessels and had lived in the town since 1812.[45] Darby Canning was a native of County Donegal and had been in Scotland for twelve years. He was a labourer in one of Greenock's shipyards.[46] McGowan's employer Quintin Leitch told the authorities that the only person whom he recognised among the mob at the prison was McGowan. Leitch stated that he told him to go home and had reason to believe that McGowan took this advice.[47] McGowan declared that he left the scene when ordered to do so.[48] McGowan, Canning and three of the others under arrest all admitted being present in the crowd at the prison but denied participating in the riot which occurred. They also declared that they did not recognise any of the perpetrators.[49] The remaining prisoners denied any involvement and instead blamed some of their fellow detainees. According to Dugald Macaulay, Canning and two of the other prisoners helped break down the prison door.[50] Andrew Foster also claimed that Canning was involved in the attack, yet stated that Macaulay was 'very active among the crowd…'.[51]

The seven men were charged with High Treason and imprisoned in Dumbarton Castle. Three months later they were released. The Advocate Depute J.A. Maconochie decided that there was not enough evidence to proceed against any of the prisoners:

> no person whatever has been recognised as active in the mob, or even sharing in the proceedings that took place, by any of the magistrates or any witness of respectability. The only proof of identification, is that afforded by the accused

themselves, who in their declarations while they severally deny being personally engaged in the tumult, mutually accuse each other.

According to Maconochie, the evidence of some of the prisoners would not be sufficient by itself to ensure the conviction of the others: 'I hardly think that a jury would feel entitled to convict upon the testimony of accomplices...without corroboration from a quarter more worthy of credit.'[52]

No other evidence of Irish involvement in the events of April 1820 has been found. However, by using the method of name-spotting it is possible to suggest further Irish participation. For example, two members of the Barrowfield Radical Committee were Thomas Connor and Barney McGarry; the Castle Street delegate to the Glasgow Secret Committee was a weaver named William Flanagan; a Duntocher radical tried for High Treason in July 1820 for his activities during the 'Radical War' was called Patrick McDevitt.[53] It is, of course, impossible to establish whether these men were of Irish birth or descent, although their names certainly suggest that this was so. However, as Thompson has noted, name-spotting is a rather 'inadequate method' of establishing Irish participation in British political agitations.[54] After all, most of the Irishmen who have already been identified as being involved in radical activities in Scotland between 1816 and 1820 — Andrew McKinlay, Hugh Dickson, Hugh Cochrane, Roger Gordon, Thomas McCulloch and William Smith — did not have 'Irish' names.

The surnames of these radicals suggest that they came from a Protestant Irish background. Indeed, some may argue that it would be most surprising if some Irishmen were not involved in the agitations of 1816–20; a large number of those who came to Scotland from Ulster were Protestants and, as shown in chapter one, certain historians have argued that the Protestant Irish found it much easier to integrate than the Catholics because of family and cultural ties, and because they shared a common religion with the Scots. For example, Gallagher claimed that 'These ties of kinship enabled local workers and Protestant immigrants to display solidarity with one another.'[55] He and several other historians have argued that it was the Roman Catholic Irish who were despised by the native workers.[56]

There is one piece of evidence in the Home Office Correspondence which could be used to support these views. On 28 December 1816 Alexander Richmond met his employers, Kirkman Finlay and James Reddie, and reported to them a conversation which he had the previous evening with 'his friend of the central committee...'. The minutes of Richmond's report state that he was informed:

No Roman Catholic admitted into the association. Enquired why so as they were considered Trust worthy in the Irish Rebellion? Answered the Priests were there in favour of the association and Insurrection. In this country the Roman Catholic clergy have preached against all interference in political matters; and their creed generally, and particularly auricular confession, render the association afraid the Roman Catholics might be the means of betraying them.[57]

From this account it could be concluded that the Irishmen involved in the secret societies in Glasgow were Protestants. Indeed, McFarland has recently done this. She also suggested that these radicals were anti-Catholic[58] and in an earlier work argued: 'Anti-Roman Catholic sentiments could find expression even at the height of popular radical agitation.'[59]

The information which Richmond passed to his employers on 28 December 1816 must, however, be handled with extreme caution. He received it from a Calton weaver named John McLachlan. This individual was the radical whom Richmond first chose to befriend in order to gain information about the secret societies.[60] In his narrative of the events of this period, published in 1824, Richmond recalled his meetings with McLachlan:

> I soon found him so completely worthless, that I could attach little credit to any of his statements…after having several conferences with this man, I found his statements so incredible and incongruous, so much at variance, at one time compared with another, that I was unable to arrive at anything definite, and, after losing nearly a fortnight, contrary to my original intention, I was obliged to make him introduce me to another of the party.[61]

The next person whom Richmond ingratiated himself with was John Campbell, one of the leading figures in the conspiracy. Richmond stated of him that: 'I…soon discovered he was much better adapted to my purpose than McLachlan, and I took the same method of getting into his confidence, by occasionally giving him small sums of money.'[62] After meeting Campbell, Richmond had few further dealings with McLachlan.[63]

Richmond's evaluation of much of the information he obtained from McLachlan means that doubts exist over the 'revelation' that Roman Catholics were excluded from the secret radical societies. There was no mention of this policy in subsequent reports from Richmond, or from Biggar, or even in the precognitions of the leading radicals arrested in February 1817. In his account of the insurrectionary activity Richmond recalled that McLachlan exaggerated the geographical extent of the conspiracy, its quantity of arms, its links with radicals in the manufacturing counties of England and with men of property and respectability, in order to impress those whom he solicited to join the organisation.[64] Perhaps it was only this information which Richmond considered 'so completely worthless' and 'so incredible and incongruous', rather than that concerning the structure, oaths and membership of the secret associations or that which stated that Roman Catholics were not permitted to join. Unfortunately, the nature of the available evidence does not allow this issue to be resolved in a satisfactory manner.

Even if it was established that the information Richmond received concerning the exclusion of Roman Catholics was indeed correct it does not necessarily follow, as McFarland has suggested, that the radicals and their societies during 1816 and 1817 were sectarian. The account which McLachlan gave could simply be interpreted as evidence that the secret societies excluded Roman Catholics for reasons of security. They did not, it seems, wish to exclude them from political participation come the revolution, as the following extract from their secret oath demonstrates:

> In the awful presence of God, I, A.B., do voluntarily swear that I will persevere in my endeavours to form a brotherhood of affection amongst Britons of every description who are considered worthy of confidence; and that I will persevere in my endeavours to obtain for all the people of Great Britain and Ireland not disqualified by crimes or insanity the elective franchise at the age of 21 with free and equal representation and annual parliaments...[65]

McFarland's evidence to support her argument that 'Anti-Roman Catholic sentiments' were expressed during major phases of the radical agitation comes from a speech given by a middle class reformer at the great meeting at Thrushgrove near Glasgow in October 1816. In it he protested against

> the late, unnecessary, ruinous, and sanguinary war, the re-establishment of the despicable family of Bourbon, the restoration of the Pope in Italy and of the Jesuits, and the Inquisition, in Spain; the extravagance of the Government, the increase of the Civil List, the exorbitant salaries of public officers, the burdens of pensions and sinecures and of the Standing Army, and the corrupt state of Parliamentary representation in Scotland.[66]

This quote does not demonstrate that the reform movement was anti-Catholic in the sense that it sought to deny members of the Catholic religion the same political rights as Protestants. It merely suggests that this particular reformer was opposed to the return of the Pope to Italy and the Jesuits and Inquisition to Spain because he, like other reformers, considered these developments, and the restoration of the Bourbon Monarchy to France, to be reactionary political measures. Indeed, one of the resolutions passed at the meeting condemned these actions as well as 'the re-establishment everywhere of that bigotry and despotism, which disgraced the darkest periods of European history; the whole filling us with the most anxious concern, not only for our own civil and religious liberties, but also for the civil and religious liberties of the whole of Europe…'.[67]

It is probable that some of the Irishmen who were members of the secret societies of 1816–20 were Protestants. It is unlikely, however, that they did not want Catholics to obtain the same political rights which they themselves were demanding. The radical agitations of this period sought the franchise for all adult males. The Protestant Irish reformers in Scotland in these years should be regarded as being part of the radical Presbyterian United Irish tradition, which was non-sectarian and which desired the same political, social and religious rights for all. This group of immigrants therefore needs to be distinguished from the Protestant Irishmen in Scotland who were joining or forming anti-Catholic Orange Lodges at this time, and pledging themselves to uphold the Protestant ascendancy in Ireland.[68] Indeed, one of the leading radicals arrested in Glasgow in February 1817 tried to convince the authorities that he had never been involved in any radical reform activity by claiming, 'That his brother and his brother-in-law are both on the contrary Orangemen and he expects to be one himself very soon.'[69]

If doubts persist concerning the attitude of the reformers of 1816–17 towards Irish Roman Catholics there is evidence which strongly suggests that the radicals actively sought the support of these immigrants during 1819. This is found in three letters written by Andrew Scott, the Roman Catholic priest in Glasgow. Two were sent to the Home Secretary Lord Sidmouth who at a meeting with Scott had requested him to provide an account of 'some of the real or supposed grievances which have tended to create a considerable degree of dissatisfaction in the minds of Roman Catholics on the west coast of Scotland, particularly in the counties of Lanark, Renfrew and Ayr'.[70] The third letter was to Bishop Alexander Cameron, Scott's superior.[71]

In his first letter to Sidmouth, in August 1819, Scott highlighted two of the major grievances of his congregation. The first was that they were refused poor relief when in poverty as a consequence of unemployment or sickness, despite being legally entitled to it; the second was the prejudices and insults they frequently encountered in the inferior courts.[72] In his second letter, sent the following month, Scott revealed that he had recently attempted to reason with members of his flock 'on the great evil and danger of being present at riots, and on the necessity of not joining with the revolutionists…'. Some of them retorted that the 'Government had never done any thing for them, and that under any government they could not be exposed to greater grievances than those they had lately experienced'.[73]

Scott was convinced that the discontent exhibited by members of his congregation was potentially very dangerous, as the Roman Catholics in the west of Scotland were

> principally Irish, of the lower orders, keen in their passions and easily inflamed. These grievances are still more magnified in their eyes by a few cunning disturbers of the public peace who are using at present every endeavour to enlist them into the ranks of the treasonably disaffected.[74]

According to Scott, during a riot in Glasgow in September 1819 the mob passed the Roman Catholic chapel on Great Clyde Street and someone suggested that they attack the building, to which 'the generality cried out: no, no, it would make a split or a division amongst us'. Scott also stated that he had been informed that earlier in the day of the riot some people travelling to a reform meeting in Paisley remarked that 'if it were not for these D...nd priests they would get all the papists to join them, and that if they could make sure of them, they would be certain of gaining their cause'.[75]

Scott was convinced that in order to secure the loyalty of the Irish Roman Catholics who he claimed amounted to about 100,000 in the western districts — clearly an exaggerated total[76] — the Government had to provide resources to build chapels for them and to pay off the debt on St Andrews in Glasgow.[77] He believed this would secure the affections and loyalty of the Irish in Scotland, and 'convert almost every man of them into agents of Government under the influence of their pastors'.[78] Scott informed Sidmouth that the Irish Catholics were unable to provide themselves with chapels, and that if the Government did this for them 'the pastors would be furnished with a lasting and powerful argument to secure their fidelity and withdraw them from the arms of the reformists and agitators'.[79] The Home Secretary's 'impression' of Scott's letters was not favourable though it is not known why this was so. Both Sidmouth and Lord Melville, the First Lord of the Admiralty, 'discountenanced' Scott's suggestions and no money was made available.[80]

This information does not, of course, reveal an Irish Catholic presence in the secret radical societies of 1819–20. It merely shows that the Roman Catholic priest at Glasgow was extremely concerned that the radicals would succeed in their attempts to recruit members of his congregation; in order to prevent this he believed that the Government had to deal with the grievances of the Irish Catholics in the west of Scotland. Some may argue that Scott was sending false information and making alarmist predictions in order to obtain funds for the construction of Catholic chapels, as the Church itself could not provide the necessary resources.

However, it is probable that Scott wrote to the Home Office in London because he was indeed greatly concerned about the activities of the radicals. The radical societies of 1819–20, like those active in 1816–17, were not hostile towards Irish Catholics.[81] Moreover, given the poverty of these immigrants and the various grievances they had regarding the Government and the local authorities, it is most unlikely that the radicals would not have desired such a potentially inflammable group to join their agitation. Indeed, in the summer of 1819 Henry Hunt and other English reformers, eager to swell the ranks of the radical movement, actively sought the support of the growing number of Irish Catholics in England.[82]

Unfortunately, because of the limitations of the available evidence it is impossible to establish how successful the Scottish societies were in gaining recruits from the Catholic community. In January 1820 Scott admitted to Bishop Cameron that in spite of all his efforts 'a few poor deluded beings' had been drawn into the ranks of the radicals.[83] Whether Scott was deliberately underestimating the extent of such involvement in order not to give the impression to his superior that he had lost control of affairs in and around Glasgow is, of course, a matter of conjecture. It might also have been that he was unaware of the extent of Catholic involvement — after all, the insurrectionary societies were secret organisations. Five years later Scott reported that the Glasgow Catholic Association, which was composed almost exclusively of Irish Catholics, contained 'well known' radicals.[84] This organisation and its activities are examined in the following chapter.

There is also evidence which can be used to suggest that a large proportion of Irish workers, both Catholic and Protestant, were at the very least supporters of the reform agitation. It has been shown that at least three Irish weavers in Calton were members of the leadership of the secret societies of 1816–17. In December 1816 the Lord Provost of Glasgow James Black informed the Lord Advocate that there had been a meeting in Calton on 11 December attended by between 600 and 900 people on the issue of poor relief. A number of 'violent resolutions' were passed and threats made by the speakers. One of the resolutions, which was adopted unanimously, stated that those present would visit the minister of the parish Dr. Burns the following morning, 'and from him demand an assurance that they and their families should immediately and adequately be sustained'. Around 200 people went to the minister's house on Wednesday 11 December and presented him with 'a memorial of the Calton weavers'. He was informed that they would return the following Monday for his reply. James Black was extremely concerned about these events. He made certain that police and cavalry were present when the crowd went to visit Burns, and informed the Lord Advocate that the military was needed in the area on the day when the inhabitants of Calton were to receive their answer. Black believed that there was a possibility that disorder would occur if relief was not given, as the memorial to the Calton minister ended by stating that the suburb's weavers hoped that Burns would 'not be the cause of us having recourse to that desperate alternative of acting in what you may be pleased to call unconstitutional to supply the cravings of nature'. The Lord Provost added: 'The very worst and most daring of our population are in this suburb — the Calton and round about it. They are almost all Irish weavers. Their threatenings have been vicious...'[85] Writing around this time the city's postmaster Dugald Bannatyne stated:

> there are strong appearances among a part of the labouring class of a disposition to disturb the public peace. These have been chiefly evinced by the working people living in a large suburb of Glasgow called the Caltoun [sic]: which contains between thirty and forty thousand inhabitants: without the jurisdiction of the municipality of Glasgow, and with no establishment of magistracy or police of its own. This is a very dangerous state for this quarter of the Town to be left in: for its population is nearly entirely composed of the labouring class, and a considerable proportion of these, of workmen, drawn from all parts of the country, and particularly from Ireland.

Bannatyne explained that about two months previously an assessment was taken of the people of Glasgow to provide for the needs of those in poverty. This, however, was not applicable to those residing in the suburbs 'and it is from there that a disturbance of the Peace is at present apprehended'.[86] The city's authorities adopted a number of measures to ensure order and plans were made to raise funds for those in poverty in the suburbs.[87]

It is evident that there was great concern in Glasgow about the large number of Irish workers in Calton. One of the first and most active of the secret seditious societies of the 1816–17 agitation was formed in this suburb and Irish weavers were active in it. During the Radical War of April 1820 Calton was one of three areas in Glasgow which were surrounded by soldiers, who then searched every house for arms and ammunition. The other two were Anderston and Bridgeton, weaving districts which also had large Irish populations.[88] Indeed, it was in Calton, Bridgeton, Anderston and in the Gorbals that the earliest schools were founded, between 1818 and 1822, for Irish Catholic children in and around Glasgow.[89]

Major centres of radical activity during 1816–20 therefore contained large numbers of Irish workers, many of whom were weavers. Murray estimated that around 30 per cent of handloom weavers in Glasgow in 1819 were of Irish birth and there were probably others of Irish parentage.[90] In Ayrshire and Renfrewshire many Irish immigrants worked at the loom.

Handloom weavers were heavily involved in the agitation of this period, as they believed that their dire economic and social condition would improve only after radical political change occurred. Trade union action was not a realistic option for them in the depression of these years, and in any case the weavers' combination had collapsed in 1813 after the failure of the great strike and the convictions of the union leadership.[91] It would appear that handloom weavers were almost unanimous in their support of the aims presented in the radical *Address* of April 1820. For example, the *Glasgow Herald* reported that the order

> to abstain from all work after the 1st day of April…has been but too implicitly obeyed. All the weavers in Glasgow and its suburbs have struck work, and our streets are crowded with them walking about idle. The weavers in Paisley and its neighbourhood, have also, we understand, ceased to work…[92]

Given such evidence it is not unreasonable to suggest that Irish handloom weavers joined their Scottish colleagues in stopping work in early April 1820 in support of the plan and aims of the Radicals.

Whereas Irish immigrants formed a large proportion of the weaving workforce at this time, in cotton spinning they predominated.[93] The spinners in and around Glasgow and Paisley, and the other workers in the mills, also stopped work during the 'Radical War'.[94] Furthermore, there is evidence that cotton spinners were active in the secret societies of these years. A leading figure in the 1816–17 conspiracy, who agreed to 'make a full and fair disclosure to the authorities', declared in his precognition 'That he understood that a great many Calton spinners had been initiated belonging to Clark's Mill and to Dunlop's Mill and in Hussey's Mill in Bridgeton…'[95] Hugh Dickson, another of those apprehended in February 1817, claimed that the insurrectionary organisation was founded by spinners: 'from what he knows it began among the Calton spinners and was by them communicated to the weavers.'[96] Colonel Norcott, who led the troops who arrested the twenty-seven man Central Committee in February 1820, reported that 'The delegates are chiefly weavers and cotton spinners'.[97] In May 1820 George Salmond, the Procurator Fiscal in Glasgow, informed a colleague that the seven cotton spinners who had been arrested in January of that year in connection with attacks on women workers at James Dunlop's Mill in Calton, and with the attempt to burn down the works, had been released on bail as all the charges could not 'be brought home to any person'. He added: 'They are again, at least the most of them, in jail as radicals.'[98] Another member of the spinners' combination, Alexander Cameron, who was reportedly one of its leading activists, fled from the city in April 1820 'on account of his connection with the

Radicals…'.[99] It is clear, therefore, that cotton spinners were involved — some more than others — in the agitation for political change between 1816 and 1820. As the overwhelming majority of spinners in this period appear to have been Irish and most spinners stopped work in April 1820, it is not unreasonable to argue that Irish spinners, like Irish weavers, went on strike in support of the radicals.

Indeed, the evidence shows that in April 1820 there was a general cessation of work in which around 60,000 people in the manufacturing areas of the west of Scotland were involved.[100] For example, Henry Monteith, Glasgow's Lord Provost, wrote to the Lord Advocate William Rae on 3 April and informed him that 'almost the whole population of the working classes have obeyed the orders contained in the treasonable proclamation by striking work. The consequence is that the multitude on the streets is immense.'[101] The Provost of Paisley wrote to Monteith that day and told him that 'The working classes here are all idle and assembled in crowds on the streets.'[102] Thus if it is impossible to establish the extent of Irish involvement in the secret radical societies of 1816–20, the evidence of the response to the call for a general strike, a vital part of the radicals' strategy, suggests that most Irish workers — Catholic and Protestant — stopped work in early April 1820 in support of the radicals and their aims.

In the introduction to this study it was noted that the historian of the Irish in Scotland, James Handley, accepted the unsubstantiated claim made by Thomas Johnston that during the reform agitations of 1816–20, 'The immigrant Irish rebels were in "the troubles" — the advanced left wing of them, almost to a man…'. According to Handley they participated because they hoped 'a successful revolt might have favourable repercussions on the conditions of their own country'.[103] It has already been argued that Irishmen were involved in the United Scotsmen Society in order to further the cause of the United Irishmen. However, although the Scottish secret societies of 1816–20 appear to have established links with Irish radicals,[104] it is highly unlikely that the vast majority of immigrants who supported the agitations did so primarily in the hope that, if successful, they would lead to reforms in their native land. It is probable that a desire to see their conditions in Scotland improve made them support the campaigns for political change. Irish workers were undoubtedly affected by the economic depression of the period, which was the principal reason why most joined the ranks of the radicals or supported their aims.[105] The precognition of Hugh Dickson, the Irish weaver who was a leading member of the conspiracy of 1816–17, makes this clear: 'That the stagnation in trade and the recent distress in the country was attributed by the Decl. and those in his neighbourhood [Calton] to the Corn Bill some time ago passed and to their not having universal suffrage and annual parliaments.'[106] Furthermore, the Catholics among the immigrants had, as has been shown, additional reasons for being hostile towards national and local government. In his letter to Lord Sidmouth in August 1819 — written before the severe economic distress of the winter of 1819–20 — Andrew Scott expressed his concern that the various grievances which the Irish Catholics had towards the authorities in Scotland combined with their economic condition made them very susceptible to the overtures of the radicals: 'They are very numerous, very poor, have nothing to lose in a revolution, and are flattered by the reformists with the hopes of ameliorating their circumstances by a revolution.'[107]

There is, on the other hand, evidence which reveals that some Irishmen were not involved in the reform agitations of these years. In October 1819 Andrew Scott informed a colleague that he was in desperate need of funds to service the debt on the Glasgow chapel because:

> Those of our Irish Catholics who had money and who cheerfully lent it on my single bill have become so frightened for fear of being murdered by the Radicals in this country that they have gone to Ireland, which is quiet at present and purchased ground there and require their money to pay it. £1,500 has been called up for this purpose…[108]

This, however, should not be used to refute the argument advanced in this chapter that large numbers of Irish Catholics in the west of Scotland supported the demands for political reform during 1819–20. What this evidence shows is that these Catholics, who were almost certainly members of the small group of Irish businessmen and shopkeepers in and around Glasgow, were greatly alarmed at the radical agitation. Middle class Scots in the city likewise feared for their lives and property in these years and formed volunteer regiments to defend them.[109] Members of the Irish Catholic business community appear to have taken the less dangerous option and simply returned home with their money.

It is evident that some Irishmen were involved in the secret radical societies of 1816–20. The extent of immigrant involvement is impossible to establish because of the limitations of the sources. Nevertheless the available evidence suggests that a sizable proportion of the Irish workforce in the west of Scotland at the very least supported the principle of political reform and stopped work in April 1820 to help the radical cause. Between 1797 and 1803 Irish immigrants were active in the United Scotsmen Society in order to assist in the struggle for an Irish Republic. In 1816–20 most of the Irish workers who were involved in the political agitations in the west of Scotland almost certainly participated not for the sake of Ireland, but for the same reasons as Scottish workers: they were suffering as a result of the economic distress of the time and became convinced that only drastic political change would end their agony.

Notes

1. SRO, Home Office Correspondence, RH2/4/98, Copy of a letter from the Lord Advocate to Richard Ryder, 6 September 1811, enclosed with A. Colquhoun to Viscount Sidmouth, 4 July 1812.

2. Tom Garvin, 'Defenders, Ribbonmen and Others: Underground Political Networks in Pre-Famine Ireland', in C.H.E. Philpin (ed.), *Nationalism and Popular Protest in Ireland* (Cambridge, 1987), pp.219–44.

3. SRO, Home Office Correspondence, RH2/4/98, Copy of a letter from the Lord Advocate to Richard Ryder, 6 September 1811, enclosed with A. Colquhoun to Viscount Sidmouth, 4 July 1812.

4. *Ibid*, Anon. to 'My Lord', 30 April 1812.

5. *Ibid*, RH2/4/97, A. Colquhoun to Richard Ryder, 19 February 1812.

6. *Ibid*, RH2/4/98, A. Colquhoun to Lord Sidmouth, 4 July 1812.

7. This paragraph and the following overview of the events of 1816–1820 are based on W. Hamish Fraser, *Conflict and Class: Scottish Workers 1700–1838* (Edinburgh, 1988), chapter 6; Norman Murray, *The Scottish Handloom Weavers, 1790–1850: A Social History* (Edinburgh 1979), chapter 9; P. Berresford Ellis and Seumas Mac a'Ghobhainn, *The Scottish Insurrection of 1820* (paperback edition, London, 1989); W.M. Roach, 'Alexander Richmond and the Radical Reform Movements in Glasgow 1816–17', *Scottish Historical Review*, LI (1972), pp.1–19; M.I. Thomis and P. Holt, *Threats of Revolution in Britain, 1789–1848* (London, 1977), chapter 3; F.K. Donnelly, 'The Scottish Rising of 1820: A Re-interpretation', *Scottish Tradition*, VI (1976), pp.27–37; Peter Holt, 'Review of P. Berresford Ellis and Seumas Mac a'Ghobhainn, *The Scottish Insurrection of 1820*', *Journal of the Scottish Labour History Society*, 3 (1970), pp.34–9.

8. Alexander B. Richmond, *Narrative of the Condition of the Manufacturing Population* (London, 1824, reprinted New York, 1971), p.77.

9. For the structure and oath of the societies see *ibid*, pp.77–80. For those of the United Scotsmen see *Report of the Committee of Secrecy of the House of Commons, 1799*, pp.11–2, 21.

10. The precognitions are located in SRO, Home Office Correspondence, RH2/4/14 and RH2/4/15, and in WRH, Lord Advocate's Papers, AD14/17/8.

11. WRH, Lord Advocate's Papers, AD14/17/8, Declaration of James McTear, 24 February 1817.

12. SRO, Home Office Correspondence, RH2/4/114, Report of 'B' [Biggar], 9 February 1817.

13. WRH, Lord Advocate's Papers, AD14/17/8, Declaration of Roger Gordon, 25 February 1817.

14. *Ibid*, Declaration of Hugh Cochrane, 25 February 1817.

15. SRO, Home Office Correspondence, RH2/4/115, Declaration of Hugh Dickson, 28 February 1817.

16. Hugh Dickson, *The Criterion, or Richmond's Narrative Exposed* (Glasgow, 1825).

17. SRO, Home Office Correspondence, RH2/4/115, Declaration of Andrew McKinlay, 28 February 1817.

18. *Ibid*, RH2/4/114, Report of 'B' [Biggar], 9 February 1817. In this report, Biggar also stated that Campbell was 'the soul of business in Calton and an Irishman who has staid long here and thinks concerned in Irish Rebellion'. However, in his precognition to the authorities, Campbell declared that he was a native of Ayrshire and had moved to Calton in December 1816. See WRH, Lord Advocates' Papers, AD14/17/8, Declaration of John Campbell, 31 March 1817.

19. Roach, 'Alexander Richmond', p.12.

20. SRO, Home Office Correspondence, RH2/4/113, 'Minutes of a conversation with Richmond, 28 December 1816', enclosed with Alexander Maconochie to Viscount Sidmouth, 2 January 1817; RH2/4/114, Report of 'B' [Biggar], 9 February 1817.

21. *Ibid*, RH2/4/114, Declaration of James Hood, 26 February 1817.

22. Roach, 'Alexander Richmond', pp.14–5.

23. *Ibid*, p.15.

24. *Ibid*, pp.14–6.

25. Richmond, *Narrative*, pp.182–3.

26. Roach, 'Alexander Richmond', p.16–7.

27. Richmond, *Narrative*, pp.166–7.

28. SRO, Home Office Correspondence, RH2/4/135, William Rae to Lord Sidmouth, 25 July 1820. See also RH2/4/132, Rae to Sidmouth, 11 April 1820.

29. *Ibid*, RH2/4/132, Alexander Boswell to 'My Lord', 22 April 1820; J.R. Fraser (ed.), *A Memoir of John Fraser of Newfield* (Paisley, 1879), p.21; John Parkhill, *History of Paisley* (Paisley, 1850), p.65.

30. SRO, Home Office Correspondence, RH2/4/131, Henry Monteith to Lord Sidmouth, 23 February 1820; R. Hamilton to Lord Sidmouth, 23 February 1820.

31. C.J. Green (ed.), *Trials for High Treason* (3 volumes, Edinburgh, 1825).

32. Thomis and Holt, *Threats of Revolution*, p.74.

33. Accounts of the events of 1819–20 by those who participated in them include Fraser (ed.) *Memoir of John Fraser*; Parkhill, *History of Paisley*, chapter 8; John Stevenson, *A True Narrative of The Radical Rising in Strathaven...* (Glasgow, 1835); SRA, MacKinnon Correspondence, TD743/1–2. See also Ellis and Mac a'Ghobhain, *Scottish Insurrection*, pp.303–49.

34. James Paterson, *Autobiographical Reminiscences* (Glasgow, 1871), pp.65–80.

35. *Ibid*, p.67.

36. Margaret and Alastair McFarlane, *The Scottish Radicals Tried and Transported to Australia for Treason in 1820* (Stevenage, 1981, First published Sydney, 1975), pp.34, 54.

37. SRO, Home Office Correspondence, RH2/4/132, Alexander Boswell to 'My Lord', 16 April 1820.

38. *Ibid*, 22 April 1820.

39. *Ibid*, 16 April 1820.

40. For the Greenock Riot see Ellis and Mac a'Ghobhainn, *Scottish Insurrection*, chapter 12; *Glasgow Courier*, 11 and 13 April 1820.

41. WRH, Lord Advocate's Papers, AD14/20/246, Declarations of Andrew Ramsay, Robert Graham Dunlop, William Findlater, James Oughterson and Quintin Leitch.

42. *Ibid*, Declaration of Quintin Leitch.

43. *Ibid*, Declaration of James Oughterson.

44. *Ibid*, Declaration of Andrew Ramsay.

45. *Ibid*, Declaration of Edward McGowan, 10 April 1820.

46. *Ibid*, Declaration of Darby Canning, 11 April 1820.

47. *Ibid*, Declaration of Quintin Leitch.

48. *Ibid*, Declaration of Edward McGowan, 10 April 1820.

49. *Ibid*, Declaration of Darby Canning, 11 April 1820; of Edward McGowan, 10 April 1820; of John Calder, 14 April 1820; of John Sinnot, 14 April 1820; and of Robert Boyle, 14 April 1820.

50. *Ibid*, Declarations of Dugald Macaulay, 10 and 11 April 1820.

51. *Ibid*, Declaration of Andrew Foster, 14 April 1820.

52. *Ibid*, Note on the Greenock Riot by J.A. Maconochie A.D. (Advocate Depute), 13 July 1820, enclosed with a letter from the Crown Agent to the Sheriff of Renfrew, 14 July 1820.

53. Ellis and Mac a'Ghobhainn, *Scottish Insurrection*, pp.162–5, 182, 211.

54. Dorothy Thompson, 'Ireland and the Irish in English Radicalism before 1850', in James Epstein and Dorothy Thompson (eds.), *The Chartist Experience: Studies in Working-Class Radicalism and Culture, 1830–1860* (London, 1982), p.123.

55. Tom Gallagher, *Glasgow, the Uneasy Peace: Religious Tension in Modern Scotland* (Manchester, 1987), p.2.

56. See chapter one.

57. SRO, Home Office Correspondence, RH2/4/113, 'Minutes of a conversation with Richmond 28.12.16', enclosed with Alexander Maconochie to Viscount Sidmouth, 2 January 1817.

58. Elaine McFarland, *Ireland and Scotland in the Age of Revolution: Planting the Green Bough* (Edinburgh, 1994), pp.237–8, 244.

59. Elaine McFarland, *Protestants First: Orangeism in Nineteenth Century Scotland* (Edinburgh, 1990), p.53.

60. Richmond, *Narrative*, pp.61–2, 66–7; Roach, 'Alexander Richmond', pp.7–8.

61. Richmond, *Narrative*, p.67.

62. *Ibid*, p.70.

63. *Ibid*, p.72.

64. *Ibid*, pp.70–1.

65. Quoted in Roach, 'Alexander Richmond', p.4.

66. Quoted in Alexander Wilson, *The Chartist Movement in Scotland* (Manchester, 1970), p.25. It was from this quote that McFarland made her conclusions. McFarland, *Protestants First*, p.53.

67. J.M. Smith (ed.), *Recollections of James Turner, Esq. of Thrushgrove* (Glasgow, 1858), p.42. At the Thrushgrove meeting another speaker stated of the Napoleonic Wars that, 'It is now clear that this nefarious contest has been carried on for no other object than the restoration of whatever was detestable, bigoted and despotic in the discarded monarchies of Europe — for no other purposes than that of again establishing "the right divine of Kings to govern wrong" and of laying the rising liberties of mankind once more prostrate at the footstool of tyranny. The Pope, the Jesuits, the Inquisition, and the Bourbons have been restored, and under their goodly auspices, Protestant massacres, and other legitimate atrocities now reign triumphant'. *Ibid*, p.27.

68. For Orangeism in Scotland at this time see McFarland, *Protestants First*, pp.47–55.

69. WRH, Lord Advocate's Papers, AD14/17/8, Declaration of John Montgomerie, 26 February 1817.

70. SRO, Home Office Correspondence, RH2/4/126, Andrew Scott to Lord Sidmouth, 23 August 1819.

71. SCA, Blairs Letters, BL5/89/7, Andrew Scott to Alexander Cameron, 13 January 1820.

72. SRO, Home Office Correspondence, RH2/4/126, Andrew Scott to Lord Sidmouth, 23 August 1819.

73. *Ibid*, Scott to Sidmouth, 22 September 1819.

74. *Ibid*, Scott to Sidmouth, 23 August 1819.

75. *Ibid*, Scott to Sidmouth, 22 September 1819.

76. By the mid-1830s the total number of Roman Catholics in the western lowlands was around 70,000. See Martin J. Mitchell 'The Establishment and Early Years of the Hamilton Mission', in T.M. Devine (ed.), *St Mary's Hamilton: A Social History* (Edinburgh, 1995), pp.2–3.

77. Scott's suggestions concerning this issue are contained in both his letters to Sidmouth.

78. SRO, Home Office Correspondence, RH2/4/126, Andrew Scott to Lord Sidmouth, 22 September 1819.

79. *Ibid*, Scott to Sidmouth, 23 August 1819.

80. *Ibid*, RH2/4/128, Lord Sidmouth to the Lord Advocate, 31 December 1819.

81. For example, the *Address to the Inhabitants of Great Britain and Ireland*, which instigated the Radical War of April 1820, called on all workers to unite to gain their lost rights. Neither this nor any other radical programme of the time gives any indication of hostility towards Irish Roman Catholics. The *Address* is reprinted in T.M. Devine and Rosalind Mitchison (eds.), *People and Society in Scotland, Volume 1, 1760–1830* (Edinburgh, 1988), p.288.

82. *Glasgow Herald*, 27 July 1819; John Belcham, 'English Working-Class Radicalism and the Irish' in R. Swift and S. Gilley (eds.), *The Irish in the Victorian City* (London, 1985), p.88; John Belcham, *Popular Radicalism in Nineteenth Century Britain* (London, 1996), p.46.

83. SCA, Blairs Letters, BL5/89/7, Andrew Scott to Alexander Cameron, 13 January 1820.

84. *Ibid*, BL5/180/1, Andrew Scott to William Reid, 7 February 1825.

85. SRO, Home Office Correspondence, RH2/4/112, James Black to the Lord Advocate, 12 December 1816.

86. *Ibid*, Dugald Bannatyne to Francis Freeling, 14 December 1816.

87. *Ibid*; see also RH2/4/112 Thomas Meek to Sir Hay Campbell, 13 December 1816.

88. *Ibid*, RH2/4/132, William Rae to Lord Sidmouth, 7 April 1820. See also *ibid*, unauthored report of 7 April 1820.

89. James Handley, *The Irish in Scotland 1798–1845* (Second edition, Cork, 1945), p.281.

90. Murray, *Handloom Weavers*, p.32.

91. *Ibid*, pp.218–9, 225–7.

92. *Glasgow Herald*, 3 April 1820.

93. See chapter one.

94. *Glasgow Courier*, 4 April 1820; SRO, Home Office Correspondence, RH2/4/131, Henry Monteith to Viscount Sidmouth, 3 and 4 April 1820; SRA, Monteith Correspondence, G1/2/33, Oliver Jamieson to Henry Monteith, 3 April 1820; *Case of the Operative Cotton-Spinners in Glasgow, in answer to the Statement by the Proprietors of Cotton Works* (Glasgow, 1825), p.25.

95. SRO, Home Office Correspondence, RH2/4/114, Declaration of John McLauchlan, 12 March 1817. See also *ibid*, Report of 'B' [Biggar], 9 February 1817 and RH2/4/113 Minutes of a Conversation with A. Richmond 28 December 1816 enclosed with Alexander Maconochie to Viscount Sidmouth, 2 January 1817.

96. *Ibid*, RH2/4/114, Declaration of Hugh Dickson, 4 March 1817.

97. *Ibid*, RH2/4/131, Copy of a letter from Colonel Norcott, 24 February 1820, enclosed with T. Bradford to H. Hobhouse, 24 February 1820.

98. WRH, Lord Advocate's Papers, AD14/20/43, George Salmond to Hugh Warrender, 10 May 1820.

99. *Ibid*, AD14/38/502, Declaration of Thomas Stewart, 19 January 1821.

100. *Glasgow Courier*, 4, 6, 8 and 11 April 1820; See also the letters from this period in SRO, Home Office Correspondence, RH2/4/131.

101. SRO, Home Office Correspondence, RH2/4/131, Henry Monteith to the Lord Advocate, 3 April 1820, enclosed with William Rae to Lord Sidmouth, 4 April 1820.

102. SRA, Monteith Correspondence, G1/2/33, Oliver Jamieson to Henry Monteith, 3 April 1820.

103. Handley, *Irish in Scotland*, p.313.

104. SRO, Home Office Correspondence, RH2/4/113, Alexander Maconochie to Viscount Sidmouth, 27 January 1817; McFarland, *Ireland and Scotland*, pp.239–40.

105. See, for example, Paterson, *Reminiscences*, pp.69–70; SRO, Home Office Correspondence, RH2/4/132, A. Boswell to 'My Lord', 16 April 1820; SRA, MacKinnon Correspondence, TD743/1–3, p.52.

106. SRO, Home Office Correspondence, RH2/4/114, Declaration of Hugh Dickson, 4 March 1817.

107. *Ibid*, RH2/4/126, Andrew Scott to Lord Sidmouth, 23 August 1819.

108. SCA, Blairs Letters, BL5/64/11, Andrew Scott to Alexander Paterson, 29 October 1819.

109. Stana Nenadic, 'The Rise of the Urban Middle Class' in Devine and Mitchison (eds.), *People and Society Volume 1*, pp.123–4; 'Political Reform and the "Ordering" of Middle-Class Protest' in T.M. Devine (ed.), *Conflict and Stablility in Scottish Society, 1700–1850* (Edinburgh, 1990), pp.77–8.

PART THREE
EMANCIPATION AND REFORM

4

The Glasgow Catholic
Association, 1823–29

According to Hamish Fraser, after the 'Radical War' of April 1820 'It was a decade before the issue of political reform revived among the working class in Scotland'[1] , and during the 1820s 'what political reform movement there was was essentially middle-class'.[2] Others share these views.[3] For example, Norman Murray states that in this decade 'reform movements played little part in Scottish social life…'.[4] It would appear that these historians are referring to campaigns for an extension of the franchise and if so their views carry some conviction. However, there was an organisation in Glasgow which existed for several years during the 1820s and was involved in an agitation for political reform — the Glasgow Catholic Association. It participated in the movement for Catholic Emancipation, which demanded an Act of Parliament to enable Roman Catholics to become Members of Parliament and allow them to hold most civil offices. Such a measure was passed in April 1829.

The only historian to have examined the Glasgow Catholic Association and its activities is James Handley.[5] He, however, did not do so in any great detail. Furthermore, Handley did not use, or perhaps was unable to gain access to, the correspondence of the Scottish priests. This source is indispensable for any discussion of the organisation. Handley's account is based on reports and letters in the city's newspapers and it is evident from his narrative that he did not fully utilise the information contained in them. What follows is a full examination of the Glasgow Catholic Association based on the correspondence and other papers of the Scottish priests, the newspapers of the period, and a history of the first two years of the society written by its secretary, William McGowan.

I

On 11 October 1823 a number of Catholics in Glasgow held a meeting in the city's Frazer's Hall and formed the Glasgow Catholic Association. The aim of the organisation was to rebut charges made in the press against the tenets of the Catholic religion. Similar defence societies had already been established in English towns and cities and their example influenced

Glasgow's Catholics. Some time after the formation of the organisation the British Catholic Association was formed to campaign for Catholic Emancipation. The Glasgow Catholic Association and the English defence societies then remodelled themselves on this new society and resolved to assist its campaign.[6] The Glasgow Association, according to William McGowan, now existed 'for the purpose of furthering the cause of catholic emancipation, and the defence of our religious principles and moral character, through the medium of the press…'[7]

In pursuance of these objectives the Association circulated a number of cheap Catholic works. The society claimed that by February 1825 it had made available several thousand copies of such publications,[8] and thus had introduced 'a new source of religious instruction both to catholic and protestant, calculated to enlighten and strengthen the faith of the former, and dispel the prejudice and ignorance of the latter'.[9] According to the first annual report of the Association, the dissemination of such materials furthered the campaign for Emancipation as it enabled the city's Catholics

> when asked to give a reasonable answer for their faith, and prove that they are Catholics from conviction and not from prejudice, or because it was the religion of their forefathers, as Protestants too generally suppose. Such associations enable the Catholics to make a united effort for the recovery of their long lost civil rights…[10]

The Glasgow Catholic Association also appointed a committee to monitor the city's newspapers. A number of articles were published by it in defence of the principles of the Catholic religion 'and in refutation of objections brought against Catholic emancipation…'.[11] According to a memorial of the Association written in February 1825 the society had, in the pamphlets it circulated and in its letters to newspapers,

> detected the base falsehoods of many itinerant slanderers of their religion and its priesthood, who support their proselytising Institutions by calumny and misrepresentation. And thus by destroying their credit, have lessened their influence, and shortened their power of doing hurt.[12]

In 1824 the Association tried to establish a library of approved Catholic works but, as will be shown, this plan foundered as a result of clerical opposition.

The leading figures in the Glasgow Catholic Association were William McGowan, his brother James, and Dr. Andrew Stewart. The McGowans were teachers in the city's Catholic schools. Stewart, the President of the society, was also a member of the British and Irish Catholic Associations,[13] organisations with which the Glasgow Association was in correspondence.[14]

The Glasgow Association, which in September 1825 claimed between six and seven hundred 'regular monthly subscribers and occasional contributors',[15] began to collect the Catholic Rent (one penny a month) in late December 1824 or early January 1825, part of which was sent to Dublin to assist the campaign of the Irish Association, led by Daniel O'Connell.[16]

The Glasgow Association was not, however, blindly attached to O'Connell. For example, it opposed the Catholic Relief Bill introduced into the House of Commons by Sir Francis Burdett in early 1825 and supported by O'Connell, as it contained two conditions attached to Emancipation which the Glasgow Association, like English radicals and many Irish ones, found highly objectionable. These were the disenfranchisement of Ireland's 40/- freeholders and the state payment of the Catholic clergy.[17] The Bill was defeated in the House of Lords and the Glasgow Association stated in late 1825 and early 1826 that it was fiercely opposed to any attempts to reintroduce a Bill with these conditions.[18] It demanded 'unqualified emancipation...'.[19] At the second annual meeting of the Association James McGowan outlined his reasons for opposing the conditions, known as 'wings'. He stated that those who advocated the 'wings' in fact wished to crush the Irish Catholic Association and destroy the unity it had created in Ireland:

> They took care, by cutting off the 40s. freeholds, that while they opened the door of parliament to Catholics, and the friends of Catholics, there was no one to vote them in; thus would they have eligibility without patronage, emancipation without profit, and ancient ascendancy would roll on as before in her chariot, unmolested by the clamour and importunity of the Irish Catholics.

McGowan opposed the proposal to pension the Catholic clergy as he believed it would fill the Church with corrupt priests 'whose obsequiousness and political intrigues would soon lose them the confidence of their people...'.[20] With the granting of Emancipation in April 1829 the Association disbanded.[21]

II

Throughout its first year the Glasgow Catholic Association received little attention from the city's priests Andrew Scott and John Murdoch. Scott in particular was unimpressed with the organisation. In February 1825 he recalled:

> As long as they were unknown we only laughed at them and never gave ourselves any trouble in public or private about them; though in their very

beginning they shewed the spirit with which they were imbibed. It was mentioned to some of them that Mr Murdoch had a curiosity to see of what description of people they were composed, and what they had to say, and that if he thought them mistaken or doing or undertaking any thing improper he would advise them as a pastor. A person assured *Mr Murdoch that if he attempted to go there, they would not allow him to speak as a pastor*, but *lock the door* and *keep him in* and *oblige him* to *hear what they had to say*, and to speak there only as an equal. Of course Mr Murdoch never went. We thought they would tire of the business and see their folly.[22]

In June 1824 the priests publicly opposed the Association for the first time as a result of its decision to raise a fund to assist in the establishment of a newspaper to promote the Catholic interest.[23] The clergymen were probably concerned that this would result in less income for the Glasgow Mission. According to William McGowan, however, some believed that the real reason behind the hostility to the Association at that time was its proposal to establish a Catholic Library, which was opposed by Scott from the pulpit 'on the ground that it would disable the people from supporting a second clergyman…'.[24] McGowan stated that this was an insult to the congregation, as he believed that if they were not able to support two priests and a library they would never prefer the latter to the former.[25] Scott's intervention, however, was sufficient to ensure that the Library was never established.[26]

The disputes concerning the Catholic library and newspaper pale in significance beside the attack launched by Scott on the Association four months later. On Sunday 24 October notices announcing the first annual meeting of the Glasgow Catholic Association were distributed in the chapel by one of its members. Murdoch told him 'to circulate no more of them; adding, that he had *not time to tell him the reason why he forbade him*'.[27] At a Committee meeting of the Association later that week one of those present stated that he understood this opposition to be principally because the day of the general meeting was a Sunday. The Committee therefore decided to change the day of the meeting and have new notices printed.[28] This had no effect on the Glasgow priests. According to McGowan, Scott, from the pulpit the following Sunday morning,

> attacked the association and its members, in the most ungenerous and violent manner, declaring the association illegal on the authority of Mr O'Connell — and that before six months, the strong arm of the law would put it down — warned the well meaning part of the congregation to keep at a distance from its meetings — declared that those who held such meetings, independent of their pastors, were as bad as protestants or presbyterians, quoting the text, 'how can they preach unless they be sent' — declaring that none of the members

were qualified, nay that none of the congregation were qualified to manage an association — the members, he said, were illiterate, none of them having received a liberal education — blamed them for meeting in a *public house*, and what was worse than all, in his opinion, meeting on a Sunday. No other society he declared, held their meetings on a Sunday, but the Glasgow association. We should at least have been allowed the credit of altering the day of the meeting… He said the association was calculated to bring scandal upon religion; and that, if any more such bills as he had seen should be circulated, the person who should do so would *never be allowed to enter the chapel.*[29]

Scott informed the congregation that such meetings were illegal on Sundays, and that circulating notices of them in the chapel would lead the city's Protestants to believe that the Catholic clergy approved of these events.[30] He added that he 'did not believe that they understood sufficiently the principles of Religion to assume to themselves the charge of defending them…'.[31]

Rather than make a public defence of the character of the organisation and its members, the Committee of the Glasgow Catholic Association met on 4 November and decided on a course of conciliation. The following resolutions were passed:

That this meeting learn with extreme regret, that the 'Glasgow Catholic Association' has been declared publicly in the chapel to be a *branch* society, and consequently illegal; and, in order to remove such impression, this meeting beg leave to state that it is not, was not, neither is it intended to be such, but an *independent* association.

That they also regret to learn, that said institution was, at the same time, declared to be calculated to bring scandal on religion; which opinion is to them a matter of astonishment, seeing that their brethren in London, Liverpool, Manchester, Preston and many other towns in England, where the Catholics are similarly circumstanced, have associated for the same purposes, and are aided and assisted by their respective clergymen.

That for the purpose of effecting a good understanding between the association and their pastors, which they consider *absolutely necessary for the good of religion* in *this place*, as well as for the prosperity of the institution, they take the liberty of laying before them the real objects of the association, which are, to promote here the circulation of approved Catholic works, and to defend our religious principles, and moral character, through the medium of the press.

That a copy of these resolutions be presented to the Rev. A. Scott and J. Murdoch, in the name of the association, by a deputation, to be appointed for that purpose, who shall be instructed to use every endeavour, consistent with the known views of their constituents, and the respect which they owe to their pastors, to bring about a *reconciliation.*[32]

A deputation was sent to Scott that evening but he refused to examine the resolutions.[33] He again questioned their qualifications and informed them 'that their education was not such as entitle them to understand politics', and added that if the society continued with its activities it 'would materially hurt the exertions of the Irish and British Catholic associations…'.[34]

Two months passed before there was another public attack on the Glasgow Catholic Association by the city's priests. On 16 January 1825, after Sunday mass, the annual meeting of the Benevolent Society was held in the chapel and according to Scott, he and Murdoch 'thought it the best opportunity to warn the people of the danger they might expose religion to in this place by meddling with things above their station and raising a mob to destroy the chapel or the property of those who had anything to lose'.[35] Scott told the meeting 'that though such an association might do in England and in Ireland, it would not do in this country — it was calculated to raise a persecution — the members of the Irish association, and the British association, were all gentlemen, and not one of the Glasgow association would be allowed to be members of the British or Irish association'.[36] He also informed them of 'the illegality of receiving ribbonmen and radicals well known' into the society.[37] The collection of the Catholic Rent, which had begun a few weeks previously, particularly troubled Scott. He stated that it was unlawful to raise the fund unless its purpose had been publicly announced[38], and that if the Rent was sent to the British or Irish Association it would render the Glasgow Association a branch society and therefore illegal.[39] Scott told those present that he had heard that a proportion of the Rent raised was to be used to support the Catholic Sunday Schools, and 'that if they meant to spend their money in circulating religious tracts in the Sundays' schools…they were usurping the power of the pastors of the Church who were alone the judges of what religious books it was proper to put into the hands of the children'.[40] After Scott finished, Murdoch spoke to the meeting and reiterated most of what his superior had said.[41]

In the defence of its principles, published in September 1825, the Glasgow Catholic Association refuted the charges made against it at the Benevolent Society meeting. It stated that it did not know whether ribbonmen were members but even if some were it would still not mean that the society was illegal;[42] it revealed that long before the Catholic Rent was collected the Association had announced in a London journal the purposes for which it was being raised;[43] the Association denied that sending a portion of the Rent to the British or Irish Association would make it a branch organisation and therefore illegal, and cited the example of Ireland where all the Associations sent the Catholic Rent to the Irish Association based in Dublin. The Glasgow Association also printed a letter from O'Connell to the Birmingham Association on the nature of branch societies to support its argument.[44] Finally, with regard to the charge that part of the fund was to be used to support the Sunday Schools, the Association denied this had ever been its intention, and noted Scott had stated that he spoke on the matter only from hearsay; moreover, the Association denied that it was improper to support the Sunday Schools — after all, the congregation had been doing so since they opened.[45]

The immediate response of the Association to the attacks made against it at the Benevolent Society meeting was not, however, to make a public defence but instead to once again seek a reconciliation.[46] It therefore sent a requisition to Scott, dated 29 January 1825, requesting him to call a meeting in the Gorbals schoolroom

> on as early a day as may best suit your convenience, for the purpose of affording an opportunity of explaining the *real* principles and objects of the Glasgow catholic association, of answering those imputations which we think have been unjustly, by you and your reverend colleague, cast upon that society, and of placing the character of that institution, and its members, in a proper point of view, before the whole Catholic public connected with Glasgow. We ask this as an act of common justice…[47]

Scott did not arrange a meeting between himself and the Glasgow Catholic Association. Instead, the following Sunday he once again made a violent attack on the Association from the pulpit and announced the reasons for his refusal to comply with the requisition.[48] In Scott's opinion

> a requisition was a *demand*, and supposed an authority in those who made it to receive what they asked *as act of justice*; that it was a new feature in the Catholic Religion for the people to call the pastors to an account for the spiritual advices, or advices connected with their spiritual welfare or the good of Religion which they considered it their duty to address from the pulpit to their flock; that it was even a schismatical if not an heretical idea because it contained an assertion that the people had a power over their pastors and could call them to account for their instructions; that it was a presbyterian principle, and only acted upon by dissenters; that the Catholic Church pointed out a different means to obtain redress if anyone thought themselves injured; that the Bishops were the sole judges of these matters and that if they had considered themselves injured they should have made their complaint to the Bishop who if he had seen reason would have given both parties a hearing and decided.[49]

The Association denied that there was anything wrong in laymen sending requisitions to their pastors.[50] In its published defence it gave two examples from Ireland of clergymen accepting requisitions and calling meetings as a result. In one of these cases the priest was the Bishop of Waterford and Lismore.[51] Furthermore, the Association denied that its requisition was calling the clergymen to account for their religious instructions, and argued that it was merely requesting that a meeting be arranged which would give its members the opportunity of explaining the principles and objects of the Association to their priests and to the Catholic congregation of the city.[52]

Scott also attacked the 119 men who signed the requisition. According to the Glasgow Catholic Association, at each mass that day he spent part of his sermon 'calling them the most offensive names, and representing those who signed the requisition as *illiterate ragamuffins*, comparing the roughness of their hand-writing to their *tattered coats*, and recommended them, if they had any money on hand, to employ it in purchasing old clothes to cover their naked members. He declared he knew little of them who signed the requisition, but by the *scandal they had given to religion*...'[53] In a letter to a colleague in Edinburgh just over a week later Scott gave the following description of the requisition's signatories:

> The Doctor's name as president is the first the two McGowans schoolmasters are next and with the exception of another drunken schoolmaster who never yet gave any proofs of his being a Catholic, of a Deistical surgeon who was reared a protestant and never yet professed the Catholic Religion, of a cork manufacturer (as they here are called) who is said to deal in stolen yarn, the whole of the rest are of the lowest and most profligate class of weavers, labourers and cotton spinners, one half of whom we know nothing of, and who have not even clothes to attend the chapel, and never attend any duties.

He also claimed that the Association had to use 'all their exertions for a fortnight' to compile the signatures, and that some were obtained under false pretences.[54] The Association later defended the characters of the signatories attacked by Scott from the pulpit:

> several of those, whose names are affixed to the document, have received a classical education, some are merchants, many shopkeepers, and the poorest is a well clad tradesman or mechanic, while against one only could he find an error in morals. Of the one hundred and twenty names, found at the requisition, eighty of them have been appointed by Mr Scott himself, from time to time, in the service of religion, by collecting money for the erection of a chapel and other purposes, catechising in Sunday schools, etc, which proves he knew these at least in another capacity than that of giving scandal to religion: and all of them, it is presumed, have contributed their mite to the erection of a magnificent temple to their God.[55]

Unfortunately, the available evidence does not allow verification of either description of those who signed the requisition.

Scott's reaction to the requisition convinced the Association that it had been left with no alternative but to appeal to Bishop Cameron to intervene.[56] In early February 1825 a memorial was sent to him which stated the principles and objects of the society and the opposition it had received from the Glasgow clergy. Its purpose was 'to remove from your Lordship's mind, any undue impression, which misrepresentation may have made, and to induce your Lordship, to interpose with your authority to protect the association, and its members from (what they deem) the unjust attacks of the Revd Mr Scott'.[57] According to William McGowan, Cameron told the deputation which presented the memorial that Scott had received no authority from him to put down the Association, nor could he, Cameron — or the Pope himself — give him such permission; he informed them that there was nothing in the objects and principles of the society which was contrary to the teachings of the Catholic Church, nor was there anything wrong with the objects to which the Catholic Rent was to be applied;[58] finally, he told the deputation that the Association would '*experience no more opposition*'.[59]

Cameron's promised intervention did not, however, take place. The Association stated that 'he either forgot his pledge, or his admonitions were disregarded'.[60] As a result, attacks on the Association by Scott and Murdoch continued to be made from the pulpit and at meetings of members of the congregation.[61] At one such gathering in April 1825 Scott reiterated his objections to the society and added two new ones. He stated that he was in France at the time of her Revolution and therefore was against the Glasgow Catholic Association 'lest it should lead to the same horrors', and he argued that the existence of the society was a major reason why there had been an unprecedented number of petitions from Glasgow against Catholic Emancipation. William McGowan later dismissed the first objection and he stated that the second was absurd. Scott, he wrote, provided no evidence to support his claim that the presence of the Association in the city had been a cause of the petitions against Emancipation. Moreover, McGowan noted that in no previous year had two petitions in favour of the measure been raised in Glasgow.[62]

Further attempts at reconciliation by the Association failed because of Scott's unwillingness to budge from his original position.[63] In August 1825 the Association resolved to appeal to Bishop Paterson to intervene, as his Lordship was in Glasgow that month.[64] A deputation from the society went to see him but he refused to meet it. He declared 'that it was inconsistent with his duty to receive a deputation from a political body'.[65] According to James McGowan, the Bishop informed the deputation 'that the subject of the association was a matter of mere opinion with which he would take nothing to do, either for or against it'.[66]

It was probably Paterson's refusal to become involved in the dispute which finally persuaded the Association to make a public defence of its activities. At the end of September 1825 it published a 122-page pamphlet, written by William McGowan, which gave the history of the Association and an account of the controversy with the clergy. Its purpose was to defend the character of the society and its members. At the second annual meeting of the Association in November the reasons for the publication were made apparent. The annual report, read by the chairman Luke Callighan,

> stated in substance that the committee had met with considerable opposition, in a quarter where it was least expected. They had made several fruitless attempts at conciliation, and were at length obliged to enter publicly on their defence and had come off victorious. They had thus secured to the Catholics of Glasgow and their posterity the right to think for themselves, and furnished a practical proof to the opposers of emancipation, that Catholics believe that the power of their clergy is only spiritual.

The President of the Association Andrew Stewart told the meeting:

> From week to week they had been misrepresented, slandered, and vilely traduced, in a place where they had no power to answer, and they were obliged to show the Catholic world that they were not the audacious violaters of their religious principles, law and justice, that they were represented to be.

James McGowan stated that as a result of the publication of the defence of their principles, the members of the Association 'had confirmed the right of thinking for themselves on political matters, and shown that their clergy had no power over them but what was strictly spiritual (hear and applause)'.[67]

Scott and Murdoch not only condemned the Association but also victimised its members. In 1825 Scott engineered the dismissal of James and William McGowan from their positions as teachers in the Catholic schools in Glasgow because they had remained in the Association after he publicly condemned it.[68] The brothers worked in the Sunday and day schools, William in those in Calton, James in those in Bridgeton. The McGowans had taught in the Sunday Schools for over twelve years and in the day schools for eight.[69] Their dismissals occurred despite petitions in their favour to the Catholic Schools Committee from the parents and guardians of the schoolchildren. Around one hundred and forty people signed the Calton petition for William McGowan and one hundred and sixty seven people in Bridgeton signed the supplication for his brother.[70] Around seventy 'of the most respectable Protestants' of Bridgeton signed a petition in favour of the latter which praised his 'upright moral character' and talents as a teacher.[71] The petitions were not allowed to be read at the Committee meeting (or meetings) which 'discussed' the McGowans' cases.[72] Prior to the dispute between Scott and the Association the teachers had apparently experienced little difficulty with those who governed the schools. According to Andrew Stewart, they 'had given much satisfaction both to the Protestant and Catholic Directors' of the Committee and this could be established from the secretary's reports.[73] Yet Scott's opposition was sufficient to ensure that they lost their positions. Even this was apparently not enough for him: James McGowan claimed in December 1825, some time after his dismissal, that he was still being persecuted by Scott. In a letter to the *Glasgow Free Press* he stated that 'lest I should succeed in raising a school, among my friends, to my own account, it has since been his constant theme, from the altar, that those who would send their children to me, were done with all church benefits…'.[74]

Some of those who were critical of Scott's treatment of the McGowans also became victims of their pastor's wrath. For example, at a supper held in March 1825, after his dismissal from the Sunday School, James McGowan was presented with a silver snuff box by a body of Roman Catholics in Bridgeton and its neighbourhood as a mark of their respect and esteem. He was also presented with an address which thanked him for his 'long and meritorious exertions' in the school. The address not only regretted McGowan's removal from his post but also strongly condemned it:

> we look on your removal from the Sunday-evening school, as being not a private, but a public evil, *and must infer that the being who could thus deprive our children of their instructor can only be compared to the man who would wilfully and deliberately extinguish the taper of light, that all might be involved in general darkness*.[75]

Those present at the supper were subsequently denied admittance to their Easter Duties. A committee for those affected wrote to Bishop Cameron on 23 April 1825 asking him to investigate the affair, and to intervene to enable them to receive the sacraments.[76] Commenting the following December, however, James McGowan stated that of the ninety to one hundred persons who were at that March soirée, 'very few have since been admitted to their religious duties, for being there present. Several when they apolied [*sic*] were openly refused, and others, hearing of the refusal, did not present themselves. Some went to strange clergymen, others remain still excluded'. According to McGowan the Glasgow clergymen had decided not to receive those who were at the presentation to him unless they acknowledged their 'error'.[77]

The Catholic parents and guardians of Calton and its neighbourhood presented William McGowan with a snuff box at a meeting held on 24 October 1825. The inscription on the box stated that the gift was a testimony of the subscribers' 'esteem and gratitude, for his zeal, ability, and long tried services, as a teacher in the Catholic schools; and as a token of their high respect for his private character, as a Christian, and public usefulness as a man'. McGowan was also presented with an address which expressed much the same sentiments as the inscription and which also regretted and criticised his dismissal, although in far milder terms than that given to James McGowan the previous March.[78] It is not known whether those who were at the presentation to William McGowan suffered a fate similar to those who honoured his brother.

What is clear is that all members of the Glasgow Catholic Association were denied the sacraments from Scott and Murdoch, whose position was that Association men would not be admitted to their duties unless they gave up their involvement in the society and renounced all connection with it.[79] These religious sanctions, combined with the frequent public condemnations of the Association from the pulpit, seem to have had an effect on some of its members. According to William McGowan, by early November 1824, after the first wave of attacks made by Scott, 'some, who did not know the length to which a pastor *should go in such cases*, or had not nerve enough to *oppose the will of the priest, though they knew him to be wrong*', decided to withdraw from the organisation.[80] Later in his pamphlet McGowan stated: 'There are several who were members of the association, and who have abandoned it, owing to the rage of persecution, and perhaps some from other motives...'.[81]

Unfortunately, there are no more reports in the press or correspondence in the Scottish Catholic Archives concerning relations between the Glasgow Catholic Association and the city's priests after 1825. It is therefore not known how many more members, if any, left the Association as a result of clerical pressure or indeed whether further measures were used by Scott and Murdoch in their campaign to crush the Association. What is clear, however, is that the dispute continued. According to the newspaper for the Irish Catholics in Glasgow in the 1860s, the *Glasgow Free Press*, the Association appealed to the Pope in 1828 against Murdoch and Scott's 'obtrusive interference and intolerable persecution'. The memorial, which was largely the work of Andrew Stewart and James McGowan, was sent to Rome on St Patrick's Day. It did not achieve its aim, perhaps because of an intervention by Bishop Paterson who was in Rome at the time on Church business.[82] With the granting of Catholic Emancipation the following year the Association disbanded. As the following chapter will demonstrate, it was not long before William McGowan and Andrew Scott became embroiled in another bitter and public controversy.

III

At first sight the ferocity of Scott's opposition to the Glasgow Catholic Association appears rather strange. After all, the aims of the society were to defend and promote the Catholic religion and to assist the campaign for Catholic Emancipation. The leading figures in the organisation were two highly respected schoolmasters. The various charges made against it by the Glasgow clergy in October 1824 and January 1825 were easily refuted by the society. It is clear that Scott was opposed to his congregation being involved in political (and other) organisations outwith clerical control or supervision. This, however, cannot fully explain his campaign against the Association and its members, particularly given the stated aims and objectives of the society.

The Glasgow Catholic Association could not understand the position taken by their clergymen. After Scott's first public condemnation in June 1824 the society *'suffered in silence his attack'* as it believed that once he saw 'the good the association would do, and the efforts both of the English and Irish clergy to forward the views of such associations, he would at least cease his opposition…'.[83] When Scott attacked the Association from the pulpit in late October 1824 it again decided not to make a public defence. According to McGowan:

> We did not wish to let it be publicly known, that any pastor of the catholic church could be capable of so acting, towards any public institution, much less towards an institution established to promote the interests of religion, and which had received the approbation of several enlightened English catholic clergymen…[84]

After Scott and Murdoch's condemnation of it at the Benevolent Society meeting on 16 January 1825, the Glasgow Catholic Association decided not to apply to Bishop Cameron or defend itself in the press, but instead sought conciliation, as it presumed 'that Mr Scott and Mr Murdoch had been induced to oppose the association, as much on account of not being acquainted with its principles, as from any other cause…'.[85] As has been shown, Scott rejected all attempts at conciliation and eventually the Glasgow Catholic Association went public in September 1825. Even then it still could not understand the clergy's opposition. The pamphlet written by William McGowan stated the following on his and his brother's dismissal from their teaching posts:

> We have heard tell of orange landlords dispossessing, of their holdings, certain of their tenants, for supporting the late Irish Catholic Association: but, who ever before heard tell of a catholic clergyman depriving, of their situations, any of his flock, for supporting an association established to promote the catholic cause? And, what is still worse, these gentlemen were not allowed to state the reasons which induced them to continue members of the association, nor to say a word in their own defence. Bishop Patterson, we are sorry to say, was induced to give his sanction and support to the measure.[86]

The reason the Glasgow Catholic Association could not understand why the clergymen should attack it in such a manner was simply that Scott and Murdoch did not publicly reveal the main reasons for their opposition. These are divulged in a lengthy letter sent by Scott to Bishop Cameron in early February 1825 in which he outlined the dispute up to that point.[87] According to Scott, towards the end of October 1824 he met James Reddie, Glasgow's first town clerk, who told him that he had seen the notices advertising the first general meeting of the Glasgow Catholic Association. Reddie spoke to Scott about the society and

> hoped that they were not radicals of the same description as those we formerly had, and that nothing serious was to be apprehended from them. He also hoped that we gave them no countenance and would use our endeavours to prevent them from raising mischief in the town, and that the whole congregation was not connected with it. He also added that the magistrates would watch them, but that they would not like to have recourse to harsh measures at first, but would trust to us to keep them from any thing improper.

It was principally because of this meeting that Scott launched his first major attack from the pulpit, on 31 October 1824, although he did not mention to the congregation that Reddie had spoken to him. A few weeks later, after New Year, Scott again met Reddie, who gave him 'a significant hint as if he thought they were going too far'. Scott recalled that Reddie 'alluded to something more than he expressed', which Scott believed to be the Catholic Rent which had recently been collected by the Glasgow Catholic Association. The following Sunday was the day of the Benevolent Society meeting at which Scott made his second major assault on the society, and in his address he condemned the raising of the Catholic Rent.

It was not only the city magistrates who were concerned about the emergence in public of the Association. Soon after Scott made his October attack on the society he was spoken to by two of the leading members of the Catholic Schools Committee

> on the impropriety of the Catholic association here, and of the still greater impropriety of these two teachers [The McGowans], servants of that committee, taking a leading part in it. I assured them that the association composed as it was had not the sanction or approbation of Mr Murdoch or of me. They said they were glad to hear it, as they were afraid that if we gave any sanction to it, it would materially hurt the interest of the schools and induce many to withdraw their subscriptions from it. They wished me to speak to Mr Kirkman Finlay on the subject as he is president of our school committee and a very large subscriber and a still better collector for it. They said that they were afraid that, if it came to his ears that the schoolmasters took a leading part in these things, he would become disgusted and withdraw his countenance from the schools.

Scott decided not to speak to Finlay as he believed that his advice to the deputation sent to him on 4 November 'would induce them to be quiet and at all events not to make a noise about their association...'. After that meeting all was quiet until New Year when collectors were appointed to raise the Catholic Rent.

During the first year of the Glasgow Catholic Association Andrew Scott and John Murdoch paid little attention to it. Once the society came to the attention of the city's magistrates and Protestant members of the Schools' Committee, who expressed disapproval of its activities, Scott decided that the Association should disband. Clearly the security and well-being of the Church and congregation took precedence, in his eyes, over a political organisation for which he and Murdoch had little time. It is clear, however, that both clergymen did not bother to enquire about the aims and objects of the Association and rejected all attempts by the society to arrange a meeting to explain them. Even if they had met, it is probable that the clergymen would have acted in the same way given their hostility to members of the congregation participating in independent political activities.

Despite Scott's denunciations from the pulpit and at Church meetings, and despite his advice to deputations and to individual members of the society, the Glasgow Catholic Association continued to campaign for Emancipation. This convinced Scott that the full weight of Church authority had to be used to crush the society. He believed that the clergy had a right to interfere in this way with such a political organisation: the Association's position was that the Church had no temporal authority over its members.[88] Scott was adamant that the McGowans in particular had to be dealt with firmly. He argued in his letter to Bishop Cameron:

If no notice be taken of the instructions given in the Sundays school by McGowan a Spirit of Rebellion will necessarily be engendered by him in the minds of the young people and kept up by him. He will take new courage from our silence and attribute that silence to a conviction that we think him in the right and will renew his efforts to spread the Evil.

This, coupled with the threat of withdrawal of financial support from the schools by Protestants, convinced Scott that the McGowans' positions were no longer tenable. Scott told Cameron that both he and Murdoch wanted to know whether they should speak to Kirkman Finlay on the affair

to let him know that we always disapproved of the association here; that the teachers of these schools always acted not only without our approbation, but in direct contradiction to our wishes; that if the committee are displeased with them we have no objections to their dismissal and shall present others for the approbation of the committee. This we consider the only method of now upholding these schools which the Catholics are not able of themselves to keep up.

The attitudes of the city magistrates and the possibility of a withdrawal of the funding of the schools by Protestants made Scott publicly condemn the Glasgow Catholic Association. When it became apparent that the society's members had not followed his instructions and indeed had insisted that he had no right to interfere in their affairs, the issue of control came into prominence. At the end of his February letter to Cameron, Scott stated:

I am fully convinced from experience that if such rebellions be not quelled in the bud, it will very soon become impossible to manage such congregations as we have here. This is the most numerous and consequently the most difficult to manage…The majority of the congregation is still free from the contagion. It is entirely confined to those few over whom the McGowans have influence, and if backed by the Bishop's authority, we would soon be able to put an end to the present trouble and by that means probably prevent future commotions.

Scott wished to know what should be done with those who had not followed his instructions and enquired whether they could be admitted to their religious duties without having retracted those views which he considered erroneous. He also asked for guidance on how he should deal with the Association in the future.

As has been demonstrated, after January 1825 the dispute between the Association and the clergy intensified. The priests continued to attack the organisation, its members and supporters were denied the sacraments, and the McGowans were dismissed from their teaching posts. It is clear,

however, that what Scott believed would happen if the society continued
to exist did not in fact occur. There is nothing in the newspapers of the
period which suggests that the presence in the city of the Association
resulted in official or popular Protestant hostility to it, the Catholic Church
or the Catholic clergy; there is no evidence in the subsequent letters of
Scott that the Glasgow magistrates were unhappy with the Association; the
withdrawal of financial support for the Catholic schools by Protestants did
not take place. The Association's meetings were open and legal and the
society claimed to have received the support of the city's 'liberal
Protestants'.[89]

The Catholic priests remained hostile because they were convinced that
if they backed down on this issue they would lose control of their
congregation. The Association had refused to bow to clerical pressure —
therefore it had to be crushed. Scott believed that to stop opposing the
Association would be extremely dangerous. For example, in a letter to
Bishop Paterson in October 1825 he stated:

> Our Association people seem now to have thrown off even the mask of
> Religion, and will require to be spoke to of their errors in strong terms in case
> they continue to frequent the chapel. Their example will corrupt many others.
> The Paddies are easily you know led astray even in their own country against
> the commands and exhortations of their pastors, and unless you speak clearly
> and strongly you will find that no pastors will be able to preserve their authority
> here, and that some anarchy of the same kind will be stirred up among them in
> Edin[r] and in all the neighbouring missions here...I know from long experience
> among them that they will attribute your silence either to a fear of meddling
> with them, or interpret it into an approbation of their conduct.[90]

Less than a fortnight later, after informing Paterson that the Association
had criticised his Lordship in print, Scott stated: 'If you trifle with these
gentry, or allow them to be admitted to their duties till they come to their
senses and renounce their error, you will find the half of the paddies in this
country in rebellion.'[91] Clearly Scott was convinced that to back down over
the issue of the Association would have disastrous consequences for the
future governance of the Glasgow Mission. Any hopes that some agreement
or compromise could be reached were finally destroyed by the publication
of McGowan's pamphlet. According to Scott it contained 'a number of
gross falsehoods and still grosser misrepresentations injurious to my
character and office of a pastor'.[92] Moreover, Bishop Paterson condemned
the publication and demanded that the members of the Association
renounce it.[93]

IV

Opposition to the Glasgow Catholic Association came not only from Scott and Murdoch but also from a section of the Catholic community in the city. It first became public on 18 April 1825 at a meeting in the Catholic schoolroom in the Gorbals. This event was organised by the two priests and those in their flock who were hostile to the society.[94] Their intention was 'to pass off this meeting for a meeting of the congregation' and to pass resolutions which praised Scott and condemned the Association.[95] In their attempt to effect this the group did not invite members of the Association to attend and took great care to prevent them from learning the time and place of the meeting. Despite this, many members of the organisation found out the arrangements and attended, although they did not form the majority of those present. Murdoch, however, moved that they be excluded.[96] In opposing this motion William McGowan 'proceeded to show that the meeting was a packed one, and could not be said to represent the sentiments of the congregation…'.[97] He added that Bishop Cameron 'had declared *that neither Mr Scott, nor the Bishop himself, nor even the Pope himself, had any right of interference with the association*'.[98] Scott denied that Cameron had made any such statement. According to McGowan, this declaration 'was the signal of confusion and disorder to the enemies of the association and free discussion'. The ensuing tumult continued for some considerable time before order was finally restored. Murdoch then announced that because of the behaviour of the Association's opponents the meeting was dissolved. Before those present left, however, Murdoch read aloud the resolutions which he had hoped would be passed that evening.[99] These condemned the activities of the Association, its members and supporters, and praised Scott for his exertions on behalf of the Catholic congregation of Glasgow over the previous two decades.[100] Murdoch also stated that copies of the resolutions would be placed in various locations and those who supported the sentiments expressed in the documents should demonstrate this by signing them. The number of people who eventually did so is not known.[101] William McGowan claimed that a number of illiterate members of the congregation allowed their names to be put on the copies by others and that 'strangers who had not resided many weeks, months or days in the place' also signed them.[102] There were allegations that women and children were pressed to do likewise.[103] Soon after the Gorbals meeting Scott received an address of loyalty from Catholics in Blackquarry, Springbank and Cowcaddens, and one from a group of those who resided in Tradeston. These contained sentiments similar to those in the resolutions which Murdoch had laid out for signatures.[104]

The following September those members of the Catholic congregation who opposed the Glasgow Catholic Association gave Scott 'a complete service of Table, and a full set of Tea Plate' and Murdoch 'an elegant Gold Watch, with a rich appropriate appendage'. The priests also received a silver gilt chalice. The total cost of the gifts was £170.[105] This largesse was a response to criticisms of Scott and Murdoch which had recently been made by the Glasgow Catholic Association,[106] although this information was not made public by the deputation which made the presentation.[107] Nevertheless, it would appear that on this occasion the supporters of the Catholic clergymen were once again attempting to give the general public the impression that they represented the overwhelming majority of Roman Catholics in the city, and that the members of the Glasgow Catholic Association formed no more than an insignificant minority of the congregation. For example, the deputation which gave Scott and Murdoch the gifts also presented each clergyman with an address which lavished praise on him. The addresses were given 'in the name of the Catholic Body of Glasgow…'.[108] This infuriated those who opposed the priests. In a letter to the *Glasgow Free Press*, 'An Old Member of the Catholic Congregation' objected to the deputation 'coming forward in the name of the whole body' and asked at what meeting of the congregation had these individuals been deputed. He claimed that hundreds of the city's Catholics 'heartily detested' the sentiments expressed in the addresses and rightly concluded that those who made the presentation to Scott and Murdoch were a 'self-appointed deputation' who had acted in response to the activities of the Glasgow Catholic Association.[109]

A number of the supporters of the two clergymen were present at a meeting of the Glasgow Catholic Association on 15 November 1825. The meeting progressed without incident until the proposal of a resolution which called on those present to 'disapprove, in the strongest manner' the role which Murdoch and Scott played in the dismissal of the McGowan brothers from their posts as teachers in the Catholic schools. According to the *Glasgow Chronicle*:

> This resolution gave rise to a scene of noise, confusion and uproar, that defies description. A number of persons, not members of the association, violently opposed the resolution. The opposite party were determined that no resolution derogatory to either the character or conduct of Mr Scott be passed. They denied that he had the power, or had been the means of the dismissal of the teachers.
>
> Mr McKay, potatoe dealer, came resolutely forward and flourished his fist in the face of the Chairman, and with a voice as loud as fury could make it, vociferated that he would rather have his head cut off that moment on the

floor where he stood, than see a vote of censure passed on their pastor. (Tremendous applause and hissing.)

As a result of this behaviour the chairman of the meeting Andrew Stewart sent for the police. He then spoke in favour of the resolution. Stewart was followed by one Hugh Curren, who defended Scott and claimed that it was in fact Bishop Paterson who was responsible for the dismissal of the McGowans. His speech resulted in another scene of great disorder. The resolution, however, was eventually carried unanimously. (Those who were not members of the Association were not entitled to vote on the motions.) William McGowan proposed the next resolution, which criticised Murdoch and Scott. It also caused uproar. James McGowan seconded it and

> said they were surely not so ignorant as to suppose that a man dressed in canonicals could do no wrong, and when they did do wrong let them oppose them like men. The men who could approve of or justify the conduct of Mr Scott and Mr Murdoch on these occasions, were not fit for emancipation.

This jibe led to the final scene of 'noise, confusion and uproar' which ended only when the police officers arrived. After this 'the business went on with becoming order and decorum'.[110]

It is evident that there was strong and organised opposition towards the Glasgow Catholic Association from within the city's Catholic community. This opposition, however, must be examined further. After all, it did not occur until April 1825, more than a year and a half after the formation of the Association and six months after Scott launched his campaign against it.

The evidence suggests that having failed to crush the Glasgow Catholic Association, Scott and Murdoch decided in April 1825 to turn members of their congregation against it. The day before the infamous Gorbals meeting was a Sunday, and at both masses Scott read out extracts from a newspaper report of a speech made by Andrew Stewart at a recent meeting of the Association, and extracts from the report in the *Glasgow Chronicle* of the presentation made to James McGowan the previous month by Catholic inhabitants of Bridgeton.[111] Stewart had criticised Scott for attacking the Association from the pulpit[112] and the Bridgeton Catholics had condemned him for dismissing McGowan from his post as teacher in the Sunday school.[113] According to William McGowan, Scott attempted to convince the congregation at each service on 17 April that in one of the extracts which he read aloud 'he had been compared to the Devil; and, in another, that the Association had spoken as if they comprehended the whole Catholic congregation…'.[114] Scott then declared that if the sentiments expressed in the extracts which he had read were those of the whole congregation 'he would willingly leave them…'.[115]

In his *Address of the Glasgow Catholic Association* William McGowan refuted the charges made by Scott. He denied that the Association had ever spoken as if it comprised the entire congregation and stated that it had in fact on many occasions expressed regret that more Catholics in the city had not become members. Moreover, the Association had 'earnestly solicited those who kept *aloof* to come forward, and co-operate with us in the same good cause'.[116] The *Address* also reprinted the report of the presentation to James McGowan. The Bridgeton Catholics, as was shown earlier, stated in their address to him that they regarded his dismissal from the Sunday school 'as being not a private, but a public evil, *and must infer that the being who could thus deprive our children of their instructor can only be compared to the man who would wilfully and deliberately extinguish the taper of light, that all might be involved in general darkness'*.[117] According to William McGowan, it was this part of the address which Scott claimed compared him to the devil. McGowan argued that the extract did no such thing: it was 'evidently a comparison used to show the *moral darkness*, which the depriving them of their Sunday-school teacher was calculated to produce…'.[118] It would appear that Scott had not simply misinterpreted the address of the Bridgeton Catholics but had deliberately distorted it in an attempt to discredit the Glasgow Catholic Association in the eyes of non-members, in order to encourage them to be hostile towards the society. William McGowan was certainly convinced that this was the reason for Scott's actions:

> He had, we may say, with the single exception of Mr Murdoch, opposed the association hitherto without engaging on his side a single auxiliary; but here an opportunity presented itself, by the susceptibility of the phrase in question of a double meaning, of engaging the feelings of the people against the association. This, together with an attempt to make it appear that the speech, from which, on the same occasion, he took some extracts, spoke of the *association* as comprehending the *whole congregation*, was the cause of the stir of CERTAIN *of the people*. For, though the association had nothing whatever to do, as a body, with the contents of any address, which the catholic inhabitants of Bridgeton thought proper to adopt, or with the phraseology or language of any speech of any member, there were few of the congregation who had the sagacity to make the necessary distinction, owing to the artful manner in which Mr Scott had compiled his paper.[119]

The support which Scott received at the Gorbals meeting the following day demonstrates that this new strategy was an instant success. Furthermore, it must also be noted that the address of loyalty which Scott received soon after this from Catholics in Blackquarry, Springbank and Cowcaddens, and that which he received from Catholics in Tradeston, condemned attacks which had supposedly been made against him in the press by the Glasgow Catholic Association.[120]

Although Andrew Scott made the allegations from the pulpit on 17 April 1825, John Murdoch was initially the principal organiser of the opposition to the society. According to William McGowan, on the day on which Scott relaunched his offensive a meeting was held in the chapel's baptism room 'at which Mr Murdoch was the principal, if not the sole, manager'. Some members of the Association learned of this event and went to the room but were told that it was a private assembly by invitation only. Indeed, Murdoch informed them '*that none had a right to be present, except those whose names would be found in a list which he had* in his pocket!!'. It was this gathering which organised the meeting in the Gorbals schoolroom the following day.[121] At the latter event Murdoch was once again the principal figure.[122] For example, it was he who prepared the resolutions which were to have been 'discussed' that evening. Moreover, McGowan claimed that during 'the violence, disorder and confusion, which that night disgraced the meeting', Andrew Scott

> *appeared* the fairest and most honourable opponent at the meeting; he appeared inclined to put an end to the dispute about the association. But not so Mr Murdoch; he was all fire and fury; he would neither give nor take any quarter. Mr Scott agreed to the proposal of Mr James McGowan, in fact seconded it, that the committee of the association and Mr Scott should retire and endeavour to settle matters, and that the meeting should be dissolved or adjourned, *sine die*, waiting the result of the conference; but Mr Murdoch would not consent. He would consent to the two parties retiring, but he would carry on hostilities against one of them, in their absence; he could by no means consent to the suppression of his darling resolutions.[123]

Finally, it was Murdoch who, after failing to restore order, dissolved the meeting and read aloud all the resolutions.[124]

It would appear, therefore, that in April 1825 Scott and Murdoch deliberately misled a section of those in their congregation who were not familiar with the activities of the Glasgow Catholic Association into believing that they, the clergymen, had been attacked by that organisation. The priests wanted to incite opposition and hostility from within the Catholic community towards the Association in order to discredit it and thus prevent it from attracting more members. Moreover, it is likely that Scott and Murdoch also wanted to demonstrate to their superiors, their colleagues and to the general public that the Glasgow Catholic Association and its activities were frowned upon by the overwhelming majority of the city's Catholic population.

The two Catholic clergymen, however, did not organise the opposition to the Association by themselves. They were ably assisted by members of the small group of Catholic businessmen in the city. For example, the chairman of the Gorbals meeting was Patrick Black, a merchant tailor in the Saltmarket, and its secretary was Charles Bryson, a hardware merchant who had premises in the Trongate.[125] Furthermore, those at the November 1825 meeting of the Glasgow Catholic Association who opposed the resolutions censuring Murdoch and Scott were described by James McGowan as 'commercial men…'.[126] These businessmen had their own particular reason for being hostile towards the Association and indeed several months prior to the events of April 1825 had privately urged Scott to crush it: in early February 1825 he informed a colleague that 'the respectable part (if we can call any part of this congregation respectable) had several times before told me that they thought we were not doing our duty when we were allowing the Catholic association to go on; that the members of it had nothing to lose, and that if any mob arose they would be the first attacked'.[127]

IV

The Glasgow Catholic Association was established for admirable reasons. The city's two Catholic priests, however, viewed the organisation with disdain during its first twelve months. In autumn 1824 the Association came to the attention of members of the city's Protestant establishment who quickly became greatly alarmed about its existence. Once informed of this Andrew Scott ordered the society to disband, in the conviction that he was protecting the position of the Catholic Church in Glasgow. It is evident, however, that those leading Glasgow Protestants whose fears Scott was made aware of had no real understanding of the Glasgow Catholic Association and its objectives. Nor had Scott and Murdoch. The two priests did not make any enquiries about the society and its aims before they launched their campaign against it. Moreover, they declined to meet representatives of the Association who wished to explain the true nature of its activities. The Glasgow Catholic Association naturally refused to be bullied into submission. The issue for Murdoch and Scott then became one of power and control as they were convinced that the society's defiance was intolerable and that members of the Catholic congregation of Glasgow had to submit to the will of their clergymen on all matters. The Association maintained that the authority of the priests was only spiritual and that they had no right to interfere in the political activities of their flock. The outcome was a bitter, dirty and very public conflict which could have been avoided had Scott and Murdoch not adopted such an intransigent position from the outset against an organisation which existed only to advance the interests of the Catholic faith and the position of Catholics in society.

Notes

1. W.H. Fraser, 'Patterns of Protest', in T.M. Devine and Rosalind Mitchison (eds.), *People and Society in Scotland Volume 1, 1760–1830* (Edinburgh, 1988), p.286.

2. W.H. Fraser, *Conflict and Class: Scottish Workers 1700–1838* (Edinburgh, 1988), p.113.

3. See, for example, Tony Clarke and Tony Dickson, 'The Making of a Class Society: Commercialisation and Working-Class Resistance, 1780–1830' in Tony Dickson (ed.), *Scottish Capitalism: Class, State and Nation from before the Union to the Present* (London, 1980), p.177; I.G.C. Hutchison, 'Glasgow Working-Class Politics', in R.A. Cage (ed.), *The Working Class in Glasgow 1750–1914* (London, 1987), pp.103–4.

4. Norman Murray, *The Scottish Handloom Weavers 1790–1850:A Social History* (Edinburgh, 1978), p.227.

5. James Handley, *The Irish in Scotland 1798–1845* (2nd edition, Cork, 1945), pp.285–6, 317–8; *The Irish in Modern Scotland* (Cork, 1947), pp.53–5.

6. SCA, Individual Mission Correspondence, IM14/3/7, The Memorial of the Glasgow Catholic Association to Bishop Cameron, 9 February 1825; William McGowan, *Address of the Glasgow Catholic Association…* (Glasgow, 1825), p.8.

7. McGowan, *Address*, p.12.

8. *Ibid*, p.9; SCA, Individual Mission Correspondence, IM14/3/7, The Memorial of the Glasgow Catholic Association to Bishop Cameron, 7 February 1825; *Glasgow Chronicle*, 2 November 1824.

9. McGowan, *Address*, p.9.

10. *Glasgow Chronicle*, 2 November 1824.

11. McGowan, *Address*, p.9; *Glasgow Chronicle*, 2 November 1824.

12. SCA, Individual Mission Correspondence, IM14/3/7, The Memorial of the Glasgow Catholic Association to Bishop Cameron, 9 February 1825.

13. McGowan, *Address*, p.29.

14. *Ibid*, p.9; SCA, Individual Mission Correspondence, IM14/3/7, The Memorial of the Glasgow Catholic Association to Bishop Cameron, 9

February 1825; SCA, Blairs letters, BL5/180/1, Andrew Scott to William Reid, 7 February 1825; *Glasgow Free Press*, 1 February 1826.

15. McGowan, *Address*, p.76.

16. *Ibid*, pp.18–23. See also *Glasgow Chronicle*, 2 November 1824.

17. *Glasgow Chronicle*, 31 May 1825; Geroid O'Tuathaigh. *Ireland before the Famine 1798–1848* (Dublin, 1992), p.69.

18. *Glasgow Chronicle*, 17 November 1825; *Glasgow Free Press*, 1 February 1826.

19. *Glasgow Free Press*, 1 February 1826.

20. *Glasgow Chronicle*, 17 November 1825.

21. *Glasgow Free Press*, 7 January 1865.

22. SCA, Blairs Letters, BL5/180/1, Andrew Scott to William Reid, 7 February 1825.

23. McGowan, *Address*, p.9.

24. *Ibid*, p.10; Handley, *Irish in Modern Scotland*, pp.57–8.

25. McGowan, *Address*, pp.10–11.

26. Handley, *Irish in Modern Scotland*, p.58.

27. McGowan, *Address*, p.12.

28. *Ibid*, p.13.

29. *Ibid*, pp.13–4.

30. SCA, Blairs letters, BL5/180/1, Andrew Scott to William Reid, 7 February 1825. As has been stated, the Association changed the day of the meeting after learning of Murdoch's opposition to it being on a Sunday. The Association also stated that if it had sometimes held meetings on a Sunday so had other associations in England. Furthermore, Scott's hostility had made it hold meetings in public houses, as he had refused the Committee the use of the old chapel schoolroom, even after having been offered money for its hire. McGowan, *Address*, p.14–5.

31. SCA, Blairs letters, BL5/180/1, Andrew Scott to William Reid, 7 February 1825.

32. McGowan, *Address*, pp16–7.

33. *Ibid*, p.17.

34. SCA, Blairs letters, BL5/180/1, Andrew Scott to William Reid, 7 February 1825.

35. *Ibid*.

36. McGowan, *Address*, p.27.

37. SCA, Blairs letters, BL5/180/1, Andrew Scott to William Reid, 7 February 1825. See also McGowan, *Address*, pp.23–4.

38. McGowan, *Address*, p.19.

39. *Ibid*, pp.20–1; SCA, Blairs letters, BL5/180/1, Andrew Scott to William Reid, 7 February 1825.

40. SCA, Blairs letters, BL5/180/1, Andrew Scott to William Reid, 7 February 1825; McGowan, *Address*, p.22.

41. SCA, Blairs letters, BL5/180/1, Andrew Scott to William Reid, 7 February 1825; McGowan, *Address*, p.30.

42. McGowan, *Address*, p.24.

43. *Ibid*, p.19.

44. *Ibid*, pp.21–2.

45. *Ibid*, pp.22–3.

46. *Ibid*, p.31.

47. *Ibid*, p.32.

48. *Ibid*, p.33.

49. SCA, Blairs letters, BL5/180/1, Andrew Scott to William Reid, 7 February 1825. See also McGowan, *Address*, p.33.

50. SCA, Blairs letters, BL5/180/1, Andrew Scott to William Reid, 7 February 1825; McGowan, *Address*, p.33.

51. McGowan, *Address*, pp.34–5.

52. *Ibid*, p.36.

53. *Ibid*, p.42. In a letter to William Reid, priest in Edinburgh, Scott said of those who signed the requisition: 'Their signatures as ragged as are their coats would be sufficient to shew what they are, and how capable they are to defend the principles of their Religion, for that is one of their objects.' SCA, Blairs letters, BL5/180/1, Andrew Scott to William Reid, 7 February 1825.

54. SCA, Blairs letters BL 5/180/1, Andrew Scott to William Reid, 7 February 1825.

55. McGowan, *Address*, p.42.

56. *Ibid*, pp.38–40.

57. SCA, Individual Mission Correspondence, IM14/3/7, Memorial of the Glasgow Catholic Association to Bishop Cameron, 9 February 1825. Most of the memorial is reprinted in McGowan, *Address*, pp.40–4. For a further appeal to Cameron, see SCA, Blairs letters, BL5/172/3 William McGowan to Alexander Cameron, 26 February 1825.

58. McGowan, *Address*, p.44.

59. *Ibid*, p.45. See also p.vi. Cameron's written reply to the Association, dated 19 February 1825, is reprinted on p.45 of McGowan, *Address*. The Association was disappointed with its contents as it believed they were 'not sufficiently explicit' as they did not allude to the Memorial or its contents and therefore were 'of no use, in removing the impression, which the

accusations of Mr Scott and Mr Murdoch have naturally made upon the public mind'. SCA, Blairs letters, BL5/172/3, William McGowan to Alexander Cameron, 26 February 1825.

60. McGowan, *Address*, p.vi.

61. *Ibid*, pp.48–103.

62. McGowan, *Address*, pp.61–3; For Scottish attitudes to emancipation see Ian A. Muirhead, 'Catholic Emancipation: Scottish Reactions in 1829', *Innes Review*, XXIV (1973), pp.26–42; Handley, *Irish in Scotland*, pp.297–8.

63. McGowan, *Address*, pp.103–6.

64. *Ibid*, p.109. In August 1825 Bishop Alexander Paterson succeeded Alexander Cameron as Vicar-Apostolic of the Lowland District of the Catholic Church in Scotland.

65. *Ibid*. See also SCA, Blairs letters, BL5/183/3, Dr. Andrew Stewart to Alexander Paterson, 31 August 1825; *Glasgow Free Press*, 7 December 1825.

66. *Glasgow Free Press*, 7 December 1825.

67. *Glasgow Chronicle*, 17 November 1825.

68. McGowan, *Address*, p.108.

69. *Glasgow Free Press*, 12 November 1825; *Glasgow Chronicle*, 17 November 1825; McGowan, *Address*, p.55.

70. *Glasgow Chronicle*, 17 November 1825; *Glasgow Free Press*, 7 December 1825.

71. *Glasgow Free Press*, 7 December 1825; *Glasgow Chronicle*, 26 November 1825.

72. *Glasgow Chronicle*, 17 November, 26 November 1825.

73. *Glasgow Chronicle*, 17 November 1825.

74. *Glasgow Free Press*, 7 December 1825.

75. The address is reprinted in McGowan's *Address*, pp.55–6, and McGowan's reply is on pp.57–61. See also SCA, Individual Mission Correspondence, IM14/3/9, Memorial of the Committee for the Snuff Box to Bishop Cameron, 23 April 1825.

76. SCA, Individual Mission Correspondence, IM14/3/9 Memorial of the Committee for the Snuff Box to Bishop Cameron, 23 April 1825.

77. *Glasgow Free Press*, 7 December 1825.

78. *Ibid*, 12 November 1825. It stated: 'While we bear grateful testimony to your eminent merits, we deeply regret that any circumstance should arise, which would deprive our youth of your useful and valuable services. This was, however, a matter over which we had no control; and are only left to lament its consequences, without being able to remedy the evil.'

79. See, for example, SCA, Blairs letters, BL5/172/3, William McGowan to Alexander Cameron, 26 February 1825; BL5/180/17, Andrew Scott to Alexander Paterson, 5 November 1825; Individual Mission Correspondence,

IM14/3/7, Memorial of the Glasgow Catholic Association to Bishop Cameron, 9 February 1825; IM14/3/11, Formula to be subscribed by all Members of the Glasgow Catholic Association so called, before their admission to their Easter Duties, n.d.; McGowan, *Address*, pp.109–10.

80. McGowan, *Address*, pp.17–8.

81. *Ibid*, p.116.

82. *Glasgow Free Press*, 2 January 1865.

83. McGowan, *Address*, p.12.

84. *Ibid*, p.14.

85. *Ibid*, p.31.

86. *Ibid*, pp.108–9. See also *Glasgow Free Press*, 12 November 1825.

87. Unless otherwise stated the following discussion is based on SCA, Blairs letters, BL5/180.1, Andrew Scott to William Reid, 7 February 1825.

88. This can be seen from the evidence in section two. See also McGowan, *Address*, pp.103–4, 111; *Glasgow Chronicle*, 13 December 1825; SCA, Blairs letters, BL5/180/9, Andrew Scott to Charles Gordon, 14 October 1825.

89. *Glasgow Chronicle*, 2 November 1824, 19 November 1825.

90. SCA, Blairs letters, BL5/180/12 Andrew Scott to Alexander Paterson, 26 October 1825.

91. *Ibid*, BL5/180/17 Andrew Scott to Alexander Paterson, 5 November 1825.

92. *Ibid*; BL5/180/15, Andrew Scott to James Kyle, 5 November 1825.

93. SCA, Individual Mission Correspondence, IM3/11, Formula to be subscribed by all Members of the Glasgow Catholic Association so called, before their admission to their Easter Duties, n.d.

94. For the Gorbals Meeting see McGowan, *Address*, pp.48–66.

95. *Ibid*, p.53. See also, SCA, Individual Mission Correspondence, IM14/3/9, Memorial of the Committee for the Snuff Box to Bishop Cameron, 23 April 1825.

96. McGowan, *Address*, pp.52–3, 61.

97. *Ibid*, p.63.

98. *Ibid*, p.64.

99. *Ibid*, pp.64–5. McGowan claimed that some members of the Association were assaulted by their opponents.

100. The resolutions and the response of the Glasgow Catholic Association to them are in *ibid*, pp.70–100.

101. *Ibid*, pp.65–6; 103.

102. *Ibid*, p.101.

103. SCA, Individual Mission Correspondence, IM14/3/9, Memorial of the Committee for the Snuff Box to Bishop Cameron, 23 April 1825.

104. *Ibid*, IM14/3/8, Address of the Catholics residing in Blackquarry, Springbank and Cowcaddens, April 1825; Oban Letters, OL2/2/4, Address from the Catholic Inhabitants of Tradeston, 4 May 1825.

105. *Glasgow Free Press*, 17 September 1825.

106. Scott also informed Kyle that those who made the presentation were 'not…very well pleased that I would not write down and give them for publication my answer to their address; but I am determined to keep out of print if I can'. SCA, Blairs letters, BL5/180/4, Andrew Scott to James Kyle, 24 September 1825.

107. The addresses and the report of the presentation made no mention of the criticisms of the priests which had been made by the Glasgow Catholic Association.

108. *Glasgow Free Press*, 17 September 1825.

109. 'An old Member of the Catholic Congregation' also stated that: 'It is no mark of the measure being popular, that very many of the oldest, and, perhaps, best members of the congregation, were never applied to for a subscription, and that a great number of those who were applied to, sternly refused. To illustrate this, I could relate many anecdotes, but let the following suffice: One man, when applied to, said, were it to send Mr S. out of Glasgow, he would willingly subscribe.' *Glasgow Free Press*, 8 October 1825.

110. This paragraph is based on *Glasgow Chronicle*, 17 November 1825.

111. McGowan, *Address*, pp.48, 54.

112. *Ibid*, pp.92–6.

113. *Ibid*, pp.55–6.

114. *Ibid*, p.54.

115. *Ibid*, p.48.

116. *Ibid*, p.100.

117. *Ibid*, pp.55–6.

118. *Ibid*, p.56.

119. *Ibid*, p.57.

120. SCA, Individual Mission Correspondence, IM14/3/8, Address from the Catholics residing in Blackquarry, Springbank and Cowcaddens, April 1825; Oban Letters, OL2/2/4, Address from the Catholic Inhabitants of Tradeston, 4 May 1825.

121. McGowan also stated that the meeting in the Baptism Room 'was composed only of such materials, as it was thought, would work into any shape or form which the workman thought proper'. McGowan, *Address*, p.51.

122. For Murdoch's role at the meeting see *ibid*, pp.53–4, 61, 64–7. See also SCA, Individual Mission Correspondence, IM14/3/9, Memorial of the Committee for the Snuff Box to Bishop Cameron, 23 April 1825.

123. McGowan, *Address*, p.67.

124. McGowan claimed that once copies of the resolutions had been placed in various locations Murdoch 'used every effort to procure signatures, that he even lectured the children in the Sunday schools upon the subject'. *Ibid*, p.101.

125. *Ibid*, p.54; SCA, Individual Mission Correspondence, IM14/2, List of the Names of Glasgow Catholics with their Addresses and Occupations (1825?); *Glasgow Free Press*, 9 September 1826.

126. *Glasgow Free Press*, 7 December 1825.

127. SCA, Blairs letters, BL5/180/1, Andrew Scott to William Reid, 7 February 1825.

5

The Reform Agitations, 1830–37

There is very little evidence in secondary sources of an Irish presence in the reform agitations in Scotland between 1830 and 1837. Handley argued that 'from the end of the Napoleonic War to the Chartist Risings the Irish immigrant had little active part in the political questions that agitated the bosom of the Scottish working class'.[1] Yet he also stated that the Irish 'joined with their comrades in the agitation for, and rejoicing over, the Reform Bill'.[2] The evidence he provided to demonstrate this, however, comes solely from a *Scotsman* report of a procession in Edinburgh of the city's trades which was held to celebrate the victories of reform candidates in the election of December 1832.[3] This poll occurred several months after the Reform Acts, which enfranchised mostly sections of the middle classes, were passed. It would appear that Handley attributed a wider significance to a single event. The other evidence of Irish participation in the agitation of 1830–32 is in an essay by J.F. McCaffrey and again reveals an Irish presence only in an Edinburgh Reform procession, on this occasion in August 1832.[4] It is surprising that there are no references in the secondary material to Irish involvement in reform activity in the west of Scotland during these years, given that this was the region in which most immigrants settled.[5]

Any study of this particular period of Scottish radicalism is heavily dependent on the contemporary press. The newspapers of the period often carried very lengthy reports of the various public meetings and demonstrations, and these accounts were not found solely in those publications which were favourable to reform. Unfortunately, the files of the major Scottish working class newspapers, *The Trades' Advocate* and *The Liberator*, have not survived. Nevertheless, the available press reports do reveal the involvement of Irish workers in the reform agitations in the west of Scotland between 1830 and 1837. Furthermore, there is also evidence of reform activity by members of the Catholic Irish business and professional community in Glasgow. This chapter will examine these groups in detail and will also discuss the attitudes of Scottish reformers to this involvement and to Ireland and Irish issues. The heavy reliance on newspapers does, however, result in difficulties. These are particularly apparent when trying to establish the nature of immigrant participation in the political campaigns, and will be addressed in the third section of this chapter.

I

From the reports of the various reform meetings and demonstrations in the west of Scotland between 1830 and 1837 it is evident that Irish involvement was greater and more significant than Handley suggested. For example, the *Scottish Guardian* stated that at the great reform demonstration on Glasgow Green on 17 May 1832, at which the number of people present was estimated at between 100 and 150,000, 'Seven Thousand Irishmen in a body marched to the field, and sent a deputy to the hustings, who was only prevented from pressing his adherence to Reform by the variety of business to be gone through'.[6] Other newspapers commented on this group and its size.[7] In October 1834 around 200,000 people assembled on the Green to hear the Earl of Durham, a noted reformer. Durham received addresses from most of the groups which had participated in the procession held prior to the meeting, including one from 'the Irish labourers of Glasgow'.[8] At the last of the great reform demonstrations in Glasgow in this period, held to honour Daniel O'Connell during his visit to the city in September 1835, the group which led the welcome procession was 'the Loyal Irish Reformers and United Labourers'.[9]

It would appear that Irish labourers, probably in the main the same people who marched in the processions in honour of Durham and O'Connell, also participated in the reform demonstrations in Glasgow in 1831 and 1832. At the Grand Reform and Coronation Procession in September 1831 around fifty groups of workers took part, including one which consisted of labourers. Reports of the event did not give the nationality of this body of workers, but the fact that most of the labourers in the city were of Irish birth or extraction suggests that it was a group of Irishmen. The principal flag under which they marched may confirm this — the *Loyal Reformers Gazette* stated that on the flag was the image of 'his Majesty crowned by Daniel O'Connell on his right and Joseph Hume on his left; on the right is the Irish harp, left, Thistle entwined with Shamrock, motto, "Royal Irish Reformers".'[10] This journal, in its account of the procession, commented that the various trade bodies were 'better dressed' than they were at the previous reform demonstration and noted that 'even the Labourers, of whom several hundreds walked, were a body of clean, well dressed, stout looking men, and carried several very handsome flags'.[11] A group of labourers was also present in the great reform procession in the city in September 1832.[12]

The newspapers of the period did not provide any more information concerning the Irish labourers who marched in the reform processions. It is probable, however, that most were Roman Catholics, as these Irish labourers greatly admired the political leader of Catholic Ireland, Daniel O'Connell. His portrait was on their banner in the reform procession in September 1831 and at the demonstration for him four years later. The address which the Earl of Durham received from the Irish labourers in Glasgow in October 1834 stated that O'Connell and other 'patriotic' Irish Members of Parliament knew better than anyone else what was needed to improve the condition of Ireland and her people. The address also argued that if the misgovernment of Ireland did not end soon, a repeal of the legislative union between Britain and Ireland should occur and an Irish parliament be established.[13] It would be remarkable if many Irish Protestants in Glasgow, or indeed anywhere else in the United Kingdom at that time, shared these sentiments. The overwhelming majority of Protestants in Ireland were from the early 1820s bitterly opposed to O'Connell. They were convinced, for a variety of reasons, that his campaigns for Catholic Emancipation and Repeal of Union sought to replace the Protestant Ascendancy in Ireland with a Catholic one which would greatly harm their social, economic, political and religious condition.[14] It is highly unlikely, therefore, that many Irish Protestant immigrants in Scotland, and in particular those who arrived after O'Connell's rise to prominence, would have supported 'the Liberator' and his policy of Repeal.

It is evident on the basis of these illustrations that Irish workers participated in the major reform demonstrations and processions in Glasgow between 1830 and 1835. It is almost certain, however, that the examples given greatly underestimate the extent of Irish involvement. At the beginning of this chapter it was noted that Handley stated that Irish workers were involved in the campaign for the Reform Bill during 1830–32. He also claimed that, 'In the processions they walked as a separate body under their own flags, which bore portraits of Wolfe Tone, Robert Emmet, and Daniel O'Connell'.[15] It has already been shown that his evidence of this apparently comes solely from a report of reform activity in Edinburgh, and it appears that the Irish in this city did indeed organise themselves into a separate body, called the United Irishmen.[16] The evidence presented thus far for Glasgow, however, demonstrates that it was Irish labourers who marched together as a group in the reform processions in the city between 1830 and 1835. It is inconceivable that it was only the labourers among the city's Irish population who were supporters of reform. It is not unreasonable to suggest, therefore, that both Catholic and Protestant Irish workers in other occupations, such as spinning and weaving, who wished to demonstrate their support for political change marched under the banner of their trade or occupation.[17] Greenock was another town in which the Irish did not participate in reform demonstrations as a separate group. In August 1832 the *Glasgow Evening Post* commented on the procession of the town's trades held to celebrate the passing of the Reform Bill:

> It would be invidious to single out any particular trade, but we were considerably pleased with the sugar boilers, mostly all Irishmen, who were well dressed and decorated with the tri-colour ribbon. They had a beautiful flag with full length portraits of Hume and O'Connell painted thereon.[18]

There is also evidence which suggests that Irish workers were involved in reform processions in Ayrshire. On 25 and 26 April 1831 the Orangemen of Girvan, who like members of the Orange Lodges elsewhere in the region appear to have been of Irish birth or descent, attacked the reform processions in the town,[19] which were 'chiefly under the management of the Scotch'.[20] This implies the involvement of some Irish inhabitants of Girvan. On both occasions the reformers' flags were captured and burned.[21] Three months later 'the Reform party, joined by the Irish Catholics' attempted to stop a 12 July parade of Orange Lodges from in and around the town.[22] Much violence ensued and a Special Constable was killed by an Orangeman who was later convicted and hanged for the crime.[23] At the trial the defence counsel asked for the proceedings to be moved out of Girvan away from public excitement because 'his clients were Orangemen, and not Reformers, while those opposed to them were Catholics and friendly to Reform'.[24]

This does not necessarily mean, however, that all Irish members of Orange Lodges in Scotland were hostile to reform. Evidence given to the Parliamentary Inquiry into Orange Lodges, published in 1835, revealed that one or two Lodges in the country had recently been dissolved because their members were 'a little irregular not only as Orangemen but as good and loyal subjects'. In other Lodges there had been those who 'under the taint of revolutionary and republican notions had become refractory and mutinous'.[25] That some Orangemen in Scotland — who might not have been of Irish birth or descent — appear to have supported reform should come as no surprise; around this time some Orangemen in England and even in Ireland supported reform activities.[26] Furthermore, the significance of the Protestant Irish in the Orange Order in Scotland must be kept in perspective: after all, in 1835 there were only forty-four Lodges in all of Scotland which, according to the institution's historian, implies a total membership of less than five hundred.[27] The vast majority of Protestant

Irishmen in Scotland were not members of the Order although this, of course, is not to suggest that they were all hostile to the principles and aims of Orangeism. Nevertheless, no evidence has been found which shows that there was significant Protestant Irish opposition to the reform agitations in Scotland. This suggests that most of these workers were either apathetic towards political change or, as is more probable, in favour of reform. After all, it was suggested in chapter three that Protestant Irish workers in and around Glasgow were involved in insurrectionary activities during 1816–20.

Irish workers who were supporters of the campaigns for reform during this period were active not only in the major reform processions and demonstrations. In May 1831 the Lord Lieutenant of Ayrshire the Earl of Glasgow was made aware of 'the dreadful state of insubordination' in the county caused by the recent parliamentary election. Disturbances had occurred and the Earl was informed that 'many of the lower orders in Ayrshire are Irishmen — and it is quite manifest that they have been excited and goaded on by persons who are actuated by the most diabolical views'.[28] In March 1834 the *Reformers Gazette*, edited and published in Glasgow by the moderate reformer Peter McKenzie, stated that among its readers were 'many intelligent Irishmen' whom it highly respected.[29] Eight months later the Tory *Glasgow Courier*, edited by the leading Orangeman William Motherwell, made some scathing remarks about a meeting of the Glasgow Political Union, which until 1836 was the city's principal reform organisation. Peter McKenzie was one of the main speakers and the paper stated that 'he had the gratification of exhibiting himself before as motley a squad of tobacco boys, Irish labourers, and tailors, as ever we had clapped eye upon. Long coats were at a sad discount, as well as hats and shoes. Bonnets, jackets and bare feet, were the order of the evening…'. The *Courier* concluded that 'altogether it was a ridiculous, laughable and grotesque affair'.[30]

At least three Irishmen were particularly prominent in the campaign in the west of Scotland for the Reform Bills. Edward Collins was one of the main speakers at a large reform meeting near Paisley on 17 October 1831 which was organised by the Renfrewshire Political Union and was attended, according to the *Glasgow Chronicle*, by between forty and fifty thousand people. The paper reported that:

> Mr COLLINS, from Ireland addressed the meeting at some length, and called on them to agitate for Reform, as had been done in Ireland, by sending deputations all over the country to get up meetings and petitions. He also defended the character of Mr O'Connell, who had done more for liberty than any other living man.[31]

Collins was also present at a lecture given in the Low Church in Paisley the following month by the leading Owenite Alexander Campbell. Campbell's topic was 'on the best mode of permanently employing and bettering the condition of the working classes', and he argued in favour of the introduction of the co-operative system. Collins spoke after the lecture had finished and 'addressed the audience at some length'. He disagreed with Campbell's remedy and urged those present 'to direct all their attention to a reform of Parliament as the first thing for relieving their distress'.[32]

By the end of 1831 Collins, who was probably a Roman Catholic,[33] had been resident in Paisley for only a few months.[34] During that short time he made a favourable impression on local reformers. In December 1831 he was unanimously elected an honorary member of the Paisley Reform Society 'out of respect for the zeal and ability he has displayed in a well written pamphlet which he has lately published, and dedicated to Earl Grey, in defence of the principles of Universal Suffrage…'. Collins seemingly received letters from the King and the Duke of Norfolk thanking him for sending them copies of the essay, and he also corresponded with other leading public figures, including several members of the Cabinet and Lord Brougham.[35]

Patrick McGowan, the Irish Catholic leader of the Glasgow Cotton Spinners whose trade union activities were discussed in chapter one, also took part in the agitation for the Reform Bills. From press reports of the processions and meetings it would appear that he was not particularly active, or perhaps prominent, in the campaign during 1831. By May 1832, however, he was one of the delegates to the Glasgow Trades Committee, which organised the role of the city's workers in the reform struggle.[36] The *Trades' Advocate* noted at this time that McGowan had 'of late been somewhat conspicuous in the cause of Reform…'.[37] He was in fact one of the speakers at probably the most famous reform meeting held in Scotland during this period of agitation — the 'Black Flag' demonstration on Glasgow Green on 12 May 1832.[38] This meeting was organised by the Trades Committee to protest against the House of Lords' obstruction of the English Reform Bill, the resignation of the reform ministry of Earl Grey, and the decision of the King to invite the anti–reform Duke of Wellington to form an administration. The demonstration took place only eighteen hours after it was called.[39] One of its organisers later recalled the excitement of the time: 'Many of us slept none that night. Flags were dyed black, emblems were prepared, veritable skulls and "other things" were provided, and the people were calm but determinedly resolved for any emergency'.[40] Another account of this event provides a vivid description of the procession to the Green. The author stated that 20,000 men came with music and a terrible array of banners and flags covered with crape. The insignia of royalty were turned upside down, and revolutionary emblems were fearlessly displayed. Skulls, *actual human skulls*, were stuck on the heads of the black staffs, and death heads and cross bones were painted on numerous banners.[41]

At the meeting a middle class reformer urged the people to tell the House of Lords that: 'It was now the Bill or the Barricades. The Reform Bill must be passed or blood should flow'.[42] Patrick McGowan's speech, which will be discussed later, was applauded by the *Trades' Advocate*:

> His speech on the hustings of the Saturday meeting did great credit to the class he belongs to, for the firmness and moderation of its sentiments, under such exciting circumstances as were then presented to a provoked and long-insulted people.[43]

McGowan was also a member of the committee which organised the reform meeting on the Green five days later. By that time the King had recalled Grey after Wellington abandoned his moves to form a ministry.[44] The demonstration on 17 May 1832 was regarded at the time as being the largest which had ever taken place in Glasgow.[45]

One of McGowan's colleagues on the Glasgow Trades Committee was James Burn, who was born in Ireland. Burn, who later wrote several books including an autobiography, became the hatter's delegate to the Committee in the summer of 1831.[46] He recalled in his memoir that he quickly became prominent in the reform campaign:

> My maiden speech at the first general meeting I attended got me elected a member of the Central Committee. Here, then, I got into the gulf-stream of political agitation, and was carried onward with amazing velocity. I was seized with a wild enthusiasm, and for the time became politically mad; my pride, too, was flattered, by being made a leader in the camp of the people. From this date I took an active part in all the proceedings of both the Whig and the Radical parties in Glasgow for several years.[47]

Six months after becoming a member of the Trades Committee Burn was elected to the Standing Committee of the Glasgow Reform Association. Burn also stated in his autobiography that he was responsible for the marshalling of the Reform Bill demonstrations on the Green and was involved in the campaigns of the city's reform candidates in the general elections of 1832 and 1837.[48]

Newspaper reports from the period confirm the leading role in the reform agitations which Burn claimed he played. For example, he was one of the speakers at a meeting on Glasgow Green in October 1831 attended by around thirty thousand people.[49] Two months prior to this there had been a meeting of the Glasgow Trades Delegates at which one of the speakers argued that they should meet when the Reform Bill passed the House of Commons to tell the Lords that 'like their ancestors, Wallace and Bruce, they were ready to draw the swords that would never be sheathed till the measure was completed'. The *Glasgow Courier* reported that this delegate, Charles MacKay, was 'interrupted by cries of order'. The hatters' delegate, whose name the paper did not give, responded to MacKay's suggestion. He

> deprecated strongly the use of such language, and hoped that they would never be led to employ any other weapons than those of reason and argument. They were not now to draw the sword on every trivial occurrence, when the end could be attained by the moral and constitutional power that lay in the people.

The *Courier* stated that 'These sentiments were loudly cheered'.[50] The speaker was almost certainly James Burn as, according to his memoir, he became the first and only representative of the hatters to these meetings a short time after he settled in Glasgow in June 1831.[51] John McAdam, one of the leading working class reformers of the time, recalled in his autobiography that Burn was one of the delegates to the Trades Committee.[52]

The contemporary press also showed that Burn continued to play an active role in political agitations after the campaign for the Reform Bills had ended. In December 1836 he was one of the founding members of the Scottish Radical Association, which called for annual parliaments, universal male suffrage, vote by ballot and a voluntary church. Later that month Burn was one of the speakers at the meeting which welcomed Feargus O'Connor to Glasgow. He also addressed the meeting of Glasgow workers held the following month to disclaim the Tory sentiments expressed in an address to Sir Robert Peel from a newly formed group of workers called the Glasgow Operative Conservative Society.[53]

It is known that Burn was born in Ireland because he stated this in his autobiography. The information which reveals that Patrick McGowan was of Irish birth or descent comes from an article on him in the *Trades' Advocate* which was reprinted in an English radical journal. No copies of the *Trades' Advocate* have been found. Reports of the activities and speeches of McGowan and Burn in the Glasgow newspapers which have survived do not mention their nationality or ethnic background. This is also the case for many other working class activists of the period.[54] It is quite possible, therefore, that among this group were some who were of Irish birth or descent.

II

The discussion thus far has focused Irish workers, with the possible exception of Edward Collins, whose occupation is not known. There is also evidence of participation in the reform movement in Glasgow by members of the group of Irish Catholic businessmen and professionals — or, to be precise, those among them who had the right to vote. The first election under the terms of the Reform Act was held in December 1832, and the number of Catholic electors in the city at that time was, according to the *Scottish Guardian*, around three hundred.[55] Almost all were of Irish birth or extraction. Elsewhere in the west of Scotland few Catholics had the franchise.[56] For example, in 1835 Andrew Scott, who was made a Bishop of the Catholic Church in 1828, was informed that only four members of the Catholic congregation at Ayr were eligible to vote; the number of Catholic families in and around the town at this time was around two hundred.[57] At the general election in December 1832 radical reformers in Glasgow were defeated and a Tory candidate, James Ewing, and a Whig reformer, James Oswald, were returned. A few Catholic electors, including Bishop Scott, voted for the victors and this led to criticism from local reformers. This in turn resulted in responses from other Catholic voters. From the material in the newspapers concerning this issue the activities of the Catholic electors in Glasgow can be examined.

The scandal first came to light in the final days of December 1832, a few days after the election had taken place. A letter to the *Reformers' Gazette* from 'An Old Reformer', dated 21 December 1832, made some very scathing remarks about the Catholic electors of Glasgow and their voting behaviour:

> Sir — During the various struggles which the Catholics had for many years before they obtained their long-withheld rights, I, in common with other Reformers in this country, contributed my part to assist their demands for justice; and what now is their return? The first opportunity they ever had, as a body, they have manifested their ingratitude. Both in Glasgow and Edinburgh, as appears from the *Scotsman* newspaper, they have given their votes to their old task-masters, and turned their backs upon those who had fought their battles against these same task-masters, and assisted in procuring their Emancipation, and the enfranchisement which the Reform Bill confers. Their conduct is quite sufficient to convince us that the Tories had great reason to say they were unworthy of political privileges. But from the fact that the Irish Catholics are always found on the liberal and independent side, I am led to believe that some secret influence must have been exercised both in this city and in Edinburgh, to induce them to support the Anti-Reform candidates.

There must certainly be some cause for the despicable conduct of these people, when compared to that of their brethren in Ireland. What will O'Connell and the other orators of the Irish Union, say to this? Will they endeavour to prove, notwithstanding, that the Catholics have uniformly been the advocates of civil and religious liberty, and the denouncers of oppression and tyranny?

Will they be able to prove that Bishop Scott, by voting for Mr Ewing, the Tory Candidate, the abettor of the Castlereagh and Wellington administrations, was walking in the footsteps of Cardinal Langton and the Barons of Runneymede? Or will they not rather be obliged to confess, that his conduct is more like that of Billy Boyton, the Conservative Goliah of Dublin, than that of the patriot above mentioned?

The editor of the journal, Peter McKenzie, promised to look into the affair.[58] Another journal, the *Radical Reformers' Gazette*, also decided to investigate. It stated that there was 'not the least doubt, that the body of the Catholics signified their intention to vote for Mr Douglas and Sir Daniel Sandford, and were restrained by a Machievalian influence, secretly exercised…'.[59] The next issues of the two publications had more to say on the matter. The *Reformers' Gazette* revealed that on the night before the election Bishop Scott attended a meeting of Catholic electors and pleaded with them to vote for Ewing and Oswald. Scott 'did not actually *command* them to vote for these two gentlemen, but he indicated pretty plainly what he expected them to do…'. This journal did not criticise Scott but was dismayed by the 'ingratitude' of the other Catholic voters towards Sir Daniel Sandford, who was described as having done 'more to secure *Catholic emancipation* than any other man in Glasgow…'.[60] The *Radical Reformers' Gazette* contained a letter from 'A Reformer' which gave a similar account of the pre-election meeting and which was very critical of the Catholics for not voting for Douglas; it claimed that of all the candidates, he 'was the only one who could redress their grievances', and because of his pledge to do so he 'lost many votes from the Protestants…'. Whereas the *Reformers' Gazette* was unwilling to censure Bishop Scott's actions, this letter to its competitor was not so charitable. It spoke of the 'perfidy' of Scott voting for Ewing after it had been 'universally understood' that he would vote for James Douglas. Moreover, Ewing had been a supporter of William McGavin, the prolific author of anti-Catholic tracts whom Scott successfully sued for libel in 1821. The letter concluded that the Bishop's support for Ewing had to be attributed solely to 'the basest of all motives' — money.[61]

The damning criticisms and allegations made against the Catholic electors of Glasgow resulted in very public responses from them. These revealed that the letters and comments concerning them were in fact

inaccurate and wholly misleading. On 18 January 1833 a meeting of the
city's Catholics was held 'for the purpose of exonerating their body from
the aspersions cast upon them of having shown ingratitude in the case of
the late elections'.[62] The meeting was chaired by one Dr. Morgan. He read
extracts from the letter of 'An Old Reformer' (which had also been
published in the *Glasgow Evening Post*), the assertions in which Morgan
'denied being applicable to the body generally'. He revealed that only
twelve Catholic electors voted for a Tory candidate. Another speaker, Mr
Tressey, condemned those who had not voted for the reform candidates as
being 'not very ripe for the franchise…The Catholics would hail the day
when Douglas and Sandford would be returned as their representatives'.
He concluded by 'proposing a vote of approbation towards Douglas and
Sandford. This proposal was loudly cheered…'. Three resolutions were
carried that night in the Lyceum Rooms, which was reported to have been
'crowded to excess'. These were:

> That the Catholics of Glasgow were much grieved at the aspersions which
> had been thrown on their body, with respect to the late elections…That they
> feel highly indignant at the political apostasy of those of their body who had
> voted for a Tory candidate…That the Catholics are convinced that their
> separated brethren both here and in Ireland will not condemn the whole body
> for the delinquency of a few, — 12 in number — who had caused the disgrace.

The meeting did not, however, deal with the matter of the involvement of
Bishop Scott. Morgan simply denied that Scott interposed during the
campaign. Furthermore, he was unwilling to allow any condemnation of
those who had voted Tory: 'The present meeting was not called to throw
odium on any one, or to calumniate any one; but merely to exonerate the
body in general from the charges made against them. They would not
interfere with those who had…the folly to vote for a Tory candidate.'[63]

The decision of the Catholic electors not to comment on the activities
of Bishop Scott during the election probably arose from an unwillingness
to fan the flames of a controversy which was currently raging in the city.
Six days prior to the meeting the *Glasgow Evening Post* published a letter
from William McGowan, the former secretary of the Glasgow Catholic
Association, which gave an account of the events of December 1832 and
the role Scott played in them.[64] In this and in subsequent letters to the
paper McGowan made a number of scathing criticisms about not only
Scott's political behaviour but also his governance of the Glasgow Mission
over the previous two decades.[65] The following discussion, however, deals
only with McGowan's version of events relating to the election of 1832.
His first letter was concerned mainly with this issue.[66] In it he stated:

as a good deal of public odium has been brought upon the Catholics as a body by the conduct of Bishop Scott in voting for Mr Ewing, which in justice should rest upon the head of Dr. Scott himself, I shall endeavour to do justice to both, and allow the public to draw their ow\n conclusions.

According to McGowan, at a meeting of Catholic electors on 3 December 1832, at which Scott was present, the following resolution was adopted:

That in order to render our support of fit and proper persons to represent the City of Glasgow in a Reformed Parliament as efficient as possible, we shall not at present pledge ourselves to any particular candidate or candidates, but shall reserve our votes till they can be most successfully employed in the election of such persons as the majority of us shall hereafter resolve to support. It being understood that none but reformers of the most liberal principles, of acknowledged talent, and of the most sterling integrity, shall receive our suffrages.

At the group's next meeting, held on 18 December (the eve of the election), Scott made a speech in favour of Oswald.[67] As this candidate did not fit the criteria laid down in the resolution adopted at the previous meeting Scott was unable to convince those present to support him. According to McGowan, Scott then introduced a motion which, if passed, would have effectively prevented a discussion of the merits of all the candidates. McGowan spoke against this and only nine men voted with the Bishop. McGowan claimed that Scott, in a fit of rage, 'left the meeting saying, that it was not the first time I had led the Catholics astray…and that he was my superior both as a scholar and a gentleman, and bawling out to those who would support Oswald, to follow him, which, about the same number that voted with him, did'. The meeting continued and the electors resolved to give their first vote to Douglas and their second to Sandford, 'provided, that from the state of the poll at 12 o'clock the next day they had reason to believe they could effect his return; and if not, to give their second votes to whatever reformer was the next highest on the poll'.

The Glasgow election did not, of course, result in victory for either Douglas or Sandford. Oswald and Ewing were returned, much to the chagrin of reformers. McGowan described the latter as 'a Tory, the abettor of the Wellington and Castlereagh Administrations, and consequently the abettor of every act of oppression and spoilation of which that vile faction had been guilty'. In his letter to the *Glasgow Evening Post*, McGowan stressed that only ten or twelve Catholic electors (including Scott) voted for Ewing and argued that the Glasgow Catholics should not be condemned because of the actions of men who were not representative of them:

I know that the poor Catholics who work in public factories, have been tortured by their fellow workers since the election on the supposition that the whole of the Catholic Electors voted for the Lord Provost, even after having promised to support Sandford and Douglas; but this I have shown was not the case, and I can assure the public that the Catholics generally, whether electors or non-electors, detest as thoroughly the conduct of the Bishop in the disposal of his votes, as the most determined Reformer can possible do. Though the Bishop has done many things during his residence in Glasgow opposed to the wishes of his people, I make bold to say that none of them nor all of them put together, have arrayed so fiercely or fixedly their feelings against him as his having voted for the Tory candidate at the election…I feel convinced that there is not a Catholic in Glasgow, of whatever situation in life, except the Bishop himself, who is a Tory in politics. They all to a man, not even excepting the few who voted with his Lordship, approve of the glorious efforts of the Irish Catholics, and other Reformers, to secure the independence of their country; and I can assure you that all the misused authority of his Lordship has not been sufficient to suppress their love of general liberty, and the detestation of tyranny and oppression upon whomsoever it may be practised. In vain has he attempted to frighten them with the horrors of Revolution and the spread of infidelity, which he thinks are synonymous with Reform.

McGowan was adamant that no Catholic clergyman had the right to interfere in the political activities of his flock. McGowan's radicalism, however, did not extend to matters spiritual: 'Upon the ground of politics, I or any other individual are the Bishop's equal, and upon the score of religious belief, I am as orthodox, and hope in God shall ever be, as those who wear mitres.' In his next letter to the *Glasgow Evening Post* McGowan expressed his hope that Catholics in Glasgow would reject any further attempts by their clergy to influence or dictate to them on political issues:

Let it be their duty to be able to draw a line of distinction between religious and political matters, and act accordingly; and take that part in the political occurrences of the day which prudence directs, and they will do more to remove the prejudice which has unfortunately long existed against them — but is now happily on the decline — than it is possible for any contrary course of conduct to accomplish.
  …these…sentiments…are better calculated to make us respected and esteemed by those who differ from us in religion, than the slavish and disgraceful policy of those who would give up their political or civil rights, to the assumed authority of any ecclesiastic, however high his dignity.[68]

The vast majority of the city's Catholic electors had, of course, already adopted such a stance when they disregarded Scott's 'advice' and voted for reform candidates in December 1832.[69]

The election controversy of 1832 was discussed briefly by Handley.[70] He suggested that William McGowan opposed Scott over the candidature of Oswald at the meeting of electors in December 1832 'less possibly from conviction of the merits of the Radical candidates than from an urge to thwart his parish priest'.[71] This is most unfair. The previous chapter demonstrated that McGowan was a committed reformer whose principled stand over the Glasgow Catholic Association led to his dismissal from his teaching post in one of the city's Catholic schools. After the general election of 1832 McGowan was involved in reform activities in Glasgow for more than a decade. He spoke at meetings in 1833 which protested against the Irish Coercion Bill[72] and the following year was one of the principal speakers at a meeting on the issue of Repeal of Union.[73] In 1835 McGowan, who appears to have been involved in the Glasgow Political Union,[74] was a member of the committee which organised O'Connell's visit to the city.[75] A year later he was active during the by-election campaign.[76] McGowan, who was employed as a teacher throughout the 1830s (though it is not known by whom), also participated in agitations concerning the working classes. For example, in January 1837 he addressed the great meeting of Glasgow operatives held to repudiate the Tory sentiments expressed in an address to Robert Peel by the Glasgow Operative Conservative Society.[77] The following October he made a speech on the utility of trade unions at a public meeting in the city which condemned the authorities for their treatment of the Committee of the Cotton Spinners Association.[78] The next two chapters will show that McGowan was involved in both Chartism and Repeal. His commitment to reform cannot be questioned.

III

It is evident that there was an Irish presence in the reform agitations in the west of Scotland between 1830 and 1837. The extent and nature of this involvement must now be examined. With regard to the first issue, the surviving evidence unfortunately permits a discussion of only the Catholic Irish in the region. In March 1833 Bishop Scott, perhaps with the election dispute and the letters of McGowan particularly prominent in his thoughts, wrote that the Irish Catholics in the west of Scotland

> have naturally keen dispositions and passions, and since the famous reform bill was mooted, they have all become keen politicians, and without proper management, are in danger of walking in the footsteps of the French Infidels in the first French Revolution of which I had the misfortune of being a witness.[79]

It is, of course, improbable that every Irish Catholic was an ardent reformer. For example, impoverished immigrants who had recently arrived in the region undoubtedly had more pressing interests and needs than campaigns for political reform. Nevertheless, the evidence presented in the previous sections, together with Scott's statement, suggests that Irish Catholic participation in the reform agitations was not confined to an insignificant minority. Furthermore, this involvement was large enough to be noted by Scottish reformers, as the following section will demonstrate.

It has been shown that Handley acknowledged that there was an Irish presence in the campaign in Scotland for the Reform. He, however, argued that the Irish were not really part of the reform movement of the time and that their participation was not of any great significance. After commenting upon the Irish in the reform processions Handley stated that 'apart from this sympathetic adherence in his adopted country to a movement that was also to the interest of Ireland he [the Irish immigrant] had not at that time identified himself, as he later came to do, with the political life of Scotland'.[80] The reason for this was that:

> The fight for Catholic Emancipation and the agitation for the repeal of the Union were more important to those who still regarded themselves as exiles than the grievances of their neighbours; and it was not until a generation of Irish, born in Scotland, had grown up to manhood that identification with the political aims of their co-workers — as, for example, during the Chartist movement of the 'forties — became a normal line of action.[81]

It will be assumed that Handley was referring to the Catholic Irish immigrants as the campaigns in Scotland for Emancipation and Repeal were almost exclusively their preserve.

The Catholic Irish in the west of Scotland were undoubtedly deeply interested in issues concerning Ireland, the Catholic Church and its adherents. In 1829 Andrew Scott informed Bishop Paterson that 'the Paddies' in the region were 'poor, ignorant people, enthusiastically attached to every thing that bears the name of Irish'.[82] Fifteen years later he told the Poor Law Inquiry that the Irish in the west 'were very national in their ideas and sentiments — rather too much so in some cases'.[83] The previous chapter showed the support given by the Irish in and around Glasgow to O'Connell's campaign for Catholic Emancipation. In the 1830s their interest in Irish issues was evident. For example, in Glasgow during the election campaign in December 1832 James Douglas, one of the candidates, addressed a large meeting of Catholic electors. His speech was concerned almost exclusively with Irish subjects:

He gave a clear and distinct explanation of the evils of Ireland inflicted by a dominant absentee church receiving immense revenue without performing any duty. He exposed the iniquity of the tithe system...He also spoke in favour of poor laws to Ireland...He was loudly cheered throughout, and the audience, which was composed almost solely of electors, separated in the highest degree satisfied.[84]

In March 1834 there was a crowded public meeting in the city, attended chiefly by Irishmen, on the subject of the repeal of the legislative union between Great Britain and Ireland; resolutions in favour of the measure were passed.[85] Later chapters will discuss the Repeal movement in the west of Scotland during the 1840s.

It is clear, therefore, that the Catholic Irish in the region were deeply interested in Irish and Catholic issues. This is perfectly understandable and should not be the subject of criticism from historians, whether direct or implied. These men and women were, after all, of Irish birth or extraction and had friends or relatives in the old country. It was only natural, therefore, that they became involved in campaigns or pressure groups concerning Ireland. Moreover, many believed that reforms or political change (such as Repeal) would lead to peace and prosperity in Ireland which would then end the need for emigration and enable them to return home.[86] Irish Catholic support for Catholic Emancipation requires no explanation.

However, Handley's argument that the Irish in the reform agitations in the west of Scotland during the 1830s were interested mainly in Irish issues and did not share 'the grievances of their neighbours' and identify with their political aims cannot be accepted for a number of reasons. Handley did not produce any evidence to support this conclusion. His assertion that the Irish had interests and aims which were separate from those of Scottish workers was influenced perhaps by his mistaken belief that Irish workers marched as separate bodies in the reform processions. Moreover, Handley's claim that 'it was not until a generation of Irish, born in Scotland, had grown up to manhood that identification with the political aims of their co-workers...became a normal line of action' is rather strange. He stated that it was not until the late 1840s that this occurred. It is clear, however, that by the early 1830s 'a generation of Irish, born in Scotland', had grown up to manhood. For example, there are numerous references in the *Report on the State of the Irish Poor in Great Britain*, compiled in 1834, to the children of Irish immigrants, born and raised in the west of Scotland.[87]

This is not to argue, however, that it was solely the Catholic Irish *born* in Scotland who identified with the political aims of Scottish workers; Handley's assertion that Irish immigrants who were involved in the reform demonstrations did not share the grievances and aims of the native reformers, and were interested mainly in Irish issues, is unconvincing. Scottish workers campaigned for the Reform Bills in the belief that if they helped to gain the franchise for the middle class that group would show its gratitude by electing men who would pass legislation to help the working class, and who would eventually extend the right to vote to all adult males. Scottish workers also believed that the franchise was their indisputable right.[88] After the Reform Acts were passed the Glasgow Trades campaigned for household suffrage, triennial parliaments and vote by ballot.[89] It soon became apparent, however, that the Reformed Parliament and most of the newly enfranchised middle class were not going to support these demands and by the end of 1836 the Trades were advocating universal suffrage, annual parliaments and the ballot.[90] Within two years they were supporting the Charter.[91] In the agitations of the 1830s and 1840s Scottish working class participants believed that political reform would result in a Parliament which would introduce legislation to improve their social and economic condition.[92] It would be foolish to suggest that Catholic Irish immigrants — as opposed to those born in Scotland of Irish parents — who marched in the reform processions were not interested in obtaining political rights, and were not interested in the benefits which political reform was expected to produce for the working classes. Catholic Irish immigrants were not isolated from the social and economic pressures of the time. Indeed, these workers, particularly those at the lower end of the economic scale, would have known them all too well.

It is, nevertheless, difficult to provide conclusive documentary proof that Irish participants in the reform agitations of 1830–37 shared the same grievances and political aims as Scottish workers. The newspaper reports of the various reform demonstrations and processions of the period, from where the evidence of Irish involvement is obtained, list or note the groups of workers which participated, but give no information on the aims and organisation of these bodies or on the background of their members. This, of course, makes the task of establishing why Irish workers were interested in reform extremely difficult. Where the press is of use, however, is in its reports of the activities of leading reformers, including the three Irishmen Edward Collins, Patrick McGowan and James Burn. By examining these accounts some indication of their political aims can be established, although it must be emphasised that, as prominent reformers, they might not have been typical of the average Irish participant during this period of political agitation.

The speeches of Collins and McGowan reveal that they had the same concerns and aims as native reformers. In his letter to the Paisley Reform Society Collins argued: 'There should be a reduction of taxes on all the necessaries of life, as their oppressive weight is so felt by the lower classes in society, as to injure the growth of a spirit of industry among the poor, and frequently to deprive them of the very necessaries of life.'[93] It has already been noted that at a public meeting in Paisley in November 1831 Collins urged the audience to become involved in the reform agitation in order to improve their conditions. Patrick McGowan shared this view. His speech from the hustings at the famous 'Black Flag' demonstration on Glasgow Green in May 1832 is worth quoting in full as it reveals the aims of one important Irish Catholic radical. McGowan seconded a resolution

and said that although the meeting viewed with surprise and indignation, the artifices of the House of Lords in attempting to dupe the people, the recent resolution of the Peers, instead of disorganising the country, had tended rather to unite more firmly all classes of society in their exertions for Reform. He believed he delivered the sentiments of 100,000 well organised operatives in this part of the country, when he stated, that they were now determined to support the upper and middle classes, in recovering their just rights and privileges. He could not for a moment suppose that the operatives would disgrace themselves by committing a single act of violence or personal insult even to their enemies, who only merited their sovereign contempt — for, although Reform had been in danger, yet that measure was not lost, and present proceedings may perhaps produce a still better measure, for no anti-reforming party will be able to divert them in their purpose with which they set out 12 months ago. The extension of the elective franchise was the only way to raise the operatives from their present degraded political condition. It was to low wages, high rates of provisions, and to political misrule that they attributed all their sufferings, and for the removal of which, every class in society must apply all their strength, and be determined in obtaining their object. Nor had the wavering of his Majesty in the present crisis, tended to shake their loyalty in the slightest degree, for they were still ready to rally around, and even spill their best blood in defending the Throne and the Constitution. But we venture to tell the King, in firm and plain language, that although we stand by in his attitude, yet we will not give up one iota of the Reform Bill. The operatives were ready to co-operate with the advocates of good order in all their exertions, which was the only sure way of certain success in obtaining the Bill, the whole, and nothing but the Bill. It is only in the late Ministry that they would place their utmost confidence, — for, suppose it were possible that another Ministry, of an opposite description, were formed, and should even offer ten Members for Glasgow, he was certain the party would be rejected with scorn. Suffice to say, on this subject, that they were determined to support the late Ministry, — for they had been found to be the true, tried and sincere friends of the country. The operatives were too intelligent to be diverted by any political scheme from the station which they had already assumed, and would speedily demonstrate that they were the true and only source of all power in the country; while those who carried on the system which had now ruined the country, would be held forth as the real, insincere advisers of the King. All that was now necessary was to be firm and temperate in their resolutions, — the only method by which they could hope to gain success. He concluded with again seconding the resolution, which was then put by the Chairman, and carried amid tremendous acclamations.[94]

It is clear from this speech that McGowan spoke as a representative of the class to which he belonged and not as an Irishman interested only in Irish issues. Moreover, as stated in chapter one, McGowan does not appear to have been involved in any campaigns concerning 'Irish' or 'Catholic' issues during this decade.

Although James Burn was the most politically active of the three Irish reformers little is known about his political aims in this period. Reports of his speeches give no indication why he advocated political change. It is probable, however, that he participated for the same reasons as McGowan and Collins as he too did not mention Irish issues. Indeed, although Burn was born in Ireland of Irish parents it is not clear, even from his autobiography, whether he in fact considered himself to be an Irishman. He left Ireland as an infant and apart from two very short spells in that country before he was twenty years of age he lived in various places in England and Scotland.[95] In his memoir Burn stated that Ireland, for the sake of her prosperity, should be independent but it is not clear whether he wrote this as an Irishman or as a concerned radical.[96] Burn's religion is not known. His natural father, who deserted his mother when Burn was an infant, had a strong hatred of Catholicism which 'like that of many of his countrymen, constituted nearly all the religion he possessed'.[97] The term 'his countrymen' perhaps indicates that Burn did not consider himself to be an Irishman. Burn's step-father, whom he regarded as his true father, was a strict Roman Catholic who had 'strong feelings of religious prejudice'.[98] Burn did not take sides and in fact described sectarian strife as being 'a natural curse to Ireland' as her people wasted their time on party feuds instead of working towards the economic and social improvement of their country.[99] It is therefore not clear whether Burn was a Protestant or a Catholic, or whether he regarded himself as an Irishman and was involved in the reform agitations mainly out of a concern for the country of his birth. However, the fact that he was involved in the campaign for the Reform Bill as the delegate for his trade suggests that he participated as a hatter and a member of his class rather than as an Irishman interested in Irish issues.

One must consider, however, whether the class concerns of trade unionists such as Patrick McGowan were shared by other Irish Catholic workers involved in the reform agitations. Press reports do not shed any light on this issue. There is, however, one important piece of evidence which demonstrates that some of these Irish Catholics, while concerned about the state of Ireland, also had the same grievances as Scottish working class reformers and identified with their political aims — the Address of the Irish labourers of Glasgow to the Earl of Durham in October 1834. The document is in the archives of the University of Edinburgh:

To the right Honourable Earl Durham

My Lord,

We, the Irish labourers, residing in Glasgow and vicinity, beg leave to approach your lordship with our congratulations upon this auspicious occasion.

We congratulate you upon the proud and enviable distinction to which your enlightened views and manly, straightforward conduct, so justly entitle you. We earnestly hope, that your statesman-like views, as to the administration of public affairs, will be adopted by his majesty's ministry, and speedily carried into effect for the amelioration of the country. We sincerely trust, that those principles of Reform, to which you lent your efficient aid, will, under your auspices be so extended, that we, who at present, have little influence in the choice of those who make the laws by which we are governed, may be invested with that important privilege. We wish to see the franchise extended and the duration of Parliaments shortened, in order that the operative classes who form the strength and sinews of the Nation, may have their interests attended to, and by a Reduction of taxation, be enabled to give their children that education and information, which are necessary to make them good and useful members of society, and faithful and loyal subjects, and to procure for themselves that moral, political and scientific instruction which the present enlightened era, renders, in a great measure, necessary.

As Irishmen, ardently attached to the interests of our native country, we tender you our most unfeigned and heartfelt gratitude, for the manly and magnanimous opposition you made to that monstrous and unconstitutional measure, the Irish *Coercion Bill*. Such disinterested and manly conduct, inspires a hope, that you will exercise your talents, and high influence, in procuring for that misgoverned, but beautiful and fertile country, those measures of amelioration and improvement, which may be recommended as necessary by her own patriotic Representatives, with Mr O'Connell at their head, who best know the wants and interests of her inhabitants.

We cannot conceal the fact, that the by-past conduct of the British Government towards Ireland, has strongly impressed us with the conviction, that nothing short of a Domestic parliament can raise that unhappy country, from the wretchedness and misery into which misgovernment has plunged her.

We shall, nevertheless, feel happy at seeing the Repeal of the Legislative union between Great Britain and Ireland, rendered unnecessary, by the wisdom and justice of British legislation.

   In conclusion, My Lord, allow us to thank you for your condescension, and to express our earnest hope and desire, that you may enjoy long life and good health, to enable you to promote the interests of our common country which we sincerely believe you are anxious to do.[100]

Similar opinions were expressed in the address to Durham from the Irishmen of Edinburgh.[101]

It has been argued that most of the Irish labourers who marched in the reform processions in Glasgow were Roman Catholics. It is probable that Catholic Irishmen in other occupations, in Glasgow and elsewhere in the west of Scotland, held the same political views as those expressed in the address of the Irish labourers. This address, therefore, supports the argument that most Catholic Irish workers who participated in the reform agitations of the period were not interested solely in Irish issues and were not merely expressing a 'sympathetic adherence in [their] adopted country to a movement which was also to the interest of Ireland'.[102] These Irishmen certainly hoped that reform would improve the condition of Ireland; but they, like Scottish workers, believed that political change would lead to an improvement in their social and economic condition.[103]

   It is more difficult to establish the political aims and priorities of the group of Irish Catholic electors in Glasgow. It has been noted that prior to the general election of December 1832 one of the reform candidates addressed a meeting of the city's Catholic electors and that most of his speech was concerned with the problems facing Ireland. This, and the fact that these men organised themselves into a separate group for the election, may be interpreted as evidence that their political aims and concerns were distinct from those of their Scottish counterparts. It is unlikely, however, that the Irish Catholic electors in Glasgow, the vast majority of whom voted for reform candidates in 1832, were interested solely or even mainly in Irish and Catholic issues. Most of them were small businessmen or professionals and as such would have taken a strong interest in the state of the country. For example, the economic and social condition of the working classes had an effect on their livelihoods. It is likely that these electors in 1832 decided to act as a separate group in order to demonstrate to the candidates that if they wanted the Catholic Irish vote they would have to be suitably sympathetic both to reform principles and to Catholic and Irish issues. At the election James Douglas and Daniel Sandford appear to have had the necessary credentials for Irish Catholic support.

IV

The support given by the Irish to the political agitations of 1830–37 was welcomed by Scottish reformers. That the Irish were permitted to march in the reform processions in the west of Scotland, whether as groups of labourers or in other bodies according to their trades or occupations, illustrates this. This, however, should come as no surprise: radical ideology was not hostile to the Irish or to Catholics, and Irishmen, both Protestant and Catholic, had been involved in earlier radical agitations with Scottish workers, as has already been shown.[104] Moreover, there is evidence which demonstrates that native reformers were particularly pleased with the participation of the Catholic Irish. For example, at the beginning of August 1832 the *Glasgow Free Press* published a letter from John McAdam, a leading member of the Glasgow Trades Committee. It was addressed to the 'Franchised and Unenfranchised Reformers' of Glasgow and its neighbourhood. McAdam wrote the letter in his capacity as secretary of the Central Committee of the City and Suburbs Political Union and in it he announced that organisation's recommendations on who to vote for at the forthcoming election. Part of the letter stated:

> We presume not to dictate to our fellow-citizens, neither do we wish to control their choice in the coming election; but when the suburbs and united districts, enfranchised and unenfranchised, are amalgamating their interests into one common focus; when the Catholic and Protestant electors of oppressed and long-suffering Ireland, in this city, burying their religious prejudices, are rallying around the sacred banner of liberty…we feel confident our endeavours to bring all classes of Reformers to act in unity will not be mistaken for conceited presumption or electioneering intrigue.[105]

Furthermore, lectures by Church of Scotland ministers on Catholicism were regarded by reformers as attempts to stir up anti-Catholic feeling in the hope that divisions in their movement would result.[106] For example, a short time before the visit of Daniel O'Connell to Glasgow in 1835, two Protestant ministers, O'Sullivan and McGhee, arrived in the city and began lecturing against Catholics and Catholicism.[107] The Glasgow reformers believed that this was not a coincidence. The city's Political Union, to which O'Connell had been elected an honorary member and councillor the previous year,[108] declared the following in its address to 'the Liberator' in September 1835:

> The vast majority of us — like our brave ancestors — are Presbyterians; but, nevertheless, we cordially stretch out the right hand of fellowship to our Catholic countrymen. Attempts, we know, are at this moment making, in this city, as elsewhere, to throw the apple of discord among us; but we will not be

the dupes of deep-laid Tory machinations, under the guise of Religion. Sir, we revere the Temple of Liberty on the wide span of the Earth; — we know that the arch of Heaven is its dome: wherefore our desire is, that the whole human race should be advanced higher and higher in the scale of being, and that *equal rights* and permanent happiness should be diffused among all.[109]

In Greenock the following month it was announced that O'Sullivan was to be present at a meeting in a local church on the Roman Catholic religion. The reformers of the town resolved to prevent this. After appealing unsuccessfully to the magistrates to withdraw their approval for the use of the church, the reformers called a public meeting to consider their next move. Here they decided to attend the meeting on the Catholic faith and elect one of their own as chairman, as the advert which announced the forthcoming event stated that no one would be allowed to speak at it without the permission of its chairman. In this way O'Sullivan would be prevented from participating. The Greenock reformers — or, as the *Scottish Guardian* described them, the 'Radicals and Papists' — obtained a large number of forged tickets and planned to arrive early and pack the meeting. The town's magistrates learned of this on the morning of the event and rescheduled it for the following day at a different church.[110] In December 1835 the *Reformers' Gazette* recalled O'Sullivan's activities during his time in Scotland and summed up what most radicals felt about his presence. The journal stated that from the very beginning it had a

notion that he was a *Reverend* demagogue, — a wolf in sheep's clothing, — a man *hired* and sent *hither* by the chief Tories, for the express purpose of exciting the religious passions or prejudices of the community, — of pitting Catholic against Protestant, and Protestant against Catholic, in the hope that thereby the bond of *civil* and political union, which has of late so happily existed between them, would be severed...[111]

One of the heroes, if not the hero, of the reform movement in Scotland at this time was Daniel O'Connell. Scottish reformers greatly admired his Catholic Association and its successful campaign for Catholic Emancipation; indeed, during the agitation for the Reform Bills both middle and working class activists in Glasgow believed that they had to model their own organisations and strategies on those which had worked so well for O'Connell and the Catholics in the previous decade.[112] Throughout the period 1830–36 O'Connell was revered by Scottish reformers because of his support for political reform. For example, in September 1831 the Glasgow Trades sent their petition for parliamentary reform to Joseph Dixon, the Member of Parliament for the Glasgow

District of Burghs, for presentation to the House of Commons. Dixon, however, returned the petition, stating that he would not present it 'owing to the language of it being disrespectful to the House'. He added that he would oblige the Trades if the petition was redrafted. A meeting of delegates from the Trades decided to reject this offer; instead it sent the petition unaltered to O'Connell, who was informed that he had been chosen to present it as a result of his 'undeviating perseverance in the people's cause…'.[113] The following spring the Church of Scotland establishment in Glasgow raised a petition to Parliament against the annual government grant to Maynooth College, a Catholic seminary in Ireland.[114] The *Loyal Reformers' Gazette* organised a counter-petition, the intention of which was to persuade the House of Commons to disregard 'the flimsy jesuitical statements of the Glasgow Maynooth Petitioners' and instead 'encourage Religious Toleration among all classes of his Majesty's subjects'.[115] The journal sent its petition, which was signed by around thirteen thousand people, to O'Connell as he was 'the best man in the house for thrashing bigots'.[116] He duly presented it to Parliament.[117] According to *the Loyal Reformers' Gazette*, the Church of Scotland petition obtained only sixteen hundred signatures.[118]

When O'Connell decided to visit Scotland in September 1835 his opponents were convinced that he would not be made welcome. For example, the Tory and Orange *Glasgow Courier* stated the following:

> We make no surmise as to how Edinburgh may receive him; but we give him this timely warning, that in this Protestant and Covenanting City, it may be dangerous for any bloodthirsty Papist and political agitator, like him, to approach it nearer than Camlachie or Tollcross. We trust this hint will be sufficient, both to the big beggarman and his paltry gang here and hereabouts; for we can assure both that the ancient spirit of the land is not yet dead, nor will any insult upon its religious feelings be tamely submitted to.[119]

Moreover, it would appear that efforts were made to rouse 'Protestant and Covenanting' Glasgow. The anti-Catholic lectures given by O'Sullivan and McGhee around this time were regarded by reformers as an attempt not only to turn the city's Protestants against the Catholics but also to incite opposition to O'Connell's visit.[120] The *Reformers' Gazette* reported that during the two weeks prior to O'Connell's arrival in Glasgow all the Church of Scotland ministers in the city attacked him from their pulpits, and some even threatened 'everlasting wo in the world to come, against all those who took part in the O'Connell Demonstration!!!'.[121]

Despite such hostility, O'Connell's visit to Scotland was a tremendous success.[122] In Glasgow the demonstration in his honour was reminiscent of those which occurred during the Reform Bill agitation and the visit of the Earl of Durham. The multitude which gathered on Glasgow Green to hear him speak was estimated by some at 100,000 strong and by others at 200,000. At this event O'Connell received an address from the Glasgow Trades which included the following sentiments:

> In you, Sir, emphatically the liberator of long misgoverned Ireland, and among the best and boldest of the British Senate, the working men of Glasgow have found a man worthy of their highest regard, and feel themselves honoured in having an opportunity of exchanging sentiments with him, on the great organic changes of national government now in progress, and in which they feel their own peculiar interests, as well as the future happiness of the whole human race, are deeply and irretrievably involved.

That evening the Trades held a soirée for O'Connell in the city's Bazaar and the following day he attended a banquet in his honour in the Town Hall. Present at the latter event were notable middle class reformers such as C.J. Tennant, Peter McKenzie, William Dixon, Sir John Maxwell, James Turner, William Weir and two Scottish Members of Parliament, A.G. Speirs and Robert Wallace. Both occasions were sell-outs.[123]

The address of the Glasgow Trades to O'Connell described him as 'the liberator of long misgoverned Ireland' and expressed a wish for that country's 'political regeneration'. These sentiments were included not simply out of courtesy towards O'Connell; concern for the condition of Ireland had been part of the programme of Scottish reformers since the beginning of the Reform Bill agitation, if not before.[124] They had a genuine conviction that Ireland was governed badly and unjustly, and that her people suffered as a result. Moreover, they believed that the situation in Ireland also affected, in many ways, the people of Scotland. For example, in June 1831 an article entitled 'Famine in Ireland', published in a pamphlet successor to the *Herald to the Trades' Advocate*, stated:

> It is melancholy to think that the 'Gem of the ocean', possessing a soil and climate superior to Britain, should be fertile only in men and massacre. The derangement of its social institutions, and the consequent ignorance and poverty of its people, have retarded the cultivation of that fruitful island, and rendered the misery of its population a never-ending theme of declamation. Were all this misery and its moral effects confined to Ireland, the picture would be dreadful enough; but when, like a devastating flood, her population and her poverty are poured out upon other countries, and thereby blight the rising hopes of a people further advanced in the march of improvement, crush their encreasing comforts, and reduce them to the same miserable level, the effects become more terribly appalling, and we perceive that ignorance and poverty,

like a hell-born pestilence, infect and destroy in their baneful and overwhelming course all that is beautiful and good.

That emigration from Ireland has been hitherto encouraged by our manufacturers, farmers and landholders, for the purpose of reducing the value of labour, none can deny — and that steam-boat traders are now giving every facility to passengers is equally certain; but if these classes who possess property do not now *see*, they will be speedily enabled to *feel* the effects of their cruel and blind selfish policy in saddling themselves not only with the subsistence of their own destitute, but the innumerable cast-off hives of another nation.

These reflections may sound harsh, but they are not applicable to the poor men themselves, whose influx in such numbers at present have called them forth. However ignorant they are in mass, there are many bright exceptions, and it must be confessed, that the warm-hearted, though rash-handed, sons of old Ireland possess qualities of heart, susceptibilities of head, and strength of limb sufficient, if properly cultivated, to render them equal, if not superior, to any people in Europe; but, in their present condition they are not fit associates for the generality of workmen in this country, and the education and improvement of our children would be retarded, and their language and manners vitiated, by being in daily contact with the rude and riotous offspring of the red-hot Hibernians.

Why should all these evils continue to afflict us? Why should the miseries of Ireland be forever a theme of declamation, and never call forth a political remedy? Why should a soil capable of yielding a hundred-fold its present amount of human subsistence be left almost a barren wilderness? Dare we point out — not the causes, for they are many and complicated — but a direct plan of immediate relief? Yes! Apply the revenues of the Church to the education of all the poor, and the support of all the destitute, as far as such revenues can reach, and if more is required, spread a strong and healthy race of labourers over the waste lands. These steps taken, and in less than twenty years every inhabitant of the 'Emerald Isle' will be sitting (if not under his own vine and fig tree) at least over his own bit of potatoe plot, to his heart's content, hale, happy, and hospitable.

NB. A memorial from a number of Operatives, requesting the Lord Provost and magistrates to call a public meeting, to consider the propriety of addressing the legislature in behalf of the Irish poor, has been presented.[125]

English working class radicals at this time were equally concerned about the influx of poverty-stricken immigrants and they too 'refused to fan any anti-Irish feeling or to raise again the old cry of "No Popery" '; instead, like their Scottish counterparts, they advocated a programme of reform for Ireland which would provide employment for her people and thus make emigration unnecessary.[126]

Some groups of English workers, such as the National Union of the Working Classes, even advocated repeal of the legislative union between

Great Britain and Ireland as the solution to the latter country's problems.[127] Scottish workers' organisations were not as radical as this in their proposals for Ireland in these years. There was no mention of Repeal in the 1831 'Famine in Ireland' article, nor was there in the address of the Glasgow Trades to O'Connell four years later. Some Scottish reformers, however, were in favour of a parliament for Ireland. For example, at the public meeting in March 1834 in Glasgow on the subject of Repeal one of the principal speakers was Abram Duncan, a leading figure on the city's Trades Committee. Duncan, who later became a prominent figure in the Scottish Chartist movement, discussed the effects of absentee landlordism in Ireland and the 'exorbitant rents' the 'miserable tenants' had to pay. He argued that English Members of Parliament were 'necessarily ignorant' of Irish affairs and therefore an Irish Parliament, with its members elected by the Irish people, had to be established to deal with domestic issues. Moreover:

> Independent of the justice of the demand of the Irish for a Repeal of the Union, for our own interest we were bound to assist them in their struggle. Had Ireland a parliament of her own, that would check absenteeism, and provide employment for her people; it would prevent their emigration into this country, and the consequent reduction of wages, for it was the overstocking of the labour market with hands that reduced the workman's wages; they were therefore, for their own interest, bound to aid the Irish nation in this great struggle. It is impossible that Scotland can be freed from the thousands of emigrants who are obliged to seek employment in this country, unless employment be provided for them at home. They were bound to rise simultaneously, and co-operate with Ireland in the attainment of their object. If Ireland had Repeal, and the people employment, there would be no need for such an army in that country to keep the people in subjection. Let then...that unnatural union between England and Ireland cease, and let equal laws and equal justice take place of the red coat and the bayonet, and grant to Ireland a Parliament of her own, which would supply the wants and wishes of her people, and remove the evils complained of.

Another Scottish working class reformer at this meeting who advocated Repeal was David Todd, who also demanded the abolition of tithes in Ireland.[128]

As noted in the previous section, this meeting, which was attended mainly by Irishmen, passed resolutions calling for Repeal. There were, however, a few dissentient voices that evening, one of which belonged to Peter McKenzie. He accepted that Ireland 'had been ruled by tyrants and despots with a rod of iron' and expressed a desire 'to see a complete and speedy reformation, or eradication, of the crimes, wrongs, and abuses of the Irish Church' and also the separation of the Church and State in Ireland.

But he maintained that Repeal would lead to separation and that this would be disastrous for both Ireland and Great Britain. Instead, McKenzie hoped 'to see an harmonious and flourishing union between these kingdoms, whereby the strength, honour, and prosperity of Great Britain will be maintained and promoted'.[129] This was not a popular point of view. According to the *Glasgow Evening Post*, 'These sentiments were far from giving satisfaction to the meeting, and the hissing, the hooting and the yelling were tremendous'.[130] In his *Reformers' Gazette* McKenzie protested that the Irishmen involved in the public meeting had no right to raise in Glasgow the issue of Repeal and argued that if they persisted with the agitation they would succeed only in 'exciting animosity and bad blood' between the people of Scotland and Ireland. The wrongs of Ireland, McKenzie insisted, should be redressed at Westminster. He also claimed that there were not 'three dozen of right-thinking Scotsmen' who would support a campaign for Repeal of Union.[131] It is, of course, impossible to establish the extent of such support, but it is clear that, whether pro-Union or pro-Repeal, Scottish reformers were greatly concerned about Ireland and her people. They were convinced that Ireland was misgoverned and that the Irish people suffered greatly as a result; they also believed the condition of Ireland had direct effects on the well-being of Scotland and the Scottish people.

This dual concern had also been evident the previous year when the Whig Administration introduced into Parliament an extremely severe Coercion Bill for Ireland. This sought to greatly restrict the activities and liberties of the Irish people, particularly in designated 'Disturbed Districts'.[132] Reformers in Scotland and England were outraged at the Bill. They regarded it as a Draconian measure which was totally unnecessary; they also feared that the Government could attempt to introduce similar legislation for the British mainland.[133] Meetings which protested against the Bill took place in Glasgow, Paisley, Edinburgh, Greenock, Dunfermline, Dundee, Kilmarnock, Irvine, Leslie, Kilbirnie and in other towns throughout Scotland.[134] On 27 February the Glasgow Political Union resolved to petition Parliament to 'throw out this infamous and tyrannical bill'. At this meeting Peter McKenzie voiced the fears of reformers:

> The liberty of the subject in every district of Ireland was proposed to be left at the mercy of three military officers; and from the well known bias of these scions of the Aristocracy, it might easily be conceived how every petty advantage would be improved to crush the slightest manifestation of public feeling. They might well tremble for the liberties of Scotland if such a flagrant subversion of the Constitution was permitted in Ireland.[135]

Two days later a great public meeting on the Bill was held in the city. It was addressed by several of Glasgow's leading reformers, including Daniel Sandford, David Walker, Abe Duncan, James Turner and Matthew Cullen.[136] Also present was Daniel McAulay, the powerloom tenter who was chairman of the Glasgow Trades Committee during the campaign for the Reform Bills. He proposed one of the resolutions and during his speech argued that Scotland should support Ireland 'equally as the friend of civil liberty — of religious liberty and of economy'.[137] McAulay concluded by stating that

> he was confident the Presbyterians of Scotland, and the Dissenters of England, would be the first to rise up for the redemption of Ireland from clerical tyranny and political degradation. As descendants of Knox, Cargill and the other Scottish Reformers, it became them to step forward and relieve the Irish Catholics; and as a parsimonious people, it was their duty as Scotchmen, to oppose a tax intended to keep up a system, which may hereafter be extended to Scotland, and be our ruin.[138]

The meeting drew up a petition to Parliament which stated 'that the measure intended to suppress the disturbances in Ireland, prior to any act being passed to remove the enormous grievances which have so long afflicted that ill-governed country, is not only uncalled for, but is a direct inroad upon the liberties of the British Empire…'.[139] Despite such opposition the Bill became law.

V

It is evident that there was an Irish presence in the reform agitations in the west of Scotland between 1830 and 1837. This involvement was not confined to an insignificant minority, but was such as to seriously alarm Bishop Andrew Scott and also be noted and welcomed by native reformers. The evidence presented in this chapter of Irish participation in political activities almost certainly underestimates the full extent of their involvement. Irish workers do not appear to have marched in the reform processions as separate groups with demands separate from those of Scottish workers; they participated in these demonstrations as members of their own particular trade or occupation. Members of the Catholic Irish business and professional group in Glasgow formed a distinct body during the 1832 election campaign, but it is probable that they did this in an attempt to persuade those standing for Parliament to be in favour of reforms for

Ireland. The Catholic Irish who were involved in the agitations had an understandable concern for issues relating to their religion and to Ireland, but this was not the sole reason they supported demands for political change. They believed, as did their Scottish counterparts, that reform would lead to an improvement in their social and economic condition.

Notes

1. James Handley, *The Irish in Scotland 1798–1845* (2nd edition, Cork, 1945), p.145.

2. *Ibid*, p.315.

3. *Ibid*; *Scotsman*, 22 December 1832.

4. John F. McCaffrey, 'Irish Immigrants and Radical Movements in the West of Scotland in the Early Nineteenth Century', *Innes Review*, XXXIX (1988), p.46; *The Journal of Henry Cockburn 1831–1854, Volume 1* (Edinburgh, 1874), p.34.

5. For example, Montgomery and Leitch, in their theses on radicalism in Glasgow and Paisley respectively between 1830 and 1848, did not provide any evidence of Irish participation in the political agitations of that period. Fiona Ann Montgomery, Glasgow Radicalism 1830–1848, Ph.D., University of Glasgow (1974); Archibald Leitch, Radicalism in Paisley, 1830–1848: and its economic, political, cultural background, M.Litt, University of Glasgow (1993). For the reform agitations of the period see also Alexander Wilson, *The Chartist Movement in Scotland* (Manchester, 1970), pp.28–41.

6. The paper also claimed that at the demonstration 'the greatest number of people were congregated that ever constituted a meeting on any question in the annals of our City — ay, and we venture to say, in those of any other district of Scotland'. *Scottish Guardian*, 18 May 1832. See also *Glasgow Evening Post and Paisley and Renfrewshire Reformer* [hereafter cited as *Glasgow Evening Post*], 19 May 1832; *Scots Times*, 19 May 1832.

7. *Scots Times*, 19 May 1832; *Glasgow Evening Post*, 19 May 1832; *Glasgow Courier*, 16 June 1832.

8. The Earl also received an address from the Irishmen of Edinburgh. *Glasgow Free Press*, 1 November 1834; *Scottish Guardian*, 31 October 1834; Edinburgh University Archives, S.R.C. 1.3, Addresses to the Earl of Durham, f.31. Address from the Irishmen of Edinburgh, 28 October 1834.

9. *Glasgow Evening Post*, 26 September 1835.

10. *Loyal Reformers Gazette*, 10 September 1831.

11. *Ibid*.

12. *Reformers Gazette*, 29 September 1832.

13. Edinburgh University Archives, S.R.C. 1.3, Addresses to the Earl of Durham, f.38, Address of the Irish labourers of Glasgow, 29 October 1834.

14. See, for example, D. George Boyce, *Nineteenth Century Ireland: The Search for Stability* (Dublin, 1990), chapters 2 and 3; Georoid O'Tuathaigh, *Ireland before the Famine 1798–1848* (Dublin, 1990), p.77; David W. Miller, *Queen's Rebels: Ulster Loyalism in Historical Perspective* (Dublin, 1978), chapter 1; Hereward Senior, *Orangeism in Ireland and Britain 1795–1836* (London, 1966), chapters 9 and 10; R.F.G. Holmes, 'Ulster Presbyterianism and Irish Nationalism', in Stewart Mews (ed.), *Religion and National Identity: Studies in Church History Volume 18* (Oxford, 1982), pp.535–48.

15. Handley, *Irish in Scotland*, p.315.

16. See, for example, W.M. Miller (ed.), *An Account of the Reform Procession in Edinburgh, 10 August 1832* (Edinburgh, 1832), p.35; *Journal of Henry Cockburn 1831–1854, Volume 1*, p.34; *Glasgow Free Press*, 28 April 1832; *Glasgow Courier*, 19 July 1832, 19 September 1835; *Scotsman*, 22 December 1832; *Scottish Guardian*, 31 October 1834.

17. In Paisley the Irish did not march as a single group. However, the cotton spinners were present in the reform demonstrations and, as chapter one showed, the majority of the town's spinners were of Irish birth or extraction. Robert Brown, *The History of Paisley, From the Roman Period Down to 1884, Volume II* (Paisley, 1886), p.264.

18. *Glasgow Evening Post*, 18 August 1832. See also PP, 1836, XXXIV, *Report on the State of the Irish Poor in Great Britain*, p.141.

19. PP, 1836, XXXIV, *Report on the State of the Irish Poor in Great Britain*, pp.xli–xlii, 150; *Glasgow Chronicle*, 22 July 1831; Handley, *Irish in Scotland*, p.308; Elaine McFarland, *Protestants First: Orangeism in Nineteenth Century Scotland* (Edinburgh, 1990), pp.55–6.

20. PP, 1836, XXXIV, *Report on the State of the Irish Poor in Great Britain*, p.xlii.

21. *Glasgow Chronicle*, 22 July 1831.

22. PP, 1836, XXXIV, *Report on the State of the Irish Poor in Great Britain*, p.xlii; SRO, Lord Advocate's Papers, AD14/31/424, Declaration of William Eaton, 2 August 1831.

23. PP, 1836, XXXIV, *Report on the State of the Irish Poor in Great Britain*, p.xlii; Handley, *Irish in Scotland*, pp.308–9; *Glasgow Chronicle*, 13 July 1831; McFarland, *Protestants First*, pp.55–6.

24. *Glasgow Chronicle*, 23 September 1831, quoted in Handley, *Irish in Scotland*, p.309.

25. Quoted in McFarland, *Protestants First*, p.61.

26. Senior, *Orangeism in Ireland and Britain*, pp.250–2; McFarland, *Protestants First*, p.61.

27. McFarland, *Protestants First*, p.56.

28. SRO, Home Office Correspondence, RH2/4/161, The Lord Justice Clerk to the Earl of Glasgow, 20 May 1831.

29. *Reformers' Gazette*, 29 March 1834. Two years earlier the journal, then named the *Loyal Reformers Gazette*, reported that it had been informed that Bishop Scott had denounced it from his pulpit. *Loyal Reformers Gazette*, 10 March 1832.

30. *Glasgow Courier*, 29 November 1834. A letter from another hostile opponent of reform published four weeks earlier gave the following description of those who attended the public breakfast for the Earl of Durham: 'there was as motley a group as the eye of mortal man ever gazed upon — half-starved weavers, idle bakers, butchers, painters, tailors, and spinners. The rear being brought up by the "repalers", staunch friends of the great Dan; in fact, a more desperate looking set it was impossible to conceive.' *Glasgow Courier*, 1 November 1834.

31. *Glasgow Chronicle*, 19 October 1831. The anti-reform *Glasgow Courier* was characteristically unimpressed: 'But not satisfied with home-spun oratory, they mounted on to the rostrum one of the Agitators of the Emerald Isle, to teach the restless spirits of Renfrewshire the immense benefits to be derived from the O'Connell system of Agitation. This scion and eulogist of the Great Dan, recommended the Political Union to send out Deputations to all parts of the country, to teach the illiterate the rudiments of Agitation...'. The paper also stated that the number of people present was only between 15–20,000. *Glasgow Courier*, 18 October 1831.

32. *Glasgow Herald*, 5 December 1831; *Glasgow Evening Post*, 3 December 1831; *Glasgow Chronicle*, 30 November 1831.

33. In a letter to the Paisley Reform Society Collins stated the following, which suggests that he was a Roman Catholic: 'It strikes me as somewhat remarkable that, differing as we do, in country, in religious principles, in early impressions and associations, in modes of thinking, and habits of life, yet that we should agree in the profession of a political creed, which agreement is, I think, a strong proof of its truth.' *Glasgow Evening Post*, 7 January 1832.

34. *Ibid*, 31 December 1831, 7 January 1832.

35. *Ibid*, 31 December 1831. In early January 1832 Collins informed the Paisley Reform Society that it was intention to leave Scotland within two months. *Ibid*, 7 January 1832.

36. Janet Fyfe (ed.), *Autobiography of John McAdam (1806–1883), with Selected Letters* (Scottish History Society, 1980), p.6.

37. Quoted in *Poor Man's Advocate*, 23 June 1832.

38. *Ibid*; *Autobiography of John McAdam*, pp.8–9; *Glasgow Sentinel*, 23 August 1862.

39. *Autobiography of John McAdam*, pp.7–10; *Glasgow Chronicle*, 14 May 1832.

40. *Autobiography of John McAdam*, p.8.

41. *Glasgow Sentinel*, 23 August 1862. The *Glasgow Courier* of 15 May 1832 described the event as a 'Revolutionary and Seditious Meeting'. It stated: 'If intimidation…was principally intended, the affair was certainly well-managed, for, marching in their ordinary apparel, under black flags, they presented a most guillotine-like aspect; but as the respectability neither of the town nor of the cause was consulted in this hurried display, we hope a similar one will never be inflicted on us.'

42. *Autobiography of John McAdam*, p.9.

43. Quoted in the *Poor Man's Advocate*, 23 June 1832. Strangely, the *Glasgow Free Press* of 16 May 1832 and the *Glasgow Chronicle* of 14 May 1832 gave the name of the speaker as William McGowan. This is obviously an error, as the working class *Trades' Advocate* (in an article on Patrick McGowan), John McAdam (one of the organisers of the meeting and a member of the Trades Committee) and the author of the *Glasgow Sentinel* articles on this reform agitation (who was also prominent in these events) all stated that the speaker was Patrick McGowan.

44. *Scots Times*, 15 May 1832.

45. *Scottish Guardian*, 28 May 1832.

46. (James Dawson Burn), *The Autobiography of a Beggar Boy* (First published 1855. This edition London, 1978, edited by David Vincent), p.139; *Autobiography of John McAdam*, p.6.

47. (Burn), *Autobiography*, p.139.

48. For Burn's account of his role in the agitations of 1831–37 see *Ibid*, pp.138–47.

49. *Glasgow Chronicle*, 24 October 1831.

50. *Glasgow Courier*, 13 August 1831.

51. (Burn), *Autobiography*, pp.138–9.

52. *Autobiography of John McAdam*, p.6.

53. *Scots Times*, 10 December 1836; *Glasgow Evening Post*, 17 December 1836, 14 January 1837. For the Glasgow Operative Conservative Association see J.T.Ward, 'Some Aspects of Working-Class Conservatism in the Nineteenth Century' in John Butt and J.T.Ward (eds.), *Scottish Themes: Essays in Honour of Professor S.G.E. Lythe* (Edinburgh, 1976), pp.147–51.

54. For a list of the Trade delegates during the Reform Bill campaign see *Autobiography of John McAdam*, p.6.

55. *Scottish Guardian*, 14 December 1832.

56. As the Introduction stated, outwith Glasgow there were very few Irish Catholics who were not members of the working classes. Moreover, not all of them would have had the vote.

57. SCA, Oban Letters, OL2/12/5, William Thomson to Andrew Scott, 8 January 1835; PP, 1836, XXXIV, *Report on the State of the Irish Poor in Great Britain*, p.146.

58. *Reformers' Gazette*, 29 December 1832.

59. *Radical Reformers' Gazette*, 29 December 1832.

60. *Reformers' Gazette*, 29 December 1832.

61. *Radical Reformers' Gazette*, 5 January 1833.

62. *Glasgow Evening Post*, 19 January 1833.

63. At the meeting it was proposed that the names of the Catholic electors who had voted for Ewing should be read aloud. Morgan and others opposed this 'on the ground that the apostates already suffered severely enough in their own consciences — and should be allowed to remain — regarded as politically lopped off from their own body'. A show of hands, however, revealed that the majority wanted the names read, but this did not occur as a list of those who had voted Tory was not at hand.

64. *Glasgow Evening Post*, 12 January 1833.

65. *Ibid*, 12 and 19 January, 22 February, 9 and 16 March 1833. For responses to McGowan's charges see *Ibid*, 26 January, 9 March 1833. See also James Handley, *The Irish in Modern Scotland* (Cork, 1947), pp.55–9.

66. The following discussion is based on *Glasgow Evening Post*, 12 January 1833.

67. According to McGowan, 'among all the reasons he [Scott] could urge in behalf of his favourite, none was so powerful, or required such a return on the part of the Catholics as this, that Mr Oswald had discounted for him a bill of £1,200!' McGowan also claimed that prior to this meeting Scott attempted to persuade some of the electors to break their pledge and support Oswald.

68. *Glasgow Evening Post*, 19 January 1833.

69. McGowan's attacks on Scott were strongly condemned by a section of the Catholic Congregation of Glasgow. It would appear, however, that this group was more angered at McGowan's invective concerning Scott's period in charge of the Catholic Church in Glasgow than about his revelations and criticisms of Scott's activities during December 1832. See *Glasgow Evening Post*, 26 January, 9 March 1833.

70. Handley, *Irish in Modern Scotland*, pp.56–7.

71. *Ibid*, p.57.

72. *Glasgow Evening Post*, 2 March 1833; *Glasgow Free Press*, 2 March 1833; *Glasgow Courier*, 2 March 1833.

73. *Glasgow Evening Post*, 22 March 1834; *Glasgow Free Press*, 29 March 1834.

74. *Glasgow Evening Post*, 2 March 1833.

75. *Ibid*, 29 August 1835.

76. *Ibid*, 13 February 1836.

77. *Ibid*, 14 January 1837.

78. *Ibid*, 28 October 1837; *Glasgow Courier*, 26 October 1837; *Scots Times*, 28 October 1837.

79. SCA, Presholme Letters, PL3/234/5, Andrew Scott to James Kyle, 22 March 1833.

80. Handley, *Irish in Scotland*, p.145.

81. *Ibid*, p.313.

82. SCA, Blairs Letters, BL5/248/16, Andrew Scott to Alexander Paterson, 23 October 1829.

83. Quoted in Handley, *Irish in Scotland*, pp.284–5.

84. *Glasgow Free Press*, 15 December 1832.

85. *Ibid*, 29 March 1834; *Reformers' Gazette*, 29 March 1834.

86. See chapter seven.

87. PP, 1836, XXXIV, *Report on the State of the Irish Poor in Great Britain*, pp. 105, 131–2, 134, 139, 142, 145–9.

88. See, for example, *Herald to the Trades' Advocate*, 5 February, 12 March, 7 May 1831; *Scots Times*, 4 August 1832.

89. See, for example, Edinburgh University Archives, SRC, 1.3, Addresses to the Earl of Durham, 1834, f.39, Address from the Working Men of Glasgow, 29 October 1834; *Glasgow Evening Post*, 19 and 26 September 1835.

90. See, for example, *Scots Times*, 10 December 1836.

91. See next chapter.

92. See, for example, *Herald to the Trades Advocate*, 5 February, 12 March 1831; *Glasgow Sentinel*, 19 July 1862.

93. *Glasgow Evening Post*, 7 January 1832.

94. *Glasgow Free Press*, 16 May 1832.

95. (Burn), *Autobiography of a Beggar Boy*, pp.40–135.

96. *Ibid*, p.74.

97. *Ibid*, p.76.

98. *Ibid*, p.42.

99. *Ibid*, p.74.

100. Edinburgh University Archives, S.R.C., 1.3, Addresses to the Earl of Durham, 1834, f.38, Address of the Irish Labourers of Glasgow, 29 October 1834.

101. *Ibid*, f.31, Address from the Irishmen of Edinburgh, 28 October 1834.

102. In June 1844 Charles Bryson, who had been active in the affairs of the Catholic community in Glasgow since the early 1820s, stated in a speech

given to a large Repeal meeting in Glasgow that: 'He had now known the Repealers of Glasgow for upwards of thirty years, of course they were not always Repealers, during that time, — (loud cheers and hear, hear) — but as Irishmen struggling for Catholic Emancipation, as Radical reformers during the agitation of the Reform Bill, and in all those other agitations for measures of civil and religious liberty, their behaviour was always worthy of the cause they were connected with. (Cheers.)' The reference to the Reform Bill campaign suggests, perhaps, that those Irishmen who participated in it had much the same reasons for doing so as the Scottish 'Radical reformers'. *Glasgow Saturday Post*, 8 June 1844.

103. In the 1830s handloom weavers were involved in the reform campaigns and they hoped that political change would lead to the establishment of Boards of Trade for handloom weaving which would regulate and protect wages and labour. It would be remarkable if those Irish handloom weavers who were undoubtedly involved in the reform agitations were not concerned about this prospect or about an improvement in their pitiful standard of life. Similarly, it would be unreasonable to suggest that Irish cotton spinners who campaigned for reform would not be interested in obtaining social and economic advancement as well as the reforms of the Factory system which the spinners hoped political change would bring. See, for example, Edinburgh University Archives, S.R.C., 1.3., Addresses to the Earl of Durham, 1834, f.14, Address of the Handloom Weavers of Scotland; f.17, Address of the Operative Cotton Spinners of Glasgow and Neighbourhood.

104. See chapters two and three.

105. *Glasgow Free Press*, 4 August 1832.

106. See, for example, *Ibid*, 31 December 1834.

107. *Reformers' Gazette*, 26 September 1835.

108. *Glasgow Evening Post*, 6 December 1834.

109. *Reformers' Gazette*, 26 September 1835.

110. The rescheduled meeting occurred without incident. *Glasgow Courier*, 17 October 1835; *Scottish Guardian*, 13 October 1835.

111. *Reformers' Gazette*, 26 December 1835.

112. *Herald to the Trades' Advocate*, 1 and 8 January 1831; *Loyal Reformers' Gazette*, 19 November 1831.

113. *Glasgow Herald*, 23 September 1831.

114. *Loyal Reformers' Gazette*, 17 March, 21 April 1832.

115. *Ibid*, 21 April 1832.

116. *Ibid*, 21 April, 26 May 1832.

117. *Ibid*, 2 June 1832.

118. *Ibid*, 16 June 1832.

119. *Glasgow Courier*, 12 September 1835. See also Montgomery, Glasgow Radicalism, p.144.

120. *Reformers' Gazette*, 26 September 1835.

121. *Ibid*. One Church of Scotland minister who attended the public dinner in Glasgow for O'Connell was the Reverend Patrick Brewster of Paisley, who later became a leading Scottish Chartist. Brewster subsequently stood trial before the synod of Glasgow and Ayr because of his presence at the event and was censured by his presbytery. See Wilson, *Chartist Movement in Scotland*, pp.32–3; Handley, *Irish in Scotland*, p.320.

122. O'Connell visited Edinburgh, Glasgow, Paisley and Greenock. See Handley, *Irish in Scotland*, pp.319–20; *Glasgow Evening Post*, 19 and 26 September 1835; *Reformers' Gazette*, 26 September 1835.

123. *Glasgow Evening Post*, 26 September 1835. See also *Reformers' Gazette*, 26 September 1835.

124. During the 1820s there was support for Catholic Emancipation from some of the reformers of the 1830s. See, for example, *Autobiography of John McAdam*, p.4; *Reformers' Gazette*, 29 December 1832.

125. *Aristocratic Spirit of the British People*, June 1831.

126. John Belcham, 'English Working Class Radicalism and the Irish', in Roger Swift and Sheridan Gilley (eds.), *The Irish in the Victorian City* (London, 1985), p.87.

127. *Ibid*, p.88.

128. *Glasgow Free Press*, 29 March 1834.

129. *Ibid*.

130. *Glasgow Evening Post*, 22 March 1834.

131. *Reformers' Gazette*, 29 March 1834.

132. Dorothy Thompson, 'Ireland and the Irish in English Radicalism before 1850' in Dorothy Thompson and James Epstein (eds.), *The Chartist Experience: Studies in Working-Class Radicalism and Culture, 1830–60* (London, 1982), p.147.

133. For the reactions of English reformers to the Bill see *ibid*, pp.127–8; Belcham, 'English Working-Class Radicalism', p.88.

134. Handley, *Irish in Scotland*, p.315; Wilson, *Chartist Movement*, p.31; *Glasgow Evening Post*, 2, 9 and 16 March 1833; *Glasgow Courier*, 19 March 1833.

135. *Glasgow Evening Post*, 2 March 1833.

136. *Ibid*. The paper's report stated that 'the room was crowded to excess, and thousands were unable to obtain admission'. See also *Glasgow Free Press*, 2 March 1833; *Glasgow Courier*, 2 March 1833.

137. *Glasgow Evening Post,* 2 March 1833.

138. The proposed tax was to pay for the upkeep of an armed police in Ireland. *Glasgow Free Press,* 2 March 1833.

139. *Glasgow Evening Post,* 2 March 1833. William McGowan spoke at the meeting and stated that: 'He was happy to see a sympathetic and friendly feeling expressed by this country towards Ireland, and begged to thank them in name of his countrymen.' See *Glasgow Free Press,* 2 March 1833.

PART FOUR
CHARTISM AND REPEAL

6
Chartism, 1838–41

There is agreement among historians about the role of the Irish in the Chartist movement in Scotland. Handley, as has already been shown, stated that the Irish did not become involved in political agitations with Scottish workers until 1848, when the Repealers and the Chartists formed an alliance. The historians of Scottish Chartism, Leslie Wright and Alexander Wilson, also maintained that it was not until 'the Year of Revolutions' that the Irish in Scotland participated to any significant extent in the campaign for the Charter.[1] To date the conclusions of these historians have not been challenged or re-evaluated.

Handley, it will be recalled, argued that until 1848 the Irish in Scotland did not identify with the political aims of native workers and were interested mainly in issues relating to Ireland and to the Catholic church. He also noted that 'In the political life of the immigrants the name of Daniel O'Connell was all potent over the period 1825–45. From the earliest years of his public life until his last days the Irish in Scotland gave him unswerving loyalty and support in word and deed'.[2] Handley, however, failed to mention that O'Connell was implacably opposed to the Chartist agitation and urged his followers not to support it.[3] O'Connell did not object to the Six Points of the Charter, namely universal male suffrage, annual parliaments, vote by ballot, payment of MPs, equal electoral districts and the abolition of property qualifications for MPs. Indeed, in June 1837 he was one of six radical Members of Parliament who pledged their support to the London Working Men's Association's proposed Bill for Parliament which would contain the Six Points. The draft Bill was finally published on 8 May 1838 as the People's Charter and the campaign for it was launched in Glasgow thirteen days later.[4] O'Connell, however, soon denounced the new movement. He condemned the violent language used by some of the Chartist leaders, including in particular his former ally and now irreconcilable enemy Feargus O'Connor. Unlike them, O'Connell believed that violence or the threat of violence — 'physical force' tactics — would never win political reforms; change would come only if reformers used peaceful, 'moral force', methods.[5] Furthermore, O'Connell and his supporters in Parliament were in alliance with the Whigs and had been since 1835. Under this informal agreement, known as the Lichfield

House Compact, the Whigs received the support of the O'Connellites on the condition that they introduced reforms for Ireland.[6] The Chartists on the other hand were deeply hostile towards the Whig Ministry of Lord Melbourne and this greatly alarmed O'Connell. He believed that

> it was a matter of the utmost importance that nothing should be done to jeopardise the Whigs' continuing hold on high office since they were attempting to honour the spirit of the Lichfield House Compact by remedying or promising to remedy some of the most deeply-felt grievances of Catholic Ireland.[7]

The Chartists' opposition to the Whig Administration convinced O'Connell that they were not concerned about the condition of Ireland.[8] He therefore urged his followers to eschew involvement in the Chartist agitation.

From the end of 1838 until his death in May 1847 O'Connell remained hostile to Chartism. This was because the movement was dominated by O'Connor and his supporters, who continued to argue that 'physical force' tactics were justifiable. Moreover, the attitudes of the O'Connorites and indeed of other Chartists to O'Connell made it unlikely that he would become favourably disposed towards their agitation; they despised him and had done since 1837. O'Connell was regarded as a traitor to the working classes because he had broken his promise to support the Charter, opposed trade unionism and supported the New English Poor Law.[9] He was also condemned for his opposition to Chartism and support for alternative political movements.[10] It is unlikely that such attacks made any impression on O'Connell. From April 1840 onwards he was devoted to his campaign for Repeal and he urged his Irish supporters in Great Britain to concentrate their energies on it and remain opposed to the Chartist agitation.

In his account of Scottish Chartism Leslie Wright agreed with Handley that it was not until 1848 that the Irish participated in a reform agitation with Scottish workers, and also accepted his explanation for this.[11] Wright, however, maintained that the advice given by Daniel O'Connell concerning Chartism was taken by the Irish in Scotland.[12] Moreover, he offered two reasons of his own for Irish non-involvement. The first was economic:

> Conditions in Ireland were so bad that even the poor comfort available in Scotland seemed highly desirable by comparison...It would be ridiculous to say they were content, but life, plus a little hope, was preferable to actual death by starvation. Perhaps it could all be summed up thus, that the Irish immigrant,

from the economic point of view, pursued a policy of 'let well alone', even if that 'well' was but a poor thing.[13]

Wright then suggested that 'the lack of education of these unfortunate people' might also have contributed to their decision not to participate in the Chartist agitation. He asked: 'What could a semi-educated immigrant make of the jargon of Chartism with its "franchise", its "equal electoral districts", and the socio-economic ideas of its leaders?'.[14] Wilson, in his study of the Scottish Chartist movement, asserted that loyalty to the views of O'Connell was the explanation for Irish political behaviour in the years until 1848.[15]

Such a consensus does not exist over the issue of Irish immigrants and the Chartist movement in England. Here a debate revolves around the work of J.H. Treble and Dorothy Thompson.[16] Treble, in an essay published in 1973, argued that although a number of Irishmen were Chartist leaders at local and national level, 'the vast majority' of immigrants in Yorkshire, Cheshire and Lancashire did not become involved in the agitation until 1848.[17] He showed that the political organisations established by the Irish in the north of England were hostile to the Chartists. Treble also found little evidence of a significant Irish presence in the movement's rank-and-file, and demonstrated that the Chartists in the north of England were fully aware that most immigrants had not joined their campaign. For Treble, the reason for Irish non-involvement was that they remained loyal to the political views of O'Connell. Thompson took issue with aspects of Treble's thesis and methodology, and asserted that in England in the years before 1848 'there was a very considerable Irish presence in the Chartist Movement'.[18] In her essay, however, she did not demonstrate this convincingly. For example, she produced evidence of local Chartist leaders who were Irish. But so had Treble. Indeed, several of the Irish Chartists discussed by Thompson had already been noted by him. Furthermore, the only substantial piece of evidence she provided of a significant Irish presence in the rank-and-file of the movement relates to Barnsley. Yet Treble had already discussed the large Irish presence among the Chartists of that town. Indeed, he specifically argued that 'until 1848 in every respect the outstanding exception to the general pattern of Irish immigrant alignments, was Barnsley…'.[19] No major work on the Irish and English Chartism has appeared since Thompson's work was published in 1982.

This and the next two chapters will examine the political activities of the Irish in the west of Scotland from 1838 to 1848. Although Handley, Wright and Wilson commented on the issue of the Irish and Scottish Chartism they, unlike Treble and Thompson for England, did not examine it in any great detail. The movement in the region for repeal of the legislative union between Great Britain and Ireland will also be discussed. Handley looked at this only briefly and Montgomery and Leitch, in their theses on radicalism in Glasgow and Paisley respectively, did not deal with the agitation at all.[20] Furthermore, in their studies of Scottish Chartism Wright and Wilson did not examine the relationship between the Chartists and the Irish Repealers in the period prior to 1848. Unfortunately, the chapters will be concerned chiefly with events in and around Glasgow. This is because the information obtained from the principal primary sources consulted for this study — the local press, the Scottish Chartist press, O'Connor's *Northern Star*, and the correspondence and papers of the Roman Catholic clergy in the west of Scotland — relates mainly to radical activities in the city and its immediate vicinity.

Although the peak years of Chartism were 1838–42 this chapter will be concerned only with events in the west of Scotland during the first three years of the agitation, from May 1838 to the spring of 1841. In the region the movement for Repeal did not emerge until the summer of 1841 and therefore the chapter will concentrate on the period before the Irish became involved in that agitation. The first section will produce evidence of Irish participation in the Chartist movement during these years. The second will argue that despite this involvement the majority of Irish Catholics, in Glasgow at least, did not in fact participate in the campaign for the Six Points. The final section will offer some reasons for this.

I

There was an Irish presence in the local leadership of the Chartist movement in the west of Scotland during the first three years of the agitation. One of these activists, Arthur O'Neill, has been known to historians for some time. Half Scottish and half Irish, O'Neill came to prominence at the Scottish Chartist Convention in 1839 when he became a member of the Universal Suffrage Central Committee. From then until he moved to Birmingham in late 1840 O'Neill promoted the principles of Chartism throughout Scotland and helped to establish local Chartist Societies. He was also in this period the principal advocate in Scotland of Christian Chartism and was in great demand as a lay preacher.[21]

The Irish-born James Burn, whose involvement in the reform agitations in Glasgow during 1831–37 was discussed in the previous chapter,[22] was also, for a brief period, active in the Chartist movement. He was one of the main speakers at the meeting in Glasgow on 3 September 1838 which established the city's Universal Suffrage Association,[23] and the following February and April he spoke at Chartist meetings in Greenock.[24] Burn moved there sometime in 1839 and ran a spirit cellar for eight months before returning to Glasgow. During his stay in the town he was active in the local Chartist movement and he also addressed Chartist meetings in Paisley and Glasgow.[25] Burn maintained the moderate and cautious stance he had taken consistently since his entry into political agitation. This eventually made him unpopular with some of Greenock's Chartists. In his autobiography Burn described a meeting he chaired in the town to discuss the call of the 1839 Chartist National Convention for workers to undertake a general strike. He opposed 'this hellish suggestion' and told his audience 'that if they wished to cover themselves with infamy, by assisting in bringing the industry of the nation to a stand, they would do well to proceed'. Burn recalled that this advice was not what some wished to hear: 'Such, however, was the infatuation of the more unthinking that I had the pleasure of being branded with the character of a renegade and a traitor to the cause.'[26] The activities of the National Convention and the hostility of some of Greenock's Chartists appear to have disillusioned Burn, and by the time he left the town and returned to Glasgow he had abandoned political agitation.[27]

However, as was explained in the previous chapter, it is not clear whether Burn, who was born in Ireland of Irish parents, actually considered himself to be 'Irish'. Doubt also exists over Arthur O'Neill, as there is no evidence in press reports of his speeches and activities that he was regarded as an Irishman or that he thought himself to be one. The issue, therefore, is essentially this: to what extent did those in the west of Scotland who considered themselves to be Irish, whether they were first, second or even third generation Irish, disregard the advice of O'Connell, the great hero of the Irish people — or to be precise of Catholic Ireland — and participate in the Chartist movement?

There is evidence that some did. At least three Irish Catholics were particularly active in the campaign in the region for the Charter during its first three years: Con Murray, William McGowan and Thomas Donnelly. Murray, from County Donegal, was secretary of the Glasgow Operative Nailmakers Society and became one of the leading O'Connorites in the city.[28] His activities will be discussed in more detail later in this chapter. McGowan, whose involvement in political movements in the 1820s and 1830s has already been detailed, was one of the main participants at the meeting in Glasgow in September 1838 which established the city's Universal Suffrage Association. During its proceedings one speaker suggested that the society should also participate in the campaign for the repeal of the Corn Laws. This proposition was opposed by James Burn and by James Moir, one of Glasgow's leading radicals. They believed that the Association should direct its activities solely towards the attainment of Universal Suffrage. McGowan agreed, and argued 'it was essential that the Association should have their energies concentrated at one given point at one given time'. He reminded those present that this strategy had been used successfully by the movements for Catholic Emancipation and the Reform Bill. McGowan argued that 'Universal Suffrage…had become more imperative than ever, and it behoved them to accomplish it, by taking example from what had proved successful with government before'.[29] The following February he was one of the speakers at the meeting in Greenock which formed the town's Chartist association.[30] There are no references in the press to McGowan playing an active role in the Chartist movement thereafter, although he continued to support its principles.[31]

Thomas H. Donnelly, a surgeon in Greenock, was during this period the most prominent Irish Catholic Chartist of the three. He chaired the February 1839 meeting in the town which resulted in the establishment of its Chartist society, and during the rest of that year and the next he played a leading role in the association.[32] In March 1840 Donnelly was the principal spokesman for the Greenock Chartists at a public meeting held to consider whether to petition for the repeal of the Corn Laws. He successfully moved an amendment which bound the meeting to petition for the Charter instead.[33] Donnelly also addressed Chartist meetings in the west of Scotland,[34] and was in demand as a lecturer. For example, in early 1840 he was asked by the Kilmarnock Working Men's Society to visit the town and employ his 'Mellesian brogue' to rouse the people into joining the Chartist agitation.[35]

Donnelly was clearly an important figure in Greenock Chartism during its early years. However, neither he nor McGowan nor Murray was a major figure in the Chartist movement in the west of Scotland in the period 1838–41. Murray later became prominent in the agitation in Glasgow, and this will be discussed in the following chapter. But in the first three years of the campaign for the Six Points the leading Chartist activists in the west of Scotland were native Scots.

There was Irish involvement in the rank-and-file of the Chartist movement in Glasgow. On 21 May 1838 a large number of trades and other bodies of reformers marched in procession to Glasgow Green to attend the great demonstration which launched the campaign in Britain for the Charter. One of the groups which participated in this event was the Loyal Irish Reformers.[36] As the previous chapter indicated, this group consisted mainly of Irish Catholic labourers in the city.[37] On 21 September 1840 a mass demonstration was held on the Green to honour John Collins, the Chartist leader from England who had recently been released from prison. In the procession of trades and districts held prior to the meeting Irish labourers were again present, although on this occasion they marched as the United Labourers.[38] Unfortunately, it is not known how many Irish labourers marched on this day or indeed in the procession in May 1838. Furthermore, it is impossible to determine how many members of the Irish community were present at these meetings. A Chartist demonstration was also held in the Green on 10 June 1839 but newspaper reports of the procession that day did not mention Irish involvement. However, these accounts did not give a complete list of the groups which marched to the meeting.[39] Given that Irish labourers participated in the 1838 and 1840 demonstrations, it is probable that they were also present at the 1839 event.

Irish workers were not, of course, employed only as labourers and it would not be unreasonable to suggest that this evidence does not represent the full extent of Irish involvement in Glasgow's Chartist demonstrations. For example, a high proportion of the workforce in cotton spinning and in dyeing in the city were Irish and the spinners and the dyers marched in the 1838 procession. So too did workers from the Govan colliery, which employed a large number of Irishmen.[40] The majority of handloom weavers in Glasgow by this time were probably Irish or of Irish descent,[41] and groups of workers from the major weaving districts in and around the city — Bridgeton, Calton, Gorbals, Hutchestown, Tradeston, Camlachie and Parkhead — participated in the Glasgow Chartist demonstrations during this period.[42] Irish workers were undoubtedly present in a number of the other occupations and districts which were represented at these events. It is, of course, impossible to establish the extent to which Irish workers marched in the processions in their trade or district grouping, or indeed whether they participated at all. But, as was argued in the previous chapter for the reform processions of 1830–35, it would be remarkable to say the least if, out of all the Irish workers in and around the city, it was solely from among the labourers that an Irish presence at these Chartist demonstrations was drawn.

Given that there was some Irish involvement in the major Chartist demonstrations in Glasgow, it is not surprising to find evidence of an Irish presence at other Chartist events in the city. In March 1841 it was reported that at a meeting of the Chartists on the second of the month a number of Irishmen participated.[43] A few days after this the yearly meeting of the Lanarkshire Universal Suffrage Association was held in the city. According to James Moir, Irishmen were in the audience.[44]

It would also appear that Irish workers were present at the debate between Feargus O'Connor and the Reverend Patrick Brewster of Paisley in the Bazaar in Glasgow on 10 January 1839. Brewster, the leading Scottish advocate of 'moral force' Chartism, was opposed to O'Connor's 'physical force' position.[45] During his speech Brewster received rough treatment from the audience, and was heckled constantly. O'Connor, in his address, claimed that at the previous night's debate in Paisley Brewster made the following statement: 'I am not for rash agitation, because I for one am determined that Ireland shall never be raised to the level of England, if I can help it.' According to a press report of the Glasgow meeting, 'tremendous uproar' resulted from O'Connor's revelation and there were calls for Brewster to be put out of the meeting. Brewster vehemently denied the accusation made by O'Connor, who then stated that the reporter present from the *True Scotsman* attended the Paisley debate and should relate to the audience what Brewster had argued. The reporter declared that O'Connor's statement was indeed true. According to the *Glasgow Courier*:

> The fury of the multitude seemed now to know no bounds — a perfect storm of hisses and uproar ensued, which lasted for some time, and raged with so much fury, that at one period the personal safety of the Rev. Gentleman seemed to be in danger.

Eventually, a vote was taken which decided that Brewster was not to be permitted to speak again at the meeting. He therefore left the building.[46]

Having been thwarted in his attempts to defend himself in the Bazaar, Brewster soon presented his version of events in a letter to the *True Scotsman*. He again denied the statement attributed to him and claimed that O'Connor had fabricated the accusation in order 'to excite the fury of the two or three hundred miserable creatures, chiefly Irishmen, so far as appeared, who, out of the three thousand present, were the principal actors in its proceedings'.[47] Unfortunately, newspaper reports of the debate do not confirm whether any Irishmen were present.[48] However, given the intensity of the reaction to Brewster's alleged statement concerning Ireland, coupled with the evidence of Irish involvement in Glasgow Chartist demonstrations and meetings between 1838 and 1841, it would not be unreasonable to suggest that Brewster was probably accurate in his description of the most hostile portion of his audience in the Bazaar.

Four days after the O'Connor–Brewster debate in Glasgow an extraordinary meeting of the Renfrewshire Political Union was held in Paisley to discuss the recent election of the militant Dr. John Taylor, a close ally of O'Connor, as the representative of the Union to the forthcoming Chartist National Convention. Brewster and a number of the leading figures in the society were opposed to Taylor and questioned the validity of his election. Chief among the doctor's supporters at the meeting was an Irishman named Archy McCallum, who in his address to the Union attacked Brewster for his links with O'Connell and for what he had allegedly said about Ireland at the debate in Paisley the previous week. McCallum's speech, and in particular his references to O'Connell, was criticised by another Irishman present, whose name was not reported. This individual also condemned the use of the threat of violence as a means to obtain the Charter. After much discussion the motion to reject Taylor as the RPU representative was not carried.[49]

Apart from this example from Paisley, the evidence presented thus far of an Irish presence in the rank-and-file of the Chartist movement has been limited to Glasgow. Unfortunately, press reports of Chartist meetings and demonstrations which occurred elsewhere in the west of Scotland do not give any indication whether Irish workers were involved in them. It would be remarkable, however, if the situation in Glasgow was unique.

II

It has been established that there was an Irish presence in the Chartist movement in Glasgow during the period 1838–41. The vital historical issue under consideration, however, is not simply whether there is evidence of Irish involvement. It is, as Treble stated, 'the extent to which the bulk of the immigrant population gave its adherence to, or withheld its support from, the Chartist cause'.[50] Fortunately, there is evidence which enables this issue to be discussed in relation to Catholic Irish participation in the campaign in Glasgow. This comes from 1840 and 1841. In February of the former year the *Scottish Patriot* published a letter from the Irish Catholic Chartist Con Murray, 'To the members of the Glasgow Catholic Total Abstinence Society'.[51] Murray had three main reasons for writing. First, he wished to explain why he had recently resigned from this temperance organisation. Murray stated that at the last meeting he attended the chairman of the Society Charles Bryson, who was also an Irishman, told those present that he was 'sure there is no person in this Hall who doubts the political honesty of Mr O'Connell; he knows what is best for Ireland'. Bryson, who had been active in the affairs of the Glasgow Catholic community since at least the early 1820s, and who by this time was a wealthy merchant and shipper,[52] then proceeded to discuss other political issues. Murray was incensed at this as Bryson had apparently violated the articles of the Society by introducing politics into its meetings. Murray, however, did not raise this issue at the time because he was convinced that he 'had a bad chance of getting justice done to by the meeting…'. He therefore decided to resign from the organisation:

> he did not object to Mr O'Connell's name being introduced, so long as it was in connection with the objects of the Society. The Chairman [Bryson] might, if he thought proper, have quoted Loyal Peter and Richmond the Spy, so long as he coupled them with the Total Abstinence cause; it was his ramming the political creed of the Whigs down my throat that caused me to leave the Society…

Secondly, Murray took issue with Bryson's claim that no-one at the meeting doubted O'Connell's political honesty. He stated that this was not true as there were a number present that evening who shared his own views concerning 'the Liberator'. These were essentially the standard Chartist criticisms of O'Connell. For example, in his letter Murray condemned O'Connell for failing to keep his promises over House of Lords reform, factory reform and universal suffrage, and for attacking trade unions and Feargus O'Connor. He also criticised O'Connell's current policies for Ireland, such as those for municipal and tithe reform. Thirdly, Murray urged the members of the Society to come to their own conclusions about Chartism and not blindly follow the lead of 'the Liberator', who misrepresented the Chartist cause:

> He has several times told you that the Chartists hate us Irishmen, our country, and our creed. Foul calumniator!…I have been among these Chartists since they commenced their agitation, and I have never seen anything of the kind; If I had I would not remain among them for one day, for I love my country and my creed. It is the love of my country that has made me a Chartist; they have always shewn the greatest kindness to Irishmen, sympathising with them in their sufferings, and, like brothers, determined to assist them in gaining their independence. I am one of those Irishmen who will not take Daniel's word for these matters. I must see the other side, and hear what they have got to say in their defence. I would advise you, my friends, to adopt this plan too, and I can assure you you will find the Chartists are not what you have been led to believe. It is the duty of every man to hear before he condemns. Enquire, therefore, of the Chartists, read their own papers, and there you will see what are their real sentiments.

Murray concluded by appealing not only to members of the Glasgow Catholic Total Abstinence Society, but also to all Irishmen in the city:

> fellow workmen, our interest is one and the same. I would call on you again to examine the grounds on which we have taken our stand against the despotic rulers of this country…I will now bid you farewell for the present, hoping the

Irishmen of Glasgow will not stay long behind their brethren of Manchester, Newcastle, Sunderland, and various other places, in joining the ranks of liberty, with a wish that every man, of whatever creed or colour he be, may yet be as free as the Almighty intended at his creation.

It is therefore evident that Murray, who was in a better position to judge than most, was convinced that the bulk of the Catholic Irish community in the city had not yet identified with Chartism.[53]

This picture of Catholic Irish political allegiance in Glasgow does not appear to have altered to any significant extent over the following year, as the aftermath of a dispute in the city in March 1841 between O'Connell's Catholic Irish supporters — the O'Connellites — and the Chartists clearly demonstrates. Early that month a public meeting was held in the Justiciary Court Hall to discuss the Irish Registration Bills of Lords Stanley and Morpeth. Stanley's measure sought to restrict the franchise in Ireland; Morpeth's Bill, which was introduced to counteract Stanley's, aimed at extending it. The meeting was called by a section of the city's Catholic Irish community. They supported the Bill of Lord Morpeth, as indeed did Daniel O'Connell. The Glasgow Chartists, while opposed to Stanley's Bill, refused to back Morpeth's measure as they were then engaged in a policy of not supporting any proposed reform other than the Charter. The Chartists attended the meeting with the intention of arguing this case and ultimately passing their own resolutions.[54] The meeting, however, rapidly degenerated into a tumultuous affair. Although the Irish Catholics arranged the event, which was scheduled to begin at 7.30 p.m., it was a public meeting, open to all. According to the *Scots Times*, the Irish Catholics endeavoured to pack it by opening the doors before six o'clock and allowing members of their body, who had been given tickets beforehand, to enter. When members of the public tried to gain admittance they were refused until all the O'Connellites with tickets had taken their seats. By the time the meeting began 'the Hall was packed to suffocation', with people standing in the aisles, the corners and in any other available spaces. The O'Connellites took the platform and moved that Bishop Murdoch take the chair. This was opposed by the Chartists who moved that one of their own, George Ross, be chosen. A show of hands took place after which the Bishop declared himself elected and proceeded to address the meeting. The Chartists objected to the way in which the vote had been taken but their appeals were ignored, the result of which was that 'turmoil commenced, as if hell had broke loose'. Murdoch and several O'Connellites spoke but could not be heard because of the uproar. A number of Chartists tried to address the gathering but were shouted down and several were assaulted. The police were called and arrests were made. Murdoch and the other organisers of the proceedings then abandoned the meeting because order could not be restored. After some time the police succeeded in taking control of the situation and the hall was eventually cleared.[55]

The Chartists were naturally aggrieved at the events of the evening and decided to call 'a *real* public meeting of the inhabitants of Glasgow' to discuss the Registration Bills. This took place two days after the Justiary Hall 'debate', on 4 March, and was held in the Bazaar, which at the time was 'the largest covered place in the city', capable of holding five thousand people; that night it 'was filled in every part'. The meeting was another highly charged affair. The *Scots Times* reported that during the election of the meeting's chairman, 'a scene of tumult ensued which baffles description — solely caused by the untameable and disorganised state of the Irish...'. Two Chartists were attacked by around twenty Irishmen for supporting the candidature of George Ross, some of the mob were arrested and police were stationed among the crowd. Ross was duly elected and the Chartists eventually succeeded in passing all their resolutions, including one which stated that those present regarded Morpeth's Bill 'as neither more nor less than another contemptible effort of the Whig Ministry to perpetuate their Administration at the expense of the cause of Justice, and would call upon every honest man to aid our exertions to establish the principles of the Charter...'. Another agreed to petition the House of Commons to urge the Queen to dismiss her ministers.[56]

From contemporary comment about the events of March 1841 it is clear that it was recognised that most of the Irish Catholics in Glasgow were not at that time involved in the Chartist movement. Reporting on the attempt to pack the meeting at the Justiciary Hall, the *Scots Times* stated that it 'had thought...that the Roman Catholics of the city — a party so powerful and united — would have been the last to have recourse to the cowardly expedient'.[57] On 9 March, five days after the debate in the Bazaar, the annual election of office bearers of the Lanarkshire Universal Suffrage Association was held in the city's Christian Chartist Church. The problem of Catholic Irish non-participation in the movement was one of the main topics of discussion.[58] In his yearly report the secretary of the Association, James Jack, made the following observations on the issue:

> he sincerely regretted that the Irish Catholics of Glasgow should so far forget their own character, and the interests of their country, as to attempt to steal public opinion in the unworthy manner they had done...He regretted the proceedings which had taken place in the Bazaar, not from any injury which could possibly result to the agitation, but because it exhibited working people divided amongst themselves — thus strengthening the hands of the general oppressor...But any evil which had been done by the momentary collision

which had taken place between the Catholics and the other inhabitants of Glasgow could easily be repaired; and he trusted that steps would be taken immediately to enlighten the Catholics on matters of politics, that they may perceive their interests to be inseparably connected with those of the Chartists. Measures of this kind would engage the attention of the Association immediately.

Con Murray agreed and argued that they should appeal directly to his fellow Irish Catholics:

> The late proceedings had led many Catholics to inquire into what Chartism was (cheers.)…and he believed that, if the Directors of the Association would get up an address to the Irishmen in Glasgow, stating simply what objects the Chartists had in view, and how they were seeking justice to Ireland, many converts would be made.

Murray's suggestion of a Chartist address to the Irish Catholics of the city was applauded by James Moir, who stated that his views on Ireland had been misrepresented by one of the city's leading O'Connellites.

The events of March 1841 clearly demonstrate that by that time the bulk of the Irish Catholic community in the city had not joined the agitation for the Charter. Unfortunately, owing to the nature of the evidence, it is impossible to establish whether the same situation existed elsewhere in the west of Scotland, although there are examples of Irish non-involvement. It has been shown that in February 1840 Dr. Thomas Donnelly, the Irish Catholic Chartist from Greenock, was invited by the Kilmarnock Working Men's Association to visit the town and its vicinity to spread the principles of Chartism. In his reply to the society Donnelly noted that he had been asked to persuade not only the native Scots but also his 'politically misled countrymen residing there…'.[59] It is not known whether the Irishmen in this part of Ayrshire subsequently altered their political views. On 11 February 1839 a Roman Catholic soirée was held in Paisley, attended by around eight hundred members of the congregation. One of the priests who spoke at the meeting was Timothy O'Meara and his address was on the current political situation. In it he urged his audience to have nothing to do with the Chartists and exhorted them to 'rally round that great man Daniel O'Connell…'. His speech concluded amid 'much applause'.[60] Whether this view of politics was common among the Irish Catholics in Paisley at this time, or in the period to mid-1841, cannot be established. No evidence has been found on the issue of the Irish and Chartism in the towns and villages of Lanarkshire. It must be noted, however, that the Chartist meeting in Glasgow in March 1841 which discussed the non-involvement of the bulk of the city's Irish Catholics in the movement was a meeting of the Lanarkshire Universal Suffrage Association. None of the delegates from outside Glasgow made any speeches or comments that evening which suggested that the situation regarding the Irish was any different in their parts of the county.

III

It is evident that many members of the Catholic Irish community in the west of Scotland did not participate in the Chartist movement in the period from May 1838 to mid–1841. In the introduction to this chapter the views of Handley, Wright and Wilson on the issue of Irish non-involvement were set out. These will now be examined critically. Handley's argument that the Irish regarded themselves as exiles, were mainly interested in Catholic and Irish issues, and did not identify with the political aims of the Scots until the late 1840s, cannot be accepted as a suitable explanation for their limited role in the Chartist movement during these years; nor can Wright's suggestion that the Irish had no great urge to become involved in the agitation because their economic condition in Scotland was at least better than what they had been used to in Ireland. After all, previous chapters have demonstrated Catholic Irish involvement in pre-Chartist radical movements in the west of Scotland and this chapter has produced evidence of some Catholic Irish participation in Chartism during 1838–41. Furthermore, not all members of the 'Irish community' were immigrants: many were born and raised in Scotland. These arguments, however, could explain the behaviour of some immigrants, particularly those who had recently arrived in the west of Scotland. Wright's suggestion that the 'semi-educated immigrant' did not understand the principles of the Charter might have been true of others. It might also have been that there were some among the Irish who were simply not interested in political issues, for example those who did not intend staying in Scotland for much longer. After all, not all natives of the west of Scotland were active in the Chartist movement.[61]

The view that the bulk of the Catholic Irish community remained loyal to O'Connell and thus refused to participate in Chartism is worth considering in greater detail, particularly as the evidence from the Irish Registration Bills dispute has already illustrated this. There are in fact many other examples of Catholic Irish loyalty to O'Connell, although these come solely from Glasgow. In August 1838 O'Connell established the Precursor Society 'to procure from the British Legislature full justice to Ireland': its principal demands were Irish municipal and parliamentary reform, and the abolition of tithes. He dissolved the Society in September 1839.[62] Branches of the organisation were established in England, and one was formed in Glasgow.[63] The members of the Glasgow Precursor Association placed their total trust in O'Connell to act in Ireland's best interests, as the following resolution, passed at a meeting in April 1839, makes clear:

> That Mr O'Connell deserves our unceasing gratitude for the invaluable services he has conferred upon the Irish people, and that to the powerful talents, the unremitting energies, and above all, to the high moral and political integrity of O'Connell are we mainly indebted for the civil and religious freedom we have already obtained, and on him do we rely for the ultimate regeneration of his native land.[64]

This conviction that O'Connell knew what was best for Ireland was articulated further by Dr. John Scanlan in June 1840 at a debate in the Lyceum Rooms in Glasgow on the political character of Daniel O'Connell.[65] Scanlan was an Irish Catholic who soon became one of the leading Repealers in the city. At the debate several of the city's most prominent Chartists — James Jack, Robert Malcolm Jun., James Moir, William Pattison, James Proudfoot and Charles McEwan — spoke against O'Connell. They condemned the positions he had taken concerning the Factory Question, trade unionism, the Tolpuddle Martyrs and the Charter, as well as his continuing support for Melbourne's ministry and the agitation for the repeal of the Corn Laws. O'Connell's current proposals for reform in Ireland were also attacked. For example, James Proudfoot argued that 'nothing but Universal Suffrage would ever remedy the abuses under which Ireland laboured. The success which attended O'Connell, conferred benefits not upon the people, but upon the middle classes of Ireland, who sent Dan and his tail to Parliament'. Scanlan defended O'Connell's conduct and policies. He argued that those present

> had no right to interfere with Ireland, whatever means she took to gain her freedom. He would ask, would a Chartist Parliament Repeal the Union? He doubted whether it would. Now, would any honest man say that Ireland should be obliged to maintain an alliance with a country that had done her no service, a country that had robbed and plundered her, and reduced her inhabitants to worse than Egyptian bondage. If not, what right had they to call in question the means Mr O'Connell thought proper to use to effect her regeneration...He considered that the people of Ireland were the best judges of what was best for themselves, and that their placing implicit reliance in the course of conduct pursued by Mr O'Connell, was the best argument as to the soundness of the views of Mr O'Connell. The best illustration of the course of agitation pursued by the Chartist leaders, was to be found in the fact, that they were now in

prison, and their followers could not release them. He believed that the people of Ireland would have to work out their own salvation.

Other O'Connellites made speeches at the debate in favour of the conduct of 'The Liberator' but eventually the Chartists' motion was carried. It stated that since the beginning of their agitation 'Mr O'Connell, along with the middle classes and the present Whig Administration, has acted unfairly, dishonestly, and ungratefully towards the industrious classes of England, Scotland and Ireland'.

As this resolution indicates, the Glasgow Chartists' criticisms of O'Connell, like those of their English counterparts, could be highly personal and insulting.[66] Indeed, at the debate Charles McEwan, after condemning O'Connell's views on trade unionism, factory reform and the tithe question in Ireland, 'concluded by asserting that the conduct of Daniel O'Connell was only equalled by that of Judas Iscariot'.[67] At the Chartist demonstration on Glasgow Green the previous year the following resolution was adopted:

> That this meeting view with feelings of indignation and contempt, the extraordinary conduct, moral turpitude, and political dishonesty of Daniel O'Connell, in his late Whiggish and mongrel address to the Chartists of Birmingham, wherein he repudiates the principle of Universal Suffrage — a principle which he voluntary advocated at upwards of one hundred public Meetings in England and Scotland, and before two hundred thousand of the citizens of Glasgow, on the very spot where we are now assembled...and farther, he having pledged himself to that principle by signing the People's Charter, proves to us his bare-faced effrontery, his unprincipled conduct and dangerous character, and that all good men and true Patriots will do well to watch the insidious letters and baneful attempts of that man to divide or divert the Chartists of Britain from their cause.[68]

These and other attacks on O'Connell[69] undoubtedly reinforced the loyalty of the Glasgow O'Connellites to their leader and also their hostility towards the Chartist movement. For example, at the June 1840 debate in the city one Mr Donnachy, an O'Connellite, 'expressed great surprise that any Irishman would have joined the Chartists, seeing that body insulted the people of Ireland by calling Mr O'Connell the Big Beggarman'. At this event Dr. John Scanlan stated that he had not wished 'his name mixed up with this discussion at all...but when he heard the calumnies and insults that had been offered to his countryman, Mr O'Connell, he could not forbear coming forward to vindicate his character from the aspersions that had been cast upon it'.[70]

It is clear that most of the politically active members of the Catholic

Irish community in Glasgow remained loyal to O'Connell and his policies for Ireland, and did not participate in the Chartist movement during 1838–41. This is not to suggest, however, that this group was simply not interested in political reform in Great Britain. The Glasgow O'Connellites, like their leader, supported Melbourne's administration during these years because they believed that it would introduce political and other reforms not only for Ireland but also for Great Britain.[71] For example, at a meeting in September 1839 of former members of the Glasgow Precursor Association a number of toasts were made including one by Charles Bryson for Lord Melbourne and his ministers. In his speech Bryson stated that

> although the Ministers had not done all they might have expected, still he believed that they had done all they could -(hear). Those who were in the habit of paying attention to passing events might see, if they had not done enough, that it was the Tory Lords, and latterly the Chartists — Tories of a worst description — (hear) — that had prevented them…It would not do for the Tories to tell them that Lord Melbourne and his coadjutors in the Government had done nothing. It would take up too much of their time to tell all they had done…But even if they had done less, it was of importance, it was their duty to do all in their power to keep the Whigs in, and the Tories out. They should do all they could to enable the present Ministry to persevere in that straightforward course of reform they had marked out for themselves, and which would tend so materially to the benefit of the country (cheers).

According to the *Glasgow Chronicle*, 'The toast was again given, and drank with the greatest enthusiasm'.[72] Bryson's sentiments were echoed by Dr. Scanlan at the O'Connellite-Chartist debate in June 1840.[73]

Indeed, there is evidence which shows that the Glasgow O'Connellites wanted an extension of the franchise and in fact supported the principle of Universal Suffrage. They, however, shared O'Connell's view — or followed his lead — that the Government would not grant Universal Suffrage and so radicals should set their sights somewhat lower.[74] For example, at the O'Connellite-Chartist debate in the city in June 1840 Dr. John Scanlan revealed that:

> For his own part he could find no fault with the People's Charter; and he believed that until the Charter Franchise was gained, the condition of the people could not be greatly improved (Loud cheers). But the question was, how were they to get it, unless they took it piecemeal. He was satisfied they would never gain the Charter Suffrage all at once. But he would say get as much of it as you can by degrees, and by peaceable and legal means…He (Dr. S.) believed that if the Chartists had agitated along with the middle classes, for a repeal of the Corn Law, they would, by this time, have had the middle classes agitating along with them for an extended suffrage.[75]

The Glasgow O'Connellites expressed similar sentiments at their debate with the Chartists in the city's Bazaar in March 1841. After their opponents moved a resolution calling on the people to support a campaign for the Six Points of the Charter, the O'Connellites 'proposed an amendment, to the effect, that while the meeting agree with the principle of the resolution just proposed, so far as universal suffrage is concerned, they think it more advisable, in the mean time, to unite in seeking that more peaceable measure, namely, household suffrage'.[76]

Two further factors which might have contributed to the decision of some Irish Catholics not to participate in Scottish Chartism during this period, and which hitherto have not been discussed by historians, were the role of Catholic priests and the role of local Catholic Irish leaders. The clergy will be examined first. It will be recalled that at the great Chartist demonstration in Glasgow in September 1840 the United Labourers, a group which consisted of Irish Catholics, marched in the procession held prior to the meeting on the Green. In its report of the event the *Scots Times* revealed that 'The United Labourers had…enrolled themselves as determined to walk in the procession', but 'The influence of a Catholic priest…who, we understand, denounced the Chartists from the pulpit the Sunday previous, and the insidious exertions of several of Dan's tail persuaded a majority of the Irishmen not to walk, and consequently this trade was awanting'.[77] More information on this issue comes from the aftermath of the dispute concerning the Irish Registration Bills. At the meeting of the Lanarkshire Universal Suffrage Association on 9 March 1841, Con Murray reminded those present that he had been a member of the Chartist deputation which invited the Irish labourers to participate in the procession. He recalled that they agreed to do so, but soon afterwards Bishop John Murdoch was made aware of their decision and 'exerted all his influence to prevent the Catholics attending, telling them he was no politician, and did not want them to interfere in politics, especially those of the Chartists'.[78] A letter 'from A Catholic Chartist, to the Right Revd Bishop Murdoch', published in the *Scots Times* on 17 March 1841, stated that Murdoch told his congregation from the pulpit 'that no Catholic ought to connect himself with Chartism, as it had been turned into a species of religion'. This, no doubt, was a reference to the Chartist Churches which had been established. The letter added that the Bishop concluded by informing his flock that, 'if they loved their God, their religion, and their country, they would stand aloof from the Chartists'.[79]

Murdoch was taken to task by both Murray and 'A Catholic Chartist' over his claim that he did not participate in political agitations. They recalled that his name had headed a large subscription list sent to the

Precursor Society in Dublin. (He subscribed one pound.)[80] 'A Catholic Chartist' also reminded him that he had chaired the meeting in the Justiciary Hall on the Irish Registration Bills. Murdoch was at this time Bishop Andrew Scott's coadjutor in the Western District, although since his superior's removal to Greenock in 1834 he had been left in charge of the Catholic Church in and around Glasgow.[81] He was not the only Catholic clergyman to participate in O'Connellite politics during the first three years of the Chartist agitation. For example, the Revs. McLauchlan of Greenock and Stewart of Glasgow were involved in the Precursor Society during its brief existence.[82]

Such clerical participation in political movements in the west of Scotland may at first appear rather strange; after all, Murdoch and Scott were extremely hostile to the O'Connellite Glasgow Catholic Association in the 1820s, and in 1832 Scott tried to persuade the Catholic electors in Glasgow not to vote for radical reform candidates at the general election.[83] However, given the hostility of the Catholic clergy in Scotland towards the Chartist movement,[84] the involvement of some of them in campaigns concerning Irish issues was perhaps the result of a conviction that clerical endorsement of 'safe' O'Connellite agitation could help encourage or persuade some Irish Catholics to become involved in it and not Chartism. Indeed, clerical advocates of O'Connellism often coupled their support for O'Connell's policies with a denunciation of Chartism. As shown earlier, Timothy O'Meara, an Irish priest based in Glasgow, did this at a meeting of the Paisley congregation in February 1839. At a meeting in Glasgow of ex-members of the Precursor Association the following September the Reverend McLauchlan of Greenock stated that those present 'wanted no ascendancy...but equality, and this they would attain by peaceful agitation, which would shake the empire to the very centre (hear, hear). But they would not be Chartists, but remain faithful subjects of their beloved Queen'.[85]

This clerical involvement in political issues greatly angered the Catholic Irish Chartists. For example, at the meeting of the Lanarkshire Universal Suffrage Association in March 1841 Con Murray condemned the role of the Glasgow priests in the Justiciary Hall debate. Using the same arguments advanced by William McGowan in his disputes with Andrew Scott in the 1820s and 1830s, Murray affirmed to his audience that 'he was a Catholic — and he trusted he was a sincere one — but although, as a Catholic, he had a right to submit to the opinion of the Bishop on points of religious doctrine, he had no right to submit to him in matters of politics'.[86]

Although the Catholic clergy in the west of Scotland appear to have been united in their hostility towards the Chartist movement, the reasons for their opposition were not always the same. For example, in his open letter to Bishop Murdoch, 'A Catholic Chartist' remarked that the Catholic priest in Greenock, Alex Smith, had accused the Chartists of being 'a set of infidels' who had 'no religion in them whatever'. This was a somewhat different view from that of Murdoch who was, among other reasons, concerned about the religious aspects of the Chartist movement.[87] Smith, who became Murdoch's coadjutor Bishop in 1847 (Andrew Scott died the previous year and was succeeded by Murdoch as Vicar-Apostolic of the Western District)[88] made his attack in 1839. It elicited a response from Dr. Thomas Donnelly, who published late that year a pamphlet entitled *An Address on the Political State of Ireland, with a Defence of Chartist Principles, against the charges of Infidelity, etc* made by the *Revd Alex Smith, Roman Catholic Clergyman, Greenock*. This work, which also argued that Universal Suffrage would solve Ireland's problems, was praised highly by the Chartist press. The *True Scotsman* stated that the pamphlet

> shows the Doctor possessed of a vigorous independent mind. His Rev. accuser is dealt with as he deserves. His unprincipled accusations are torn to pieces; and if the reverend gentleman be not devoid of conscience, he must have bitterly regretted his calumnious attacks on the Catholic Chartists, and Chartists generally. We think his soul must have quailed within him when perusing the well merited castigation he has received from the Doctor. The pamphlet answers a far higher end than being a reply to the accuser: it contains much valuable information. It points out the ills of Ireland in a clear and forcible manner; it points out the evils it has suffered by its connection with Britain; it points out its…capabilities for making its population happy; it points out the delusive nature of O'Connell's cry 'Justice to Ireland', and exposes his treachery to his country and the cause of liberty. In all these and other topics, it contains much valuable information, and is worthy of perusal by all interested in the procurement of equal justice.

The *Scottish Patriot* was equally lavish in its praise. It stated 'that a better Address upon the subject we have seldom read', and urged its readers to obtain a copy.[89] In February 1840 Donnelly claimed that he had 'received assurances from no less than thirteen different parts of the country' that his Address had 'been the means of instructing [his] countrymen in their rights, and stimulating many of them to join with the patriotic men of their adopted country, in claiming their civil and political privilege'.[90]

As the example of the Irish labourers and the September 1840 Chartist demonstration in Glasgow has shown, Catholic clergymen sometimes succeeded in preventing members of their congregations from joining the Chartist cause. In other instances their efforts might have simply reinforced

Catholic Irish hostility towards the agitation. It seems unlikely, however, that priests in the west of Scotland adopted the same measures towards Catholic Chartists as Scott and Murdoch used against members of the Glasgow Catholic Association in the 1820s, for example denying the sacraments to those who refused to follow clerical 'advice'. Such behaviour would undoubtedly have been reported in the Chartist and radical press. There is, however, evidence that at least one priest, though admittedly not in the west of Scotland, was unwilling to tolerate the presence of a Catholic Chartist in his church. In July 1842 Con Murray delivered a lecture in Campsie on Chartism. The following day he went to the local chapel whereupon he was physically thrown out by its priest.[91]

Finally, the role of Irish Catholic leaders must be examined in relation to the issue of Irish Catholic non-involvement in Chartism during the first three years of the agitation. Glasgow Chartists certainly believed that individuals such as Charles Bryson and Dr. John Scanlan were in a great measure responsible for the political position adopted by the bulk of their fellow countrymen.[92] At the March 1841 meeting of the Lanarkshire Universal Suffrage Association its secretary, James Jack, commented on the events earlier that month concerning the Irish Registration Bills. He told those assembled that:

> He by no means blamed the great body of the Irish Catholics, but those amongst them who, having the power, misled their worst informed countrymen...He was sorry to see that the leaders of the Irish Catholics in Glasgow had instilled into the minds of their countrymen that the people of Glasgow were opposed to the interests of Ireland. There could be nothing more erroneous, more totally false than this. It was unworthy of the Catholic leaders thus to deceive and irritate one class of men against another.

Con Murray agreed with Jack and suggested that the Association present an address to the Irish Catholics which explained Chartist principles. Moreover, he argued that the Chartists should take the fight to the Catholic Irish leaders:

> Another thing which he thought would do much good, would be to challenge the Catholic leaders to public discussion, on the merits of the questions at issue between them. He thought this would open the eyes of his countrymen, and make them join hands with the Chartists in seeking justice for all (cheers).

It would appear that Murray had forgotten that such debates occurred in the city the previous June, evidently with little or no success as far as the Chartists were concerned. Nevertheless, his suggestion received the approval of the meeting.

It is impossible to establish the extent to which Catholic Irish leaders in Glasgow were responsible for their countrymen's hostility or apathy towards Chartism. They certainly tried to ensure that the Chartists did not make large numbers of recruits from Catholic Irish ranks. Charles Bryson's use of his position as chairman of the Glasgow Catholic Total Abstinence Society to advance O'Connellite views has already been noted. It would also appear that Bryson and Dr. John Scanlan were involved in the events which led to Bishop Murdoch 'advising' the Irish labourers not to participate in the 1840 Chartist demonstration in Glasgow. Con Murray reminded the March 1841 meeting of the Lanarkshire Universal Suffrage Association that Murdoch acted after being informed of the Irish labourers' intention to march in the procession by 'the very party who got up the disgraceful meeting in the Justiciary Hall', who solicited 'him to shake the thunders of the church over the heads of the Irish labourers, to prevent them attending the demonstration'. In his open letter to Murdoch in the *Scots Times* on 17 March 1841, 'A Catholic Chartist' described this group as 'the respectables in the Bridgegate...those conscientious men, the drunkard makers, the pawn-brokers, and the rag merchants...'. It would appear, therefore, that this group of shopkeepers and businessmen who actively supported O'Connell used their position within the Catholic Irish community to advance their political views and campaign against Chartism.[93]

Despite almost three years of agitation the Glasgow Chartists had failed to persuade the vast majority of Irish Catholics in the city to join their campaign for political reform. One of the main reasons for the political position taken by the Irish Catholics was that they remained loyal to O'Connell. In March 1841 the Glasgow Chartists began to seriously address the issue of Catholic Irish non-participation. Their task was soon made more difficult by the establishment in the city of a society which supported the campaign for repeal of the Act of Union between Great Britain and Ireland. This movement was, of course, led by Daniel O'Connell.

Notes

1. Leslie C. Wright, *Scottish Chartism* (Edinburgh, 1953), pp. 16–20; Alexander Wilson, *The Chartist Movement in Scotland* (Manchester, 1970), pp. 141, 216–7, 222–3.

2. James Handley, *The Irish in Scotland 1798–1845* (2nd edition, Cork, 1945), p. 317.

3. Dorothy Thompson, 'Ireland and the Irish in English Radicalism before

1850', in James Epstein and Dorothy Thompson (eds.), *The Chartist Experience: Studies in Working-Class Radicalism and Culture, 1830–1860* (London, 1982), pp.133–4; J.H. Treble, 'O'Connor, O'Connell and the Attitudes of Irish Immigrants towards Chartism in the North of England 1838–1848', in J. Butt and I.F. Clarke (eds.), *The Victorians and Social Protest: a Symposium* (Newton Abbot, 1973), pp.34–43.

4. Dorothy Thompson, 'Ireland and the Irish in English Radicalism', p.133; Edward Royle, *Chartism* (2nd edition, London, 1988), pp.19–21; J.T. Ward, *Chartism* (London, 1973), pp.82–5; 93–5.

5. Treble, 'O'Connor, O'Connell and the Attitudes of Irish Immigrants', p.38.

6. Oliver McDonagh, *The Emancipist: Daniel O'Connell, 1830–1847* (London, 1989), pp.167–94; D. George Boyce, *Nineteenth Century Ireland: The Search for Stability* (Dublin, 1990), pp.66–74; Gearoid O'Tuathaigh, *Ireland Before the Famine* (2nd edition, Dublin, 1990), pp.181–4.

7. Treble, 'O'Connor, O'Connell and the Attitudes of Irish Immigrants', pp.36–7.

8. *Ibid*, p.38.

9. *Ibid*, pp.38–9; Ward, *Chartism*, pp.110–3.

10. Treble, 'O'Connor, O'Connell and the Attitudes of Irish Immigrants', pp.50–1; Ward, *Chartism*, pp.126, 146; James Epstein, *The Lion of Freedom: Feargus O'Connor and the Chartist Movement, 1832–1842* (London, 1982), pp.126–7, 267–71.

11. Wright, *Scottish Chartism*, pp.18–9.

12. *Ibid*, pp.19–20.

13. *Ibid*, p.19.

14. *Ibid*, p.20.

15. Wilson, *Chartist Movement*, p.141.

16. Treble, 'O'Connor, O'Connell and the Attitudes of Irish Immigrants', pp.33–70; Thompson, 'Ireland and the Irish in English Radicalism', pp.120–51.

17. Treble, 'O'Connor, O'Connell and the Attitudes of Irish Immigrants', p.34.

18. Thompson, 'Ireland and the Irish in English Radicalism', p.123.

19. Treble, 'O'Connor, O'Connell and the Attitudes of Irish Immigrants', p.41.

20. F.A. Montgomery, Glasgow Radicalism, 1830–1848, Ph.D. thesis, University of Glasgow (1975); Archibald Leitch, Radicalism in Paisley, 1830–1848: and its economic, political, cultural background, M.Litt. thesis, University of Glasgow (1993).

21. Alexander Wilson, 'Chartism in Glasgow', in Asa Briggs (ed.), *Chartist Studies* (London, 1959), pp.273–7.

22. See previous chapter, pp.150–1.

23. *Scots Times*, 5 September 1838.

24. *Ibid*, 27 February 1839; *True Scotsman*, 23 February 1839; *Glasgow Chronicle*, 15 April 1839.

25. (James Dawson Burn), *The Autobiography of a Beggar Boy* (1st published 1855. This edition edited by David Vincent, London, 1978), pp.150–2; *True Scotsman*, 22 February 1839; *Scottish Patriot*, 12 July, 14 September 1839.

26. (Burn), *Autobiography of a Beggar Boy*, pp.150–1.

27. *Ibid*, p.157. For another example of Burn's cautious attitude see *Scottish Patriot*, 12 July 1839.

28. *Scottish Patriot*, 15 February, 28 March 1840; *Scots Times*, 3 March 1841; *Northern Star*, 18 September 1841.

29. *Scots Times*, 5 September 1838. See also *Glasgow Chronicle*, 5 September 1838.

30. *Scots Times*, 27 February 1839. James Burn was also one of the speakers.

31. See, for example, *Glasgow Saturday Post*, 15 January 1842.

32. *Scots Times*, 27 February 1839; *True Scotsman*, 23 February; 2 and 23 March; 6 April; 14 September 1839; *Scottish Patriot*, 14 September 1839, 16 May 1840; *Glasgow Chronicle*, 16 September 1839.

33. *Scottish Patriot*, 7 and 14 March 1840.

34. *Ibid*, 20 June 1840.

35. *Ibid*, 22 February 1840. Donnelly regretted that he was unable to accept the invitation at that time.

36. *Glasgow Chronicle*, 21 May 1838; *Glasgow Courier*, 22 May 1838; *Glasgow Argus*, 21 May 1838; *Scots Times*, 23 May 1838.

37. See chapter 5.

38. *True Scotsman*, 26 September 1840; *Scots Times*, 23 September 1840, 10 and 17 March 1841; *Northern Star*, 26 September 1840.

39. *True Scotsman*, 15 June 1839; *Scots Times*, 12 June 1839; *Glasgow Argus*, 13 June 1839; *Glasgow Chronicle*, 12 June 1839; *Glasgow Courier*, 11 June 1839.

40. Handley, *Irish in Scotland*, pp.118–9.

41. See chapter 1.

42. See Notes 26, 28 and 29.

43. *Scots Times*, 10 March 1841.

44. *Ibid*, 17 March 1841.

45. Wilson, *Chartist Movement*, Chapters 4 and 8; Tony Clarke and Tony Dickson, 'Class and Class Consciousness in Early Industrial Capitalism: Paisley 1770–1850', in Tony Dickson (ed.), *Capital and Class in Scotland* (Edinburgh, 1982), pp.46–9.

46. *Glasgow Courier*, 12 January 1839.

47. Brewster claimed that what he had in fact said that evening in Paisley was that he would not join with O'Connell 'in his peculiarly Irish agitation, which he says is to bring Ireland on a level with England. If he will not join in our movement, which will effect this by a shorter process, I will not consent to wait for lagging Ireland, but will try to keep England a-head of him, and give him fresh work for agitation'. Brewster said that this, 'if not the very words', was 'the substance and meaning' of what he said. *True Scotsman*, 26 January 1839.

48. See, for example, *Ibid*, 19 January 1839; *Scots Times*, 12 January 1839; *Glasgow Argus*, 14 January 1839; *Northern* Star, 19 January 1839.

49. This paragraph is based on Clarke and Dickson, 'Class and Class Consciousness', p.48; Wilson, *Chartist Movement*, pp.66–68; *True Scotsman*, 19 January 1839; *Glasgow Chronicle*, 16 January 1839; See also *Scots Times*, 19 January 1839; *Glasgow Argus*, 17 January 1839.

50. Treble, 'O'Connor, O'Connell and the Attitudes of Irish Immigrants', p.34.

51. *Scottish Patriot*, 15 February 1840.

52. Bryson is described as a merchant and shipper in *Glasgow Chronicle*, 11 September 1839. An indication of the extent of his wealth is found in the following extract from a letter from Bishop Scott to Bishop Kyle, dated 7 May 1839: 'Bryson at Glasgow has sold St Margaret's Place with appendages at £10,000 str. He paid £11,000 for it. His circumstances compelled him to sell it, and everyone is surprised that he got so much for it, but he takes in payment to the value of £3,000 in goods…He has given up his shop and warehouse and is now engaged in the wood trade from St Johns in Nova Scotia to New Brunswick. He got a pretty large ship built there and brought her lately to Greenock loaded with timber, but in spite of the sale of St Margaret's Place, he was obliged to borrow money on the vessel nearly to the amount of its value at 5 percent and to ensure her a for a very heavy sum.' SCA, Presholme Letters, PL3/285/13, Andrew Scott to James Kyle, 7 May 1839.

53. For further correspondence concerning Murray and the Glasgow Catholic Total Abstinence Society see *Scottish Patriot*, 14 and 28 March 1840.

54. *Scots Times*, 10 March 1841; *Glasgow Saturday Post*, 6 March 1841.

55. *Scots Times*, 10 March 1841.

56. *Ibid*. See also *Glasgow Saturday Post*, 6 March 1841; *Northern Star*, 13 March 1841.

57. *Scots Times*, 10 March 1841.

58. The following discussion of this meeting is based on *ibid*, 17 March 1841.

59. *Scottish Patriot*, 22 February 1840.

60. *Glasgow Chronicle*, 15 February 1839.

61. Wilson, *Chartist Movement*, passim.

62. MacDonagh, *The Emancipist*, pp.177–82.

63. Treble,'O'Connor, O'Connell and the Attitudes of Irish Immigrants', pp.42–3; *Glasgow Chronicle*, 5 April 1839.

64. *Glasgow Chronicle*, 5 April 1839. See also *Scots Times*, 6 April 1839.

65. The remainder of this paragraph is based on *Scottish Patriot*, 27 June 1840.

66. For the attitudes of Chartists in England to O'Connell see Treble, 'O'Connor, O'Connell and the Attitudes of Irish Immigrants', p.39.

67. *Scottish Patriot*, 27 June 1840.

68. *Glasgow Chronicle*, 12 June 1839.

69. For the attitudes of Chartists in Scotland to O'Connell see Wilson, *Chartist Movement*, pp.105, 117, 157–61.

70. *Scottish Patriot*, 27 June 1840.

71. For Glasgow O'Connellite support for the Whig Ministry see, for example, *Glasgow Chronicle*, 11 September 1839; *Scottish Patriot*, 27 June 1840; *Scots Times*, 10 March 1841.

72. *Glasgow Chronicle*, 11 September 1839.

73. *Scottish Patriot*, 27 June 1840.

74. For O'Connell's views on political reform in Great Britain see Epstein, *Lion of Freedom*, pp. 126–7, 267.

75. *Scottish Patriot*, 27 June 1840.

76. *Glasgow Saturday Post*, 6 March 1841.

77. *Scots Times*, 23 September 1840.

78. *Ibid*, 17 March 1841.

79. *Ibid.* The author of the letter informed Murdoch that he believed that of the 'thousands' of Catholics in Britain who were 'stern advocates of the Charter' there was not one who took 'anything to do with their [the Chartists'] religious worship'. He added that the Chartists did not interfere 'with those who hold different views of religion' and did not 'calumniate and misrepresent the doctrines of the Catholic Church'.

80. In March 1839 the *Glasgow Courier* reported that Murdoch had recently become a member of the Precursor Association 'on the motion of Mr O'Connell'. *Glasgow Courier*, 30 March 1839.

81. *Scottish Catholic Directory*, 1867, p.140.

82. *Glasgow Chronicle*, 11 September 1839.

83. See chapters 4 and 5.

84. For examples of hostility towards Chartism from Catholic clergymen in Scotland see *Glasgow Chronicle*, 15 February, 11 September 1839; *True Scotsmen*, 29 February 1840; *Scots Times*, 17 March 1841; *Northern Star*, 23

July 1842. For the attitudes of priests in England see Treble, 'O'Connor, O'Connell and the Attitudes of Irish Immigrants', pp.48–50.

85. *Glasgow Chronicle*, 11 September 1839.

86. *Scots Times*, 17 March 1841.

87. *Ibid.*

88. *Scottish Catholic Directory*, 1867, p.141.

89. *True Scotsman*, 29 February 1840; *Scottish Patriot*, 14 December 1839. The former paper produced an extract from the pamphlet. This was not the first occasion on which Donnelly was involved in a controversy with the Catholic clergy. See SCA, Oban letters, OL2/31/3, Dr Donnelly to Andrew Scott, 8 January 1838 and OL2/32/4 Dr Donnelly to Andrew Scott, 8 March 1838.

90. *Scottish Patriot*, 22 February 1840.

91. *Northern Star*, 23 July 1842.

92. All the evidence on the role of Irish Catholic leaders in Glasgow comes from the report of the annual meeting of the Lanarkshire Universal Suffrage Association and the 'letter from a Catholic Chartist, to the Right Revd Bishop Murdoch', both of which are in *Scots Times*, 17 March 1841.

93. Bryson and Scanlan were two of the leading O'Connellite participants in the debates with the Glagow Chartists in March 1841.

7

Chartism, Repeal and Complete Suffragism in Glasgow, 1841–42

This chapter will examine the movement in Glasgow for the repeal of the Act of Union of 1800 and the Chartist response to it. The relationship between the city's Irish Repealers and Complete Suffragists will also be discussed. The chapter will cover the period from May 1841 to December 1842 and thus complete the examination of the Irish and Chartism between 1838 and 1842, the peak years of the movement. It is regrettable that the discussion will be concerned only with developments in Glasgow. However, the sources consulted for this period, which were outlined in the introduction to the previous chapter, have produced evidence of the political activities of the Irish which relates almost exclusively to the city.

I

In April 1840 Daniel O'Connell founded the Loyal National Repeal Association and revived the movement for the repeal of the Act of Union. He wanted an Irish Parliament because he believed that the Irish people should have control of their own domestic affairs. O'Connell did not, however, envisage a legislature on the lines of that which was abolished in 1800: under his proposals the Catholic interest would receive its just representation. O'Connell had campaigned for Repeal during the first half of the 1830s, but was unable to arouse much support for the cause in either Ireland or Britain. He suspended the agitation in 1835 after concluding his agreement with the Whigs. By 1840 O'Connell had become convinced that Melbourne's ministry was doomed and would soon be replaced by a Tory administration hostile to the interests of the majority of the Irish nation. He therefore relaunched the campaign for an Irish Parliament.[1]

The Irish in Britain participated in the revived agitation. Between 1840 and 1843, in towns and cities throughout the country, they formed societies which organised meetings, lectures and petitions on Repeal, and which contributed funds to the movement's headquarters in Dublin. These Repealers agreed with O'Connell that it was the right of their fellow countrymen to have their own representative legislature; they were also convinced by the argument that an Irish Parliament would lead to the economic regeneration of their native land which would not only stop Irish emigration, but also enable Irish workers in Britain to return home.[2]

The Glasgow Repeal Association was founded by the city's O'Connellites a short time after their dispute with the Chartists in March 1841 over the Irish Registration Bills.[3] Although the date of its formation is not known the organisation certainly existed by early May, two months before the Tories returned to power.[4] It appears to have made satisfactory progress during its first year. At a Repeal meeting in November 1841 its chairman, after listening to the report of the society's proceedings since the previous May, stated that

> he hoped they all felt gratified at the progress they had made, and for his part he was convinced that the repeal agitation was only in its infancy. Letters had been received from several districts, which had not yet been organised, asking the assistance of some of their members to effect that object, and he had no doubt, from this and other symptoms, but their cause would go on, daily increasing in strength.[5]

Large attendances were reported for this and for subsequent meetings organised by the society. For example, nearly two thousand people attended a Repeal soirée in the City Hall in January 1842. William McGowan was one of the principal speakers at this event.[6] The following month the Association organised a public meeting in the Lyceum Rooms which unanimously adopted the Irish National Petition for Repeal. According to the *Glasgow Saturday Post*, the hall was 'excessively crowded'.[7] The petition, which was reported to have been signed by around thirty thousand inhabitants of Glasgow, was sent to the House of Commons in March 1842.[8] Despite these successes the Association experienced some financial difficulties during its first twelve months. At a meeting of the Repealers in June 1842 the secretary of the society, Dr. Eneas McDonnell, regretted that over the previous year they had not subscribed a larger amount of money to the Repeal Fund in Dublin. He attributed this to the effects of the trade depression and to the high level of unemployment in the city.[9]

II

It is probable that the establishment of the Repeal society in Glasgow did not surprise the city's Chartists. After all, by January 1841 the large Irish communities in Manchester and Liverpool had founded similar organisations, and it is likely that the Glasgow Chartists, being fully aware of the strength of Irish support in the city for O'Connell and his policies, believed that it would not be long before they too were faced with an agitation for Repeal. Indeed, in November 1840 a number of the leading Chartists in Glasgow discussed how their movement should react to such a development.[10] Robert Malcolm Jun. supported Repeal and argued that the Chartists should not oppose a movement in Glasgow for it, a view shared by James Moir. James Jack was not so generous. He argued that if the O'Connellites in the city called a public meeting to discuss Repeal, the Chartists, consistent with their policy of attending all public political meetings to advocate their programme of reform, had to attend the event and put forward the Charter as the solution to Ireland's grievances:

> If the people of Ireland wished a parliament of their own, they had a right to have it, and the people of England or Scotland would not deny that right. But although that the people of Glasgow were willing enough to give the Irish whatever sort of government they desired, it was altogether out of the question to suppose that the Chartists would allow a public meeting to sanction an agitation for the repeal of the Irish union, when they had crushed an agitation for a repeal of the Corn Laws (cheers). It must not go forth to the world that the public of Glasgow had turned Irish repealers. The Irishmen in Glasgow might call a meeting of themselves and agitate their favourite measure; but if they appealed to the public, the Chartists would assuredly step in and oppose them.

Robert Malcolm disagreed with the policy of the Chartists attending every political meeting to put forward the Six Points, as he believed it resulted only in hostility towards them and division among reformers. He argued that it would be counter-productive to antagonise the Repealers, as he was convinced that the House of Commons would not grant Repeal and

> he could imagine the probability of a junction of the Repealers on their being defeated in their attempt for Repeal with the Chartists of the three countries. And what a prospect for them! Mr O'Connell, backed by his millions, agitating with the masses of England and Scotland for the Charter, the whole Charter, and nothing less (cheers). With this view, and holding these sentiments, he was of opinion that if they were not prepared to give their countenance to the Repeal agitation, that they ought not to oppose it.

Matthew Cullen stated that he would 'be very cautious as to the terms upon which he agreed to give the Repealers any assistance', given 'the ignominious and disgraceful way Mr O'Connell had treated and spoken of the Chartists...'. The meeting ended, however, without forming a strategy on how to deal with a Repeal movement in Glasgow.

Unfortunately, the available sources do not reveal the reaction of the Glasgow Chartists to the foundation of the city's Repeal Association. It is probable, however, that this development concerned them greatly. The dispute over the Irish Registration Bills in March 1841 highlighted to the city's Chartists the fact that, despite almost three years of agitation, they had failed to gain many supporters from O'Connellite ranks. Now they were faced with a rival movement, led by O' Connell, which was already very popular among Irish communities in England. Furthermore, it is likely that the strategies advanced by James Jack and Robert Malcolm jun. in November 1840 on how the Chartists should react to a Repeal agitation in Glasgow were no longer regarded as viable options. The Chartist intervention at the public meeting on the Irish Registration Bills had aroused O'Connellite wrath in the city and widened further the gulf between the two groups; the aftermath of the dispute showed that the Chartists were planning to launch a campaign to gain O'Connellite support, which suggests that Malcolm's argument that the Chartists should not interfere with a Repeal campaign would not have been seen as a suitable course of action. It is probable, therefore, that the launch of the Repeal agitation in Glasgow in 1841 was regarded by the city's Chartists as a very serious obstacle to their ambition to win over members of the Catholic Irish community. A new plan had to be devised.

Chartists in several of the principal towns and cities in England were, of course, also faced with the problem of how to deal with the Repeal movement, and eventually a strategy was devised. The O'Connorite National Charter Association, the Chartist organisation for England, decided in September 1841 to raise another Chartist petition to Parliament. The petition differed from the previous one as it also demanded the repeal of the Act of Union between Great Britain and Ireland, and the repeal of the English Poor Law Amendment Act. The call for repeal of Union was, of course, included to make Chartism more attractive to the Irish. The Chartist argument was that Repeal on its own would not improve the condition of Ireland and her people — it had to be accompanied by the political reforms embodied in the Charter.[11] According to Treble, 'Once sounded this message which had received the personal endorsement of O'Connor, was to be heard from Chartist platforms in virtually every major town in the North of England.'[12] The new programme was also adopted enthusiastically by O'Connor's supporters in Glasgow. From September to December 1841, at meetings in and around the city on the condition of Ireland, they argued that only Chartism and Repeal would regenerate that country. Con Murray was one of the leading promoters of the new message as was another Irish Catholic, Dennis McMillan. Indeed, it was during this period that McMillan first became prominent in the Chartist movement in Glasgow.[13]

It is difficult to establish how successful the Chartism and Repeal policy was during these months in persuading Glasgow O'Connellites to join the agitation for the Six Points. For example, in September Con Murray gave a lecture in Bridgeton on Irish politics. The *Northern Star* reported that as Bridgeton was 'a district which contains upwards of 7000 Roman Catholics, the hall was crowded to excess, besides the numbers who congregated outside'. During the meeting Murray and several other Chartists, including Dennis McMillan, attacked O'Connell and his policies. The *Northern Star* claimed that these speeches and the general discussion which followed resulted in 'Dan's backers' admitting 'that they were now convinced' by the Chartist arguments. A resolution was adopted which stated that those present sympathised with the condition of the people of Ireland and would assist the campaign for Repeal and the Charter. The 'entire assembly' also voted to hold a procession and demonstration to welcome O'Connor on his visit to Glasgow the following month.[14] The report did not, however, give a figure for the size of O'Connell's support at the beginning of the lecture, and accounts of subsequent meetings did not indicate whether similar political conversions occurred. Indeed, the report of the Bridgeton meeting in O'Connor's *Northern Star* is the only one available, and it is possible that the correspondent might have been less than truthful in his account, in order to give the reader 'evidence' that the new Chartist policy was a magnificent success in Glasgow.

The demonstration for O'Connor, who had been released from prison in August after serving a sentence of sixteen months for his Chartist activities, took place on Glasgow Green on 11 October. At this gathering he received from the Irish Chartists in the city an address which praised him and attacked his critics, and which supported the decision to campaign for Repeal and the Charter.[15] Unfortunately, nothing more is known about this group. It is therefore impossible to determine the extent to which it included new adherents to the Chartist cause. It might simply have been composed mainly of the Irish workers who had participated in previous Chartist demonstrations and meetings in the city.

O'Connor's visit to Glasgow in October 1841 was part of a tour of Scotland he made during that and the following month. During its final three weeks O'Connor engaged in a series of debates in a number of towns and cities with his old adversary Patrick Brewster on 'the best means of obtaining the Charter'. Their final contest was held in the Bazaar in Glasgow on 4 November. By a huge majority this public meeting supported O'Connor and his policies; it also produced a vote of no confidence in Brewster. According to the *Northern Star*, prior to the meeting 'two hundred O'Connellites marched into the Hall in a body, resolved, right or wrong, to vote against O'Connor', but at the end of the debate actually supported him, 'their hearts having warmed to their countryman…'. O'Connor, in his account of events, stated that at the conclusion of the night's business, 'The hustings was charged by the Irishmen, who seized me by the neck and limb, claimed me for their own, and literally dragged me through the meeting, jumping and cheering till I thought the building would come down.'[16]

Once again it is extremely difficult to assess the significance of this event, or indeed the accuracy of the account of it given that O'Connor's *Northern Star* was the only newspaper which gave information on the O'Connellites' role in the debate. Leslie Wright accepted that the Irish were present, and offered the following reason why they supported O'Connor over Brewster: 'faced by a renegade Irishman and an alien cleric the former might prove more popular.'[17] It must also be added that O'Connor argued that the Chartists should campaign for Repeal whereas Brewster maintained that they should concentrate solely on the Six Points, and not mix them up with other issues and demands.[18] Whether the support for O'Connor from these 'two hundred O'Connellites' continued after the excitement of the debate had passed is not known.[19]

As has been demonstrated, it is impossible to determine the exact impact the Chartism and Repeal package had during the last quarter of 1841 on the political views of O'Connell's supporters in Glasgow. It might have won over some, but it is probable that it did not result in a large increase in Irish support for the Chartist movement. If this had occurred, it would surely have been seized upon by the Chartists and trumpeted by them at their meetings for all to hear. Press reports of their activities, other than the two examples from the *Northern Star* already discussed, did not suggest that this occurred. Similarly, accounts of Repeal meetings in Glasgow around this time did not give the impression that a major transfer of Irish political allegiances had taken place. For example, at a meeting of the city's Repealers in the Lyceum Rooms on 9 November those present heard the secretary's report of the proceedings of the society since early May. Neither the report nor the speeches made that evening expressed concern about the activities of the Glasgow Chartists: in fact, they did not mention them at all.[20]

The attempts by O'Connor's supporters in the city to gain more Irish support for the Chartist cause in fact suffered a major setback in November 1841, when a meeting of the Glasgow Chartists resolved to oppose the decision of the National Charter Association to include repeal of the Act of Union and repeal of the English Poor Law Amendment Act in the new National Petition. This, however, was merely a prelude to the events of

January 1842, when the Scottish Chartist Convention, held in Glasgow, also decided — on the casting vote of its chairman — not to endorse the National Petition. Those who opposed the NCA's plan did not necessarily do so out of hostility towards Repeal or indifference to the problems of Ireland. For example, one of the leading opponents of the National Petition was Robert Malcolm jun. who, as has already been stated, supported Repeal and in fact became active in the agitation for it once the Chartist movement went into decline. The vast majority of those who rejected the petition of the National Charter Association appear to have done so as a matter of principle. They believed that a Chartist petition should concentrate solely on the Six Points and not include any proposals, such as repeal of Union and repeal of the Poor Law Amendment Act, which were supported by only a section of the Chartist movement, 'no matter how large or small that section...'. Furthermore, this group, which included most Scottish Chartist leaders, might have used the issue of the National Petition to humiliate O'Connor, as they were opposed to the dominant role which he and his followers played in the movement and to their attempts to promote a petition and policies on which the Scottish Chartists had not been consulted. Indeed, the rejection of the National Petition was not the only defeat suffered by O'Connor, who was present at the debates and who spoke in favour of the plans of the NCA. The Convention passed a resolution expressing 'satisfaction at the growing progress of Chartist principles among the middle classes', which O'Connor had tried to amend to 'a vote of thanks to the working-classes for the resistance they had made, and were still making, to oppression and oppressors'. The Convention also condemned the policy of intervening at public meetings to advocate the Six Points of the Charter. Finally, the Scottish Convention asserted its independence by making arrangements to raise its own petition.[21]

O'Connor was furious at these defeats. Over the following few weeks he launched a virulent campaign in the *Northern Star* against the Glasgow Chartists. It eventually succeeded. On 7 February the city's Chartists voted by at least two to one to reverse their decision of November 1841 and adopt the National Petition of the NCA instead of that prepared by the Scottish Convention. Con Murray was, not surprisingly, one of the principal proponents of the English petition at this meeting: he argued that it should be supported 'because it contained a recognition of the right of Ireland to a repeal of the Legislative Union'.[22]

Soon after this a number of Glasgow Chartists attended a public meeting in the city's Lyceum Rooms, held to consider whether to petition Parliament for a repeal of the British-Irish Act of Union. The meeting, which was arranged by the Glasgow Repealers, resolved to do so and those present also pledged themselves to assist the agitation for an Irish parliament. Charles Bryson, on behalf of the Repealers, singled out for praise the presence of the Chartists at the event and stated:

> He was of opinion that it was a pity for any dispute to arise between Irishmen and Chartists. (Hear, hear and approbation). Their object was the same, and he declared he would sign a petition for the Charter the moment it was presented to him. (Cheers.) He was a Chartist out and out, and the reason why he had not hitherto mingled so much amongst them as he would otherwise have done, or induced his countrymen to do so, was not because he had any doubt of the justice of their principles, but because he could not join with some of their leaders. (Applause.)

Once all the resolutions of the meeting had been adopted John Colquhoun, one of the leading O'Connorites in the city and an active supporter of the National Petition, addressed the audience and denied that the Chartists had ever advocated the use of physical force to achieve their aims. He then pledged his support to the campaign for Repeal and urged the meeting to support the agitation for the Charter. Bryson 'rejoiced' at Colquhoun's speech and 'trusted that if his friends wished well to the cause of Ireland, that they would come forward in great numbers, and sign the Repeal Petition, this would be a proof of their sincerity. (Applause)'. [23]

That the Chartists received such a friendly reception at this meeting in February 1842 may at first appear somewhat surprising given the hostility of the Glasgow O'Connellites towards the Chartist movement during its first three years. The Chartists, however, had now adopted Repeal as part of their programme and naturally this was welcomed by the O'Connellites. More importantly, by that time the Glasgow Repealers had come to the conclusion that, because of the changed political situation in Great Britain, they needed the support of the Chartists. Since July 1841 the Tories had been in power and were regarded by O'Connell and his supporters as hostile to the interests of the majority of the Irish nation. Indeed, the likely prospect of a Tory government was one of the reasons why O'Connell relaunched his Repeal campaign. [24] The Tories had no intention of establishing an Irish parliament and the Glasgow Repealers became convinced that their agitation would not succeed unless it received the backing of all groups in society, including the Chartists. [25]

To obtain such support the Glasgow Repealers argued that it was in the interest of all Scottish workers to aid O'Connell's movement. For example, at the aforementioned meeting in the Lyceum Rooms the following resolution was adopted:

That British labourers, trades people, and artizans having their wages reduced and places occupied through Irish enterprise and industry, being forced annually upon the shores of this realm, we calculate on the intelligent of both countries aiding the Irish in obtaining the repeal of an act fraught with such disastrous consequences, which robs Ireland of her wealth, her prosperity, and her sons, whilst it overwhelms Britain with Irish competitors in every branch of human industry.[26]

Similar arguments were used by the Repealers in the north of England who sought assistance from native workers.[27] The Glasgow Repealers also believed that theirs was a just cause which therefore deserved the support of everyone.[28]

The Glasgow Repealers welcomed the backing given by the city's Chartists to their agitation, but were still unwilling to form any sort of alliance with them. The Chartist movement in Britain continued to be dominated by O'Connell's arch-enemy Feargus O'Connor, and despite the qualities of the Glasgow Chartists the Repealers would not unite with them so long as this was the case. They also still believed that the Chartists intended to use unconstitutional means to obtain their demands, as 'A Glasgow Repealer' made apparent in a letter to the *Glasgow Saturday Post* soon after the February meeting in the Lyceum Rooms. He, however, along with Repealers such as Bryson, longed for the day when the two parties could campaign together:

when they [the Chartists] repudiate physical force doctrines, as they did at our meeting, we, with the approbation and counsel of our illustrious leader O'Connell, will aid them in obtaining their just and constitutional demands, whilst we cordially accept their proffered assistance in obtaining ours. This is as it should be. It is by one mighty, widespread, but unanimous combination of the people against their oppressors, that any good can at present be achieved. Thus reciprocally acting in unison, what ministry or junto of lordlings dare refuse us our just demands! Our great object is to unite all classes in one mighty moral phalanx to overthrow Toryism and monopoly.[29]

Although they had adopted Repeal as part of their programme, the Glasgow Chartists in February 1842 were unable to persuade the city's Repealers to join the campaign for the Six Points. Nevertheless, they were probably pleased with the progress which had been made. After all, in March 1841 the Chartists engaged in two very bitter and violent debates with the O'Connellites; eleven months later several O'Connorites attended a Repeal meeting at which their presence was warmly welcomed. The Glasgow Chartists, however, were soon faced with a rival organisation in the city which advocated the Six Points and which also sought an alliance with the Repealers — the Complete Suffrage Association.

III

The Complete Suffrage movement was founded by Joseph Sturge, who was a corn factor from Birmingham and a member of the Anti-Corn Law League.[30] He was one of a number of middle class reformers who by autumn 1841 had become extremely alarmed at the extent of class conflict in England. To help eliminate this, Sturge argued that a 'Reconciliation between the Middle and Labouring Classes' should occur based on a joint campaign for an extension of the franchise. He advanced this view at a conference of the Anti-Corn Law League held in Manchester in November 1841 and received the support of many of the delegates, who probably also believed that now the Tories were in power the campaign for repeal of the Corn Laws would be bolstered if it received widespread support from working class reformers. Sturge and Sharman Crawford, a radical Member of Parliament, were authorised by these delegates to produce a manifesto which set out their agreed aims and which would be signed by them. The resulting document became known as the Sturge Declaration:

> Deeply impressed with conviction of the evils arising from class legislation, and of the sufferings thereby inflicted upon our industrious fellow-subjects, the undersigned affirm that a large majority of the people of this country are unjustly excluded from that fair, full and free exercise of the legislative franchise to which they are entitled by the great principles of Christian equity, and also by the British Constitution...[31]

Copies of the declaration were soon distributed throughout Great Britain, and in December the Birmingham Complete Suffrage Union was formed to promote a cross-class alliance for parliamentary reform. Over the next few months the Sturge declaration was adopted at a number of meetings across the country, and Complete Suffrage societies and provisional committees were established by middle- and working-class reformers.

The declaration was also signed by a number of leading Chartists, including William Lovett, John Collins, Henry Vincent and Robert Lowery, all of whom were moderates opposed to O'Connor's dominance of their movement. They had become convinced by this time that the Chartists would achieve their aims only in alliance with middle-class reformers, and therefore welcomed Sturge's proposals. O'Connor, however, did not agree with this assessment of Chartism's prospects. Furthermore, he did not trust the new movement and noted how his opponents within the National Charter Association had been quick to associate themselves with it. For O'Connor, Complete Suffragism was

Complete Humbug, a plot to gain working class support for corn–law repeal. If middle class radicals were sincere in their desire to aid the working class in their struggle for political democracy, they should declare for the Charter and join the ranks of the Chartist movement.[32]

Chartists who joined or sympathised with the Complete Suffragists became the victims of violent attacks by O'Connor, his supporters and the *Northern Star*.

In April 1842 the Complete Suffragists held their founding conference in Birmingham. Despite the hostility of the O'Connorities to the movement, Lowery, Vincent, Collins and Lovett were among the delegates. The Conference adopted all Six Points of the Charter as its policy. However, despite the wishes of the Chartist delegates, the name 'Charter' was not chosen: the middle–class delegates were hostile to the term because of the reputation for violence that Chartism had as a result of the activities of a number of its adherents. According to Epstein, 'Middle class radicals had no intention of becoming part of the Chartist movement. Implicit in the middle–class rejection of the name "Chartist" was the suggestion that the working–class radicals repudiate the tone and history, established leadership and organisation of Chartism'.[33] Lovett was made aware of the hostility towards the term and decided not to propose its adoption. Instead, a final decision on the issue was postponed to a future conference. The Birmingham conference also established the rules of 'The National Complete Suffrage Union' and elected a forty-eight member general council, which included Lovett, Vincent and Collins. On 21 April the Complete Suffrage petition was presented to Parliament: it was rejected by 226 votes to 67. Eleven days later the Chartist National Petition was likewise introduced. It too was defeated.

Despite the presence of leading figures in their movement at the Birmingham conference, Chartists in most areas of England remained loyal to O'Connor and the *Northern Star*. However, 'In a few localites, most notably Birmingham, Bath, Brighton...differences between O'Connor and leaders sympathetic to the CSU led to rifts within the Chartist ranks...'.[34] This occurred in Glasgow. In January 1842 Sturge visited the city. A public meeting adopted his declaration and a provisional committee, which included several leading middle class reformers, was appointed to establish a Complete Suffrage society.[35] Most of the leading figures in the Glasgow Chartist movement soon became involved in Complete Suffragism: James Jack, Malcolm McFarlane, James Hoey, Robert Malcolm jun., William Thomson, Walter Currie, James Walker, Charles McEwan and William Pattison all became committee members of the Glasgow Complete Suffrage Association when it was founded on 19 May 1842.[36] Thomson was later elected its secretary, and McFarlane one of its Vice-Presidents.[37] These Chartists had opposed O'Connor and his policies at the Scottish Convention in January 1842. Afterwards O'Connor launched a fierce campaign in the *Northern Star* against 'the rotten leaders of Glasgow' who were 'all Whigs — not a drop of Chartist blood in their veins'. It will be recalled that this was successful; in February a meeting of the Glasgow Chartists adopted the National Petition of the NCA despite the expressed opposition of those leading activists who had contributed to its rejection at the Scottish Convention the previous month.[38] This was a major defeat for O'Connor's opponents and, according to Wilson, thereafter they 'were unwilling to seek any further reconciliation' with him.[39] Thus isolated, these Chartists, who like Lovett and Vincent believed that the only way to achieve the Six Points was through an alliance of the middle and working classes, saw the Complete Suffrage movement as a vehicle to promote their aims and ideals. But they did not see themselves as abandoning Chartism: 'For them the emergence of Joseph Sturge and Complete Suffragism was a welcome promise that Chartism might yet be able to throw off the tutelage of O'Connor. They saw no incompatibility between support for Sturge and their responsibilities to the older movement, from which they had no apparent intention of divorcing themselves.'[40]

The Complete Suffrage movement in Glasgow also received the support of the city's Irish Repealers. For example, the following resolution was adopted unanimously at a large Repeal meeting in the City Hall in June:

> we hereby pledge ourselves to agitate for Complete Suffrage and other measures of reform, and that we will combine legally with Liberals of all classes to resist Toryism and oppression, and raise the working classes of these countries to that station that justice demands, and which has been so long withheld from them by our common oppressors, the British aristocrats and British legislators.[41]

Furthermore, four leading members of the Glasgow Repeal Association — Charles Bryson, Dr. John Scanlan, Dr. Henry Gribben and Peter McCabe — were elected to the committee of the Glasgow Complete Suffrage Association at its founding meeting in May.[42] Bryson later became one of the Vice-Presidents of the society.[43] He also chaired a meeting in the City Hall in September, attended by around 2000 people, at which Henry Vincent lectured on the principles of Complete Suffragism.[44]

It is not difficult to understand why the Glasgow Repealers became such enthusiastic supporters of the Complete Suffrage movement. This and the previous chapter have demonstrated that the city's O'Connellites were in favour of the Six Points of the Charter. They could not, however, give their support to the Chartist agitation so long as it was dominated by their leader's bitter enemy Feargus O'Connor. Complete Suffragism finally gave O'Connell's followers in Glasgow an opportunity they could take to participate in a national campaign for the Six Points. It was not an O'Connorite movement — indeed, it included most of O'Connor's leading opponents within English and Scottish Chartism. Moreover, the Complete Suffragists wanted to unite the middle class and the working class in a peaceful reform campaign. As has been shown, the Glasgow Repealers were convinced that their movement would succeed only if it was part of a wider reform agitation, supported by all groups in society. Bryson reiterated this at a Repeal meeting in June 1842 when he proposed a resolution supporting Complete Suffragism:

> It was now necessary that they should throw aside all minor points of difference, and promote that union amongst Reformers without which no great movement could hope to be successful...It was their interest to embrace into their views all who, in common with themselves, were struggling to get quit of the yoke of their aristocratic oppressors, and the Complete Suffragists, as rational, peaceable, and constitutional reformers, were in every way entitled to their co-operation and assistance.[45]

Finally, and perhaps most importantly, O'Connell had given his blessing to the Complete Suffrage agitation.[46]

Leading Scottish Complete Suffragists in Glasgow were, not surprisingly, delighted that the city's Irish Repealers had decided to support their movement. For example, Walter Currie spoke at the Repeal meeting in Glasgow in June which passed resolutions in favour of Complete Suffragism:

> He would confess that to-night he had been almost electrified, not more with the union and enthusiasm of the audience than with the power and eloquence of the speakers. It did his heart good to witness such a meeting, and to feel with them in sentiment and action. Irishmen and Scotsmen had hitherto been taught by the ruling few, and by their clerical teachers, that it was good to hate, oppose, and injure each other, and that they had no interests in common. The march of intelligence, however, had dispelled these nostrums, and the people now felt and acted upon the principle that union was strength, and a bad government the enemy of both. Irishmen had been dubbed aliens in language and religion. Aliens! indeed, and why? Because they dared to worship the God of their fathers, and adhered to the tenets of the Catholic faith. Aliens forsooth! and did their oppressors think that Scotsmen sympathised in such a sentiment? No, no, while they united with their Irish brethren in behalf of their common interests they could not forget that to a catholic Wallace and a catholic Bruce they owed the small shreds of freedom they enjoyed at the present day (Tremendous cheering). While they united with their Irish brethren they could

not forget that the catholics had been the first to strip the shackles from the persecuted quakers — (renewed cheering) — and that wherever the voice of the patriot, or the cry of suffering humanity had been heard there were Irishmen to sympathize — to struggle — and, if need be, to die. Who would not give them praise for what they had done — the devil himself could not deny their many good qualities.

Robert Malcolm jun. addressed this meeting and he too praised the Glasgow Repealers for giving their support to the Complete Suffrage agitation.[47] Similar sentiments were expressed at a meeting of the city's Complete Suffrage Association the following month.[48]

The Glasgow O'Connorites were, by contrast, understandably dismayed by the actions of the Repealers. In a lecture given in the Christian Chartist Church in June 1842, Con Murray appealed to the Irishmen among the crowded audience to support the Chartists. He argued that 'If they wished for Repeal, the Chartists were their best, their only friends', and to demonstrate this he reminded them that several of the leading members of the Glasgow Complete Suffrage Association had not so long before opposed the Chartist National Petition, 'because the claims of the people of Ireland were recognised in it'.[49] Such arguments, however, made little impression on the city's Irish Repealers.

IV

When the Complete Suffrage movement was established in Glasgow, O'Connor's supporters in the city denounced it and its followers in much the same manner as their leader and the *Northern Star* had done. After April, however, such attacks ceased, and though still opposed to the agitation the O'Connorite Chartists 'seemed to be honouring a truce'. In May the Lanarkshire Universal Suffrage Association, which had gone into rapid decline after most of its leading members left for the Complete Suffrage movement, was finally put to rest. It was replaced by the Glasgow Charter Association, an organisation dominated by O'Connor's most prominent supporters in the city such as James Moir, George Ross, John Colquhoun, Con Murray and Dennis McMillan.[50] O'Connorite attacks on Complete Suffragism in Glasgow were renewed in October when the Complete Suffrage Association, emboldened perhaps by the success of recent visits to the city by Sturge and Vincent,[51] began to campaign more vigorously for support. A section of the Glasgow Charter Association led by Con Murray and John Colquhoun resolved to oppose this development. They attended meetings organised by the Complete Suffragists in order to defeat the motions of their rivals. They were not always successful.[52]

O'Connor had suspended his attack on Complete Suffragism in July: in the autumn he renewed hostilities. He was concerned about the growth of the rival movement and the support it continued to receive from his opponents within Chartism[53] — Complete Suffragism was, after all, 'widely regarded as an attempt to supplant the leadership of O'Connor and the NCA'.[54] O'Connor's campaign soon intensified when the Complete Suffrage Union announced the arrangements for its National Conference, to be held in Birmingham on 27 December. The conference was to decide 'on an act of parliament, for securing the just representation of the whole people; and for determining on such peaceful, legal and constitutional means as may cause it to become the law of these realms'.[55] One half of the conference delegates were to be chosen by meetings of electors, the other half by meetings of non-electors. O'Connor saw in this the opportunity to destroy the Complete Suffrage movement. He urged his followers to attend these events and put forward their own candidates. If chosen, they were to attend the Birmingham conference and demand that 'the Charter and nothing but the Charter' be adopted. In dozens of towns and cities throughout the country O'Connor's supporters followed this advice and contested delegate elections. In most instances they were successful, although such victories were usually won under dubious or disputed circumstances.[56] This occurred in Glasgow. On 29 November the public meeting to elect the city's representatives to the Birmingham conference was held in the City Hall. According to the *Glasgow Chronicle*, the O'Connorites packed the meeting with supporters 'from every town and village within 7 miles of Glasgow', and elected George Ross of the Glasgow Charter Association chairman of the meeting. The Complete Suffragists' candidate was Dr. Eneas McDonnell, an Irish Catholic who was a leading figure in the city's Repeal movement.[57] The O'Connorites went on to pass their resolutions and elect their candidates for all six delegate places who pledged themselves to support only the Charter, 'name and all'.[58]

At the Complete Suffrage conference in Birmingham the following month O'Connorite Chartists and supporters of 'Complete Suffrage' Chartists such as Lovett and Collins constituted the majority of delegates.[59] On its first day Sturge and his middle-class supporters revealed that they had not changed their position on the use of the term 'Charter'. They proposed that their secretly prepared ninety-eight clause Bill of Rights, which included the Six Points, be adopted as the policy of the movement. This was, as Epstein stated, 'an attempt to disassociate middle-class radicalism from the "anarchy and confusion" associated with the Chartist adherents of O'Connor.'[60] Lovett, who had not been consulted on the 'Bill of Rights', reaffirmed his commitment to 'The Charter'; for him it advocated 'just and equal representation…in plain and definite language, capable of being understood and appreciated by the great mass of the people…[and for which] vast numbers had suffered imprisonment, transportation and death…'.[61] The Sturgeites refused to budge. Lovett, O'Connor and almost all the Chartist delegates then united to pass a motion which adopted the 'Charter' instead of the 'Bill of Rights' as the policy of the movement. As a result, Sturge and his followers withdrew from the conference and reconvened elsewhere. The attempt to establish a cross-class reform alliance had failed.

Notes

1. D. George Boyce, *Nineteenth Century Ireland: The Search for Stability* (Dublin, 1990), pp.58–77; Gearoid O'Tuathaigh, *Ireland Before the Famine* (Second edition, Dublin, 1990), pp.160–85; J.H. Treble, 'O'Connor, O'Connell and the Attitudes of Irish Immigrants towards Chartism in the North of England 1838–48', in J. Butt and I.F. Clarke (eds.), *The Victorians and Social Protest: a Symposium* (Newton Abbot, 1973), pp.44–5. Chapter five noted that a public meeting in Glasgow in March 1834, attended chiefly by Irishmen, passed resolutions in favour of Repeal. The meeting also appointed a committee to establish a Repeal Association in the city. It would appear, however, that this society never progressed past the planning stage as there were no reports of a Repeal society in Glasgow until 1841. *Glasgow Free Press*, 29 March 1834.

2. Treble, 'O'Connor, O'Connell and the Attitudes of Irish Immigrants', pp.45–7; Lynn Hollen Lees, *Exiles of Erin: Irish Migrants in Victorian London* (Manchester, 1979), p.225; *Glasgow Saturday Post*, 26 February, 2 July 1842; *Glasgow Chronicle*, 10 June 1842.

3. *The Scots Times'* report of the Irish Registration Bills dispute sometimes refers to the City's Irish Catholics as 'O'Connellites' and on other occasions uses the term 'Repealers'. However, no evidence has been found which demonstrates that a Repeal Association had been established in the city by March 1841. Moreover, Repeal is not mentioned in any of the speeches of the O'Connellites or of the Chartists. The report in the *Glasgow Saturday Post* which deals with the Registration Bills dispute states that 'the supporters of the government measure' were 'principally Irishmen, and whom, merely for the sake of distinction, we shall term Repealers…'. It is probable that the *Scots Times* also used the term for this reason. *Scots Times*, 10 March 1841; *Glasgow Saturday Post*, 6 March 1841. See also *Scotch Reformers' Gazette*, 6 and 20 March 1841; *Glasgow Herald*, 5 March 1841; *Glasgow Courier*, 6 March 1841.

4. *Glasgow Saturday Post*, 13 November 1841; *Glasgow Courier*, 11 November 1841.

5. *Glasgow Saturday Post*, 13 November 1841.

6. McGowan had been the secretary of the Repeal meeting in the city in 1834. At the soiree in January 1842 he expressed his support for both the Repeal Movement and the Six Points of the Charter. Unlike others who were active in the Glasgow Repeal Association around this time, McGowan acknowledged that O'Connell was not infallible: 'He concluded by saying, in reference to Mr O'Connell, that many were not satisfied with the conduct of that gentleman; but he had had much to do, and it would not therefore be surprising if he had done something wrong; if he had faults, however, he was even then like the sun in its evening splendour, he pleased more, although he dazzled less. (Great Cheering.)' After this event there are no more references in the press to McGowan taking an active part in the campaign for Repeal. *Ibid*, 15 January 1842.

7. *Ibid*, 26 February 1842. See also *Ibid*, 2 July 1842 and *Glasgow Chronicle*, 10 June 1842 for other comments on the size of Repeal meetings.

8. *Glasgow Saturday Post*, 19 March 1842.

9. *Glasgow Chronicle*, 10 June 1842.

10. This paragraph is based on *Scots Times*, 18 November 1840.

11. Treble, 'O'Connor, O'Connell and the Attitudes of Irish Immigrants', pp.56–7; Alexander Wilson, *The Chartist Movement in Scotland* (Manchester, 1970), p.172; Leslie C. Wright, *Scottish Chartism* (Edinburgh, 1953), p.135; Edward Royle, *Chartism* (2nd edition, London, 1988), pp.29–30; D.G. Wright, *Popular Radicalism: The Working-Class Experience, 1780–1880* (London, 1988), p.126.

12. Treble, 'O' Connor, O'Connell and the Attitudes of Irish Immigrants', p.57.

13. *Northern Star*, 18 and 25 September, 9 October, 11 and 18 December 1841.

14. *Ibid*, 18 and 25 September 1841.

15. *Ibid*, 16 October 1841; *Glasgow Saturday Post*, 16 October 1841; *Glasgow Courier*, 12 October 1841.

16. *Northern Star*, 13 November 1841; Wilson, *Chartist Movement in Scotland*, pp.168–71; Wright, *Scottish Chartism*, p.135.

17. Wright, *Scottish Chartism*, p.135.

18. Wilson, *Chartist Movement in Scotland*, p.170; *Glasgow Chronicle*, 5 November 1841.

19. It is possible that these Irishmen were not active Repealers determined, initially at least, to oppose O'Connor, but were in fact a 'rent-a-mob', hired by O'Connor's opponents. In the *Northern Star* O'Connor stated that the Irish had been 'canvassed' to oppose him and that he was told 'that our enemies had calculated upon a large muster of Irish to take satisfaction for

my defence of my character against the unmanly, malicious, and continuous assaults of Mr O'Connell'. Furthermore, the reported leader of these 'two hundred O'Connellites' was one John Campbell: this individual does not appear in any reports of the activities of the Glasgow Repeal Association. *Northern Star*, 13 and 20 November 1841.

20. *Glasgow Saturday Post*, 13 November 1841. See also *ibid*, 15 January 1842.

21. Wilson, *Chartist Movement in Scotland*, pp.171–72; Wright, *Scottish Chartism*, pp.135–6; *Glasgow Saturday Post*, 8 January 1842; *Glasgow Courier*, 11 January 1842; *Northern Star*, 8 January, 5 February 1842.

22. Wilson, *Chartist Movement in Scotland*, p.173; Wright, *Scottish Chartism*, pp.136–7; *Glasgow Saturday Post*, 12 February 1842; *Northern Star*, 22 and 29 January, 19 February 1842.

23. *Glasgow Saturday Post*, 26 February 1842.

24. Boyce, *Nineteenth Century Ireland*, pp.74–5; O'Tuathaigh, *Ireland Before the Famine*, p.185.

25. *Glasgow Saturday Post*, 19 March 1842.

26. *Ibid*, 26 February 1842.

27. Treble, 'O'Connor, O'Connell and the Attitudes of Irish Immigrants', pp.46–7.

28. *Glasgow Saturday Post*, 15 January 1842.

29. *Ibid*, 19 March 1842.

30. For the Complete Suffrage Movement in England and Scotland see Wright, *Scottish Chartism*, pp.138–42; James Epstein, *The Lion of Freedom: Feargus O'Connor and the Chartist Movement* (London, 1982), pp.287–93; Alexander Wilson, 'The Suffrage Movement', in Patricia Hollis (ed.), *Pressure from Without in early Victorian England*, pp.174–79; Ward, *Chartism*, pp.158–60, 165–7; Dorothy Thompson, *The Chartists: Popular Politics in the Industrial Revolution*, (pbk edition, Aldershot, 1986), pp.261–70.

31. Quoted in Wilson, 'Suffrage Movement', p.84.

32. Quoted in Epstein, *Lion of Freedom*, p.288.

33. Epstein, *Lion of Freedom*, p.290.

34. *Ibid*, p.291.

35. Wilson, *Chartist Movement in Scotland*, p.174.

36. *Glasgow Saturday Post*, 28 May 1842; *Glasgow Chronicle*, 30 May 1842.

37. *Glasgow Chronicle*, 1, 8 August 1842; *Glasgow Saturday Post*, 30 July, 8 August 1842.

38. Wilson, *Chartist Movement in Scotland*, pp.172–3; 'Chartism in Glasgow', pp.280–1.

39. Wilson, *Chartist Movement in Scotland*, p.174.

40. *Ibid.*

41. *Glasgow Saturday Post*, 2 July 1842. For a similar resolution, see *Glasgow Chronicle*, 10 June 1842.

42. *Glasgow Saturday Post*, 28 May 1842; *Glasgow Chronicle*, 30 May 1842.

43. *Glasgow Saturday Post*, 6 August 1842; *Glasgow Chronicle*, 8 August 1842.

44. *Glasgow Chronicle*, 28 September 1842.

45. *Ibid*, 10 June 1842.

46. Wilson, 'Suffrage Movement', p.87; Ward, *Chartism*, p.159; Treble, 'O'Connor, O'Connell and the Attitudes of Irish Immigrants', p.221.

47. *Glasgow Chronicle*, 10 June 1842.

48. *Ibid*, 11 July 1842.

49. *Northern Star*, 25 June 1842.

50. Wilson, *Chartist Movement*, pp.175–6; 'Chartism in Glasgow', pp.281–2; *Glasgow Chronicle*, 30 November 1842.

51. On 21 and 23 September 1842 Henry Vincent gave lectures in the Glasgow City Hall on Complete Suffragism. Over two thousand people attended both events. On 3 October Vincent was present, along with over a thousand others, at a banquet in the same venue held to honour Joseph Sturge and Sharman Crawford. See *Glasgow Chronicle*, 26 September 1842; *Glasgow Saturday Post*, 8 October 1842; Wilson, *Chartist Movement*, p.176; Wright, *Scottish Chartism*, p.154; Montgomery, Glasgow Radicalism, p.217.

52. Wilson, *Chartist Movement*, p.177; *Glasgow Saturday Post*, 5 November 1842.

53. Wright, *Popular Radicalism*, p.134.

54. Epstein, *Lion of Freedom*, p.290.

55. Quoted in Wilson, 'Suffrage Movement', p.87.

56. Epstein, *Lion of Freedom*, pp.292–3; Wright, *Scottish Chartism*, p.154; Wilson, 'Suffrage Movement, pp.88–9.

57. In his address McDonnell 'spoke chiefly of the position of his own country (Ireland) in reference to the question of Complete Suffrage, and denounced in energetic terms the Tory faction as the common enemy of Chartists, Complete Suffragists, and Irish Repealers, against the rule of whom all their exertions were necessary'. *Glasgow Chronicle*, 30 November 1842.

58. The Glasgow Complete Suffragists wanted the delegates chosen to attend the Birmingham Conference to support the Six Points of the Charter, but to have a free vote in the choice of the name of the new organisation which would campaign for them. Moreover, they wanted the delegates to support all motions which would pledge the society to campaign for an end of monopolies of the Church and the State and for a repeal of the Corn Laws. Wilson, *Chartist Movement*, p.177; *Glasgow Chronicle*, 30 November 1842.

59. For the December Conference see Wilson, 'Suffrage Movement', pp.89–91; Ward, *Chartism*, pp.165–6; Epstein, *Lion of Freedom*, pp.292–3; Wright, *Scottish Chartism*, pp.154–5. Con Murray attended the Conference as a delegate for Campsie. See *Glasgow Chronicle*, 30 December 1842.

60. Epstein, *Lion of Freedom*, pp.292–3.

61. Quoted in Ward, *Chartism*, p.166.

8
Repeal, 1843–48

After 1842 the Chartist movement in Great Britain went into rapid decline and did not re-emerge as a force of any major significance until 1848. There were a number of reasons for its weakened state during this period. In England, 'Relative economic prosperity no doubt helped to dampen the enthusiasm of the rank-and-file',[1] and this improvement in trade, coupled with the failure of Chartism to achieve its aims in 1842, also resulted in workers turning towards trade union activity as a means of improving their social and economic condition. Furthermore, the large number of arrests and convictions of Chartists involved in the strike wave of July to September 1842 greatly weakened the movement in England as did the continual conflicts and quarrels among Chartist leaders and within Chartist organisations.[2] As a result of all these factors, 'at the local level, Chartists were left high and dry, a dedicated rump without an active mass following' between 1842 and 1847.[3]

In Scotland the movement had been in a 'disorganised state… throughout the summer of 1842', largely owing to the schism resulting from the emergence of Complete Suffragism and the effects of the trade depression. In October 1842 an attempt was made to reorganise the movement and establish an effective national organisation, but this soon failed because of a lack of funds.[4] By 1843 the number of local Chartist associations had fallen to less than forty and 'These survived in varying degrees of disappointment and apathy…'[5] As in England, the Chartist movement in Scotland between 1842 and 1847 was plagued by internal divisions. Furthermore, the Chartists and Complete Suffragists were unable to settle their differences and unite.[6] These divisions, the lack of a national organisation and the Chartists' failure to achieve any success all contributed to the collapse of Scottish Chartism as a mass agitation.

The Complete Suffrage movement likewise went into decline after 1842, mainly because of the collapse of the Birmingham Conference and the failure to establish a cross-class reform alliance. There was still a Suffrage society in Glasgow but, as has been indicated, much of its time was spent in competition with the city's Chartists.[7] The Irish Repealers in Glasgow appear to have abandoned the Suffrage agitation: no longer were resolutions in favour of it passed at Repeal meetings, and those Repealers who were prominent in the city's Complete Suffrage Association in 1842 do not seem to have been involved in the organisation thereafter. The Repealers were probably disenchanted with the movement after the events in Birmingham in December 1842 and, in the absence of any other suitable campaign for the Six Points, decided to concentrate on Repeal. Moreover, despite the fact that a number of Scottish and English Complete Suffragists supported Repeal their movement would not adopt the cause as part of its policy during 1843.[8]

This chapter contains three sections. The first will look at the progress of the Repeal movement in the west of Scotland from 1843 to O'Connell's death in May 1847. The second will examine the role of the Catholic clergy in the agitation during the same period. The final section will discuss the events of 1848, when the Repealers and the Chartists finally participated in a joint campaign for reform.

I

The Repeal movement in the west of Scotland made spectacular progress during 1843. At a meeting of the Glasgow Repealers in July, Dr. Eneas McDonnell told those present: 'In every part of Scotland there were Irishmen, and in every part of Scotland there were repealers. (Great cheers.) They were in Edinburgh, in Dundee, in Airdrie, in Paisley, in Greenock, in vast numbers...'[9] That month Bishop Scott reported that in the western counties, 'All our poor people are mad about repeal, and they are convinced that before two months an Irish parliament will be sitting on College Green in Dublin.'[10] These claims are supported by an editorial in the *Glasgow Saturday Post*, again from July:

> While O'Connell thus virtually rules Ireland, the natives of that ill-used country are making active demonstrations for his support in both England and Scotland. In Scotland in particular, there is not a town of any importance that has not had its repeal meeting and sent off its contribution to the repeal fund. Indeed, such is now the number of the natives of Ireland in all our principal towns, and such is their zeal and energy, that were any demonstration against the repeal of the union to be attempted, the repealers would be almost certain to muster, and carry the declaration of public opinion in their favour.[11]

Newspapers of the period also demonstrated the increased popularity of the movement in the west of Scotland. During the first nine months of 1843 there were reports of crowded Repeal meetings at Greenock,[12] Airdrie,[13] Paisley,[14] and in and around Glasgow.[15]

There are several likely reasons for the rapid growth of the Repeal movement during this period. The decision of the Glasgow Repealers to forsake the Complete Suffrage agitation probably resulted in their energies becoming concentrated solely on promoting Repeal. The improvement in trade from late 1842 onwards, the subsequent fall in unemployment and the return of relative economic prosperity undoubtedly contributed to the increase in Repeal activity: sympathisers who had been unemployed or underemployed now had the extra funds to enable them to join Repeal societies and contribute to the Repeal Fund in Dublin. Finally, and perhaps most importantly, at the beginning of the year O'Connell told the Irish people that if they became more active in the campaign, 1843 would be the 'Repeal Year'. In Ireland the people responded magnificently to O'Connell's appeal and so apparently did the Irish community in the west of Scotland.[16]

A major part of O'Connell's strategy during 1843 was the holding of huge Repeal demonstrations. These 'monster meetings', over forty of which occurred in the provinces of Leinster, Munster and Connaught during the summer and autumn, attracted hundreds of thousands of his followers. The purpose of these events was to demonstrate to Peel's Government the extent and strength of support in Ireland for a domestic legislature. The Prime Minister certainly took note of these gatherings — but his response was not what O'Connell had expected. During these months Peel became increasingly alarmed at the 'monster meetings' and at other aspects of O'Connell's campaign. Matters came to a head in October over the demonstration to be held at Clontarf. Peel banned this meeting and sent troops to the area to prevent any attempts to defy the proscription. O'Connell decided not to proceed with the event. A week later he and a number of his colleagues were arrested and charged with conspiracy, and the following February were convicted and imprisoned. The proceedings were an outrage as Catholics were excluded from the jury empanelled for the trial. In September 1844 the Law Lords recognised the unjust nature of the trial and conviction and released O'Connell and his allies.[17]

The actions of Peel's ministry greatly angered O'Connell's supporters in the west of Scotland. The decision to suppress the Clontarf demonstration and other Repeal meetings in Ireland was condemned by the Glasgow Repealers at a public meeting in the city's Lyceum Rooms, 'which was crowded to overflowing...'.[18] The packing of the jury for the trial of O'Connell and his supporters resulted in protest meetings of Catholics at Dumbarton, Duntocher, Barrhead and Paisley.[19] The Glasgow Repealers received petition sheets from the headquarters of the Repeal movement in Dublin which was raising a petition to Parliament to investigate the trial and other Irish grievances, and according to the *Glasgow Saturday Post* 15,000 signatures were collected in the city in three days. The sheets were then returned to Dublin.[20] O'Connell's imprisonment led to a meeting of three to four thousand Glasgow Repealers in the City Hall, at which they expressed their 'indignation and detestation at the conduct of the Peel Government towards Ireland' and O'Connell, their sympathy for him and his imprisoned supporters, and their determination to continue the agitation for Repeal.[21] Similar meetings were held at Airdrie and Paisley.[22] When O'Connell and his fellow prisoners were liberated the Repealers of Glasgow organised a public meeting in the City Hall to celebrate the occasion. The *Glasgow Saturday Post* reported that 'This was a highly respectable meeting, and certainly one of the most numerous ever held within doors in this city, or within the walls of our City Halls since its erection'.[23]

It was not only the Repealers who were outraged at the measures taken by Peel's administration. On 18 December 1843 a large public meeting was held in Glasgow's City Hall to take 'into consideration the late interference of the Peel Ministry with the right of public meeting and petitioning in Ireland'. This meeting, at which nearly three thousand inhabitants of the city were present, was called by the Lord Provost, who had received 'a numerously signed requisition from Town Councillors, electors and others' for such an event. The meeting, which was addressed by councillors, bailies, Repealers and Complete Suffragists, condemned the actions of the Government. Those present sympathised with the plight of the Irish people and were also concerned about the possible implications of Peel's measure, as the following resolution, passed unanimously, demonstrates:

> That it is the duty of all classes of Reformers, at the present crisis, to come forward and assist the Irish people by firm and prudent co-operation, to vindicate the right of public meeting and free discussion. This co-operation is the more necessary as there is imminent danger that should the Government succeed in suppressing the right of public meeting in Ireland they may not hesitate to adopt the same coercive measures in the sister kingdoms.[24]

Similar arguments had been used ten years previously at public meetings in the west of Scotland which condemned the Irish Coercion Bill. Scottish reformers also protested against the trial and imprisonment of O'Connell and his allies. For example, the meeting in January 1844 of Paisley's Roman Catholics called as a result of the packing of the jury for O'Connell's trial was attended by the town's Provost and other 'Liberal Protestants'.[25] Six months later a public meeting in the town sent an address of support and sympathy to O'Connell and resolved to petition for his release. The chairman of the meeting was Patrick Brewster, the former Chartist leader, and the chairman of the committee which organised the night's proceedings was William Aitken, another of Paisley's leading reformers.[26] Shortly before this event a similar meeting was held in Airdrie by the Repealers of that town and vicinity; also present were several of the leading members of Airdrie's Complete Suffrage Association.[27]

Patrick Brewster was one of two prominent Scottish reformers who not only sympathised with O'Connell's plight and with the condition of the Irish people, but also participated in the Repeal movement in the west of Scotland during these years; the other was the former Chartist leader from Glasgow, Robert Malcolm jun. At a Repeal meeting in Paisley in July 1843 Brewster stated why he supported the agitation:

> As a citizen of the world, and a friend of the human race, he felt an interest in the success of every nation bravely struggling to be free. It was not possible that he could remain indifferent to the magnanimous and constitutional and peaceful struggle of his Irish brethren — the most oppressed people in the world. Their success would be a step in the great march of the world's deliverance…[28]

Malcolm was by far the more active Repealer of the two. During 1844 and 1845 he addressed several Repeal meetings in Glasgow at a time when he was one of the leading members of the city's Complete Suffrage Association. Malcolm was a sub-editor for the *Glasgow Saturday Post* and he ensured that the activities of the city's Repeal movement were fully reported and publicised. For this and for other services to the cause he was held in high esteem by the Glasgow Repealers, who presented him 'with a massive silver snuff-box filled with sovereigns' at a soirée held in his honour in November 1844.[29]

As well as protesting against the Government's policies for Ireland and its treatment of O'Connell, the Repeal societies in the west of Scotland during 1843 and 1844 continued to hold meetings on Repeal, collect the Repeal Rent, and generally promote their cause.[30] A great emphasis was placed on providing members with knowledge of current events. The societies organised meetings at which speakers addressed the audience on political issues and on the present position and prospects of Repeal.[31] The Glasgow Repeal Reading Room was established in the city's Saltmarket Street; it was supported not only by Repealers but also by 'Scotsmen and Englishmen, and by men of different religious and political opinions'. At a meeting of its members and friends in October 1844 James Partridge, a prominent Glasgow Repealer, praised the institution in glowing terms:

Its existence and spirited support he looked upon as evidence of the improved state of the times, and the desire for knowledge which now seemed to actuate all classes of the community. Instead of drinking and quarrelling, as in times past, on the Saturday and other evenings of the week, he was glad to observe that his own Irish countrymen flocked to the reading-room, and those of them who could not read for themselves, were furnished with all the news of the week from newspapers of every grade of politics, by means of the reading aloud of some of their more fortunate brethren. And this public reading seemed to be highly appreciated by those for whose advantage it was adopted…

The Room was not solely for the use of Repealers, but was open to anyone who wished to use it. Moreover, it was believed that for the Room to be a success it needed to 'be conducted on strictly total abstinence principles'.[32] A similar Repeal Reading Room existed in Calton at this time.[33]

It is evident from the newspapers of the period that from late 1844 to May 1846 the Repeal societies in the west of Scotland remained active.[34] However, for the twelve months before O'Connell's death in May 1847 it is impossible to give an account of the Repeal movement in the region because of the lack of reports on the agitation.[35] Therefore it is not known whether there were any major divisions in the Repeal societies as a result of the activities of the radical Young Ireland group, which seceded from the Loyal National Repeal Association in July 1846.[36] This split 'produced serious disaffection among many Repeal Societies' in the north of England, and 'a sizeable minority' of Repealers in this region eventually joined the Irish Confederation, founded in January 1847 by the Young Irelanders to rival the Repeal Association.[37] The absence of evidence means that the effect of the Young Ireland secession on the Repeal movement in the west of Scotland in the year to O'Connell's death is not known.

II

In Ireland the vast majority of the Catholic clergy supported Repeal and indeed were actively involved in O'Connell's campaign.[38] According to Treble this was also the case in England. He added that nowhere was this clerical commitment to the cause 'more apparent than in Lancashire and Yorkshire where with few exceptions the clergy, whether of Irish or English extraction, played a prominent part in organising Repeal Associations at the local level'.[39] In the west of Scotland the situation was somewhat different: it would appear that in this region only the Irish priests among the Catholic clergy were active in the agitation. Furthermore, their involvement occurred despite the expressed opposition to the campaign and to clerical participation in it from Bishops Murdoch and Scott.

During 1842 and for much of 1843, John Ryan, an Irish priest at St Andrew's chapel in Glasgow,[40] was a prominent figure in the city's Repeal organisation.[41] He was also very popular within the movement. For example, near the end of a Repeal meeting in June 1842:

> The Chairman…stated that as the chief business of the evening was finished, the meeting might call upon any gentleman they might be anxious to hear. Loud cries for the Rev. Mr Ryan came from all parts of the house, that gentleman rose amidst great cheering, and delivered a long and eloquent address, teeming with rich historical associations…The reverend gentleman threw an occasional dash of poetry into his address, and during its delivery he was rapturously applauded. At its close the audience rose simultaneously to their feet and cheered enthusiastically.[42]

Ryan's speeches at several other meetings elicited a similar response.[43] In the autumn of 1843 Ryan, who had recently recovered from illness, returned to Ireland for good. In September the Repealers of Glasgow held a farewell soirée for him which, according to the *Glasgow Saturday Post*, 'was crowded almost to suffocation long before the proceedings commenced; a large and respectable assemblage of the fair sex forming no inconsiderable portion of the audience'. The newspaper added:

> The occasion was one of deep and heartfelt emotion, not only to the Repealers of Glasgow, to whom the Rev. Mr O'Ryan has endeared himself by his eloquent and zealous advocacy of their cause, but also to a large body of Catholic admirers to whom his services have been doubly dear.

Ryan was presented with an address, a gold watch and a purse containing fifty sovereigns.[44]

After this there were no more reports in the press of priests at Glasgow being present at Repeal meetings or soirées in the city. This was not because the clergymen were hostile or indifferent to the cause, although this might have been the case with some. Rather, it was a consequence of Bishop Murdoch's decision to ban them from participating in the city's Repeal movement.[45] (His reasons for doing so will be examined shortly.) Furthermore, it would appear that priests elsewhere in the Western District of the Scottish Catholic Church[46] were also forbidden to participate in the campaign for Repeal. Nevertheless, it is clear that this order was not obeyed by all of the Catholic priests serving in the lowland counties of the District. In August 1844 Bishop Scott revealed to Bishop Kyle of the Northern District that he, Scott, had been informed, by one of the priests at Paisley, 'that privately with our Irish clergy, repeal is the go' and 'though they do not publicly assist at meetings' — no doubt because of the ban — most of their time was spent among their congregations furthering the cause.[47]

One of the most active of those Irish priests who privately promoted Repeal was Hugh Quigley, who had been stationed at St Mary's in Calton since his ordination in 1842. In the winter of 1844 he was transferred to St Kieran's in Campbeltown.[48] On 22 November a soirée was held for him in Glasgow to mark the occasion, 'and also as a mark of respect for his liberal and enlightened advocacy of the cause of civil liberty and the repeal of the Irish legislative act of union'. Those present that evening were addressed by Charles Penny, a member of St Mary's congregation. His speech caused a sensation:

> Persons took upon them to assign various reasons for Mr Quigley's departure from amongst them; but the reverend gentleman had himself informed them that he was going at the order of his clerical superior, and that with Catholics was considered in accordance with the will of God. But they (his admirers and they were many) could not conceal their astonishment that so many of their talented countrymen, their eloquent and amiable Irish priests, were taken from them as soon almost as they became endeared to the people, or in any manner became beloved and popular amongst them. (Hear, hear, and great excitement.) They found that as soon as they raised their voices in the cause of liberty for their bleeding country, that they left Glasgow. (Hear, hear, and 'true, true'.) The reason of this he did not know; but, as a Catholic, and as an Irishman, he regretted to see these talented gentlemen taken away at the time they were capable of doing most good. (Cheers.) He was not calling in question the authority of any person in these matters; he only regretted the circumstances that occasioned them, and he was sure they equally joined with him in expressing regret that those clergymen who ably advocated their cause should thus be taken away from them. (Hear, hear.)

According to the *Glasgow Saturday Post*, several gentlemen addressed the meeting, 'all of whom concurred in, and followed up the remarks of Mr Penny as to the occasion of the Rev. Mr Quigley's departure'.[49]

By late 1844 the transfer of pro-Repeal Irish priests was evidently a cause of great concern to Glasgow's Catholic Irish community, and there was a belief among many that such priests had been moved because of their political activities.[50] The following March, however, a letter from Penny was published in the *Glasgow Saturday Post* in which he stated that Murdoch had solemnly declared that these allegations were false, and as a result Penny was willing to retract the assertions he made at the soirée for Quigley.[51] Whatever Murdoch's reasons were for the removal of other Irish priests it would appear that Quigley was indeed transferred because of his political activities: one of his successors at St Kieran's recalled that Quigley was 'relegated' to Campbeltown because he had 'earnestly advocated "Repeal"…'.[52]

Bishop Murdoch was opposed to the Repeal agitation and to the involvement of his priests in it. For over three years, however, he did not make these views public, perhaps because he did not wish to lose favour with his flock. In December 1844 he finally decided to make his position known, apparently in response to the soirée held the previous month for Quigley. According to a letter from 'One of St Mary's Congregation' published in the *Glasgow Saturday Post* on 14 December 1844, earlier that month in the Calton chapel Murdoch made 'an unwarrantable attack' on Repeal. In a seemingly scathing tirade he condemned Quigley 'for his conduct as a Repeal agitator' and denounced those who attended the soirée in honour of the Irish priest. Murdoch also attacked the Calton Repeal Reading-Room, which he described as 'a den of sedition'. The newspaper informed its readers that it had inquired into the incident and had been told that during his address Murdoch declared:

> Let other bishops do as they pleased — let them, if they chose, erect the standard of Repeal where they pleased — he would not condemn or find fault with them. His own opinion was against Repeal, and he considered further that political agitation was not the province of priests, and he would not consent to his priests or clergy here (in Glasgow) occupying their time with Repeal or political agitations.

Murdoch's use of St Mary's to discuss political issues was condemned by the paper and by its correspondent, who also strongly criticised his Bishop for attacking Repeal and its supporters.[53]

Murdoch and Scott's reasons for ordering their priests not to participate in the Repeal agitation must now be examined. In his outburst at St Mary's Murdoch stated that he 'would not consent to' the Catholic clergy in Glasgow 'occupying their time with Repeal or political agitations'. Yet, as was demonstrated in a previous chapter, Murdoch and other priests at Glasgow had been involved in the Precursor organisation and in the agitation concerning the Irish Registration Bills. Furthermore, in September 1842 the *Glasgow Chronicle* revealed that the Sturge Declaration was signed earlier that year by 'the seven Catholic Clergymen of Glasgow', and that these priests had been invited by the Glasgow Complete Suffrage Association to attend its banquet for Sharman Crawford and Joseph Sturge in the City Hall in October 1842.[54] Two, William Gordon and John Ryan, attended the event.[55] In January and February 1844 meetings of Catholics were held at Dumbarton, Duntocher, Barrhead and Paisley to protest against the exclusion of Catholics from the jury for O'Connell's trial, and were chaired by the local priests.[56] It would appear that the involvement of Catholic clergymen in these activities was not condemned or opposed by the bishops. Therefore it was not politics as such that Murdoch and Scott were opposed to their priests' participating in; rather, it was those agitations of which they disapproved. Repeal was one such campaign.

The reasons for Murdoch and Scott's opposition to the Repeal movement are not all known. One of them, however, was financial. The Catholic Church in the Western District, or for that matter in Scotland, was not a wealthy institution. In the decades since the beginning of Irish emigration to the region it had struggled to raise funds for the building of chapels and the recruitment of priests. By the late 1830s progress had been made, although a number of the churches in the western lowland counties remained heavily in debt. By this time the Church had raised enough money to begin a period of expansion, and in the remainder of the decade and throughout the 1840s plots of land were purchased and places of worship erected on them. Debts remained on these new buildings but the practice was, as with Catholic churches built prior to the late 1830s, that the money owed would be repaid eventually by the new congregations through collections and their weekly contributions.[57] Bishop Scott was convinced that the Repeal movement in the west of Scotland, through its collection of the Repeal Rent, deprived the Catholic Church of vital funds. The sums of money sent to Dublin were often considerable. For example, during May 1843 the districts in and around Glasgow raised £129.12s.6d.; during the second half of the year the Rent collected by the Glasgow Repealers amounted to £304. 3s. 4d.[58] In January 1845 Scott informed Bishop Kyle that:

> Trade is tolerably good at present though wages be low. But we do not feel much of the goodness of the trade in the way of seat rents or penny collections. Our poor Irish especially in Glasgow from the spouters among them down to the most unlettered are all taken up with repeal at present and with the discussion of the Charitable bequests bill, about which the greater part of them understand no more than they do of the Greek alphabet.[59]

The following month Scott stated to Kyle: 'Would to God that Irish agitation was settled one way or another. It is doing us here at present an immensity of harm.'[60] Furthermore, the Irish priests in the western lowland counties had encouraged their congregations to give to the Repeal Rent. In a letter to Kyle in August 1844 Scott stated of his Irish priests that, 'almost all their time is taken up going about privately among the people, exhorting them to contribute for repeal, but never say a word about contributing for paying off the debts of the chapels'.[61]

Indeed, it is probable that Scott and Murdoch's ban on clerical involvement in the Repeal movement was imposed largely as a result of the enthusiasm which their Irish clergymen showed for the agitation. (No evidence has been found which reveals that Scottish Catholic clergymen supported the campaign, either publicly or privately.) It is unlikely that the Bishops' opposition was caused mainly by the fact that the Irish priests were encouraging members of the Catholic community to give money to the Repeal Rent: Murdoch and Scott arguably had a far more important reason for not wanting the Irish clergymen to become involved in the movement. This concerned the issue of power and control in the Scottish Catholic Church. Scott had never wanted Irish priests to serve in the west of Scotland. In January 1826 he informed Bishop Paterson that he was 'strongly convinced that the Glasgow mission in particular would be most seriously injured by bringing an Irishman to it, even for a few months'. According to Scott, it was

> natural even for Scotchmen in a foreign land to draw together. Irishmen have the same feelings, but less prudence. There has been a cry to get Irishmen to Glasgow, and most certainly an Irish priest would soon associate with his countrymen and naturally fall, into all the habits he was accustomed to see between his own country priests at home and their flocks. He would appear to have all their hearts, which might flatter too much a young mind, and if he had not extraordinary prudence, all Episcopal authority would soon be set aside. This has happened elsewhere. He would also impart to them everything that passed, and many things that he ought not to do...I should fear the total ruin of the Glasgow mission in its present circumstances from such a step.[62]

Three years later James Gibbons, an Irish priest who had been dismissed from his mission at Tombae in the north-east of Scotland because of his excessive drinking, arrived in Glasgow and inflamed the Irish Catholics in the city against the Scottish Bishops and priests. Gibbons told them that he had been discharged because he was an Irishman and 'that the Irish Catholics being the most numerous body of Catholics in all the South of Scotland, have a right to be served by Irish priests and governed by Irish bishops...'.[63] At the end of the year he returned to Ireland.[64] In 1832 Revd Byrne, another Irish priest, was stationed in the Western District at Paisley. He soon became convinced that he was suffering an injustice because priests who were junior to him were being placed at the Glasgow Mission. Byrne believed that his seniority entitled him to be moved to Glasgow before these clergymen.[65] He was incensed at this and in the autumn he stirred up the Irish Catholics in the Glasgow and Paisley Missions against Bishop Scott and the Scottish priests by telling them about his 'injustice' and by claiming that he was 'persecuted merely because he was an

Irishman…'.[66] He continued this campaign until December 1833 and then apparently left the District.[67]

The activities of Gibbons and Byrne undoubtedly confirmed Scott's fears about the consequences of introducing Irish priests into the western lowland counties. By the late 1830s, however, the shortage of Scottish priests coupled with the increasing size of the Catholic community in the west of Scotland led to a major recruitment of priests from Ireland. At the beginning of 1838 there were twenty-seven priests and two bishops in the Western District, all of whom were Scottish. Six years later the number of priests had risen to thirty-four, of whom eleven were Irish. Moreover, ten of the twenty priests in the lowland counties of the District — Ayrshire, Dunbartonshire, Lanarkshire, Renfrewshire and Wigtownshire — were from Ireland.[68] It was, of course, in these counties that the overwhelming majority of the Irish Catholics in the Western District lived. Although the Irish clergymen in the District were recruited by Murdoch and Scott, it is likely that the Bishops viewed this development with some trepidation given their previous experience of priests from Ireland. They would have been concerned that the Irish in the region would become strongly attached to the Irish clergymen and that this could have serious consequences for discipline and for the effective running of the Church if, for example, a dispute again arose between the native clergy and the Irish priests. It is probable, therefore, that in an attempt to prevent the natural bond between Irish priests and people becoming firmer, Murdoch and Scott decided that their Irish clergymen should not become involved in the agitation for Repeal. The adoration heaped upon John Ryan for his participation in the campaign during 1842–43 showed the Bishops just how popular a priest-Repealer could be; this was again demonstrated by the response of the Catholic Irish Repealers to the transfer of Hugh Quigley in November 1844.

Indeed, Murdoch and Scott's fears concerning the close relationship between Irish priests and people, and the problems for the Scottish Catholic Church which could result from it, were confirmed by the subsequent behaviour of Quigley, and of another Irish priest John McDermott, Quigley's predecessor at Campbeltown and the founder in 1845 of the mission at Dalry.[69] In April 1846 Scott informed Bishop Kyle that:

> We have been sadly plagued with two or three of the Irish priests who have been with us now for some years. They seemed to wish to govern the District themselves, and would not obey Dr. Murdoch but in as far as they thought proper. At last when scolded for disobedience and other things two of them viz. Hugh Quigley and John McDermot threw up their charge and asked for an exeat. They were taken at their word.

Shortly after the two priests were given formal permission to find employment under another bishop they attended a Repeal meeting in Glasgow at which, according to Scott, Quigley 'made a most violent harangue against Dr. Murdoch, adding that as he was no longer under the control of tyrannical superiors he would speak his mind quite freely'. Scott added that the priests had 'raised it seems by their calumnies a very bad feeling among the Catholics of Glasgow against Dr. Murdoch'.[70] The following month they left the Western District for good. A relieved Scott described them to Kyle as 'the most self conceited ungovernable beings that ever I knew among clergymen'.[71]

III

At the end of section one of this chapter it was stated that there is little evidence available concerning the Repeal agitation in the west of Scotland during the twelve months before the death of Daniel O'Connell. The same is true of the period from May 1847 (when O'Connell died) to March 1848. Indeed, in December 1847 a crowded public meeting of Repealers in Glasgow was held 'for the purpose of reviving the cause...and promoting its advancement...'. It passed the following resolution:

> That in working for the repeal of the legislative union, we will adopt the peaceful, legal and constitutional mode of agitation which was founded and practised by the lamented O'Connell; and in future we will be guided by the counsel and advice of his illustrious son John, and the committee of the Loyal National Repeal Association of Ireland.[72]

There were two main reasons for the lack of Repeal activity in the region during 1847. The first was financial. On 15 February 1847 a public meeting of Glasgow Repealers was held in the city's Blackfriars Street Church. Its chairman Charles Bryson

> said it was not to be expected that much could be done at the present time, in a pecuniary point of view, to forward the Repeal cause, on account of the wide-spread distress which prevailed over every part of the country, and the high price of provisions; but still it was their duty to agitate the question, and keep the claims of Ireland's sons before the public mind of the country.[73]

The state of the economy did not improve during the remainder of the year[74] and this would almost certainly have had an effect on the activities of Repeal societies. The second and undoubtedly more important cause of the continuing lull in the agitation in the west of Scotland concerned events in Ireland. The Repeal meeting in Glasgow in February 1847 pledged its support to the campaign led by Daniel O'Connell.[75] At that time, however, the Loyal National Repeal Association was experiencing major difficulties as a result of the Irish Famine, and by the time of O'Connell's death 'was disintegrating rapidly'. John O'Connell, the 'Liberator's' son and political heir, was unable to turn the situation around, with the result that 'By 1848 the Repeal Association was simply irrelevant in a famine-stricken land.'[76] Given the collapse of the LNRA it is not surprising that there was little Repeal activity among its supporters in the west of Scotland. In spring 1848, however, the Repeal movement in the region burst into life and remained active for several months.

Two major Repeal meetings were held in Glasgow during March 1848. The first, on 17 March, took place in the Lyceum Rooms, which was 'crowded to excess' with 'hundreds…unable to gain admittance'. The meeting pledged its support to the campaign being conducted by John O'Connell and the Loyal National Repeal Association.[77] Ten days later the Lyceum Rooms was the venue for a public meeting of those in the city who supported Repeal. According to the *Glasgow Saturday Post*, 'The hall was densely filled, and large numbers could not gain admission'. Resolutions supporting Repeal and pledging those present to campaign for it were carried unanimously. Unlike the previous Repeal meeting, this was organised by those in the city who supported the Irish Confederation. Given the paucity of information concerning the Repeal agitation in the west of Scotland between May 1846 and March 1848 it has been impossible to establish both when the split within the Glasgow Repeal movement occurred and which organisation — the LNRA or the Irish Confederation — was supported by the majority of the city's Repealers. Nevertheless, followers of the LNRA attended the public meeting in the Lyceum Rooms on 27 March 1848. One of them, James Welsh, declared:

> This was a time when all major differences should be buried in oblivion, and when all should meet as brethren for Ireland, and fraternise with their brother Repealers. (Cheers.) It was in this spirit that he now came forward to fraternise with…that section of Repealers called Young Ireland. He trusted that from that night there would be no Young Ireland or Old Ireland in Glasgow, but all for Ireland. (Hear, and cheers.)

The presence of supporters of the Repeal Association at the event was welcomed by several speakers that evening. Furthermore, one of the resolutions carried unanimously at the meeting stated that those present were

> of the opinion that, at this crisis, it is the duty of all true democrats, particularly Repealers, to fling aside all minor differences and party prejudices, and firmly

cement a union that will securely defeat Ireland's oppressors, and establish her independence; and to accomplish that desirable object, we pledge ourselves to fraternise and act together for the salvation of our common country.[78]

It is evident from subsequent newspaper reports of Repeal activity in Glasgow that 'Young Irelanders' and 'Old Irelanders' did indeed unite and campaign for their cause.[79] It is not clear, however, whether this reunified movement received the support of all of those who had been involved in the agitation, whether as followers of the LNRA or of the Irish Confederation, prior to March 1848.[80] Repeal societies elsewhere in the west of Scotland, for example at Paisley, Johnstone, Dalry and Coatbridge, also became active once more during this period.[81]

This upsurge in Repeal activity was almost certainly caused by events in Ireland. The February 1848 revolution in France gave much hope and encouragement to Ireland's Repealers and led to an improvement in relations between the LNRA and the Irish Confederation. Furthermore, the latter organisation was greatly invigorated by the events in Paris and quickly formed an alliance with the resurgent Chartist movement in England. In the north of England, Chartists and Confederates held joint meetings at which they pledged themselves to campaign for Repeal and the Charter. The Irish Confederation was convinced that in the aftermath of the French Revolution the British Government, faced with a strong and united Chartist–Repeal movement, would be forced to establish an Irish Parliament. Some within the organisation, however, had another reason for wanting an alliance with the Chartists. They believed that if the Government refused to grant Repeal an Irish Rebellion was a distinct possibility, and if this were to occur it would have a better chance of success if a simultaneous rising of Confederates and Chartists took place in England, as troops who would be needed in Ireland would have to remain on the British mainland.[82] The Repealers in the west of Scotland were caught up in the excitement of the times and, like their brethren in Ireland and in England, were also greatly encouraged by the French Revolution.[83] They believed an Irish Parliament was at last within reach and that they had to play their part in the final act of the struggle. For example, one of the resolutions passed at the public meeting of Repealers in the Lyceum Rooms on 27 March 1848 stated:

That we the Repealers of Glasgow, are now convinced that the period of Ireland's redemption is at hand, and that, to achieve the reconstruction of that country's nationality, we must no longer confide in the effacy of prayers and petitions, but sternly demand the right of self-legislation to protect Ireland's interests.

At the same meeting James Welsh urged Repealers to unite and argued: 'This was the proper time for Ireland to look to her interests — she should not allow the present opportunity to pass, as she might never have another'.[84]

The Chartist movement in Scotland, like its counterpart in England, witnessed a revival in its fortunes in spring 1848, and for the same reasons. The deepening economic distress led many once again to political agitation in the hope that it would result in an improvement in their social and economic condition; the French Revolution and the likelihood that the long hoped-for union of Chartists and Repealers would finally become a reality encouraged the Chartists greatly and roused them into action.[85]

The Repealers and Chartists in the west of Scotland, as in the east of the country[86] and in England, formed alliances in 1848. One of the main speakers at the public meeting of Repealers in the Lyceum Rooms in Glasgow on 27 March 1848 was James Adams, who was by that time the leading figure in the city's Chartist movement[87], and at the conclusion of the evening's proceedings three cheers were given for William Smith O'Brien and John Mitchel of the Irish Confederation, John O'Connell, Repeal, Feargus O'Connor and the Charter.[88] On 7 April the Chartists and Repealers held a public meeting in the City Hall which, according to the *Glasgow Saturday Post*, was attended by not less than 6,000 people and was 'crowded to excess'. Those present pledged themselves to campaign for the Charter and Repeal. They also resolved to contribute to the defence fund of the recently arrested Irish Confederate leaders Smith O'Brien, Mitchel and Thomas Meagher, who were all charged with sedition.[89] Ten days later the two parties held a large Charter and Repeal demonstration on Glasgow Green[90] and throughout the summer several more joint meetings and demonstrations took place in the city.[91] Fraternal meetings of Repealers and Chartists also occurred elsewhere in the west of Scotland during this period, for example at Paisley, Johnstone, Coatbridge and Dalry.[92] The Repealers in the region, like the Confederates in Ireland and in England, had become convinced that their agitation would be successful only if they acted in concert with the Chartist movement.[93]

As occurred in the north of England,[94] some Repealers in the west of Scotland in spring 1848 advocated the use of 'physical force' measures. For example, at the Repeal meeting in the Lyceum Rooms in Glasgow on 27 March John Daly stated the following:

> The Chartists were with them — the Chartists of Great Britain were with them — 500,000 Chartists had with uncovered heads solemnly vowed that blood spilled in Ireland should be dearly avenged in England. (Loud cheers). Prayers and petitions were the weapons of slaves and cowards, arms were the weapons

used by the free and brave. (Cheers.) These were not times for men to mince their words — these were not times to shrink from a determination to stand forth as volunteers to assist their friends in Ireland. It might be asked what could they do here to assist their countrymen? Why, they could keep the army in Scotland.

At this point the chairman of the meeting interrupted Daly and called him to order. Daly, however,

> contended he was not out of order. They had prayed for a hundred years and what had they got? (A voice — 'nothing') Yes, they had got something; they had got starvation, famine, pestilence, and the Malthusian doctrines fostered in their land; and was that a time to call him to order? The way to petition was to present their petitions on the points of pikes (loud cheers.)...They would be glad to have a bloodless revolution if they could obtain their rights, but they would have it, bloody or not.[95]

Daly was one of the leading figures in the resurgent Repeal agitation.[96] For example, he was one of the speakers at a meeting of the Repealers and Chartists on 8 May, held 'for the purpose of taking into consideration the propriety of forming a National Guard' to protect the reform movement in the city from attempts by the Government or the local authorities to crush it. Daly argued that it was imperative that every man in England, Scotland and Ireland obtained arms. However, no decision was made concerning the establishment of such an organisation.[97] In fact, National Guards were not formed anywhere in the west of Scotland during this period.[98]

The Repeal and Chartist movements in Glasgow began to disintegrate during May 1848. For example, on 2 June a public meeting of Chartists and Repealers was held in the City Hall to condemn the trial and conviction of John Mitchel; the *Scotch Reformers' Gazette* reported that 'The assemblage was not nearly so numerous as some of the meetings held a few weeks ago...'. Ten days later the two parties held a joint demonstration on Glasgow Green which was attended by between only 6,000 and 7,000 people. The *Scotch Reformers' Gazette* described it as 'a miserable failure'. Others shared this view.[99] It is not clear what caused this rapid decline in support for both agitations.

The Government was not willing to entertain either Repeal or the Charter and from April 1848 onwards it embarked on a policy of repression against both movements. As a result, some leaders of the Irish Confederation came to the conclusion that rebellion was the only way by which they could obtain Repeal. In England, Chartists and Confederates held secret meetings, and armed and drilled; the authorities were aware of this and became convinced that a rising was being planned to coincide with an insurrection in Ireland.[100] There is evidence which suggests that some Chartists and Repealers in the west of Scotland also seriously considered whether to rebel, although it must be emphasised that there is, compared with the situation for England, very little information available concerning seditious activities in the region. The *Scotch Reformers' Gazette* reported that in the last week of June the authorities in Glasgow learned that the manufacture of pikes and daggers was taking place in the Anderston district, 'for physical force purposes, after the approved recommendation, we suppose, of these Chartist and Repeal scoundrels'. The authorities raided the premises involved and seized the weapons. The blacksmiths who made them, however, had managed to flee before the search occurred.[101] On 22 July the same newspaper reported that 'some pike and treason meetings' had taken place near Maryhill at which advice was given on the manufacture of pikes and the use of weapons.[102] Around this time Irish Confederate leaders were apparently informed that 'several hundred Irishmen in Scotland' had been preparing for a rising for some time and were willing to come to Ireland should the need arise.[103]

Increasingly repressive measures introduced in Ireland by the Government eventually pushed members of the Irish Confederation into their ill-fated rebellion in County Tipperary in late July. The rising was put down with little difficulty and its leaders were tried and transported.[104] Events in Ireland, however, did not lead to an insurrection in Britain. The Confederates and Chartists in England were too weak and unorganised, and the authorities, who were well aware of the activities of the would-be revolutionaries, experienced few problems in breaking the conspiracy in Liverpool, Manchester and London during July and August.[105] In the west of Scotland the 'physical force' movement does not appear to have been as extensive or significant. Unlike for England, there is no evidence of seditious or insurrectionary activity in the region during the Tipperary fiasco or in its aftermath, and there was no round-up of revolutionary Chartists and Repealers.[106] Indeed, the lack of evidence means it is impossible to establish whether revolutionary conspiracies similar to those in England even existed in the west of Scotland at that time.[107] Nevertheless, by the end of the summer of 1848 the campaigns in the United Kingdom for Repeal and the Charter were over: the Government had been able to crush both agitations with ease.[108] After these defeats the Irish in Scotland, like native workers, did not participate to any significant extent in movements for political reform for almost twenty years.[109]

Notes

1. D.G. Wright, *Popular Radicalism: the Working Class Experience, 1780–1880* (London, 1988), p.133.

2. *Ibid*, pp.127–31, 133, 148; Edward Royle, *Chartism* (2nd edition, London, 1988), p.33.

3. Royle, *Chartism*, p.33.

4. Alexander Wilson, *The Chartist Movement in Scotland* (Manchester, 1970), pp.179, 186–97.

5. *Ibid*, p.197.

6. *Ibid*, Chapter 15.

7. *Ibid*, p.179; Alexander Wilson, 'The Suffrage Movement', in Patricia Hollis (ed.), *Pressure from Without in early Victorian England* (London, 1974), p.91; Leslie C. Wright, *Scottish Chartism* (Edinburgh, 1953), p.155.

8. J.H. Treble, 'O'Connor, O'Connell and the Attitudes of Irish Immigrants towards Chartism in the North of England 1838–48', in J. Butt and I.F. Clarke (eds.), *The Victorians and Social Protest: a Symposium* (Newton Abbot, 1973), p.221; *Glasgow Saturday Post*, 7 December 1844; *Glasgow Examiner*, 7 December 1844.

9. *Glasgow Saturday Post*, 22 July 1843. See also *ibid*, 5 August 1843 for similar claims.

10. SCA, Presholme Letters, PL3/309/18, Andrew Scott to 'My Dear Lord' [Bishop Kyle], 12 July 1843.

11. *Glasgow Saturday Post*, 29 July 1843.

12. *Glasgow Chronicle*, 12 July 1843.

13. *Glasgow Saturday Post*, 8 July 1843.

14. *Ibid*, 29 July, 23 September 1843.

15. *Glasgow Chronicle*, 3 July 1843; *Glasgow Saturday Post*, 11 February, 6 May, 10 June, 22 July, 19 August, 16 September 1843.

16. Gearoid O'Tuathaigh, *Ireland Before the Famine* (2nd edition, Dublin, 1990), p.189.

17. *Ibid*, pp.189–90; D. George Boyce, *Nineteenth Century Ireland: The Search for Stability (Dublin, 1990)*, pp.83–91.

18. *Glasgow Saturday Post*, 21 October 1843.

19. *Ibid*, 27 January, 3 and 10 February 1844.

20. The sheets arrived in the city on 4 March and were sent back to Dublin on 9 March. The *Glasgow Saturday Post* suggested that 'Had a public meeting been called, or public meeting been given previously, there can be no doubt but double the number of names might have been got, as a great number of

Scotchmen signed it who never took any part in Irish affairs before'. *Glasgow Saturday Post*, 16 March 1844.

21. *Ibid*, 8 June 1844.

22. *Ibid*, 6 and 13 July 1844.

23. *Ibid*, 14 September 1844; *Glasgow Examiner*, 14 September 1844. Henry Vincent was one of the speakers at the meeting.

24. *Glasgow Saturday Post*, 23 December 1843.

25. *Ibid*, 3 February 1844.

26. *Ibid*, 13 July 1844; *Glasgow Examiner*, 13 July 1844.

27. *Glasgow Saturday Post*, 6 July 1844.

28. *Ibid*, 29 July 1843. Brewster also chaired a Repeal meeting in the town two months later. See *ibid*, 23 September 1843. Apart from these two references I have found no other evidence of Brewster participating in the Repeal movement in Paisley during 1843 and 1844. It must be noted, however, that there are not many other examples of Repeal activity in the town during these years.

29. *Ibid*, 3 February, 2 and 9 March, 8 June, 17 August, 26 October, 30 November 1844; 11 January, 22 March, 31 May, 12 July, 20 September 1845. *Glasgow Examiner*, 22 March 1845; Wilson, *Chartist Movement in Scotland*, p.202; Alexander Wilson, 'Chartism in Glasgow' in Asa Briggs (ed.), *Chartist Studies* (London, 1959), p.273.

30. See, for example, *Glasgow Saturday Post*, 3 and 17 February, 2 and 9 March, 11 May 1844.

31. See, for example, *ibid*, 4 and 18 May, 17 August 1844.

32. Those present at the meeting also believed that 'the dissemination of useful knowledge' was the only means of making them 'good citizens and proper members of society'. *Ibid*, 26 October 1844.

33. *Ibid*, 14 December 1844.

34. *Ibid*, 11 and 18 January, 22 March, 31 May, 12 and 19 July, 20 September 1845; 31 January, 14 February, 18 March, 16 May 1846; *Glasgow Examiner* 22 March, 29 November 1845, 31 January 1846.

35. For example, I have found only one report in the *Glasgow Saturday Post* of a Repeal meeting in Glasgow in the period from May 1846 to May 1847. This was in February 1847. *Ibid*, 20 February 1847.

36. For the Young Ireland Movement see O'Tuathaigh, *Ireland Before the Famine*, pp.186–202; Boyce, *Nineteenth Century Ireland*, pp.78–84, 115–18.

37. Treble, 'O'Connor, O'Connell and the Attitudes of Irish Immigrants', pp.60–1.

38. O'Tuathaigh, *Ireland Before the Famine*, p.188; Hoppen, *Ireland since 1800*, p.27.

39. Treble, 'O'Connor, O'Connell and the Attitudes of Irish Immigrants', p.48.

40. Sometimes Ryan is named as O'Ryan. Johnson listed him as being one of the priests at St Andrews during 1842–43 but did not provide a biography of him. Christine Johnson, 'Scottish Secular Clergy, 1830–1878: the Western District', *Innes Review*, XL (1989), p.144; Bernard J. Canning, *Irish-Born Secular Priests in Scotland 1829–1979* (Inverness, 1979), p.345.

41. *Glasgow Chronicle*, 10 June 1842; *Glasgow Saturday Post*, 15 January, 2 July 1842; 6 May, 10 June, 3 and 22 July 1843.

42. *Glasgow Chronicle*, 10 June 1842.

43. *Glasgow Saturday Post*, 10 June, 22 July 1843.

44. *Ibid*, 16 September 1843. The paper also reported that 'in addition to the immense numbers almost wedged together within the buildings, hundreds occupied the staircases and the passages, and the street in front of the church was completely blocked up'.

45. *Ibid*, 14 December 1844.

46. The Western District was composed of the counties of 'Argyllshire, Ayrshire, Bute and Arran, Dunbartonshire, Lanarkshire, Renfrewshire, Wigtownshire, the Hebrides or Western Islands and the Southern part of Inverness-shire...' *Scottish Catholic Directory* for 1839, p.37.

47. SCA, Blairs Letters, BL6/442/15 Andrew Scott to James Kyle, 28 August 1844. This information from Scott, along with the fact that I have found no evidence of priests participating in Repeal meetings outside Glasgow, suggests that a ban on the Catholic clergy becoming involved in the movement was imposed not only in the city but also elsewhere in the Western District.

48. Canning, *Irish-Born Secular Priests*, p.334.

49. *Glasgow Saturday Post*, 23 November 1844. The paper also reported that the meeting was attended not only by Catholics but also by 'liberal Protestant inhabitants of Glasgow...'.

50. See also, *ibid*, 29 March 1845.

51. *Ibid*.

52. Michael Condon quoted in Canning, *Irish-Born Secular Priests*, p.334. In the period from 1838 to the end of 1844 at least seven other Irish priests left Glasgow. The Revs. Caissey, Enraght, O'Meara and Wallace returned to Ireland, all of whom having been only on loan to the Western District. John Ryan, who returned home in 1843, might also have been on loan; John Scanlan was transferred to Hamilton; Daniel Gallagher was moved to Airdrie in 1840 but returned to Glasgow the following year. Johnson, 'Scottish Secular Clergy', pp.110–40; Canning, *Irish-Born Secular Priests*, pp.39, 95, 113, 314, 376; *Glasgow Saturday Post*, 16 September 1843.

53. *Glasgow Saturday Post*, 14 December 1844. The author of the letter stated of Murdoch 'that his warmth of feeling, his menacing style of address, and his violent declamation on the question of Repeal agitators, seemed anything but judicious…'

54. *Glasgow Chronicle*, 26 September 1842.

55. *Glasgow Saturday Post*, 8 October 1842.

56. *Ibid*, 27 January, 3 and 10 February 1844. John Bremner, the priest who chaired the Paisley meeting, stressed to his audience that he was no politician and would not give an opinion on Repeal. For Bremner, the exclusion of Catholics from the jury was an attack on their civil rights: 'Trial by jury is our palladium. Meddle with it and our liberties are gone. As Catholics, the step which we got by the Emancipation Act will be slipped from beneath our feet, if we do not look to ourselves and protest against the present conduct of the Irish executive in these state trials, and as British subjects…we shall speedily become bond slaves like the Russians, if we do not, by every constitutional means in our power, struggle to keep from our wrists the chains with which a Tory government would bind us up, depriving us of liberty, and fattening us on our heart's blood'. Bremner was also outraged at the treatment of O'Connell: 'When I behold the liberator of the slave, the emancipator of the Catholic, the champion of the dissenter, the hero of reform, and the saviour of his country, seized upon by a base, bloody, and tyrannical horde of Tories, while 40,000 armed men keep sentry upon him, I behoved to have neither head nor heart, reason nor religion, if such a spectacle did not wind up my feelings to their highest pitch of intensity.' *Ibid*, 3 February 1844. The following month he stated to a colleague that if the people did not petition over the issue of the State Trials and 'if the silent system is…followed, then any ministry may trample the nation under their feet'. SCA, Blairs Letters, BL6/407/1, John Bremner to 'My Dear Friend', 1 March 1844.

57. For the development of the Catholic Church in the west of Scotland during the period 1790–1850 see Martin J. Mitchell, 'The Establishment and Early Years of the Hamilton Mission', in T.M. Devine (ed.), *St Mary's Hamilton, 1846–1996: a Social History* (Edinburgh, 1995), pp.1–14; John F. McCaffrey, 'The Stewardship of Resources: Financial Strategies of Roman Catholics in the Glasgow District, 1800–70', in W.J. Sheils and Diana Wood (eds.), *The Church and Wealth* (Studies in Church History Vol.24) (Oxford, 1987), pp.359–70.

58. *Glasgow Saturday Post*, 10 June 1843, 3 February 1844.

59. SCA, Blairs Letters, BL6/483/2, Andrew Scott to James Kyle, 11 January 1845. The aim of the Charitable Bequests Act of 1844 was to protect Catholic charities in Ireland. O'Connell opposed the Act because it was part of the Peel Government's programme of reforms for Ireland, the aim of which was to dampen the enthusiasm for Repeal. According to Scott the

Irish Catholics in Glasgow also opposed the Act. O'Tuathaigh, *Ireland Before the Famine*, p.193; Dickson, *Nineteenth Century Ireland*, pp.89–91.

60. SCA, Blairs Letters, BL6/483/3, Andrew Scott to James Kyle, 6 February 1845.

61. *Ibid*, BL6/442/15, Andrew Scott to James Kyle, 24 August 1844.

62. Quoted in Christine Johnson, *Developments in the Roman Catholic Church in Scotland, 1789–1829* (Edinburgh, 1983), pp.138–39.

63. *Ibid*, p.139.

64. Christine Johnson, 'Secular Clergy of the Lowland District, 1732–1829', *Innes Review*, XXXIV (1983), p.71.

65. SCA, Presholme Letters, PL3/214/16, Andrew Scott to James Kyle, 22 October 1832.

66. *Ibid*, PL3/214/20, Andrew Scott to James Kyle, 21 November 1832.

67. *Ibid*, PL3/234/17, Andrew Scott to James Kyle, 11 December 1833. See also Bernard Aspinwall, 'Scots and Irish clergy ministering to immigrants, 1830–1878', *Innes Review*, XLVII (1996), p.48.

68. *Scottish Catholic Directory* for 1838, pp.56–59; *Ibid*, for 1844, pp.60–61; Johnson, 'Scottish Secular Clergy', pp.110–40.

69. Canning, *Irish-Born Secular Priests*, p.245.

70. SCA, Presholme Letters, PL3/327/5, Andrew Scott to James Kyle, 29 April 1846. See also PL3/327/7, Scott to Kyle, 10 May 1846. The meeting to which Scott referred might have been that which took place in the Lyceum Rooms on 14 April 1846 to present the secretary of the Glasgow Repealers with gifts in honour of his exertions on behalf of the cause. Quigley and McDermott were both present. The report of Quigley's speech, however, did not demonstrate that he publicly criticised Murdoch. See *Glasgow Saturday Post*, 15 April 1846. For a brief account of Quigley's activities see Canning, *Irish-Born Secular Priests*, p.334.

71. SCA, Blairs Letters, BL6/517/6, Andrew Scott to James Kyle, 28 May 1846.

72. *Glasgow Saturday Post*, 25 December 1847.

73. *Ibid*, 20 February 1847.

74. Wilson, *Chartist Movement in Scotland*, pp.216–7.

75. One of the speakers at the meeting 'denounced the confederation of the Young Ireland party as inimical to the interests of Ireland and the cause of Repeal…' Also, one of the resolutions passed at the meeting condemned divisions in the Repeal movement.

76. O'Tuathaigh, *Ireland Before the Famine*, p.197. See also Dickson, *Nineteenth Century Ireland*, p.115.

77. *Glasgow Saturday Post*, 18 March 1848. See also *Scotch Reformers' Gazette*, 18 March 1848.

78. *Glasgow Saturday Post*, 1 April 1848. See also *Scotch Reformers' Gazette*, 1 April 1848.

79. See, for example, *Glasgow Saturday Post*, 8 April, 24 June 1848.

80. For example, five Glasgow Repealers who were prominent supporters, during 1847, of the campaign of the LNRA, were particularly active in the agitation of 1848, namely Peter McCabe, James Welsh, Andrew Dournan, Edward Kelly and D. Henry. However, several leading pro-LNRA Repealers in the city do not appear to have been involved in the reunified movement: there are no references to Charles Bryson, John Tracey, John Cunningham, Daniel Burns, John Lynch and Dr. Henry Gribben in newspaper reports of the activities of the Repealers from March 1848 onwards.

81. *Northern Star*, 22 April, 17 and 24 June, 27 July 1848.

82. W.J. Lowe, 'The Chartists and Irish Confederates: Lancashire, 1848', *Irish Historical Studies*, XXIV (1984), pp.176–9; Treble, 'O'Connor, O'Connell and the Attitudes of Irish Immigrants', pp.64–8; O'Tuathaigh, *Ireland Before the Famine*, pp.199–200; John Belcham, English Working Class Radicalism and the Irish, 1815–50', in Roger Swift and Sheridan Gilley (eds.), *The Irish in the Victorian City* (London, 1985), pp.89–91; Lynn Hollen Lees, *Exiles of Erin: Irish Migrants in Victorian London* (Manchester, 1979), p.228; D.N. Petler, 'Ireland and France in 1848', *Irish Historical Studies*, XXIV (1985), pp.493–496.

83. One of the resolutions passed at the Repeal meeting in the Lyceum Rooms on 17 March 1848 hailed 'with satisfaction the triumph of Frenchmen over a despotic government'. The public meeting of Repealers in the same place ten days later was held 'for the purpose of congratulating the French people on the attainment of their freedom'. One of the speakers at the latter event asked: 'was it by prayers and petitions that they [The French people] now enjoyed the blessings of liberty? Was it praying and petitioning that caused Metternich to fly for his life? Were Irishmen to be bound when the rest of the states in Continental Europe were receiving their freedom by the use of constitutional means. (Cheers.) Ireland should, would, and must be free, if Irishmen would unite and act in consistency with one another in the great struggle. (Cheers.)' *Glasgow Saturday Post*, 18 March, 1 April 1848.

84. *Ibid*, 1 April 1848.

85. Wright, *Popular Radicalism*, p.136; Royle, *Chartism*, p.43; Wilson, *Chartist Movement*, pp.216–7. It would appear that there was an Irish presence in the resurgent Chartist Movement in the west of Scotland. For example, one of the leading figures in Glasgow Chartism at this time was one William Docherty. Other prominent activists in the region who had 'Irish names' included James and David McMullen, James Daly and James McGonegal. In Hamilton, a public meeting was held on 6 April 1848 and one of the resolutions passed at it stated the following: 'That this meeting being composed of Englishmen, Irishmen and Scotchmen, equally unrepresented

in the legislature, resolve to throw aside all national prejudices, and make an united struggle to obtain the People's Charter.' Moreover, the chairman of the meeting was an Irishman named Hugh O'Neil. See *Northern Star*, 17 February, 22 April, 13 May, 17 June 1848; John F. McCaffrey, 'Irish Immigrants and Radical Movements in the West of Scotland in the Early Nineteenth Century', Innes Review, XXXIX (1988), p.54; Wilson, *Chartist Movement in Scotland*, p.230.

86. Wright, *Scottish Chartism*, pp.194–201.

87. Alexander Wilson, 'Chartism in Glasgow', pp.284–5. For the Chartist movement in Scotland in 1848 see Wilson, *Chartist Movement in Scotland*, chapter 16.

88. *Glasgow, Saturday Post*, 1 April 1848; *Scotch Reformers' Gazette*, 1 April 1848.

89. *Glasgow Saturday Post*, 8 April 1848; *Scotch Reformers' Gazette*, 8 April 1848.

90. *Glasgow Saturday Post*, 22 April 1848; *Scotch Reformers' Gazette*, 22 April 1848; *Northern Star*, 29 April 1848; Wilson, *Chartist Movement in Scotland*, pp.226–7.

91. These included two more meetings on Glasgow Green. *Glasgow Saturday Post*, 13 May, 3 June 1848; *Scotch Reformers' Gazette*, 13 May, 3 and 17 June, 5 August 1848.

92. *Northern Star*, 22 April, 17 June, 22 July 1848; *Glasgow Saturday Post*, 17 June 1848.

93. See, for example, *Glasgow Saturday Post*, 1 and 8 April 1848.

94. Treble, 'O'Connor, O'Connell and the Attitudes of Irish Immigrants', p.69.

95. *Glasgow Saturday Post*, 1 April 1848. The *Scotch Reformers' Gazette* was appalled at this meeting, which was attended by Young Irelanders, supporters of the LNRA and by the Chartist James Adams. It stated: 'We have no hesitation in characterising the meeting as one of the most disgraceful, for its atrocity and violence, ever held in this city.' *Scotch Reformers' Gazette*, 1 April 1848.

96. See, for example, *Glasgow Saturday Post*, 8 April, 3 and 24 June 1848.

97. *Ibid*, 13 May, 1848; *Scotch Reformers' Gazette*, 13 May 1848.

98. National Guards were, however, formed in Edinburgh, Aberdeen and Dundee. Indeed, in Edinburgh Irishmen appear to have been involved in the organisation. See Wilson, *Chartist Movement in Scotland*, pp.228–32; Wright, *Scottish Chartism*, pp.194–9.

99. *Scotch Reformers' Gazette*, 3 and 17 June 1848; Wilson, *Chartist Movement in Scotland*, p.233.

100. O'Tuathaigh, *Ireland Before the Famine*, p.200; Wright, *Popular Radicalism*, pp.137–8; Royle, *Chartism*, pp.47–8; Treble, 'O'Connor, O'Connell and the Attitudes of Irish Immigrants', p.69; Belcham, 'English Working Class Radicalism', pp.91–2; Lowe, 'Chartists and Irish Confederates', pp.180–9.

101. *Scotch Reformers' Gazette*, 1 July 1848.

102. *Ibid*, 22 July 1848.

103. James Handley, *The Irish in Scotland, 1798–1845* (2nd edition, Cork, 1945), p.316.

104. O'Tuathaigh, *Ireland Before the Famine*, pp.200–1.

105. Lowe, 'Chartists and Irish Confederates', pp.180–191; Treble, 'O'Connor, O'Connell and the Attitudes of Irish Immigrants', p.69; Belcham, 'English Working Class Radicalism', pp.91–2; Wright, *Popular Radicalism*, p.138; Royle, *Chartism*, p.49.

106. The Catholic clergy in the west of Scotland might have played some part in preventing insurrectionary activity. In August 1848 Bishop John Murdoch informed Bishop Kyle that in Glasgow 'all the Young Irelanders are raging against the Irish priests because they used their influence to keep the people from joining Mad O'Bryan and his mad associates'. It is not clear, however, whether Murdoch was referring to the Irish priests in the west of Scotland or to those in Ireland. Murdoch had no time for the Irish rebels: 'It is really a pity that some of these stupid fools did not get a skinful of bullets.' SCA, Blairs Letters, BL6/587/13, John Murdoch to 'My Dear Lord'[Kyle] 20 August 1848.

107. Archibald Alison, who was Sheriff of Lanarkshire at the time of O'Brien's rising in Tipperary, recalled in his memoir that he was informed of the revolt at 2 a.m. He 'immediately despatched instructions to the military authorities to call out the pensioners, put the troops under arms, and occupy in force the principal points of the city [Glasgow]; and before the citizens generally awoke this was done, so that no immediate danger was to be apprehended. Before night the train from Liverpool brought the accounts of the cabbage garden conflict, and the failure of the insurrection. The danger was over...' Alison did not mention the existence of any insurrectionary groups in the city at this time. Archibald Alison, *Some Account of my Life and Writings, Volume I* (Edinburgh, 1883), pp.594–5.

108. Wilson, *Chartist Movement in Scotland*, pp.217, 232–40; Treble, 'O'Connor, O'Connell and the Attitudes of Irish Immigrants', p.69; O'Tuathaigh, *Ireland Before the Famine*, pp.201–2; Royle, *Chartism*, pp.47–9; Wright, *Popular Radicalism*, pp.237–8.

109. Wilson, *Chartist Movement in Scotland*, chapters 17 and 18; James Handley, *The Irish in Modern Scotland* (Cork, 1947), pp.261–9; I.G.C. Hutchison, 'Working-Class Politics' in R.A. Cage (ed.), *The Working Class in Glasgow, 1750–1914* (London, 1987), pp.107–9.

Conclusion

In the introduction to this book it was shown that the dominant historical view of the Catholic Irish in Scotland in the first half of the nineteenth century is that they were despised on account of their religion and because most were employed as strike-breakers or low-wage labour. As a result of this hostility, it has been argued, the Catholic Irish formed separate and isolated communities in the towns in which they settled in significant numbers. Furthermore, they were unable or unwilling to participate in trade unions, strikes and radical reform movements with native workers, and politically were interested mainly in Irish and Catholic issues. The Protestant Irish immigrants, on the other hand, are said to have integrated with little difficulty, mainly because of their religious beliefs and because many had family and cultural ties with Scotland.

The prevailing view of the Catholic Irish is not compatible with much of the evidence surveyed in this study. With regard to industrial action, it is indisputable that some Irish workers were used as cheap or blackleg labour. There is, however, evidence that others participated in strikes and trade unions. For example, the Irish — Catholic and Protestant — appear to have constituted the majority of the membership of the formidable Glasgow Cotton Spinners' Association throughout this period; and Irish workers formed a large proportion, perhaps even the majority, of those involved in the handloom weavers' unions in and around Glasgow by the late 1830s. The examples of the Irish as strike-breakers relate mainly to the coal and iron industries of Lanarkshire and Ayrshire from the second half of the 1830s onwards. Yet there is also evidence that Irish colliers and miners in these counties participated in strikes. It would appear that some of these workers were employed initially as blackleg or cheap labour, but once part of the labour force were just as willing as Scottish workers to engage in industrial action when wages or conditions came under threat.

It is undeniable that the Catholic Irish in the west of Scotland were deeply interested in Catholic and Irish issues. In the 1820s members of that community in Glasgow established an association which participated in the campaign for Catholic Emancipation, and this society lasted for over five years despite intense opposition to it from the city's priests and a section of the congregation. For most of the 1840s the Catholic Irish in the region were enthusiastic supporters of O'Connell's campaign for repeal of the legislative union between Great Britain and Ireland, much to the chagrin of their bishops.

This is not to suggest, however, that the Catholic Irish were not interested in the issues which concerned the native population. Indeed, given their lowly economic and social position the Catholic Irish were not isolated from the problems which faced Scottish workers who were in the same or similar circumstances. In the late 1790s and early 1800s Irish immigrants helped establish and man the revolutionary Society of United Scotsmen, and it is probable that they did so in order to assist the cause of the United Irishmen. Members of the Catholic Irish community in the west of Scotland participated in subsequent agitations for political change, but were undoubtedly involved for the same reasons as the Scots: they were convinced that reform would lead to a marked improvement in their social and economic condition, and also believed that it was indisputable that they should have the franchise. There is evidence that Irish workers were among the leaders of the secret radical societies of 1816–20 and it would appear that the aims of these revolutionary organisations were supported by a large number of Irish immigrants in the region, both Catholic and Protestant. There was a significant Catholic Irish presence in the pre-Chartist reform agitations of the 1830s and there is evidence that some were active in the campaign for the Charter. However, the bulk of the politically active members of the Catholic Irish population of Glasgow, and probably elsewhere in the west of Scotland, were not involved in the Chartist movement. This was not because they were apathetic towards the Charter: they did not participate because the dominant figure in the Chartist agitation was their hero Daniel O'Connell's arch-enemy Feargus O'Connor. Indeed, once the Complete Suffrage movement adopted the Six Points as its policy O'Connell's Catholic Irish supporters in Glasgow became enthusiastic supporters of it. They were not to know that within a few months both Complete Suffragism and Chartism would to go into rapid decline. In 1848 the O'Connellites in the west of Scotland finally allied with the Chartists and campaigned for Repeal and the Charter. But it was too little, too late.

It is now evident that the Catholic Irish in the west of Scotland in the first half of the nineteenth century were not as isolated and despised as some historians have claimed. Many members of that community participated in strikes, trade unions and political movements with native workers. Scottish reformers welcomed the Catholic Irish presence in the political agitations. When the bulk of the Catholic Irish in Glasgow eschewed involvement in the campaign for the Six Points the city's Chartists sought ways to bring them back into the ranks of the radical movement.

Of course not every Scottish worker was a striker, a trade unionist or a political reformer. Perhaps those who engaged in or sought joint action with the Catholic Irish were more enlightened and less bigoted than those who did not. In order to establish the extent of Catholic Irish integration in the west of Scotland during this period more research clearly needs to be undertaken. For example, the attitudes of the rest of the native urban working class and of the middle class towards the Catholic Irish need to be examined, as does the issue of inter-marriage with the Scottish population. The role of the Catholic Irish in activities such as riots, popular disturbances and the temperance movement must be investigated. Moreover, in light of the findings of this study the Catholic Irish experience in Scotland during the second half of the nineteenth century will also have to be reassessed.

Bibliography

Primary Sources

MANUSCRIPT SOURCES

Edinburgh University Archives
Forty-three Papers relating to the Earl of Durham, mainly congratulatory
    addresses from reformers, on the occasion of his visit to Glasgow in 1834,
    SRC.1.3, D2654/2

Glasgow Archdiocesan Archives
Baptismal Register, 30 June 1808–28 December 1815, RH21/62/11
Condon Diaries, WD5

National Library of Scotland
C.H. Hutchison, Ms. Diary 1820–48, MS 2733.
Melville Papers, Scotland 1808–38, MS 1054.

Scottish Catholic Archives
Blairs Letters
Dunkeld Diocese Correspondence
Individual Mission Correspondence
Oban Letters
Presholme Letters
Scottish Mission Correspondence

Scottish Record Office
Home Office Correspondence, Scotland, RH2/4
Justiciary Court Records, JC26, JC45
Lord Advocate's Papers, AD14
Melville Castle Muniments, GD51

Strathclyde Regional Archives
Hibernian Society of Glasgow Minute Book, 1792–1824, TD200/7
John MacKinnon Correspondence, TD 743
Letterbooks of the Association of Master Cotton Spinners, 1810–1811, T-MJ/99
Letterbooks of the Cotton Spinners, 1816, T-MJ/100
Monteith Correspondence, G1/2/1–52
Papers of Sir John Maxwell, Eighth Bt. of Pollock, T-PM.117
Papers of Sir John Maxwell, Ninth Bt. of Pollock, T-PM.117

Newspapers and Periodicals

Ayr Observer
Chartist Circular
Glasgow Argus
Glasgow Chronicle
Glasgow Courier
Glasgow Examiner
Glasgow Evening (Saturday) Post and Paisley and Renfrewshire Reformer
Glasgow Free Press (Founded 1823)
Glasgow Free Press (Founded 1851)
Glasgow Herald
Glasgow Observer
Glasgow Sentinel
Greenock Advertiser
Herald to the Trades' Advocate
(Loyal) Reformers' Gazette
Monthly Liberator
New Liberator
Northern Star
Poor Man's Advocate
Radical Reformers' Gazette
Scotch Reformers' Gazette
Scots Times
Scotsman
Scottish Guardian
Scottish Patriot
Spirit of the Union
Trades Examiner
Tradesman
True Scotsman
Weavers' Journal

Parliamentary Papers

1799	*Report of the Committee of Secrecy of the House of Commons*
1816 III	*Report of the Minutes of Evidence Taken Before the Select Committee on the State of the Children Employed in the Manufactories of the United Kingdom*
1817 IV	*First Report of the Select Committee of Secrecy*
1824 V	*Reports from the Select Committee appointed to inquire into the State of the Law respecting Artisans leaving the Kingdom and residing abroad; the exportation of Tools and Machinery; and the Combination of Workmen and Others to raise wages, or to regulate their Wages and Hours of Working.*

1825 IV — Report from the Select Committee appointed to inquire into the effects of the Act 5 Geo. 4, c.95, in respect to the conduct of Workmen and others in the United Kingdom, and how far it may be necessary to repeal and amend the said Act.

1826 IV — Report from the Select Committee on Emigration from the United Kingdom

1826–27 V — Reports from the Select Committee on Emigration from the United Kingdom

1831–2 XV — Report from the Select Committee on the 'Bill to regulate the Labour of Children in the Mills and Factories of the United Kingdom'.

1833 VI — Report from the Select Committee on Manufactures, Commerce and Shipping

1833 XX — First Report of the Central Board of His Majesty's Commissioners for inquiring into the Employment of Children in Factories.

1834 X — Select Committee on Handloom Weavers' Petitions.

1835 XIII — Analysis of the Evidence taken before the Select Committee on Handloom Weavers (1834–35)

1835 XVII — Report from the Select Committee appointed to inquire into the origin, nature, extent and tendency of Orange Institutions in Great Britain and Colonies

1835 XL — Reports made to the Secrecy of State by the Inspector of Factories, in Pursuance of the 45th Section of the Factories Regulation Act

1836 XXXIV — Report on the State of the Irish Poor in Great Britain

1836 XLV — Reports by the Inspectors of Factories

1837 XXXI — Reports by the Inspectors of Factories

1837–38 VIII — Reports from the Select Committee on Combinations of Workmen

1837–38 XXVIII — Reports by the Inspectors of Factories

1837–38 — Reports from the Commissioners of Religious Instruction, Scotland

1839 XIX — Reports by the Inspectors of Factories

1839 XLII — Reports from the Assistant Commissioners on Handloom Weavers

1840 X — Reports from the Select Committee on the Act for the Regulation of Mills and Factories

1840 XXIII — Reports by the Inspectors of Factories

1840 XXIV — Report of W.E. Hickson on the Condition of Handloom Weavers

1841 VI — Reports by the Inspectors of Factories

1841 VI — First and Second Reports from the Select Committee on Emigration, Scotland

1841 IX — Report from the Select Committee on the Act for the Regulation of Mills and Factories

1841 X — Reports by the Inspectors of Factories

1842	*Report on the Sanitary Condition of the Labouring Population of Scotland in Consequence of an Inquiry directed to be made by the Poor Law Commissioners*
1842 IX	*Report from the Select Committee on Payment of Wages*
1842 XVI	*Children's Employment Commission (Mines): Appendix 1*
1842 XXII	*Reports by the Inspectors of Factories*
1843 VII	*Select Committee on Distress in Paisley*
1843 XXVII	*Reports by the Inspectors of Factories*
1844 XVI	*Reports of the Commissioner appointed under the provision of the Act 5 and 6 Vict. c.99, to inquire into the operation of that Act and into the State of the Population in the Mining districts*
1844 XVII	*First Report of the Commissioners for inquiring into the State of Large Towns and Populous Districts*
1844 XXVIII	*Reports by the Inspectors of Factories*
1845 XVIII	*Second Report of the Commissioners for Inquiring into the State of the Large Towns and Populous Districts*
1845 XXV	*Reports by the Inspectors of Factories*
1845 XXVII	*Reports of the Mining Commissioner*
1846 XX	*Reports by the Inspectors of Factories*
1846 XXIII	*Report from the Select Committee on Railway Labourers*
1846 XXIV	*Reports of the Mining Commissioner*
1847 XV	*Reports by the Inspectors of Factories*
1847 XVI	*Reports of the Mining Commissioner*
1847–48 XXVI	*Reports of the Mining Commissioner*
1847–48 XXVI	*Reports by the Inspectors of Factories*
1849 XXII	*Reports of the Mining Commissioner*
1850 XXIII	*Reports of the Mining Commissioner*
1851 XXII	*Reports of the Mining Commissioner*

COMTEMPORARY BOOKS, PAMPHLETS, MEMOIRS EARLY HISTORIES, ETC

Alison, Archibald, *Some Account of my Life and Writings* (2 Vols. Edinburgh, 1883)

Baird, C.R., 'Observations upon the Poorest Class of Operatives in Glasgow in 1837', *Journal of the Statistical Society of London*, I (1838)

Bishop Bridge Murder! The Trial and Sentence of Doolan, Redding and Hickie, for the murder of John Green, Ganger on the Edinburgh and Glasgow Railway (Glasgow, 1841)

Bremner, D., *The Industries of Scotland: Their Rise, Progress and Present Condition* (First published 1869. This edition London, 1969)

(Burn, J.D.), *The Autobiography of a Beggar Boy* (First published 1855. This edition, London, 1978).

(Burn, J.D), *Commercial Enterprise and Social Progress: or Gleanings in London, Sheffield, Glasgow and Dublin* (London, 1858)

(Burn, J.D), *A Glimpse into the Social Condition of the Working Classes during the Early Part of the Present Century* (London, 1868)

Campbell, John, *Recollections of Radical times, Descriptive of the last hour of Baird and Hardie and the Riots in Glasgow, 1848* (Glasgow, 1880)

Catholic Directory for Scotland, 1831–1914

Cleland, James, *Enumeration of the Inhabitants of the city of Glasgow and its connected suburbs*, (Glasgow, 1820)

Cleland, James, *The Rise and Progress of the city of Glasgow, comprising an account of its Public Buildings, Charities and other Concerns* (Glasgow, 1820)

Cleland, James, *The Former and Present State of Glasgow* (Glasgow, 1840)

Cockburn, Henry, *Memorials of his own times* (Edinburgh, 1856)

Cockburn, Henry, *The Journal of Henry Cockburn 1831–54* (2 Vols., Edinburgh, 1874)

Crosshill Execution. The Life and Behaviour, Since Condemnation of Dennis Doolan and Patrick Redding (Glasgow, 1841)

Dickson, Hugh, *The Criterion, or Richmond's Narrative Exposed*, (Glasgow, 1825)

Fraser, James Roy, (ed.), *A Memoir of John Fraser of Newfield* (Paisley, 1879)

Gilmour, David, *Paisley Weavers of Other Days* (Edinburgh, 1898)

Glasgow Electors: List of the Names and Designations of the Persons who voted in the First election of Two members to serve in Parliament for the City of Glasgow under the Scotch Reform Bill, 18 and 19 December 1832. Collated from the Original Lists (Glasgow, 1832)

Green, C.J., *Trials for High Treason* (3 Volumes, Edinburgh, 1825)

Hamilton, Janet, *Poems, Essays and Sketches* (Glasgow, 1885)

Hammond, William, *Recollections of William Hammond, a Glasgow Handloom Weaver* (Glasgow, 1884)

(Hay, Robert), *Catholicity in Glasgow Thirty Years Ago* (Glasgow, 1863)

Howell, T.B., and Howell, T. Jones, (eds.), *A Complete Collection of State Trials and Proceedings for High Treason and Other Crimes and Misdemeanours*, Vol. XXVI (London, 1819)

Howie, J., *An Historical Account of the Town of Ayr for the last Fifty Years* (Kilmarnock, 1861)

MacKenzie, Peter, *Narrative of the late occurrences at the Cotton Mills in Glasgow; In answer to the Statement of these occurrences by the proprietors* (Glasgow, 1825)

MacKenzie, Peter, *The Trial of James Wilson for High Treason with an account of his execution at Glasgow, September 1820* (Glasgow, 1832)

MacKenzie, Peter, *An Exposure of the Spy System pursued in Glasgow during the years 1816–20, with copies of the original letters of Andrew Hardie* (Glasgow, 1833)

McGowan, William, *Address of the Glasgow Catholic Association* (Glasgow, 1825)

Marshall, James, *The Trial of Thomas Hunter, Peter Hacket, Richard McNiel, James Gibb and William McLean, the Glasgow Cotton Spinners* (Edinburgh, 1838)

Miller, W.M., (ed.), *An Account of the Reform Procession in Edinburgh, 10 August 1832* (Edinburgh, 1832)

New Statistical Account of Scotland (Edinburgh, 1845)

Parkhill, John, *The History of Paisley* (Paisley, 1857)

Parkhill, John, *The Life and Opinions of Arthur Sneddon* (Paisley, 1860)

Paterson, James, *Autobiographical Reminiscences* (Glasgow, 1871)

Report of a Trial in the Jury Court, Edinburgh, on 25 June 1821, for an Alleged Libel: In the Case of Revd Andrew Scott, roman Catholic priest, Glasgow, versus, W. McGavin, author of a work entitled 'The Protestant', and Others (Glasgow, 1821)

Richmond, Alexander B., *Narrative of the Condition of the Manufacturing Population and the Proceedings of Government which led to the State Trials in Scotland* (First published 1824. This edition New York, 1971)

A Short Account of the Life and Hardships of a Glasgow Weaver...Written by Himself (Glasgow, 1834)

Smith, J. (ed.), *Recollections of James Turner, Esq. of Thrushgrove* (Glasgow, 1854)

Somerville, Alexander, *The Autobiography of a Working Man*, London, 1848)

Statement by the Proprietors of Cotton Works in Glasgow and the Vicinity; Case of the Operative Cotton-Spinners in Glasgow, in Answer to the Statement by the Proprietors of Cotton Works; Reply by the Proprietors of Cotton Works in Glasgow and the Vicinity to the Case of the Operative Cotton-Spinners (Glasgow, 1825)

Stevenson, John, *A True Narrative of the Radical Rising in Strathaven* (Glasgow, 1835)

Swinton, A., *Report of the Trial of Thomas Hunter, Peter Hacket, Richard McNeil, James Gibb and William McLean, Operative Cotton Spinners in Glasgow* (Edinburgh, 1838)

Tait, William, *Exposure of the Spy System of 1816–17* (Glasgow, 1835)

Thom, William, *Rhymes and Recollections of a Handloom Weaver* (London, 1847)

Tone, W.T.W., (ed.), *Life of Theobald Wolfe Tone* (Washington, 1826)

Trades Edition of the Cotton Spinners Trial (Glasgow, 1838)

Trial and Self Defence of Alexander Campbell, Operative, Before the Exchequer Court, Edinburgh, for Printing and Publishing 'The Tradesman', Contrary to the Infamous Gagging Act (Glasgow, 1835)

Trial for Libel in the Court of Exchequer, Guildhall, London, Saturday and Monday, December 20–22, 1834. Richmond versus Simpkin and Marshall (Glasgow, 1835)

Trial of Andrew McKinley, Before the High Court of Justiciary, at Edinburgh, on 26 July 1827, for Administering Unlawful Oaths (Edinburgh, 1818)

Urie, John, *Reminiscences of Eighty Years* (Paisley, 1908)

Secondary Sources

BOOKS

Anson, P.F., *The Catholic Church in Modern Scotland* (London, 1937)

Arnot, R. Page, *A History of the Scottish Miners* (London, 1955)

Aspinall, A., (ed.), *The Early English Trade Unions* (London, 1949)

Bartlett, Thomas and Hayton, D.W., (eds.), *Penal Era and Golden Age: Essays in Irish History, 1690–1800* (Belfast, 1979)

Belcham, John, *Popular Radicalism in Nineteenth Century Britain* (Basingstoke, 1996)

Bewley, Christine, *Muir of Huntershill* (Oxford, 1981)

Boyce, D. George, *Nineteenth Century Ireland: The Search for Stability* (Dublin, 1990)

Boyce, D. George, *Nationalism in Ireland* (3rd edition, London, 1995)

Boyce, D. George, and O'Day, Alan, (eds.), *The Making of Modern Irish History: Revisionism and the Revisionist Controversy* (London and New York, 1996)

Boyle, John W., *The Irish Labour Movement in the Nineteenth Century* (Washington, 1988)

Briggs, Asa, (eds.), *Chartist Studies* (London, 1959)

Brotherstone, Terry, (ed.), *Covenant, Charter and Party: Traditions of Revolt and Protest in Modern Scottish History* (Aberdeen, 1989)

Brown, Callum G., *The Social History of Religion in Scotland since 1730* (London, 1987)

Brown, Callum G., *The People in the Pews: Religion and Society in Scotland since 1780* (1993)

Brown, Robert, *The History of Paisley, From the Roman Period Down to 1884, Vol. II* (Paisley, 1886)

Bruce, Steve, *No Pope of Rome: Anti-Catholicism in Modern Scotland* (Edinburgh, 1985)

Butt, John and Clarke, I.F., (eds.), *The Victorians and Social Protest: a Symposium* (Newton Abbot, 1973)

Butt, John and Ward, J.T., (eds.), *Scottish Themes: Essays in Honour of Professor S.G.E. Lythe* (Edinburgh, 1976)

Butt, John and Ponting, Kenneth, (eds.), *Scottish Textile History* (Aberdeen, 1987)

Bythell, Duncan, *The Handloom Weavers: A Study of the English Cotton Industry during the Industrial Revolution* (Cambridge, 1969)

Cage, R.A., (ed.), *The Working Class in Glasgow 1750–1914* (London, 1987)

Campbell, A.B., *The Lanarkshire Miners: A Social History of their Trade Unions, 1775–1874* (Edinburgh, 1979)

Campbell, R.H., *Scotland Since 1707: The Rise of an Industrial Society* (2nd edition, Edinburgh, 1977)

Canning, Bernard, *Irish-Born Secular Priests in Scotland 1829–1979* (Inverness, 1979)

Chapman, Sydney, J., *The Lancashire Cotton Industry: A Study in Economic Development* (First published 1804. This edition, Clifton, 1973)

Checkland, Olive and Checkland, Sydney, *Industry and Ethos: Scotland, 1832–1914* (2nd edition, Edinburgh, 1989)

Clark, Anna, *The Struggle for the Breeches: Gender and the Making of the British Working Class* (London, 1995)

Clark, S., and Donnelly, J.S., (eds.), *Irish Peasants: Violence and Political Unrest 1780–1914* (Manchester, 1983)

Colley, Linda, *Britons: Forging the Nation, 1707–1837* (London, 1992)

Connelly, Sean, *Religion and Society in Nineteenth Century Ireland* (Dublin, 1985)

Corish, Patrick, J., (ed.), *Radicals, Rebels and Establishment* (Belfast, 1985)

Cowan, R.M.W., *The Newspaper in Scotland: A Study of its First Expansion* (Glasgow, 1946)

Cullen, L.M., *An Economic History of Ireland Since 1660* (London, 1972)

Cullen, L.M., *The Emergence of Modern Ireland* (London, 1981)

Cullen, L.M., and Smout, T.C., (eds.), *Comparative Aspects of Scottish and Irish Economic and Social History, 1600–1900* (Edinburgh, 1977)

Cullen, L.M., and Furet, F., (eds.), *Ireland and France Seventeenth-Twentieth Centuries: Towards a Comparative Study of Rural History* (Paris, 1980)

Cummings, A.J.G., and Devine, T.M., (eds.) *Industry, Business and Society since 1700: Essays presented to Professor John Butt* (Edinburgh, 1994)

Damer, Sean, *Glasgow: Going for a Song* (London, 1990)

Davis, Graham, *The Irish in Britain 1815–1914* (Dublin, 1991)

Devine, T.M., (ed.) *Improvement and Enlightenment* (Edinburgh, 1989)

Devine, T.M., (ed.), *Conflict and Stability in Scottish Society, 1700–1850* (Edinburgh, 1990)

Devine, T.M., (ed.), *Irish Immigrants and Scottish Society in the Nineteenth and Twentieth Centuries* (Edinburgh, 1991)

Devine, T.M., (ed), *Scottish Emigration and Scottish Society* (Edinburgh, 1992)

Devine, T.M., (ed.), *Scottish Elites* (Edinburgh, 1994)

Devine, T.M., *Exploring the Scottish Past: Themes in the History of Scottish Society* (East Linton, 1995)

Devine, T.M., (ed.), *St Mary's Hamilton: A Social History, 1846–1996* (Edinburgh, 1995)

Devine, T.M., and Dickson, David, (eds.), *Ireland and Scotland 1600–1850: Parallels and Contrasts in Economic and Social Development* (Edinburgh, 1983)

Devine, T.M., and Mitchison, Rosalind, (eds.), *People and Society in Scotland, Vol.I, 1760–1830* (Edinburgh, 1988)

Devine, T.M., and Jackson, Gordon, (eds.), *Glasgow, Volume I: Beginnings to 1830* (Manchester, 1995)

Dickinson, H.T., *British Radicalism and the French Revolution 1789–1815* (Oxford, 1985)

Dickson, David, *New Foundations: Ireland 1660–1800* (Dublin, 1987)

Dickson, David, and Gough, H., (eds.), *Ireland and the French Revolution* (Dublin, 1990)

Dickson, David, Keogh, Daire and Whelan, Kevin, (eds.), *The United Irishmen: Republicanism, Radicalism and Rebellion* (Dublin, 1993)

Dickson, Tony (ed.), *Scottish Capitalism: Class, State and Nation from before the Union to the Present* (London, 1980)

Dickson, Tony (ed.), *Capital and Class in Scotland* (Edinburgh, 1982)

Digby, Anne and Feinstein, Charles, (eds.), *New Directions in Economic and Social History* (Basingstoke, 1989)

Donnachie, Ian and Whatley, Christopher, (eds.), *The Manufacture of Scottish History* (Edinburgh, 1992)

Duckham, Baron, F., *A History of the Scottish Coal Industry, Vol. I: 1700–1815* (Newton Abbot, 1967)

Duncan, Robert, *Steelopolis: The Making of Motherwell c. 1750–1939* (Motherwell, 1991)

Dyos, H.J., and Wolff, Michael, (eds.), *The Victorian City: Images and Realities, Volume 2* (London, 1973)

Elliott, Marianne, *Partners in Revolution: The United Irishmen and France* (London, 1982)

Elliott, Marianne, *Wolfe Tone: Prophet of Irish Independence* (London, 1989)

Ellis, Peter Berresford and Mac a'Ghobhainn, Seamus, *The Scottish Insurrection of 1820* (Pbk. edition, London, 1989)

Epstein, James, *The Lion of Freedom: Feargus O'Connor and the Chartist Movement, 1832–1842* (London, 1982)

Epstein, James, and Thompson, Dorothy, (eds.), *The Chartist Experience: Studies in Working Class Radicalism and Culture, 1830–60* (Basingstoke, 1982)

Evans, Eric J., *The Forging of the Modern British State: Early Industrial Britain, 1783–1870* (2nd edition, Harlow, 1996)

Ferguson, William, *Scotland: 1689 to the Present* (Pbk. edition, Edinburgh, 1978)

Fitzpatrick, D., *Irish Emigration 1801–1921* (Dublin, 1984)

Foster, John, *Class Struggle and the Industrial Revolution: Early Industrial Capitalism in three English Towns* (Pbk. edition, London, 1977)

Foster, R.F., *Modern Ireland, 1600–1972* (Pbk. edition, London, 1989)

Fraser, W. Hamish, *Conflict and Class: Scottish Workers, 1700–1838* (Edinburgh, 1988)

Fraser, W. Hamish, *Alexander Campbell and the Search for Socialism* (Manchester, 1996)

Fraser, W. Hamish, and Morris, R.J., (eds.), *People and Society in Scotland, Volume II, 1830–1914* (Edinburgh, 1990)

Fraser, W. Hamish, and Mavor, Irene (eds.), *Glasgow, Volume II: 1830–1912* (Manchester, 1996)

Fry, Michael, *Patronage and Principle: A Political History of Modern Scotland* (Pbk. edition, Aberdeen, 1991)

Fry, Michael, *The Dundas Despotism* (Edinburgh, 1992)

Fyfe, Janet, (ed.), *Autobiography of John McAdam (1806–1883) with selected Letters* (Edinburgh, 1980)

Gallagher, Tom, *Glasgow, The Uneasy Peace: Religious Tension in Modern Scotland* (Manchester, 1987)

Garvin, Tom, *The Evolution of Irish Nationalist Politics* (Dublin, 1981)

Gibbon, Peter, *The Origins of Ulster Unionism: The Formation of Popular Protestant Politics and Ideology in Nineteenth Century Ireland* (Manchester, 1975)

Glasgow Women's Studies Group, *Unchartered Lives: Extracts from Scottish Women's Experiences, 1850–1982* (Glasgow, 1983)

Goldstrom, J.M., and Clarkson, L.A., (eds.), *Irish Population, Economy and Society* (Oxford, 1981)

Goodwin, A., *The Friends of Liberty: The English Democratic Movement in the Age of the French Revolution* (London, 1979)

Gordon, Eleanor, *Women and the Labour Movement in Scotland 1850–1914* (Oxford, 1991)

Handley, James, *The Irish in Scotland* (2nd edition, Cork, 1945)

Handley, James, *The Irish in Modern Scotland* (Cork, 1947)

Handley, James, *The Navvy in Scotland* (Cork, 1970)

Harrison, R., (ed.), *The Independent Collier: The Coal Miner as Archetypal Proletarian Reconsidered* (London, 1978)

Hickey, John V., *Urban Catholics: Urban Catholicism in England and Wales from 1829 to the Present Day* (London, 1967)

Hollis, Patricia, (ed.), *Pressure from Without in early Victorian England* (London, 1974)

Holmes, Colin, (ed.), *Immigrants and Minorities in British Society* (London, 1978)

Hoppen, K. Theodore, *Ireland since 1800: Conflict and Conformity* (Harlow, 1989)

Hunt, E.H., *British Labour History, 1815–1914* (London, 1981)

Jackson, J.A., *The Irish in Britain* (London, 1963)

Johnson, Christine, *Developments in the Roman Catholic Church in Scotland, 1789–1829* (Edinburgh, 1983)

Johnston, Thomas, *The History of the Working Classes in Scotland* (Glasgow, 1920)

Jones, David, *Chartism and the Chartists* (London, 1975)

Kearns, Gerry and Withers, Charles, W.J., (eds.), *Urbanising Britain: Essays on Class and Community in the Nineteenth Century* (Cambridge, 1991)

Kennedy, Liam and Ollerenshaw, Philip, (eds.), *An Economic History of Ulster, 1820–1940* (Manchester, 1985)

King, Elspeth, *The Hidden History of Glasgow's Women: The Thenew Factor* (Edinburgh and London, 1993)

Kirby, R.G. and Musson, A.E., *The Voice of the People, John Doherty 1798–1854: Trade Unionist, Radical and Factory Reformer* (Manchester, 1975)

Knox, W.W., *Hanging By A Thread: The Scottish Cotton Industry, c. 1850–1914* (Preston, 1995)

Lees, Lynn Hollen, *Exiles of Erin: Irish Migrants in Victorian London* (Manchester, 1979)

Lenman, Bruce, *An Economic History of Modern Scotland* (London, 1977)

Lenman, Bruce, *Integration, Enlightenment and Industrialisation: Scotland , 1746–1832* (Edinburgh, 1981)

Levitt, Ian and Smout, Christopher, *The State of the Scottish Working Class in 1843* (Edinburgh, 1979)

Loades, David, (ed.), *The End of Strife* (Edinburgh, 1984)

Logue, Kenneth, J., *Popular Disturbances in Scotland, 1780–1815* (Edinburgh, 1979)

Lowe, W.J., *The Irish in Mid-Victorian Lancashire* (New York, 1989)

Lunn, Kenneth, (ed.), *Hosts, Immigrants and Minorities: Historical Responses to Newcomers in British Society 1870–1914* (Folkestone, 1980)

Lynch, Michael, *Scotland: A New History* (London, 1991)

Lythe, S.G.E. and Butt, John, *An Economic History of Scotland 1100–1939* (Glasgow and London, 1975)

McCarthey, Mary, *A Social Geography of Paisley* (Paisley, 1969)

McCord, Norman, *The Anti-Corn Law League 1838–1846* (2nd edition, London, 1968)

McCord, Norman, *British History, 1815–1906* (Oxford, 1991)

McCluskey, Raymond, *St Joseph's Kilmarnock, 1847–1997: A Portrait of a Parish Community* (Kilmarnock, 1997)

McCluskey, (ed.), *The See of Ninian: A History of the Medieval Diocese of Whithorn and the Diocese of Galloway in Modern Times* (Ayr, 1997)

MacDonagh, Oliver, *The Emancipist: Daniel O'Connell, 1830–47* (London, 1989)

MacDonald, D.F., *Scotland's Shifting Population, 1770–1850* (Glasgow, 1937)

MacDougall, Ian, (ed.), *Essays in Scottish Labour History* (Edinburgh, 1979)

McFarland, Elaine, *Protestants First: Orangeism in Nineteenth Century Scotland* (Edinburgh, 1990)

McFarland, Elaine, *Ireland and Scotland in the Age of Revolution: Planting the Green Bough* (Edinburgh, 1994)

McFarlane, Margaret and McFarlane, Alastair, *The Scottish Radicals Tried and Transported to Australia for Treason in 1820* (Stevenage, 1981)

McLeod, Hugh, *Religion and the Working Class in Nineteenth Century Britain* (Basingstoke, 1984)

McRoberts, David, (ed.), *Modern Scottish Catholicism, 1878–1978* (Glasgow, 1979)

Machin, G.I.T., *The Catholic Question in English Politics 1820–1830* (Oxford, 1964)

Marshall, William S., *The Billy Boys: A Concise History of Orangeism in Scotland* (Edinburgh, 1996)

Marwick, W.H., *The Life of Alexander Campbell* (Glasgow, 1963)

Marwick, W.H., *A Short History of Labour in Scotland* (Edinburgh, 1967)

Mason, Roger, (ed.), *Scotland and England 1286–1815* (Edinburgh, 1987)

Mason, Roger, and MacDougall, Norman, (eds.), *People and Power in Scotland: Essays in Honour of T.C. Smout* (Edinburgh, 1992)

Mathieson, W.L., *The Awakening of Scotland: A History from 1747–1797* (Glasgow, 1910)

Maxwell, W., *The History of Co-operation in Scotland* (Glasgow, 1910)

Meikle, H.W., *Scotland and the French Revolution* (Glasgow, 1912)

Menzies, Gordon, (ed.), *History is my Witness* (BBC, 1976)

Mews, S., (ed.), *Studies in Church History, Vol. 18: Religion and National Identity* (Oxford, 1982)

Michie, Michael, *An Enlightenment Tory in Victorian Scotland: The Career of Sir Archibald Alison* (East Linton, 1997)

Miller, D.W., *Queen's Rebels: Ulster Loyalism in Historical Perspective* (Dublin, 1978)

Miller, Kerby, *Emigrants and Exiles: Ireland and the Irish Exodus to North America* (Oxford, 1985)

Mitchison, Rosalind, *A History of Scotland* (London, 1970)

Mitchison, Rosalind, *Life in Scotland* (London, 1978)

Mitchison, Rosalind, and Peter Roebuck (eds.), *Economy and Society in Scotland and Ireland 1500–1939* (Edinburgh, 1988)

Morris, R.J., *Class and Class Consciousness in the Industrial Revolution 1780–1850* (Basingstoke, 1979)

Murray, Norman, *The Scottish Handloom Weavers, 1790–1850: A Social History* (Edinburgh, 1978)

Musson, A.E., *British Trade Unions, 1800–75* (1972)

Neal, F., *Sectarian Violence: The Liverpool Experience, 1819–1914* (Manchester, 1987)

O'Farrell, Patrick, *The Irish in Australia* (Kensington, 1987)

O'Ferrall, Feargus, *Catholic Emancipation: Daniel O'Connell and the Birth of Irish Democracy* (Dublin, 1985)

(continued)

O'Sullivan, Patrick, (ed.), *The Irish World Wide, Vol. I: Patterns of Migration* (Leicester, 1992)

O'Sullivan, Patrick, (ed.), *The Irish World Wide, volume 5: Religion and Identity* (Leicester, 1996)

O'Tuiathaigh, Gearoid, *Ireland before the Famine* (2nd edition, Dublin, 1990)

Philipin, C.H.E., (ed.), *Nationalism and Popular Protest in Ireland* (Cambridge, 1987)

Read, D and Glasgow, E., *Feargus O'Connor* (London, 1961)

Renwick, R., (ed.), *Extracts from the Records of the Burgh of Glasgow, vols. ix–xi* (Glasgow, 1914–16)

Robson, Robert (ed.), *Ideas and Institutions of Victorian Britain* (London, 1967)

Roebuck, Peter (ed.), *From Plantation to Partition: Essays in Ulster History in Honour of John McCracken* (Belfast, 1981)

Royle, Edward, *Chartism* (2nd edition, London, 1988)

Rule, John, *The Labouring Classes in Early Industrial England, 1750–1850* (London, 1986)

Rule, John, (ed.), *British Trade Unionism, 1750–1850: The Formative Years* (London, and New York, 1988)

Saville, John, *1848: The British State and the Chartist Movement* (Cambridge, 1987)

Senior, H., *Orangeism in Ireland and Britain, 1795–1836* (London, 1966)

Sherry, F.A., *The Rising of 1820* (Glasgow, 1968)

Shiels, W.J., and Wood, Diana (eds.), *Studies in Church History Vol. 23: Voluntary Religion* (Oxford, 1986)

Shiels, W.J., and Wood, Diana (eds.), *Studies in Church History Vol. 24: The Church and Wealth* (Oxford, 1987)

Shiels, W.J., and Wood, Diana (eds.), *Studies in Church History Vol. 25: The Churches, Ireland and the Irish* (Oxford, 1989)

Slaven, Anthony, *The Development of the West of Scotland: 1750–1960* (London, 1975)

Smout, T.C., *A History of the Scottish People* (Pbk. edition, London, 1972)

Smout, T.C., (ed.), *The Search for Wealth and Stability* (London, 1979)

Smout, T.C., *A Century of the Scottish People, 1830–1850* (Pbk. edition, Glasgow, 1986)

Stevenson, John, *Popular Disturbances in England, 1700–1832* (2nd edition, London, 1992)

Strawthorn, J., *Ayrshire, the Story of a County* (Ayr, 1975)

Swift, Roger and Gilley, Sheridan (eds.), *The Irish in the Victorian City* (London, 1985)

Swift, Roger and Gilley, Sheridan (eds.), *The Irish in Britain, 1815–1939* (London, 1989)

Thale, Mary (ed.), *Selections from the Papers of the London Corresponding Society, 1792–99* (Cambridge, 1977)

Thomis, Malcolm I. and Holt, Peter, *Threats of Revolution in Britain, 1789–1848* (London and Basingstoke, 1977)

Thompson, Dorothy, *The Chartists: Popular Politics in the Industrial Revolution* (Pbk. edition, Aldershot, 1986)

Thompson, E.P., *The Making of the English Working Class* (Pbk. edition, London, 1968)

Walker, Graham, *Intimate Strangers: Political and Cultural Interaction between Scotland and Ulster in Modern Times* (Edinburgh, 1995)

Walker, Graham, and Gallagher, Tom (eds.), *Sermons and Battle Hymns: Protestant Popular Culture in Modern Scotland* (Edinburgh, 1990)

Walker, William, *Juteopolis: Dundee and its Textile Workers, 1885–1923* (Edinburgh, 1979)

Walsh, James, *History of the Catholic Church in Scotland* (Glasgow, 1874)

Ward, J.T., *The Factory Movement 1830–1855* (London, 1962)

Ward, J.T., (ed.), *Popular Movements, c. 1830–1850* (London, 1970)

Ward, J.T., *Chartism* (London, 1973)

Wells, Roger, *Insurrection: The British Experience, 1795–1803* (Gloucester, 1983)

Whatley, Christopher A., *The Industrial Revolution in Scotland* (Cambridge, 1997)

Williams, G.A., *Artisans and Sans Culottes: Popular Movements in France and Britain during the French Revolution* (London, 1968)

Williams, T.D., *Secret Societies in Ireland* (Dublin, 1973)

Wilson, Alexander, *The Chartist Movement in Scotland* (Manchester, 1970)

Wilson, Gordon M., *Alexander McDonald: Leader of the Miners* (Aberdeen, 1982)

Wright, D.G., *Popular Radicalism: the Working-Class Experience, 1780–1880* (London, 1988)

Wright, Leslie C., *Scottish Chartism* (Edinburgh, 1953)

Young, James D., *The Rousing of the Scottish Working Class* (London, 1979)

Young, James D., *Women and Popular Struggles* (London, 1985)

Articles and Essays

Anderson, William James, 'David Downie and the "Friends of the People" ', *Innes Review*, XVI (1965)

Aspinwall, Bernard, 'The Formation of the Catholic Community in the West of Scotland: Some Preliminary Outlines', *Innes Review*, XXXIII (1982)

Aspinwall, Bernard, 'Popery in Scotland: Image and Reality, 1820–1920', *Records of the Scottish Church History Society*, 22 (1986)

Aspinwall, Bernard, 'Children of the Dead End: The Formation of the Modern Archdiocese of Glasgow, 1815–1914', *Innes Review*, XLIII (1992)

Aspinwall, Bernard, 'Scots and Irish Clergy Ministering to Immigrants, 1830–1878', *Innes Review*, XLVII (1996)

Belcham, John, 'Henry Hunt and the Evolution of the Mass Platform', *English Historical Review*, 93 (1978)

Belcham, John, 'Republicanism, Popular Constitutionalism and the Radical Platform in early Nineteenth Century England', *Social History*, 6 (1981)

Belcham, John, 'English Working-Class Radicalism and the Irish, 1815–1850', in Swift and Gilley (eds.), *Irish in the Victorian City*

Bolin-Hort, Per, 'Managerial Strategies and Worker Responses: A New Perspective on the Decline of the Scottish Cotton Industry', *Journal of the Scottish Labour History Society*, 29 (1994)

Brims, John D., 'The "Scottish Jacobins", Scottish Nationalism and the British Union', in Mason (ed.), *Scotland and England*

Brims, John D., 'From Reformers to "Jacobins": The Scottish Association of the Friends of the People' in Devine (ed.), *Conflict and Stability*

Brims, John D., 'Scottish Radicalism and the United Irishmen' in Dickson, Keogh and Whelan (eds.), *United Irishmen*

Brown, Callum G., 'Religion and Social Change' in Devine and Mitchison (eds.), *People and Society Vol.I*

Brown, Callum G., 'Religion, Class and Church Growth' in Fraser and Morris (eds.), *People and Society Vol.II*

Burgess, Keith, 'Workshop of the World: Client Capitalism at its Zenith, 1830–1870', in Dickson (ed.), *Scottish Capitalism*

Butt, John, 'Labour and Industrial Relations in the Scottish Cotton Industry during the Industrial Revolution', in Butt and Ponting (eds.), *Scottish Textile History*

Cage, R.A., 'The Standard of Living Debate: Glasgow, 1800–1850', *Journal of Economic History*, 43 (1982)

Cameron, Kenneth, J., 'William Weir and the Origins of the "Manchester League" in Scotland, 1833–39', *Scottish Historical Review*, LVIII (1979)

Campbell, A.B., 'The Scots Colliers' Strikes of 1824–1826: The Years of Freedom and Independence', in Rule (ed.), *British Trade Unionism*

Clarke, Tony and Dickson, Tony, 'The Making of a Class Society: Commercialization and Working-Class Resistance, 1780–1830', in Dickson (ed.), *Scottish Capitalism*

Clarke, Tony and Dickson, Tony, 'Class and Class Consciousness in Early Industrial Capitalism: Paisley, 1770–1850' in Dickson (ed.), *Capital and Class*

Clarke, Tony and Dickson, Tony, 'Social Concern and Social Control in Nineteenth Century Scotland: Paisley, 1841–1843', *Scottish Historical Review*, LXV (1986)

Clarke, Tony and Dickson, Tony, 'The Birth of Class?' in Devine and Mitchison (eds.), *People and Society, Vol.I*

Colley, Linda, 'The Apotheosis of George III: Loyalty, Royalty and the British Nation, ,1760–1820', *Past and Present*, 102 (1984)

Collins, Brenda, 'Irish Emigration to Dundee and Paisley during the First Half of the Nineteenth Century' in Goldstrom and Clarkson (eds.), *Irish Population, Economy and Society*

Collins, Brenda, 'Proto-Industrialisation and pre-Famine Emigration', *Social History*, 7 (1982)

Collins, Brenda, 'The Origins of Irish Immigration to Scotland in the Nineteenth and Twentieth Centuries', in Devine (ed.), *Irish Immigrants*

Crawford, W.H., 'Landed Tenant Relations in Ulster 1609–1820', *Irish Economic and Social History*, II (1975)

Crawford, W.H., 'The Evolution of the Linen Trade in Ulster before Industrialisation', *Irish Economic and Social History*, XV (1988)

D'Arcy, F.A., 'The Artisans of Dublin and Daniel O'Connell, 1830–47: an Unquiet Liaison', *Irish Historical Studies*, XVII (1970)

Darragh, James, 'The Catholic Population of Scotland since the Year 1680', *Innes Review*, IV (1953)

Donnelly, J.S., 'Republicanism and Reaction in the 1790s', *Irish Economic and Social History*, XI (1984)

Donnelly, F.K., 'The Scottish Rising of 1820: A Re-interpretation', *Scottish Tradition*, VI (1976)

Donnelly, F.K., and Baxter, J.L., 'Sheffield and the English Revolutionary Tradition, 1791–1820', *International Review of Social History*, 20 (1975)

Donovan, Robert Kent, 'Voices of Distrust: The Expression of Anti-Catholic Feeling in Scotland, 1778–1781', *Innes Review*, XXX (1979)

Dyer, Michael, ' "Mere Detail and Machinery": The Great Reform Act and the Effects of Redistribution on Scottish Representation, 1832–1868', *Scottish Historical Review*, LXII (1983)

Elliott, Marianne, 'The "Despard Conspiracy" Reconsidered', *Past and Present*, 75 (1977)

Elliott, Marianne, 'The Origins and Transformation of Early Irish Republicanism', *International Review of Social History*, XXIII (1978)

Elliott, Marianne, 'Irish Republicanism in England: The First Phase, 1797–99' in Bartlett and Hayton (eds.), *Penal Era and Golden Age*

Elliott, Marianne, 'The Defenders in Ulster' in Dickson, Keogh and Whelan (eds.), *United Irishmen*

Ferguson, William, 'The Reform Act (Scotland) of 1832: Intention and effect', *Scottish Historical Review*, XLV (1966)

Fitzpatrick, David, 'Unrest in Rural Ireland', *Irish Economic and Social History*, XII (1985)

Fraser, W. Hamish, 'The Glasgow Cotton Spinners' in Menzies (ed.), *History is my Witness*

Fraser, W. Hamish, 'The Glasgow Cotton Spinners, 1837' in Butt and Ward (eds.), *Scottish Themes*

Fraser, W. Hamish, 'A Note on the Scottish Weavers' Association, 1808–1813', *Journal of the Scottish Labour History Society*, 20 (1985)

Fraser, W. Hamish, 'Patterns of Protest', in Devine and Mitchison (eds.), *People and Society, Vol.I*

Fraser, W. Hamish, 'Alexander Campbell and some "lost" Unstamped Newspapers', *Journal of the Scottish Labour History Society*, 31 (1996)

Fraser, W. Hamish, 'Owenite Socialism in Scotland', *Scottish Economic and Social History*, 16 (1996)

Gallagher, Tom, 'The Catholic Irish in Scotland: in Search of Identity', in Devine (ed.), *Irish Immigrants*

Garvin, Tom, 'Defenders, Ribbonmen and Others: Underground Political Networks in Pre-Famine Ireland', in Philpin (ed.), *Nationalism and Popular Protest*

Graham, Thomas, ' "A Union of Power"? The United Irish Organisation: 1795–1798' in Dickson, Keogh and Whelan (eds.), *United Irishmen*

Holmes, R.F.G., 'Ulster Presbyterians and Irish Nationalism', in Mews (ed.), *Religion and National Identity*

Holt, Peter, 'Review of P. Berresford Ellis and Seamus Mac a'Ghobhainn, *The Scottish Insurrection of 1820*', *Journal of the Scottish Labour History Society*, 3 (1970)

Hutchison, 'Glasgow Working Class Politics' in Cage (ed.), *Working Class in Glasgow*

Johnson, Christine, 'David Downie: A Reappraisal', *Innes Review*, XXXI (1980)

Johnson, Christine, 'Secular Clergy of the Lowland District, 1732–1829', *Innes Review*, XXXIV (1983)

Johnson, Christine, 'Scottish Secular Clergy, 1830–1878: The Western District', *Innes Review*, XL (1989)

Knox, W., 'The Political and Workplace Culture of the Scottish Working Class, 1832–1914' in Fraser and Morris (eds.), *People and Society Vol.II*

Lawlor, James M., 'Benefactors of the Early Glasgow Mission: 1793 and 1797', *Innes Review*, XXXV (1984)

Lobban, 'The Irish Community in Greenock in the Nineteenth Century, *Irish Geography*, VI (1971)

McCaffrey, John F., 'Roman Catholics in Scotland in the nineteenth and twentieth centuries', *Records of the Scottish Church History Society*, 21 (1983)

McCaffrey, John F., 'The Stewardship of Resources: Financial Strategies of Roman Catholics in the Glasgow District, 1800–70', in Shiels and Wood (eds.), *The Church and Wealth*

McCaffrey, John F., 'Irish Immigrants and Radical Movements in the west of Scotland in the Early Nineteenth Century', *Innes Review*, XXXIX (1988)

McCaffrey, John F., 'Irish Issues in the Nineteenth and Twentieth Century: Radicalism in a Scottish Context?' in Devine (ed.), *Irish Immigrants*

McCalman, Stuart D., 'Chartism in Aberdeen', *Journal of the Scottish Labour History Society*, 2 (1970)

Marwick, W.H., 'Early Trade Unionism in Scotland', *Economic History Review*, V (1935)

Miller, David W., 'Irish Catholicism and the Great Famine', *Journal of Social History*, 9 (1975–1976)

Miller, David W., 'Presbyterianism and "Modernization" in Ulster' in Philpin (ed.), *Nationalism and Popular Protest*

Mitchell, Martin J., 'The Establishment and Early Years of the Hamilton Mission', in Devine (ed.), *St Mary's Hamilton*

Mitchell, Martin J., 'The Catholic Community in Hamilton, c.1800–1914' in Devine (ed.), *St Mary's Hamilton*

Montgomery, Fiona A., 'Glasgow and the Movement for Corn Law Repeal', *History*, 64 (1979)

Montgomery, Fiona A., 'The Unstamped Press: The Contribution of Glasgow 1831–36', *Scottish Historical Review*, LIX (1980)

Montgomery, Fiona A., 'Glasgow and the Struggle for Parliamentary Reform, 1830–1832', *Scottish Historical Review*, LXI (1982)

Muirhead, Ian, 'Catholic Emancipation: Scottish Reactions in 1829', *Innes Review*, XXIV (1973)

Muirhead, Ian, 'Catholic Emancipation in Scotland: The Debate and Aftermath, Part Two', *Innes Review*, XXIV (1973)

Nenadic, Stana, 'The Rise of the Urban Middle Class', in Devine and Mitchison (eds.), *People and Society Vol. I*

Nenadic, Stana, 'Political Reform and the "Ordering" of Middle-Class Protest' in Devine (ed.), *Conflict and Stability*

O'Higgins, Rachel, 'The Irish Influence in the Chartist Movement', *Past and Present*, 20 (1961)

O'Higgins, Rachel, 'Irish Trade Unions and Politics, 1830–50', *Historical Journal*, 4 (1961)

Roach, W.M., 'Alexander Richmond and the Radical Reform Movements in Glasgow in 1816–17', *Scottish Historical Review*, LI (1972)

Sloan, William, 'Employment Opportunities and Migrant Group Assimilation: the Highlanders and Irish in Glasgow, 1840–1860', in Cummings and Devine (eds.), *Industry, Business and Society*

Smith, A.W., 'Irish Rebels and English Radicals, 1798–1820', *Past and Present*, 7 (1955)

Straka, W.W., 'Reform in Scotland and the Working Class', *Scottish Tradition*, II (1972)

Thompson, Dorothy, 'Ireland and the Irish in English Radicalism before 1850', in Epstein and Thompson (eds.), *Chartist Experience*

Treble, J.H., 'The Attitude of the Roman Catholic Church towards Trade Unionism in the North of England, 1833–1842', *Northern History*, 5 (1970)

Treble, J.H., 'The Navvies', *Journal of the Scottish Labour History Society*, 5 (1972)

Treble, J.H., 'The Irish Navvies in the North of England, 1830–1850', *Transport History*, 6 (1973)

Treble, J.H., 'O'Connor, O'Connell and the Attitudes of Irish Immigrants towards Chartism in the North of England, 1838–48', in Butt and Clarke (eds.), *The Victorians and Social Protest*

Walker, Graham, 'The Protestant Irish in Scotland', in Devine (ed.), *Irish Immigrants*

Walker, W.M., 'Irish Immigrants in Scotland: Their Priests, Politics and Political Life', *Historical Journal*, XV (1972)

Ward, J.T., 'The Factory Reform Movement in Scotland', *Scottish Historical Review*, XLI (1962)

Werly, John M., 'The Irish in Manchester, 1832–49', *Irish Historical Studies*, XVIII (1973)

Whatley, Christopher A., 'Women, Girls and Vitriolic Song: a "Note" on the Glasgow Cotton Strike of 1825', *Journal of The Scottish Labour History Society*, 28 (1993)

Whatley, Christopher A., 'Women and the Economic Transformation of Scotland c.1740–1830', *Scottish Economic and Social History*, 14 (1994)

Wilson, Alexander, 'Chartism in Glasgow' in Briggs (ed.), *Chartist Studies*

Wilson, Alexander, 'The Scottish Chartist Press', *Journal of the Scottish Labour History Society*, 4 (1971)

Wilson, Alexander, 'The Suffrage Movement', in Hollis (ed.) *Pressure from Without*

Wilson, Gordon M., 'The Strike Policy of the Miners in the West of Scotland', in MacDougall (ed.), *Essays in Scottish Labour History*

Young, James D., 'The Making of the Scottish Working Class', *Bulletin of the Society for the Study of Labour History,* 28 (1974)

Young, James D., 'Struggle without consciousness: The myth of an un-class', *Bulletin of the Society for the Study of Labour History,* 54 (1989)

THESES

Brassey, Z.G., The Cotton Spinners in Glasgow and the West of Scotland, c.1790–1840: A Study in Early Industrial Relations (M.Litt, University of Strathclyde, 1974).

Brims, J.D., The Scottish Democratic Movement in the Age of the French Revolution, (Ph.D., University of Edinburgh, 1983).

Burns, C.M., Industrial Labour and Radical Movements in Scotland in the 1790s, (M.Sc., University of Strathclyde, 1971).

Hutchison, I.G.C., Politics and Society in Mid-Victorian Glasgow (Ph.D., University of Edinburgh, 1974).

Leitch, Archibald, Radicalism in Paisley, 1830–1848: and its economic, political, cultural background (M.Litt, University of Glasgow, 1993)

Montgomery, Fiona A., Glasgow Radicalism, 1830–1850 (Ph.D., University of Glasgow, 1974)

Roach, W.M., Radical Reform Movements in Scotland from 1815 to 1822 with Particular Reference to Events in the West of Scotland (Ph.D., University of Glasgow, 1970)

Sloan, W., Aspects of the Assimilation of Highland and Irish Migrants in Glasgow, 1830–1870 (M.Phil, University of Strathclyde, 1987)

Sweeney, Irene, The Municipal Administration of Glasgow 1833–1912: Public Service and the Scottish Civic Identity (Ph.D., University of Strathclyde, 1990)

Treble, J.H., The Place of Irish Catholics in the Social Life of the North of England 1829–1851 (Ph.D., University of Leeds, 1969)

Whatley, C.A., The Process of Industrialisation in Ayrshire, c.1707–1871 (Ph.D., University of Strathclyde, 1975)

Wilson, G., The Miners of the west of Scotland and their Trade Unions 1842–74 (Ph.D., University of Glasgow, 1977).

Index